Childhood, Agency, and Fantasy

Children and Youth in Popular Culture
Series Editor: Debbie Olson, Missouri Valley College

Children and Youth in Popular Culture features works that interrogate the various representations of children and youth in popular culture, as well as the reception of these representations. The series is international in scope, recognizing the transnational discourses about children and youth that have helped shape modern and post-modern childhoods and adolescence. The scope of the series ranges from such subjects as gender, race, class, and economic conditions and their global intersections with issues relevant to children and youth and their representation in global popular culture: children and youth at play, geographies and spaces (including World Wide Web), material cultures, adultification, sexuality, children of/in war, religion, children of diaspora, youth and the law, and more.

Advisory Board: LuElla D'Amico, Whitworth University; Markus P.J. Bohlmann, Seneca College; Vibiana Bowman Cvetkovic, Rutgers University; Adrian Schober, Australian Catholic University, Melbourne

Titles in the Series

Childhood, Agency, and Fantasy: Walking in Other Worlds, edited by Ingrid E. Castro
Children and Childhood in the Works of Stephen King, edited by Debbie Olson
Child and Youth Agency in Science Fiction: Travel, Technology, Time, edited by Ingrid E. Castro and Jessica Clark
Critical Childhood Studies and the Practice of Interdisciplinarity: Disciplining the Child, edited by Magdalena Zolkos and Joanna Faulkner
Posthumanist Readings in Dystopian Young Adult Fiction: Negotiating the Nature/Culture Divide, by Jennifer Harrison
The Sidekick Comes of Age: How Young Adult Literature is Shifting the Sidekick Paradigm, by Stephen M. Zimmerly
Female Adolescent Sexuality in the United States, 1850-1965, by Ann Kordas
Tweencom Girls: Gender and Adolescence in Disney and Nickelodeon Sitcoms, by Patrice A. Oppliger
Representing Agency in Popular Culture: Children and Youth on Page, Screen, and In Between, edited by Ingrid E. Castro and Jessica Clark
The Feeling Child: Affect and Politics in Latin American Literature and Film, edited by Philippa Page, Inela Selimović, and Camilla Sutherland
The Rhetorical Power of Children's Literature, edited by John H. Saunders
Children in the Films of Steven Spielberg, edited by Debbie Olson and Adrian Schober
The Child in World Cinema, edited by Debbie Olson
Girls' Series Fiction and American Popular Culture, edited by Luella D'Amico
Indians in Victorian Children's Narratives: Animalizing the Native, 1830-1930, by Shilpa Bhat Daithota
The Rhetorical Power of Children's Literature, edited by John Saunders
Misfit Children: An Inquiry into Childhood Belongings, edited by Markus P. J. Bohlmann
The Américas Award: Honoring Latino/a Children's and Young Adult Literature of the Americas, edited by Laretta Henderson
Critical Childhood Studies and the Practice of Interdisciplinarity: Disciplining the Child, edited by Magdalena Zolkos and Joanna Faulkner

Childhood, Agency, and Fantasy

Walking in Other Worlds

Edited by Ingrid E. Castro

LEXINGTON BOOKS
Lanham • Boulder • New York • London

Chapter Illustrations by Breck Young © 2020.

Published by Lexington Books
An imprint of The Rowman & Littlefield Publishing Group, Inc.
4501 Forbes Boulevard, Suite 200, Lanham, Maryland 20706
www.rowman.com

6 Tinworth Street, London SE11 5AL, United Kingdom

Copyright © 2021 by The Rowman and Littlefield Publishing Group, Inc.

All rights reserved. No part of this book may be reproduced in any form or by any electronic or mechanical means, including information storage and retrieval systems, without written permission from the publisher, except by a reviewer who may quote passages in a review.

British Library Cataloguing in Publication Information Available

Library of Congress Cataloging-in-Publication Data

Library of Congress Control Number: 2020942613

ISBN 978-1-4985-9429-5 (cloth)
ISBN 978-1-4985-9431-8 (pbk)
ISBN 978-1-4985-9430-1 (electronic)

To my fiancé Breck for his love,
To my mother Maryke for her hope,
To my mentor Maureen for her support,
To my dog Moxie for her companionship.

Contents

Acknowledgments   ix

ADVENTURE/OTHERWORLD   2

1   Where Do We Belong? Childhood Studies, Agency, Citizenry, and Fantasy   3
Ingrid E. Castro

DREAM/GOOD VS. EVIL   40

2   A Futile Rage against the Machine: The Triumph of *The 5,000 Fingers of Dr. T*   41
Peter W. Y. Lee

IMAGINATION/TRANSFORMATION   72

3   Developing Children's Agency through Play with Imaginary Companions   73
Kostas Magos and Sophia Kremmydiotou

HEROISM/SUPERNATURAL   94

4   Arcadia Is in the Hands of Teenagers: Team Power in Guillermo del Toro's *Trollhunters*   95
Tara Moore

MAGIC/JOURNEY — 116

5 The Boy Who Lives: Agentic Locations of Friendship Identity, Peer Culture, and Interpretive Reproduction in *Harry Potter* — 117
Ingrid E. Castro

MYTHOLOGY/QUEST — 150

6 All in the Family: The Agency of Demigods and Godlings in the Mythic World of Rick Riordan — 151
Michele D. Castleman

CONFLICT/JUSTICE — 172

7 Young People's Agency in Online Fan Spaces — 173
Parinita Shetty

PORTALS/TIME — 200

8 Girls' Agency through Supermobility: The Power of Imagined Futures in Young Adult Fantasy Literature — 201
Ida Fadzillah Leggett

MOVEMENT/POWER — 226

9 Being Scared in the Dark: Paradoxes, Perils, and the Promise of Fantasy for Urban Girls of Color — 227
Ingrid E. Castro and Ana Lilia Campos-Manzo

Index — 263

About the Contributors — 277

Acknowledgments

The construction of this book comes with gratitude to many people. First, thank you to the chapter authors, all of whom were patient through the review and publication process. Second, thanks to all of the great women and editors at Lexington who worked on making this book a reality: Judith Lakamper, Shelby Russell, Courtney Morales, Megan Murray, and Becca Beurer. I am grateful to Debbie Olson, editor of Lexington's Children and Youth in Popular Culture Series, who enthusiastically supported the ideas behind this project.

Children's fantasy books are often accompanied by a small picture at the heading of each chapter, a thumbnail piece of art that depicts a bit about what is coming next. I asked myself, "Why not?" This intertextual and intertwined approach, merging the conventions of one kind of book into another, is rare. Paraphrasing Maurice Sendak, we need to break down those walls between books for children and books for adults. Bringing the art of children's fantasy into the structure of academic scholarship reflects true interdisciplinarity, something I believe we need to do more often. So, my fiancé Breck Young drew the small illustrations that accompany each section in this volume and he also contributed the dynamic cover painting. While I thank him on the dedication page, it is worth repeating: you are my favorite and I am so glad you are the other pea in our pod.

Working on this book in the midst of the coronavirus pandemic was a struggle. As I am sure all of you can attest to, concentrating on writing is difficult when a trip to the grocery store seems like the end of days. I miss my coworkers, students, friends, and family. Mostly, I miss the routineness of life, the everyday banality of it. And I miss easy choices. But, I look outside and the sun shines brilliantly, the sky is azure blue, and the leaves rustle gently in the wind. The birds are chirping and a baby bunny is eating weeds in my backyard. So, while all is not right with the world, it's not all wrong either. Hopefully a bit more than fantasy, like Rod Serling I too dream of what seems like the impossible becoming more than probable—humanity will embrace once again, and that will be a wonderful day.

Adventure/Otherworld

Chapter 1

Where Do We Belong?

Childhood Studies, Agency, Citizenry, and Fantasy

Ingrid E. Castro

As I sit down to write the Introduction to this collection of chapters on children's agency in fantasy, we are in the throes of COVID-19. Worldwide, children are banned from going to school, seeing their friends, playing at the park, and visiting their grandparents. A few weeks ago, Josh Gad, who voices Olaf in Disney's fairy tale *Frozen* and its sequel (2013 & 2019) stated, "I think nostalgia is so important right now because we all want to go back to simpler times. We all are hoping for something we can connect with that reminds of us better days" (Elber 2020). I will return to the project Gad conceived of during social distancing measures later in this chapter, but suffice it to say I agree with Gad that it seems now, more than ever, we need a little (or a lot) of fantasy in our lives, regardless of whether we classify as children or adults.

In 1962, narrating *The Twilight Zone* episode "The Fugitive," Rod Serling famously claimed that fantasy is "the impossible made probable." He created *The Twilight Zone* (1959–1964) because he was frustrated with conservative television networks and sponsors, finding that he could circumvent criticism and censorship while tackling the political and social problems of his era through a combination of fantasy writing and morality fable (PBS 2003). Fantasy continues to serve such purposes—when we watch a fantasy tale on television or film, when we read a fantasy story, when we play a fantasy game, we are simultaneously enveloped in commentary about the real world while exploring another imaginary one further afield. In thinking about Serling's point in creating *The Twilight Zone*, it is evident he was agentically staking his rights as a citizen to express that which concerned or fascinated him most about the social world and time to which he belonged. This connection is what we also find in children's agentic motivations in or with fantasy: childhood is, after all, part of the fabric that encircles our humanity.

What does, or does not, encompass fantasy is overwhelmingly a matter of opinion, and there is a related ongoing debate as to how fairy tale and fantasy differ. Perhaps part of the reason people find it hard to classify fantasy is due to the difficulty in defining fairy tale as a genre. As Zipes (1988) explains, "It is nearly impossible . . . because it has become more of a cultural institution than anything else" (7). Overall, academics find that the fairy tale is an element of fantasy, part of its roots. Maria Nikolajeva (2003) outlines differences between the two—she says fantasy is postmodern in its use of technology while the fairy tale is archaic in its folk traditions, and fantasy allows for more experimentation, nonlinear time, and multiple-world depiction compared to fairy tales. Nevertheless, she also makes undeniable connections between fantasy and fairy tale in that they draw on similar attributes, characters, and plotlines (Nikolajeva 2003). Greenhill and Matrix (2010) claim fairy tale films *are* fantasy films, especially when created for young adults. Others cite differences between fairy tale and fantasy or between recognized subdivisions of fantasy, but quickly dismiss them in the genres' modern iterations: "I mention these distinctions if only to discard them" (Lehtonen 2013, 9); "We need to break the old binaries like a bad habit" (Honeyman 2010, 12). I concur with such suggestions while in the pursuit of expanding critical analyses and intertextual understandings, and thus proceed in this introduction discussing fairy tale and fantasy as a complementary unit. In general, it is agreed that fantasy

> evokes wonder, mystery, or magic—a sense of possibility beyond the ordinary, material, rationally predictable world in which we live . . . modern fantasy is clearly related to the magical stories of myth, legend, fairy tale, and folklore from all over the world . . . . Fantasy . . . elicits wonder through elements of the supernatural or impossible. It consciously breaks free from mundane reality. (Mathews 2011, 1–2)

Though encompassing so much potential, a general circulating belief dismisses fantasy as "mere escapism" (Roberts and MacCallum-Stewart 2016, 3). Some, however, establish fantasy as an important cultural form—a subversive, unique, eclectic, and revolutionary genre that, similar to how Serling deployed *The Twilight Zone*, questions cultural, social, and political norms and offers alternative potential outcomes that can engender agency, liberation, or real change (Lehtonen 2013; Mathews 2011; Nikolajeva 2003; Roberts and MacCallum-Stewart 2016; Willis 2009).

In many ways, contrasting views on fantasy are similarly found in perspectives of childhood. People still make the claim that childhood is an existence full of innocence and wonder and free of trouble or strife, a time adults repeatedly call on when expressing wish fulfillment or lamenting the conditions of those "few" children who cannot fully relish childhood as it is purportedly meant to be enjoyed. There are a multitude of fantasy films that depict adults morphing into children, and children transforming into adults, which overarchingly "say much more about adults' and children's fantasy investments in the idea of childhood than they do about the realities of children's lives; and they are often imbued with nostalgia for a past Golden Age of freedom and play" (Buckingham 2000, 9). David Buckingham (2000) is referring to both the imagined glory of childhood and the blanket protectionism that constricts children to smaller and smaller spaces and mutates childhood into a glimmer of its supposed former self (see Swauger, Castro, and Harger 2017).

While researching this introductory chapter, I came across a most curious and invigorating interview of Maurice Sendak, conducted 50 years ago by children's literature authority and librarian Virginia Haviland (1971). Much like another beloved fantasy book, *Alice in Wonderland* (1865), I followed the rabbit holes and came across a second just as illuminating feature piece on Sendak published in *The New Yorker* (Hentoff 1966). Maurice Sendak, most famous for writing and illustrating *Where the Wild Things Are* (1963), had very strong opinions on the genre of fantasy and children's positionality in society. He believed creativity, that quality rooted in both imagination and reality, could not exist without fantasy (Haviland 1971). He stated, "fantasy is so all-pervasive in a child's life: I believe there's no part of our lives, our adult as well as child life, when we're not fantasizing, but we prefer to relegate fantasy to children . . . . Children do live in fantasy and reality; they move back and forth very easily in a way that we no longer remember how to do" (Haviland 1971, 264). Bill Corsaro (1992) notes the very same thing in his work on children's peer cultures and interpretive reproduction. He explains that adapting to developing social worlds leads to children's "use of current abilities in new ways or even the abandonment or withering away of certain skills. For example, children's spontaneity and their skills in creating and maintaining fantasy events often may dissipate or become rusty with lack of use in the progression through childhood cultures to adult culture" (Corsaro 1992, 162). Thus, fantasy for both children and adults is situated in the process of being found, and then lost, and perhaps found again.

Sendak was vehemently against the idea of relegating fantasy to children only, setting out to write and illustrate books for all people. The author dreamed of "a time when children's books were not segregated from adult books, a time when people didn't think of children's books as a minor art form" (Haviland 1971, 280). Here, one need only think of the currently popular phrase placed on 18 and overs consuming young adult fantasy literature—"reading down"—a label that judges children's literature as inferior in sophistication and complexity. Connected, Sendak argued that the separation between children's fantasy books and adult books was (and, I agree, continues to be) based on how children are, often superficially and discriminatorily, viewed qualitatively different from adults. He said, "I would like to do away with the division into age categories of children over here and adults over there, which is confusing to me and I think probably confusing to children" (Haviland 1971, 280). Pointing out the link made between the physicality of children and relegating children's literature to a lower art form, while also honoring the bookmakers who captured his esteem and fascination during his childhood, Sendak explained, "those illustrators and writers that attracted me were the ones who did not seem at all to be hung up by the fact that their audiences were small people. They were telling the truth, just the way it was" (Haviland 1971, 274). Of course, this trend continues today with that demeaning phrase "reading down," which clearly invokes iconicity—an immediate picture of lower spatiality coupled with the quality of smallness or meaninglessness many adults attribute to children's bodies, their beliefs, and their material cultures.[1] Against such views, Sendak believed young children were "fluid . . . like moving water," extremely capable people who deserved to read about (and in that act face their own) truths of childhood and truths of life (Hentoff 1966).

The irony is not lost that in the 1960s Sendak's *Where the Wild Things Are* was banned from schools and libraries because psychologists considered the book to be "damaging and traumatizing," "too dark," and "too much for little children" with its "unvarnished story of rebellion, fear, punishment, and escape" (Cleveland 2015; Spillman 2013). Even so, the book won the Caldecott Medal for outstanding children's picture book. Critics of the age occasionally appreciated Sendak's humanistic approach to children and childhood, themselves pointing out children's special abilities and children's key role in intergenerational family relationships: "Boys and girls may have to shield their parents from this book. Parents are very easily scared" (review quoted in Hentoff 1966). Protectionism is not, actually, a 1990s and beyond phenomenon, as many childhood studies scholars claim. Instead, protectionism was alive and well in the 1960s when Sendak criticized its futility—"Too many parents and too many writers of children's books don't respect the fact that kids know a great deal and suffer a great deal . . . . The need for half-truth books is the most obvious indication of the common wish to protect children from their everyday fears and anxieties, a hopeless wish that denies the child's endless battle with disturbing emotions" (Hentoff 1966).

Adults make essentialist links between childhood and fantasy because fantasy and fairy tales are labeled the stuff of children, not adults. *Once upon a time* is interchangeable with *There once was a child*; historically, the tradition of the fairy tale is at its core the practice of adults mounting morality lessons to teach or, perhaps better said, control children. As Sendak asserted, the genre was (and still is) rife with false narratives of children and protectionist discourses about childhood (see Castro 2005). Even so, fantasy is a genre in which "literally anything could happen," that depicts "creative possibilities" with "oceanic scope" (Mathews 2011, xi; Roberts and MacCallum-Stewart 2016, 2). In this project, fantasy makers have at times recognized that the genre is a perfect conduit to explore children's "eternal questions about identity, power, love, lust, and belonging—the human condition" (Greenhill and Matrix 2010, 10). Taking the stance that fantasy and fairy tales are not "low" art forms presented to "immature" or "incomplete" consuming children is a growing trend. As a result, modern fantasy stories increasingly portray children's potential for modifying their world(s), while its young characters simultaneously recognize and contend with power differentials that influence such processes of change (Beauvais 2012).

Childhood studies, specifically its social science branches, tackle such concerns more broadly. The "new" sociology of childhood sought to redefine the child and reconceptualize childhood from the late 1970s onward. In these efforts, "new" sociology of childhood theorists reframed children as people who are social agents, situated within their specific contexts and capable of expressing their own worldviews. The subdiscipline expressed a clear vision of how to move forward, making the inclusion of children in participatory research designs an imperative. In childhood studies, elements of voice, agency, and structure now combine with children's geographies to emphasize the importance of place, space, time, and generationality. These foundations must be theoretically and empirically positioned by the arenas children most frequently occupy: in considering the social locations of families, schools, and neighborhoods (among others), the multiplicity of youth's lives is better encapsulated in our academic work. Finally, the "new" sociology of childhood named peer groups as the leading shared location of children's socialization instead of adult cultural and social milieus. As such, sociologists embraced that peers and peer cultures are the reigning spaces for children to try out ideas, fall in line with rules, play out their fantasies and fears, and accept, reproduce, or change ideologies and social norms found in society as a whole.

There is, of course, continual modification to such advancement efforts. What was once considered revolutionary thinking—removing the child from the realm of yet-to-become adult—is now thought of as a practice that perhaps took the child out of childhood a bit too much. Instead, children should be viewed as both being and becoming, scholars acknowledging that in addition to honoring children being themselves, children should be honored for becoming in childhood, just as, I am sure all agree, adults both be and become in adulthood. As Lee (1998) and Uprichard (2008) explain, children are still developing forward toward adulthood, and naming their becomings along with their beings opens up how we value children as both current and future social change agents in their practices and resolutions. Similarly, Buckingham (2019) emphasizes that, moving forward, childhood studies needs to find a third space that intertwines the individual with the social, the biology with the structure, or, put another way, the psychology with the sociology (see also Kuczynski, Harach, and Bernardini 1999). Only in this application will we be able to truly interrogate agency that is not static, but temporal and fluid, removing children's agency from the capability approach and placing it into the realm of performances, connections, practices, materials, networks, and translations (Buckingham 2019; Prout 2000). In addition, researchers and theorists stress that now, more than ever, we must reconsider children's citizenship and belongingness holistically, recognizing children as a national and international group with rights and concerns. Reflecting this charge is the 1989 United Nations Convention on the Rights of the Child agreement, established to ensure the rights of children globally. For while children are still situated solidly in childhood, they are carers and workers, they are learners and translators, they are creators and consumers, and they are leaders and organizers.

With its portals, age-shifting, power struggles, and exploration of spaces small and large, fantasy is perhaps the best genre to apply childhood studies interests in the tension between being, becoming, and belonging. Some "new" sociology of childhood scholars explore the role fantasy plays in children's lives. Bill Corsaro (2015) covers fantasy, fairy tales, myths, and legends in his discussion of children's culture; he also details the importance of children's fantasy play with peers. I examine fairy tale and fantasy films to advance theories on children's agency, constructions of innocence, gender dynamics, and generational relationships (Castro 2005, 2016, 2019a). And Allison James (1993) explains how children's self-created fairy tales are thematically groundbreaking and thus identity fortifying, wherein children tell stories with

> endings as being dependent upon choices made in interpersonal relationships and upon strategic social action. It is through radically reappraising their own social behaviour and relationships, rather than through magic or illusion, that the heroes and heroines of the children's stories gain mastery over their own fate and construct a social identity for themselves. (James 1993, 135)

There are, of course, other examples, but suffice it to say that social scientists rarely cross over into humanities products to further their research or make their points. Similarly, those paramount foundations of the "new" social studies of childhood—voice, agency, structure, generation, and citizenry—are generally less attended to or not taken up with as much vigor in humanities work on children and childhood. Interestingly, I find when researchers housed in the humanities make such connections in fairy tale and fantasy scholarship, it is more likely to happen when they focalize on gender, specifically girls and girlhood. For example, Sanna Lehtonen's (2013) book explores girls' mobility and age-shifting in fantasy texts, Sarah Hentges (2018) offers a book on girls in dystopian fiction, and Day, Green-Barteet, and Montz (2014) similarly put forth an entire edited volume on dystopian fiction and female rebellion (granted, the latter two texts hedge more toward science fiction than fantasy). Again, while there are obviously many more examples available, the point I am making is that if you query "fairy tale/fantasy" with "agency" or "citizenship" or "generation," few results appear, regardless of discipline or search engine.

Overall, analyses of boys in fantasy tend to circulate around Peter Pan, Harry Potter, and Charlie Bucket.[2] Certainly, there are many other boys' journeys in fantasy and fairy tale that deserve attention. Such stories have the capacity to position boys' friendships and adventures within "interdependency, reciprocity, and shared knowledge and work," while also contextualizing "the emergence of their expertise, creativity, and agency" (Clark and Castro 2019a, 3 & 4). One such fantasy film is *The Goonies* (1985), a powerhouse project with shared film credit between Steven Spielberg (story), Chris Columbus (screenplay), and Richard Donner (director). Briefly, *The Goonies* is about a team of youth (Mikey, Chunk, Data, Mouth, Brand, Andy, and Stef, five boys later joined by two girls) who go on an adventure, hoping to find rumored pirate's treasure hidden in the bowels of their Astoria, Oregon hometown. The boys, who fashion themselves Goonies because they come from the working-class side of town called the Goon Docks, want to find the "rich stuff" to pay off their parents' debts and stave off country club developers seizing their families' properties to construct a golf course. Following an old treasure map and finding the entrance to hidden subterranean caves under an abandoned restaurant by the sea, the youth successfully circumvent a variety of booby traps that in earlier decades thwarted an adult treasure hunter. Eventually, the children reach One-Eyed Willy's immense pirate ship, the *Inferno*, that contains the captain's hidden treasure, but are forced to relinquish their bounty to the dangerous on-the-lam Fratelli family (who earlier took Chunk captive in the restaurant). In the end, the Goon Docks, the children's families, and most importantly the Goonies' peer group and culture are saved by a pile of jewels discovered inside Mikey's marble bag.

In this fantasy film, children are certainly agentic. They know their rights as Goonies peer group members and as Astoria citizens, endeavor to keep the Goon Docks safe from capitalistic developers, protect their Goonies culture with tenacity, and support each other all the while during their "last crazy

Figure 1.1 (From left): Data (Ke Huy Kwan), Mikey (Sean Astin), Brand (Josh Brolin), Mouth (Corey Feldman), and Chunk (Jeff Cohen) discover the treasure map to "rich stuff" in Brand and Mikey's attic: *The Goonies* (1985).

Goonie adventure." There is a hopefulness that shines through the film, with characters believing they can make an agentic positive difference in their own and their parents' lives and their town, while also calling on their individual talents and underestimated power as children when facing threats stemming from the crime-riddled Fratelli family. Some of the film's most quotable lines come from Mikey (arguably the lead role), who after explaining how the children's lives will change if they have to move, permanently severing their peer group's ties, encourages the group: "We got a chance! . . . Goonies never say die!" The belief the Goonies have in themselves, specifically because they are children, is placed at the forefront of the film, also acknowledging that it is okay for children to have missteps along their journeys. As Mikey tells new Goonie member Andy, "I believe in you. Goonies always make mistakes, just don't make any more." Mikey urges the group to continue on their path forward: "Our parents, they want the bestest stuff for us. But right now, they gotta do what's right for them, 'cause it's their time, their time up there. Down here, it's our time, it's our time down here."

Interestingly, the latter scene enframes *The Goonies* adventure as the literal depiction of children's "citizenship from below," wherein the children act together in underground caves, with movement toward a common goal using mutual respect and self-made rules (Liebel 2008). Mikey's speeches, with realistic words an "ordinary," asthmatic, awkward boy of thirteen might use to convince his peers to go on an adventure, say much about fantasy, agency, generationality, and citizenry. Mikey recognizes the connection family members have to one another and how emotional investments span across generations. He also clearly points out the holistic belongingness the children have to one another and to their town. Finally, he references the integral and combined roles power, space, and time serve in children's lives, elements central to twenty-first-century childhood studies scholarship (see, for example, Arai 2011; Christensen, James, and Jenks 2000; Holloway, Holt, and Mills 2019; Leonard 2007; Moss 2010). Children's material culture is also overwhelmingly present in *The Goonies*. From seemingly random references to pop culture of the age, Chunk playing video games and sharing a Baby Ruth candy bar, Data's Nike slick shoes, to the boys riding their bikes through the woods to reach the restaurant, boys' material culture is central to their adventure.[3] In addition, the fact that the town is ultimately saved by the jewels remaining in Mikey's marble bag, something the Fratelli trio overlooked while shedding the children of their treasures, is an insightful and critical commentary on just how little children's material and play cultures are recognized or valued by adults in charge.

The movie was a resounding success, a summer blockbuster that was one of the top ten grossing films of 1985—it was allotted a hefty budget (at the time) of $19 million and grossed $124 million worldwide. Even so, it has a host of bloopers, the most egregious of which are found at the end of the film when there are a few lines referencing the children battling an octopus, a scene that wound up on the cutting room floor. And yet, fans do not seem to mind; perhaps these mistakes contribute to part of the film's charm. Returning to Josh Gad, during COVID-19 he conceived of a web project called *Reunited Apart*. His first special (virtually) gathered the stars, filmmakers, and Cyndi Lauper, the singer of *The Goonies* theme song, together thirty-five years after its debut. In the video, Gad explains *The Goonies* "forever change[d] the course of my life," naming the film "the godfather of its generation." He says *The Goonies* raised the bar for the fantasy genre, and two of the film's stars make connections between *The Goonies* and classic fantasy stories: Robert Davi (Jake Fratelli) quotes Donner claiming at the time of making the film, "This will be the *Wizard of Oz* of this time period," and Corey Feldman (Mouth) asserts, "It's the *Willy Wonka* of our generation" (Gad 2020).

So why is all this filmmaking backstory important? *The Goonies* is an exemplar of the lasting power fantasy can have in our collective memories, and just how much its fantasy predecessors and children's material and pop culture tie-ins matter to public reception and target audience success. Most children who grew up in the '70s or '80s likely saw the movie, continuing to have fond memories of the characters and quotable dialogue as adults. In evidence, at the time of writing this chapter, a mere three weeks have passed since upload and Gad's *Reunited Apart: The Goonies* special already has over 2.4 million views on YouTube. As further proof, there are large *Goonies* event gatherings in Astoria, Oregon every ten years or so to celebrate milestone anniversaries of the film; up to 1,500 people a day continue to visit and take pictures of the Astoria house that served as Mikey and Brand's home; and in 2017 *The Goonies* was selected for preservation by the Library of Congress U.S. National Film Registry for being "culturally, historically, or aesthetically significant." Contributing to the nostalgia, most film critics agree a movie like *The Goonies* will never be made again. This claim is made because today's filmmakers shy away from the construction of immense interactive sets, instead turning to cheaper, quicker, and easier CGI green screen backdrops, and the movie includes a litany of tropes that are now found to be culturally insensitive.[4] Related, in 1985 the film was rated PG instead of PG-13, likely due to Spielberg's pull in Hollywood. As Roger Ebert (1985) explained, "his kids say 'shit' a lot, and it is a measure of Spielberg's insight that the word draws only a PG rating for the movie; Spielberg no doubt argues that most kids talk like that half the time, and he is right." At the time of filming, Spielberg said of the movie, "We're just making an ordinary adventure here, ordinary fantasy, nothing extraordinary happens in this picture at all ... they get bored one day and they have the most extraordinary adventure than any adult could possibly imagine."[5] And perhaps it is this quality of "ordinary fantasy," above all else, that continues to capture the imagination of generations of children and adults: "*The Goonies* is a classic '80s movie, but it's endured for more than 30 years because it's also timeless—the rip-roaring story of a tight-knit group of friends fighting land developers and criminals in search of treasure and adventure" (Boone 2016).

The film's monumental set, which included a labyrinth of caves, custom-built waterslide, and the pirate ship *Inferno* built-to-scale, was visited by a variety of Hollywood heavyweights during filming (including Paul Rubens aka Pee-wee Herman, Clint Eastwood, Dan Aykroyd, Tim Burton, and Harrison Ford)—as Cyndi Lauper says during *Reunited Apart*, "Everyone visited the set!" (Gad 2020).[6] Drawing on Spielberg's knack for (capitalistically) merging his films, pop culture, and children's material culture products together (i.e., *E.T.* and Reese's Pieces), he asked Lauper to write and perform the theme song, *The Goonies 'r' Good Enough*.[7] She explained, "Steven really liked my videos and thought my image and what I was about matched the movie. He wanted to merge those two identities" (Jerome 1985). The song was accompanied by two sequential narrative videos (also directed by Donner) that combined span over twelve minutes; the first video came out prior to *The Goonies* release, the second after the film's debut. This project was the first two-part music video, the first movie-theme video, and the first music video to use a studio feature's storylines, characters, sets, and filmmakers for production (Jerome 1985). The video features hot pop culture ephemera of the 1980s—hibachi grilling in the cave, child stars of the film,

Where Do We Belong?

Figure 1.2 (From left): Mikey (Sean Astin), Data (Ke Huy Kwan), Stef (Martha Plimpton), and Mouth (Corey Feldman) are Goonies once again, complete with treasure map, in Cyndi Lauper's (second from right) groundbreaking music video: *The Goonies 'r' Good Enough* (1985).

girl group The Bangles, various cars, a laundry list of famed professional wrestlers, and a cameo from Spielberg himself.[8]

A few years ago, I published a piece examining the portrayals of children's innocence and agency in the works of Steven Spielberg (see Castro 2016). At the time, I was told by one of the editors that I had to exclude *The Goonies* from my discussion since no scholar had yet solidly established the film as decidedly Spielberg's. Thus, since apparently no one (at least not academically) has officially claimed the connection between Spielberg and *The Goonies*, I will do so here in this exploration of fantasy, childhood, and agency. While in that chapter I did detail the following key revelation about who directed *The Goonies*, I am reemphasizing the point here to assist in my argument and because the quote is buried in an endnote. In his autobiography, Sean Astin (Mikey) says that while filming *The Goonies*, Donner

> was something of a drill sergeant: "Get over here kid! Hit your mark! Say your line! Now get out of the way." He was a bombastic leader on the set . . . . Steven was different. The tenor and the ambience when he was directing scenes (and they really were like codirectors) was much gentler, more whimsical. They're

both extraordinary directors, of course, but as a kid I presumed that Steven had a more natural appreciation for the spirit of adventure. (Astin 2004, 135)

Donner, as it turns out, was not exactly prepared to work with so many child actors.[9] Donner explained his frustration while he was making the movie:

> It is the most difficult thing I ever thought I was going to get into. I never anticipated what it was going to be like. Because individually they are wonderful, they are nuts, they are the warmest craziest little things that have come into my life. But in a composite form, you get them all together and it's mind-blowing . . . and yet, it's probably the most gratifying experience because in an odd sort of way, a lot of their energy and excitement is rubbing off on me.

Here, Donner is commenting on the power children's peer groups have in the lives of adults, finding that Spielberg's vision for the film, combined with the whirlwind seven children together can cause, is generationally, and particularly to adults like him, challenging but ultimately worth navigating. As further evidence, every critical review of *The Goonies* in 1985 (that I read) identified Spielberg as the person in charge of the film. I offer two:

> There used to be children's movies and adult movies. Now Spielberg has found an in-between niche, for young teenagers who have fairly sophisticated tastes . . . . He supervises the formula and oversees the production, assigning the direction to stylish action veterans . . . . "Goonies," like "Gremlins," walks a thin line between the cheerful and the gruesome, and the very scenes the adults might object to are the ones the kids will like best: Spielberg is congratulating them on their ability to take the heavy-duty stuff . . . . His technique is to take his thirteen-and fourteen-year-olds and let them act a little older than their age. (Ebert 1985)

> Made under the aegis of Steven Spielberg, and crammed with every pop cultural artifact from Mad Magazine to Michael Jackson's sister, "The Goonies" doesn't even pretend to court the grown-up set. So there may be those who share the sentiments of the "Goonies" character who declares, "I feel like I'm babysitting, except I'm not getting paid," but that hardly matters. There isn't a child in America who won't want to see "The Goonies" this summer . . . . Mr. Spielberg did not direct "The Goonies"; he didn't have to. (Maslin 1985)

At the time of filming, Donner admitted, "Spielberg [is] looking over my shoulder all of the time, which I happen to love because I guess he's the biggest kid of them all and he comes up with the best ideas." In my original content analysis research, I found that *The Goonies* portrays very high levels of youth agency; higher, in fact, than Spielberg's agentic child supermovie *E.T.* In addition, *The Goonies* is the only film of Spielberg's wherein children's agency is enacted for the benefit of the group/society more than for the self or one other person. Also, the children in *The Goonies* are fully realized beings who express their hopes for the future clearly to adults and one another. Between Spielberg's codirecting (according to Astin), Spielberg's arrangement for Lauper to take on the theme music for the film (in Part 1 of her video Lauper even cries out, "Steven Spielberg, how do I get out of this one?" and he answers, "Well, the first thing you sh . . . I don't know"), reviews that name Spielberg the captain of this particular ship, and Donner explaining that Spielberg endlessly hovered around him on set, I think it is high time we recognize Steven Spielberg as maybe not the sole creative force, but certainly the auteur of *The Goonies*—the movie belongs to him. Not doing so does a disservice to Spielberg, for *The Goonies* is a standout exemplar of his life's work, wherein the power of children's peer group agency functions in the name of citizenry and holistic belongingness within a fantasy narrative that, albeit "ordinary," continues to inspire wonderment at the "real" children depicted within.

Connected to such themes, a much more recent fairy tale fantasy narrative of belongingness, identity, and citizenship emerges in Seanan McGuire's novella *Every Heart a Doorway* (2016). A winner of both the Hugo and the Nebula awards, the book is acknowledged for its portrayal of youth's abilities to navigate identity, space, and time: "Growing up isn't a linear process, McGuire puts forth, but a jumpy, chaotic one full of retrograde steps and conflicting rhythms. And innocence is a double-edged sword—something to be yearned for as well as distrusted" (Heller 2016). The novella focuses on Nancy, a new arrival to *Eleanor West's Home for Wayward Children*. Eleanor runs a boarding school for children who have returned to the mortal plane from portal worlds. These children were presented doorways into various fantastical places characterized by major and minor directional qualities, which reflect traveling children's inner characteristics: Logic, Nonsense, Wicked, Virtue, Linearity, Whimsey, Reason, Neutral, Wild, and Rhyme.[10] The school welcomes children who enjoyed their adventures and are struggling to adjust to life back with their parents on the earthly plane, who continue to identify their portal worlds as their true homes, and who then bond together in their newfound expressions, identities, and desires. As Nancy explains, "[my parents] didn't understand me *before* I went away, and now, I might as well be from another planet" (McGuire 2016, 132). Children in the novella thus paradoxically come together as citizens of differing, yet similar, experiences. The students are "united in their marginality from central social (adult) institutions, all these children share temporarily a common, generational culture, while clearly adopting different cultural stances to it with respect to their individual biographical locations" (James, Jenks, and Prout 1998, 88). Children at the school return to the mortal plane for various reasons: they age out of being welcomed by the fairies, do something to offend the occupants of otherworlds, are not sure they want to stay in their portal worlds, or wish to see their families one last time before permanently committing to the other realm. Once children leave their alternate worlds, it is nearly impossible for most of them to find their way back—doorway portals are notoriously difficult to find and rarely appear twice. Eleanor works to help her students adjust while encouraging them to stay hopeful that their door, or a similar one, may open up again in the future. The portal worlds and Eleanor's boarding school certainly qualify as liminal spaces since these are liberating places of fluidity where children agentically claim and perform their identities, finally free from the constraints and scrutiny of their parents and society as a whole (Arai 2011; Cashmore 2014; Clark and Castro, 2019a).

Variation in children's identities is key to the novella, and the characters' beings and becomings span a multiplicity of ages, genders, and sexualities. Fantasy is a space that, while traditionally heteronormative, can provide in its modernity the queering of stories that challenge, disrupt, or transgress popular notions or conventions of time, gender, and sexuality (Campbell 2010; Kenneally 2016; Lehtonen 2013; Nikolajeva 2003; Roberts and MacCallum-Stewart 2016). Time runs differently in portal worlds; as a result, while shorter periods pass on earth, children emerge with a wealth of experience. In such fantasy transformations, new forms of agency are possible (Lehtonen 2013). Magical aging in fantasy "symbolizes the exceptional ability . . . to cross borders and escape the limits of the material body, as well as the social expectations associated with gendered and aged bodies," and characters in fantasy "may easily live a whole life in the imaginary world while no time will pass in their own reality" (Lehtonen 2013, 164–5; Nikolajeva 2003, 143). Sometimes in fantasy, characters have lasting marks to physically prove the alternate aging processes that accompany their traveling and identity transformations; for example, Nancy returns from the Underworld with bone-white hair merely streaked with black since she lived years and years there, but only six months passed on earth.

The novella tracks Nancy's first days at Eleanor's school, her arrival coinciding with a killing spree that she, as the new girl, is suspected of perpetrating by many of the students. Along the way, Nancy makes several good friends in Sumi, Kade, Jack, and Christopher.[11] McGuire calls on a traditional fantasy and children's literature setting, the boarding school, a location that frequently contains narratives of friendships and loyalty, often an isolated place yet young characters experience no homesickness (Gruner 2009).[12] In the school, the children are not passive learners or followers; instead, they are agentic "makers of fashion, gender, social identity, and selves" (Musolf 1996,

315). Kade, for example, runs a clothing exchange program from his attic room. Children arrive at Eleanor's school with suitcases containing clothing they preferred (or likely agreed to prefer) to wear prior to their portal travels. Such structural hurdles to children agentically expressing and actively defining their identities reflect the controlling and unequal power positions that can exist between children and adults (Brannen, Haptinstall, and Bhopal 2000; Jenkins 1998; Pufall and Unsworth 2004; Wyness 2006). So, Nancy opens a suitcase packed by her parents that is filled to the brim with bright, rainbow-colored, cheerful clothes. After her time in the Underworld, she now prefers simple, drab, loose-fitting outfits with no embellishment. Detailing the influence of time and power relations in children's lives, Hood-Williams (2001) explains, "Control over what you wear is linked to controls over where you go and also where you go when" (108). We can consider this control twofold: first, the more obvious, and frankly mundane, control adults have over their children while at home, purchasing clothing and packing children's suitcases on the way to boarding school. However, we can also view control as an agentic process of experience. Time and place and movement through their doorways ("where you go when") changes the children's desires and motivations to control what they wear instead of relinquishing control to adults—would these children attempt to dress differently had they not traveled in the first place? So, Kade's primary role among his peers is to switch out fashion between different students based on self-determined social/gender identities in the now, not before.

Children's parents in *Every Heart a Doorway* are at once criticized, loved, and pitied. The school is, at its core, established because of the disconnect between traveling children and their parents: "the people they loved most in all the world—all this world, at least—dismissed their memories as delusions, their experiences as fantasy, their lives as some intractable illness" (McGuire 2016, 11). When Nancy, with the help of her roommate Sumi, calls on Kade to trade in her clothing, Kade explains, "Parent's don't always like to admit that things have changed. They want the world to be exactly the way it was before their children went away on these life-changing adventures, and when the world doesn't oblige, they try to force it into the boxes they build for us" (McGuire 2016, 38).[13] While several of the children comment that their parents love them, in Kade's words we find recognition that if these children remained in their earthly homes after their adventures, there would be an assumption of "submission to adult expectations of passivity, innocence, and complacency," which would "not leave much room for children to invoke agency" (Castro 2016, 123). As Nancy says, her parents' "love wanted to *fix* her, and refused to see she wasn't broken" (McGuire 2016, 83). In their movements toward expressing their wants, needs, and desires, the traveling children agentically present themselves to themselves and to other students in a reflection, a mirror of their otherworld citizenry, those very places that fashioned their newly formed or until-doorway hidden identities.

Nancy desperately wants to return to the Halls of the Dead, but Kade had a much different experience traveling—he was ejected from Prism for being exposed as a boy. Kade was born a girl, Katie, but the Fairyland's dying King recognized Kade's inner truth and named her as a male heir, the Goblin Prince in Waiting. The Rainbow Princess court fairies were so upset at the "deception" that they threw Kade out of their world. As a result, Kade asserts that while he does not want to go back to Prism, he would do his adventure all over again because

> I grew up there . . . . I figured out who I was there. I kissed a girl with hair the color of cabbages and eyes the color of moth-wings, and she kissed me back, and it was wonderful. Just because I wouldn't go back if you paid me, that doesn't mean I want to forget a *second* of what happened to me. I wouldn't be who I am if I hadn't gone to Prism. (McGuire 2016, 70)

Given Prism's fairies are not accepting of Kade's true self and Kade's parents reject his transgender identity, only willing to welcome him back into their home if he reverts to Katie, the liminal space of Eleanor's school is the sole place where he can be fully expressive. Thus, locality becomes the central crux of citizenry and identity performance for the children, with settings "marked by a plurality of understandings of what it means to belong" (Hall, Coffey, and Williamson 1999, 510). Related, Jack/Jacqueline and Jill/Jillian are identical twin sisters who grew up mislabeled by their parents: Jack was treated as the "pretty" one even though she wanted to be the "smart" one and vice versa. After living in the Moors for five earth years,[14] Jack presents as very literal, no-nonsense, and masculine in dress (glasses, jeans, button-down shirt, vest, bowtie, and slicked-back hair) while Jill presents as a frivolous, feminine stereotype with a weak constitution (pink or pastel lacy, low-cut dresses with ribbons adorning her long curly hair). Each sister dresses in the manner that was expected of her (in her role and by her master) while in the Moors. Finally, Nancy knows she is asexual prior to her journey, but goes through the motions of dating boys to satisfy her parents. Once emerging from the portal, Nancy's process of connecting to new friends at Eleanor's school includes internal struggles on how best to make her peers understand her sexuality, and the novella literally, and perhaps unfortunately, depicts her asexuality through her gender- and color-neutral wardrobe expressions. As Gilbert and colleagues (2017) explain, at school, "Cast as a set of possibilities, sexuality becomes less a description of a sexual orientation than an invocation, a fantasy, a performance" (3). In all the children, there is a hybridity of identities connected to transformation: door travelers, age transcenders, gender claimers, sexuality holders. These identities challenge simplistic categories and binaries, promoting "a complex, fluid, and often contradictory understanding of identities" (Kustatscher, Konstantoni, and Emejulu 2018, 480).[15] In these processes of sexuality and gender identity awakening or growth, portal stories have the capacity to highlight "power associations and imbalances . . . centralizing and making transparent the ways in which literary fantasy attacks real-world problems" (Campbell 2010, 6).

Some scholars trouble "new" sociology of childhood, children's geographies, and childhood studies core concepts or beliefs surrounding agency. Problematizing appears in various forms, but I cover two here. The first is related to voice and movement: agency proponents frequently call on these two elements as proof of children's innate capabilities. Children are lauded for defying the adult, organizational, and national structures that try to silence or truncate them, encompassing: (1) what children say and how they say it (the LOUDER! the better) and (2) how children proceed, where they go, and what they use to get there. However, singularly citing children's use of voice is not advisable as a benchmark of agency because their voices (or interpretations of their voices) are not free from adult distortion, mediation, or ongoing dialogue (Wyness 2015). In my exploration of children's agency enacted in high-structure environments, I find that children sometimes express their voice through parents, wherein children are agentic within structure and among adult rule (Castro 2017). In this work, I conclude that high-structure militates agency, but does preclude agency (Castro 2017). Also, merely listening to children's voices does not guarantee that evaluating adults will know or understand children and their motivations, and at times it is inappropriate for adults to listen to children's voices (Kraftl 2013; Moore 2014).

Thus, we must delve into silence: does not agency also matter when children speak softly, or are silenced, or decide not to speak, or use others as conduits for their voices? Silence is an aspect of voice, so we need "To attend to that which is vocally absent but meaningfully present . . . *to make silence speak*. But to attend to silence requires a radical rethinking" (Spyrou 2016, 10). And as to movement, are not those children who are motionless because of physical disabilities or who are constrained by their restrictive geographical or social surrounds still agentic in their immobility? Kraftl (2013) asserts that children's mobility is rarely independent, and therefore movement is not necessarily an adequate indicator of agency. Pluquailec (2018) explains that childhood studies scholars notoriously approach agency with an eye toward normativity, excluding children who have atypical embodiments, marking out those children's movements as less valuable or agency reductive. As Sharkey (2006) reminds us, "children respond to and shape their environment in very different ways, and agency matters in *any* context" (828, italics added).[16] Thus, movement is not so much an indicator of agency in the actual moving, but instead a better indicator of children's agency is how they move differently or when they decide whether or not to move at all.

Every Heart a Doorway depicts such criticisms and reevaluations through Nancy's embodiment. Nancy summons her silence while actively honoring her own and others' emotions; for example, when Kade explains why he will never return to Prism, "Nancy hadn't known what to say to that, and so she hadn't said anything at all. Increasingly that felt like the safest option she had" (McGuire 2016, 72). So, Nancy agentically calls on silence for protection of self as well as out of respect for her peers. Though silence was a talent she possessed prior to the portal, she honed that ability while in the Underworld. Importantly, silence in that place implied a natural state of being, and learning how to be more silent was a virtue of the quality and expectations of her otherworld space: "in the Halls of the Dead, no one spoke unless they wanted to be listened to" (McGuire 2016, 149). Fisher (1990) explains that in the genre, silence "provides a means of 'listening' to the 'reality' of the fantasy world and to the wisdom . . . meaning is preserved by wordlessness" (48). Complimentary to silence, Nancy also has the great talent of remaining still—in fact, it is her silence and stillness that ultimately saves her from the killer roaming the school. Nancy claims that in her life "she had chosen stillness," and it was the very recognition of that choice that led to her doorway opening into the Halls of the Dead, a place "where she had a prayer of being happy" (McGuire 2016, 86). Nancy's choice of immobility continues while she is at school, wherein "She knew what she needed, and what she needed was to be still" (McGuire 2016, 156). Her peers come to value her abilities; for example, Kade observes Nancy's silence and stillness with wonder:

> ...she did what she always did when she was confused or frightened: she froze, becoming a girl-shaped statue.
> "Whoa . . . . That's some trick. Do you actually turn into stone, or does it only seem like you do? . . . You're holding really, really still, but you're not inanimate. How are you doing that? Are you even still breathing? I can't do that."
> "The Lady of Shadows required that everyone who served her be able to hold properly still . . . . I'm sorry. I tend to freeze up when I get nervous." (McGuire 2016, 123)

Nancy's stillness and silence are intricately tied to her emotions—her deep communion with her inner needs and desires. Lori Campbell (2010) explains that fantasy and portal travel functions as a way inward. She states that movements between worlds via portals "externalize the protagonist's most intimate and usually unacknowledged needs . . . a venture into the ultimate undiscovered country of the self" (Campbell 2010, 10–11). In both her silence and her stillness while occupying the Halls of the Dead, Nancy was recognized and revered by the Lord of the Dead and Lady of Shadows, leading to their invitation for Nancy to stay.[17] Nancy contemplates her stillness and silence as elements that are normative to her being: "maybe her ability to be still was preternaturally honed. It didn't feel like anything special. It just felt *correct*, as if this was what she should have been all the time, always" (McGuire 2016, 156). And so, silence and stillness as a combined talent is enframed by *Every Heart a Doorway* as something innate and natural, bringing with it core protections of body and emotion for self and others. Spyros Spyrou (2016) states that silence is a part of children's "complexity and fullness," and he advises that we must approach it with "care and respect" (18). In this framework, contextualization of children's agency, voice, and movement can be expanded beyond the loud and fast, shifting into the quiet and static.

The second issue relates to children's spirit, intent, and morality. All too often, children's agency is appreciated resolutely. Problematizing approaches to children's agency in this category must first start with childhood studies' broad and uncritical assumptions that all children's agency is good, children who exercise agency are virtuous, and agency guarantees children's independence (Holloway, Holt, and Mills 2019; Lee 1998; Punch 2016). In fact, children's agency is not singularly liberatory and will always include an element of deviance; thus, it should not wholly be viewed as "a positive force in the world" since, in the very least, children frequently break certain rules to enact it (Holloway, Holt, and Mills 2019, 461; James 2011; Wyness 2006, 2015). Not all children employ agency in the spirit of goodwill toward constructive betterment of themselves or others or in pursuit of more utopic societies. Perhaps the reason children's agency is paraded about with such affirmation relates to the lasting romantic depiction of children as innocent in the broader context of power relations (Castro 2016; Gittens 1998; Holloway, Holt, and Mills 2019). In this connection, innocence is frequently associated with those characteristics of children that are attached to negative connotations of passivity, weakness, vulnerability, and helplessness (see Castro 2016). Paradoxically, scholars may simultaneously (and subconsciously) embrace childhood innocence as the reason for why they believe children will always be good and positive agents while they concomitantly avoid characterizing children as passive, weak, vulnerable, and helpless, seeing these traits, along with innocence, as antithetical to and preclusive of agency. However, these elements are not necessarily negative, and Samantha Punch (2016) asserts children's vulnerability must be considered in any examination of agency.[18] As Punch (2016) explains, we are too often intent on qualifying children's agency as either morally positive or negative and instead should view children's agency as a continuum, but if we remain intent on binary assumptions, then generational order and contexts children are entrenched within *must* be taken into account to understand agency more fully.

A good example of "the darker side" of children's agency is found in the characterizations of Jack and Jill. In the Moors, each sister was finally able to live as she wished, with Jack working as a scientist under Dr. Bleak to learn the art of resurrection, while Jill, serving a vampire, became a rampant killer who was ejected from the Moors by Dr. Bleak. Jack asserts that "if she'd been a little smarter," then Jill could have stayed in the Moors and "would have been a beautiful monster" (McGuire 2016, 160).[19] At *Eleanor West's Home for Wayward Children*, Sumi is killed first, followed by several other girls, a part of each girl's body removed while still alive (hands, eyes, brain).[20] Combining their talents and knowhow, Nancy, Kade, Jack, and Christopher eventually discover the person committing these gruesome murderous dismemberments is Jill, who hatches a plan to build a "perfect girl" (à la Frankenstein's monster) so that every portal door will open for her and she can finally return home to the Moors and her vampire Master. Buckingham (2019) cautions against essentializing children's agency since, "Agency is not always a positive thing, and it can have negative consequences" (286). The spirit of Buckingham's (2019) statement is reflected in *Every Heart a Doorway*—I contend the duality of possibility and intent in agency is "like the duality of the doors: they changed lives, and they destroyed them, all with the same, simple invitation. *Come through, and see*" (McGuire 2016, 105). There is no definitive in the doors, just as there is no definitive in children's agency and no definitive in children's lives. The element of context is integral when unpacking Jill's actions and motivations. Childhood studies scholars emphasize that it is dangerous to ignore the context of events and surrounds when interrogating children's agency, their voices, and their movements (see, for example, Castro 2017; France 2004; James 2011; Pufall and Unsworth 2004; Punch 2016). In their widely cited work on agency as a concept and element of personal and social life, Emirbayer and Mische (1998) explain that "temporal-relational contexts support particular agentic orientations, which in turn constitute different structuring relationships of actors toward their environments" (1004). In all the children's experiences in the novella, an ambivalence exists as a result of their movements into otherworld doorways and back out onto the rough mortal plane, which obviously structures their agentic motivations, feelings of belongingness, and pledged citizenry (see Jans 2004).

Since nearly all children at the boarding school want to return to their otherworlds, some claim they would do nearly anything to get there. Jill is the child who acts on this desire, and so her "beautiful monster" self that was fashioned in the Moors is unleashed on the school. Jenkins (1998) states that in children's agency and culture there are "moments of hegemonic incorporation and moments of resistance. The same girl or boy may sometimes conform and sometimes disobey" (28). In this dance, children "play a variety of roles . . . although many of those roles might also be culturally determined, they are often differently situated within and between cultures so that each child brings to those roles their own interpretation" (James and James 2004, 214). Just as agency is not an *absolute* for children, so too should we accept that the tenor of their agency is not *resolute*. Children participate in interpretive reproduction, and in the case of the characters in *Every Heart a Doorway* this process encompasses what students learn in their otherworlds and how these skills are interpreted or reproduced, positively or negatively or neutrally, on the earthly plane. The time and space constraints the children bring with them between worlds contain "contested meaning, conventions of placing and avenues of possibilities" (Christensen, James, and Jenks 2000, 153; James, Jenks, and Prout 1998). Yes, one such possibility in a fantasy tale is that an agentic child chooses to hurt others in the pursuit of escape to where she feels most welcome. Jack explains:

> ...that's the thing people forget when they start talking about things in terms of good and evil . . . . For us, the places we went were home. We didn't care if they were good or evil or neutral or what. We cared about the fact that for the first time, we didn't have to pretend to be something we weren't. We just got to *be*. That made all the difference in the world . . . . It didn't care about whether something *could* be done. It was about whether it *should* be done, and the answer was always, always *yes*. (McGuire 2016, 57 & 82)

In her work on children's geographies, Gill Valentine (1996) outlines that "despite the complex and multiple realities of young people's lives, representations of childhood have repeatedly drawn on simplified oppositional significations of angels-devils. At different moments one or other of these binary understandings of childhood has temporally dominated popular imaginings of what it means to be a child" (596). Jack's explanation of the Moors, and by extension all of the students' doorway travels, emphasizes two things—first, the dichotomy of good versus evil/angel versus devil is not only limiting to children in its moralistic absolute, it also strains children's bodies and emotions. Second, Jack makes the point that instead of this dichotomy, adults should view children through the very agency continuum Punch (2016) stresses, wherein alternate, non-partisan approaches open up possibility in childhood's beings and becomings. Fairy tale and fantasy stories have strengths and "delusional repercussions" (Honeyman 2010, 178); as previously discussed, while traditionally fairy tales were constructed to maintain and restrain children within societal or adult measures of good morality, in fantasy's modernity there is fluidity and potentiality in children's agentic acts. Thus, *Every Heart a Doorway* truthfully reflects that some children who undergo exceptional experiences can find it difficult to adjust to a hostile and unwelcoming dominant culture (Cashmore 2014). In this sense, the children moving through their doors and then returning to a place they no longer consider home dictates a change in their agendas and citizenship alliances, wherein time and travel have altered their desires and motivations, delimiting the visions of who they were there and who they are here (see James 2011; James, Curtis, and Birch 2008; Jenkins 1998). In their otherness, "affective geographies of their distant, other worlds . . . are vital to what children's lives are" (Jones 2009, 201). *Every Heart a Doorway* presents children's lives as messy, sad, hopeful, and destructive, and in that message, we can possibly admit that adultist approaches to children's agency are, perhaps, also messy, sad, hopeful, and, yes, potentially destructive.

With that said, it is in the attempt to recognize children's agency, honor their integral place in society, and interrogate their sense of belongingness and holistic citizenry, in whatever shape, measure, or tenor these elements take, that we move forward in our collective purpose and shared knowledge. The fantasy forms found in this book span film, novels, television, social media, and games and play. In thinking on how to organize these works, I call on many characteristic elements of fantasy. The "genre of modern fantasy is characterized by a narrative frame that unites timeless mythic patterns with contemporary individual experiences. Its stories at their hearts are about the relationship between the individual and the infinite" (Mathews 2011, 1). So, each chapter is indexed and contextualized by two topics that are integral to fantasy and reflected in the author's analysis, just as this introductory chapter is headed Adventure/Otherworld. While some of the chapters in this book explore children's agency as represented in fictionalized works, others are situated in empirical research and observation and yet the children continue to embody the creativity, hope, heart, and infiniteness that typify the genre. The authors hail from a range of disciplines, including Sociology, Anthropology, Education, History, and English. Their works combine children's agency theories with interrogation of those various elements that make up childhood, encompassing: material and peer cultures, protectionism and alienation, identity formation and group bonds, leisure and work, generationality and family relationships, school and home, and opened and closed spaces and places. As a unit, the chapter authors approach children's agency from different viewpoints and bravely expose the negative, in addition to the positive, qualities of children and their surrounds.

Reflecting Dream/Good vs. Evil, Peter W.Y. Lee offers "A Futile Rage against the Machine: The Triumph of *The 5,000 Fingers of Dr. T*." This film was the live-action Hollywood pursuit of Theodor Geisel/Dr. Seuss.

Focalizing on one boy's dream of overcoming the dictatorial machine known as adult rule, *The 5,000 Fingers of Dr. T* (1953) depicts how it is sometimes difficult for children to overcome regimes of control in their lives (Qvortrup 2008). With a boy who desires a father and who wants to play baseball instead of practicing piano, the dream entails overthrowing his evil piano teacher by making a machine from bits of his boyhood material culture to save himself along with a mass of boys enslaved to play, as a unit, Dr. T's immense piano. The boy also imagines a plumber to function as his father figure, his mother's new husband, and his buddy, reflecting and ultimately embracing nuclear heteronormative family benchmarks of the era. Lee states that the mixed content of this fantasy led to its poor reception in theaters, perhaps because Geisel's initial, and much stronger, messages of boyhood agency and criticisms of capitalism were softened or completely cut from the film.

Imagination and Transformation are addressed in Kostas Magos and Sophia Kremmydiotou's "Developing Children's Agency through Play with Imaginary Companions," an empirical piece that studies young children and their imaginary friends in Athens, Greece. The children transform dolls, stuffed animals, action figures, and invisible beings into their fantasy imaginary companions. Children and friends do everything from treasure hunting to spending the day together shopping and eating. Dynamics between playfulness, space, time, and material culture as children imagine elsewheres, while still remaining at home, highlight children's creative agency in their active meaning-making (Burke 2005; Jans 2004). Magos and Kremmydiotou find that play with imaginary companions does not necessarily always encompass positive, happy emotions; sometimes, imaginary friends are antagonistic or influence bad behavior, but imaginary friend play reveals the ability of children to reflect on the self, show care toward others, or work through beliefs they have regarding aspects of Greek culture.

Tara Moore's "Arcadia is in the Hands of Teenagers: Team Power in Guillermo del Toro's *Trollhunters*" considers Heroism and Supernatural elements. del Toro is well-known for depicting supernatural influences in the lives of children and their families, and he continues to do so in this animated series for Netflix. Over three seasons, the children in *Trollhunters* (2016–2018) navigate changing expectations connected to their everyday lives aboveground and their shared supernatural powers below. The hero protagonist endeavors to balance teenage life between his mother, peers, and school while serving in his magically chosen role. As they age, material and magical spaces surrounding the agentic young characters of *Trollhunters* eventually coalesce; thus, "it is precisely through the dynamic and fluid movement of children in, out and around the home that their own sense of belonging . . . is constituted" (Christensen, James, and Jenks 2000, 153). Moore makes some convincing thematic comparisons between *Trollhunters*' chosen hero and his triumphs and struggles and "The Chosen One" heroine and her journey found in the beloved fantasy television series *Buffy the Vampire Slayer* (1997–2003).

In the next chapter, I offer "The Boy Who Lives: Agentic Locations of Friendship Identity, Peer Culture, and Interpretive Reproduction in *Harry Potter*." Exemplifying Magic/Journey themes, J.K. Rowling's Harry Potter series (1997–2007) is *the* benchmark of modern fantasy, with its seven books globally capturing the hearts of children and adults alike. Calling on "new" sociology of childhood theory blended with children's geographies work, I discuss the friendships and culture formed between students at the magic school Hogwarts. Starting with the underutilized "children's islanding" theories of Helga Zeiher (2001, 2003), elements of children's friendships (sharing, solidarity, trust, and secrecy) further contextualize the chapter, with special attention paid to what I view as the most important friendship made during Harry's journey, that with Luna Lovegood. Empowerment for Harry and his friends emerges from individuality but also cohesion, choice but also preternatural selection (Lehtonen 2013). Harry and his peer group show their capacity for interpretive reproduction—embracing, altering, or (re)creating various material culture artifacts during their childhood. In the shared space of Hogwarts and beyond, they agentically come together to formulate their identities and collectively accomplish shared goals.

Michele D. Castleman's "All in the Family: The Agency of Demigods and Godlings in the Mythic World of Rick Riordan" illustrates Mythology/Quest. Focalizing on children of gods, Castleman discusses various fantasy series of Rick Riordan (Percy Jackson; Kane; Magnus Chase, etc.) that present characters framed out by identity, diversity, and intersectionality. Children in his stories negotiate family dynamics that are laden with multifaceted internal conflicts, parental abandonment and abuse, and intergenerational power struggles. Riordan's books contain the message that "children and young people's social identities involve complex, shifting, and potentially contradictory forms of being and belonging in terms of their multiple positions in relation to gender, social class, race, ethnicity, age, religion, sexuality, disability/ability, and more" (Kustatscher, Konstantoni, and Emejulu 2018, 476). Contextualized by their relationships with other demigods and their experiences living among mortal humans, young characters approach prophesies and quests with newfound powers, agentic courage, and deep dedication to fairness.

"Young People's Agency in Online Fan Spaces," written by Parinita Shetty, broaches Conflict/Justice that plays out on Facebook fan sites for popular fantasy texts. Observing social media spaces and posts dedicated to Harry Potter and Percy Jackson, Shetty finds that youth's creative conversation, agentic participation, and community engagement flourish there.

A central quality of liminality is present online, wherein class and age differences are diminished and youth's cultural productions offer the promise of and potential for challenging the social order and contributing to social change (Corsaro 2005; James, Jenks, and Prout 1998; Kenny 2019; Wyness 2015). Fan participants are usually empathetic, expressing solidarity while imagining characters' omitted contexts, alternate trajectories, or post-novel outcomes. Posters tackle inequality, oppression, and injustice, conversing about real-world issues using the books' characters and themes as a frame of reference in the attempt to diminish stigma or further understand prejudice and discrimination. While conflict between participants does happen, cohesion emerges from youth's moral agency and creative activism working toward political and social transformation.

Theories on Portals/Time are expanded in Ida Fadzillah Leggett's "Girls' Agency through Supermobility: The Power of Imagined Futures in Young Adult Fantasy Literature." The author proposes a new type of movement in fantasy literature—supermobility—that emerges from novel geographies and agentic identities presented to girl readers in Laini Taylor's *Daughter of Smoke and Bone* trilogy (2011–2014). Taylor's books embrace magic, religion, and myth, with characters descending from aliens, angels, and chimaera, and when combined with the protagonist's cultural knowledge, artistic joie de vivre, and global travel via portals, girls are given a vision of unlimited potential. The books answer the call from girls who are "in the search for grand narratives of resistance," presenting childhood as something that can always change or be reconstituted within and between time (Renold and Ringrose 2008, 316; Shanahan 2007). Leggett asserts that this fairy tale fantasy story expands and empowers global girls' imaginaries, wherein they can envision more possibilities for their identities, girlhoods, and lives in the alternative gender scripts emerging from Taylor's powerful literary characters.

Finally, I join Ana Lilia Campos-Manzo for "Being Scared in the Dark: Paradoxes, Perils, and the Promise of Fantasy for Urban Girls of Color." Girls' Movement/Power in urban streets, neighborhoods, and life is limited due to gendered messages of fear. In this qualitative piece based on interviews with girls of color, Campos-Manzo and I find that girls' movements are truncated twofold: parents limit girls' presence on the streets while girls self-monitor their own travel in the city. Some girls witness street violence, while others talk of predatory men; darkness ushers in heightened fear and danger for the girls. Hope emerging from play brings a sense of power into their lives, with tween girls of color coopting a locker room to play scary games in the dark. The girls (surreptitiously) claim the locker room as a children's place, into which they attribute lost meanings of joy and freedom while redefining their gendered subjectivities and reconfiguring their embodied girlhood experiences (Lehtonen 2013; Rasmussen 2004; Skelton 2000). Urban girls of color bravely "taking back the night" via fantasy play and pop culture performance demonstrates how children can creatively reconnect to one another within and outside of the paradoxes of fear that encircle and structure their lives.

Fantasy and fairy tales frequently include a protagonist who has dissatisfaction in life, leading to the act of "simultaneously running away from something and running toward something else" (Castro 2005, 220). When this character is the oft-forgotten child or the child who is searching for a place to belong, breaking spells and enacting agency through individual choice leads to the onset of emancipation and transformation of the self (Castro 2005; Lehtonen 2013; Zipes 1988). The children of modern fantasy are placed in a variety of uncanny circumstances, and they strive to agentically claim their own power while raging against others who characterize them as weak, vulnerable, or traumatized (see Cashmore 2014; Castro 2019b). The sense of purpose underlying children acting independently in unfamiliar environments offers a "small glimmer of light in a somewhat dark story" (James, Curtis, and Birch 2008, 95). Owain Jones (2009) asserts, "children are always, in some respects, on their own, in other places" (200). Perhaps this fact is why children and adults delve into fantasy with such ferocity—we find our own hope in the possibility of wandering children meeting someone who or coming across something that encourages them to feel not so alone. The fantastic journey of the child always seems better when friends are made and tasks are faced together. As Cyndi Lauper said after making her music video, "Goonies have each other. I was singular, alone. I wished when I was small that I had friends. I never was lucky enough to have friends like these kids in the film" (Jerome 1985). The wistfulness in her memory and reflection is likely the reason we find ourselves repeatedly returning to our favorite fantasy novels and films—the characters and storylines become something akin to our friends, keeping us company when we need them most.

Fantasy offers us a version of childhood that is "a rich and complicated space/time of varied experiences" (Talley 2011, 122). Each of the chapters in this book relate to children's holistic citizenry in and through fantasy: it is through their creativity, relationships, and trials and tribulations that children reflect upon their just discovered, newly formed, or partially hidden identities as members of cultures, locales, and worlds close and faraway. In doing so, children in fantasy, or children consuming fantasy, or children who employ fantasy in their lives further explore childhood in its various forms, enacting agency on behalf of themselves and others in the pursuit of satisfying curiosity, claiming space and place, resolving lost history, or journeying toward their next great adventure.

NOTES

1. See Castro (2017) for a discussion of children's smallness representing "small, insignificant views" (166; see also Wyness 2006).
2. For those who do not recognize the latter name, he is the main character in *Charlie and the Chocolate Factory* (1964).
3. See Giunta (2019) for more on the importance of boys' bikes in the suburbs and children's mobile material culture found in Spielberg's predecessor film *E.T. the Extra-Terrestrial* (1982) and Netflix's web series that pays homage to all things '80s, *Stranger Things* (2016–present). Also, see Clark and Castro (2019a) on the central role material culture plays in the portrayal of adventure and agency in boyhood.
4. Reasons for this assessment include, but are not limited to, the ethnic stereotyped portrayals of Data and the Fratelli family and the fat shaming of Chunk: "It's hard to imagine a kids movie being made nowadays with something like the truffle shuffle in it" (TheJournal.ie. 2015). Other fantasy films from the '80s have been altered to fit twenty-first-century hyperprotectionist standards held by adults toward children. For example, the streaming service Disney+ recently edited *Splash* (1984) to remove nudity from the mermaid Madison by covering up actor Daryl Hannah's bare backside with CGI hair and blurring her naked body. In 2001, Spielberg himself decided to postedit *E.T.* 20 years after its initial release, removing law enforcement officer's guns and replacing the offending items with CGI walkie-talkies. Ten years later, however, the director changed his mind and announced the next iteration of *E.T.* would return the guns: "I tried [changing a film] once and lived to regret it. Not because of fan outrage, but because I was disappointed in myself. I got overly sensitive to [some of the reaction] to E.T., and I thought if technology evolved, [I might go in and change some things] . . . it was OK for a while, but I realized what I had done was I had robbed people who loved E.T. of their memories of E.T." (Leitch 2011). Both *Splash* and *E.T.* were originally rated PG, but what were considered non-sexualized or non-threatening integral elements of plotlines in the '80s are now deemed gratuitous and not "family friendly." See Castro (2005, 2016) for why '80s films, specifically, depict children with more freedom and autonomy.
5. This quote from Steven Spielberg and all of the following quotes from Richard Donner are retrieved from *The Goonies* DVD Special Feature documentary "The Making of *The Goonies*."
6. Adding to the crossover between the "real" stars and the "fictional" Goonies children, Donner says, "I never let the kids see this boat, they were banned from the stage, from day one, from the start of its construction." The first day of filming on the *Inferno*, Donner brought the children in with their backs to set, so when the actors see the ship for the first time, so too do the Goonies; thus, the awed wonder of the children caught on film is real. These types of true reaction shots are no longer possible with green screen movie making. To note, the *Inferno* was destroyed after filming because the moviemakers could not find anyone who wanted the immense ship.
7. Proving the lasting cachet of *The Goonies*, a few years ago a line of Funko Pop! figures were made in the likenesses of Mikey, Chunk, Data, Mouth, and Sloth (the

abused and malformed adult third child of the Fratelli family, who Chunk befriends while in captivity. Sloth greatly assists the children in escaping the Fratellis and getting out of the pirate caves, and he is invited to live with Chunk and his family in the last scene of the film). The toy figures, released in 2013 and 2014 for about $10, now resell for between $70 and $400, Data and Sloth the priciest. Oswell (2013) states that "Children's agency is not set against commercialisation, but facilitated through it. It is through marketisation that children have been endowed with greater personhood" (210). Certainly true, I however think we can agree that most children would never be able to afford one of these Goonies figurines today, instead becoming fodder for avid adult collectors of toys and film memorabilia. Thus, we have evidence of how children's material and play culture is occasionally coopted by adult commercial and capitalistic culture.

8. All children from the film were in Lauper's music video except for Kerri Green (Andy), who was already filming the much-loved Pygmalionesque fairy-tale-turned-on-its-head movie *Lucas* (1986). Hibachi grill restaurants with Asian chefs performing tricks with food were wildly popular in the suburbs during the '80s. While gaining fame in the mid- to late '80s, The Bangles were relatively unknown at the time of filming Lauper's video. The cars in the video are a Woody Wagon, Camaro Z28, and just-then available in the U.S. Mitsubishi Mirage, the latter of which the wrestlers lift off the ground in the video. The wrestlers notably include André the Giant, Captain Lou Albano, Rowdy Roddy Piper, and The Iron Sheik, among others. Of all the wrestlers appearing in the video, André the Giant is still best known today. Often referred to as a "gentle giant," he was highly regarded by all who knew and worked with him prior to his untimely death from congestive heart failure, caused by acromegaly and gigantism. Shepard Fairey built his pop culture print and clothing empire OBEY: André the Giant Has a Posse on the shoulders of André the Giant's image, and outside of wrestling André the Giant is probably best known for his beloved pirate character Fezzick in the live-action fairy tale favorite *The Princess Bride* (1987). Wrestling, of course, is the literal translation of fantasy into the Cyndi Lauper music video, for in addition to the popularity of WWF (World Wrestling Federation) at the time, wrestling of this caliber is in itself the most fantasy-oriented sport, with its performance of rich character roles, elaborate costumes, ring-acting, and spoofy feuds.

9. Shockingly (though he seems to say it, at least partially, in jest), a clip from "The Making of *The Goonies*" shows Donner at the time of filming saying, "I think the uniquest part of working with kids, this many kids in a film, is that every night I'm contemplating suicide." However, considering the film as a working product, he says that in contrast to the all-children scenes, he does not like the ones filmed with the adults. In Gad's (2020) *Reunited Apart*, Spielberg explains that after *The Goonies* wrapped, Donner retreated to his home in Hawaii for some rest and relaxation after experiencing such a "difficult" time wrangling all the kids in the movie. In a wildly orchestrated prank, Spielberg then bought the child actors tickets to Hawaii, depositing them all on Donner's doorstep.

10. Jack explains that children's inner attributes attract the doors and it is those sympathetic elements that enable children (at least the ones who come to Eleanor's school) to be happy in their otherworlds.

11. Like Nancy, Christopher also went to an Underworld, a Día de los Muertos sort of place. Kade undergoes discrimination from one of the children at the school because of his sexuality, while Nancy comes under attack from students who went to light and bright Fairyworlds because Underworlds are often viewed as bad, scary, and improper places by the rainbows and candy crowd. Christopher, however, does not suffer from such bullying because he gets in with the "cool" kids at school and he purposely hides his unique Underworld talent to avoid being outcasted—he can talk to the bones of the dead with a flute made out of an ulna.

12. The children are in fact homesick, but not in the traditional sense of earthly home. They miss their portal homes.

13. See Clark and Castro (2019b) and Cashmore (2014) for further discussion of children not being believed, recognized, responded to, or valued for their special knowledge by the adults in their lives.

14. The Moors world type is not specified in the novella, but Eleanor mentions that Netherworlds exist, so perhaps that is where the Moors is located.

15. See Castro (2019b), Clark and Castro (2019a), Kraftl (2013), and Prout (2000) for more on hybridity, identity, social relationships, and childhood.

16. Also, see James (2011) for a discussion of the importance of incorporating local contexts into understanding the experience of being a child.

17. Nancy is sent back to the earthly plane by the Lord so that she can be absolutely sure she wants to forever remain in the Halls of the Dead. While in the Underworld, she often thought of her parents, but once she returns to earth, all she desires is to get back through the doorway.

18. As an example, I find that girls' physical agency can importantly come from control and power borne out of gendered and ageist assumptions of children's innocence, weakness, vulnerability, and helplessness (Castro 2019b; see also Esser 2016; Kitzinger 2015). In that work, I discuss the agency of a fictional posthuman girl who uses those key assumptions of childhood and girlhood to overtake an adult male attacker intent on killing her. Calling on those purported negative qualities, she pretends to cry and reaches for a hug so as to mete out her deadly blow, saving herself and all other posthumans who remain on earth (Castro 2019b).

19. Jack explains that she was not the one evicted from the Moors. Jack accompanied Jill back to earth because she felt it was the right thing to do given their family ties. Eventually, it is revealed that Jack's door to the Moors was always open, she just never went back through it because of protectiveness for and allegiance to her twin sister.

20. The school is predominantly populated by girls since fairies are prone to entice girls into their otherworlds (according to McGuire 2016). A clear commentary on gender socialization, the text states that girls are not paid attention to or missed nearly as much or quickly enough in comparison to boys, leading to more girls experiencing successful transitions between earth and portal worlds.

REFERENCES

Arai, Lisa. 2011. "Growing Up: Moving Through Time, Place and Space from Babyhood to Adolescence." In *Children and Young People's Spaces: Developing Practice*, edited by Pam Foley and Stephen Leverett, 118–30. Hampshire: Palgrave Macmillan.

Astin, Sean. 2004. *There and Back Again: An Actor's Tale*. New York, NY: St. Martin's Press.

Beauvais, Clémentine. 2012. "Romance, Dystopia, and the Hybrid Child." In *Contemporary Adolescent Literature and Culture: The Emergent Adult*, edited by Mary Hilton and Maria Nikolajeva, 61–76. Surrey: Ashgate.

Boone, Brian. 2016. "The Untold Truth of *The Goonies*." *Looper*. September 19, 2016. https://www.looper.com/24998/untold-truth-goonies/.

Brannen, Julia, Ellen Haptinstall, and Kalwant Bhopal. 2000. *Connecting Children: Care and Family Life in Later Childhood*. London: Routledge/Falmer.

Buckingham, David. 2000. *After the Death of Childhood: Growing Up in the Age of Electronic Media*. Cambridge: Polity.

———. 2019. "Afterword: Agency and Representation in Children's Media Culture." In *Representing Agency in Popular Culture: Children and Youth on Page, Screen, and In Between*, edited by Ingrid E. Castro and Jessica Clark, 283–8. Lanham, MD: Lexington Books.

Burke, Catherine. 2005. "'Play in Focus': Children Researching Their Own Spaces and Places for Play." *Children, Youth and Environments* 15 (1): 27–53.

Campbell, Lori M. 2010. *Portals of Power: Magical Agency and Transformation in Literary Fantasy*. Jefferson, NC: McFarland & Company.

Cashmore, Judith. 2014. "Children in Exceptional Circumstances." In *The SAGE Handbook of Child Research*, edited by Gary B. Melon, Asher Ben-Arieh, Judith Cashmore, Gail S. Goodman, and Natalie K. Worley, 197–207. Los Angeles, CA: SAGE.

Castro, Ingrid E. 2005. "Children's Agency and Cinema's New Fairy Tale." In *Sociological Studies of Children and Youth, Volume 11*, edited by David A. Kinney and Katherine B. Rosier, 215–37. Amsterdam: Elsevier.

———. 2016. "Children, Innocence, and Agency in the Films of Steven Spielberg." In *Children in the Films of Steven Spielberg*, edited by Adrian Schober and Debbie Olson, 121–40. Lanham, MD: Lexington Books.

———. 2017. "Contextualizing Agency in High-Structure Environments: Children's Participation in Parent Interviews." In *Researching Children and Youth: Methodological Issues, Strategies, and Innovations—Sociological Studies of Children and Youth, Volume 22*, edited by Ingrid E. Castro, Melissa Swauger, and Brent Harger, 149–73. Bingley: Emerald.

———. 2019a. "The Spirit and the Witch: Hayao Miyazaki's Agentic Girls and Their (Intra)Independent Genderational Childhoods." In *Representing Agency in Popular Culture: Children and Youth on Page, Screen, and In Between*, edited by Ingrid E. Castro and Jessica Clark, 255–82. Lanham, MD: Lexington Books.

———. 2019b. "The *Emergence* of Agency After Bionuclear War: Posthuman Child—Animal Possibilities." In *Child and Youth Agency in Science Fiction:*

Travel, Technology, Time, edited by Ingrid E. Castro and Jessica Clark, 251–72. Lanham, MD: Lexington Books.

Christensen, Pia, Allison James, and Chris Jenks. 2000. "Home and Movement: Children Constructing 'Family Time.'" In *Children's Geographies: Playing, Living, Learning*, edited by Sarah L. Holloway and Gill Valentine, 139–55. London: Routledge.

Clark, Jessica, and Ingrid E. Castro. 2019a. "Girl Zombies and Boy Wonders: The Future of Agency Is Now!" In *Child and Youth Agency in Science Fiction: Travel, Technology, Time*, edited by Ingrid E. Castro and Jessica Clark, 1–21. Lanham, MD: Lexington Books.

———. 2019b. "ZuZu's Petals and Scout's Mockingbirds: The Legacy of Children's Agency in Popular Culture." In *Representing Agency in Popular Culture: Children and Youth on Page, Screen, and In Between*, edited by Ingrid E. Castro and Jessica Clark, xi–xxxi. Lanham, MD: Lexington Books.

Cleveland, Hannah. 2015. "Five Children's Books You Didn't Know Were Banned." *Reading Partners*. September 28, 2015. https://readingpartners.org/blog/five-childrens-books-you-didnt-know-were-banned/.

Corsaro, William A. 1992. "Interpretive Reproduction in Children's Peer Cultures." *Social Psychology Quarterly* 55 (2): 160–77.

———. 2005. "Collective Action and Agency in Young Children's Peer Cultures." In *Studies in Modern Childhood: Society, Agency, Culture*, edited by Jens Qvortrup, 231–47. Hampshire: Palgrave Macmillan.

———. 2015. *The Sociology of Childhood* (4th ed.). Thousand Oaks, CA: SAGE.

Day, Sara K., Miranda A. Green-Barteet, and Amy L. Montz. 2014. "Introduction: From 'New Woman' to 'Future Girl': The Roots and the Rise of the Female Protagonist in Contemporary Young Adult Dystopias." In *Female Rebellion in Young Adult Dystopian Fiction*, edited by Sara K. Day, Miranda A. Green-Barteet, and Amy L. Montz, 1–14. New York, NY: Routledge.

Ebert, Roger. 1985. "The Goonies." *Roger Ebert.com*. January 1, 1985. https://www.rogerebert.com/reviews/the-goonies-1985.

Elber, Lynn. 2020. "'Goonies' Cast, 'Flintstones' Rescue TV Viewers in Pandemic." *Las Vegas Sun*. April 30, 2020. https://lasvegassun.com/news/2020/apr/30/goonies-cast-flintstones-rescue-tv-viewers-in-pand/.

Emirbayer, Mustafa, and Ann Mische. 1998. "What Is Agency?" *American Journal of Sociology* 103 (4): 962–1023.

Esser, Florian. 2016. "Neither 'Thick' nor 'Thin': Reconceptualising Agency and Childhood Relationally." In *Reconceptualising Agency and Childhood: New Perspectives in Childhood Studies*, edited by Florian Esser, Meike S. Baader, Tanja Betz, and Beatrice Hungerland, 48–60. Oxon: Routledge.

Fisher, Leona W. 1990. "Mystical Fantasy for Children: Silence and Community." *The Lion and the Unicorn* 14 (2): 37–57.

France, Alan. 2004. "Young People." In *Doing Research with Children and Young People*, edited by Sandy Fraser, Vicky Lewis, Sharon Ding, Mary Kellett, and Chris Robinson, 175–90. London: SAGE.

Gad, Josh. 2020. "Reunited Apart: The Goonies." *YouTube*. April 27, 2020. https://www.youtube.com/watch?v=-SF_VyXQpyo.

Garris, Mick. 1985. "The Making of *The Goonies*." Directed by Mick Garris. Documentary: Special Feature, *The Goonies* DVD. USA: Amblin Entertainment, Warner Brothers Pictures.

Gilbert, Jen, Jessica Fields, Laura Mamo, and Nancy Lesko. 2017. "Tending Toward Friendship: LGBTQ Sexualities in US Schools." *Sexualities*. DOI: 10.1177/1363460717731931.

Gittens, Diana. 1998. *The Child in Question*. Hampshire: Macmillan Press.

Giunta, Joseph. 2019. "'Why Are You Keeping This Curiosity Door Locked?' Childhood Subjectivities and Play As Conflict Resolution in the Postmodern Web Series *Stranger Things*." In *Child and Youth Agency in Science Fiction: Travel, Technology, Time*, edited by Ingrid E. Castro and Jessica Clark, 25–53. Lanham, MD: Lexington Books.

Greenhill, Pauline, and Sidney E. Matrix. 2010. "Introduction—Envisioning Ambiguity: Fairy Tale Films." In *Fairy Tale Films: Visions of Ambiguity*, edited by Pauline Greenhill and Sidney E. Matrix, 1–22. Logan, UT: Utah State University Press.

Gruner, Elisabeth R. 2009. "Teach the Children: Education and Knowledge in Recent Children's Fantasy." *Children's Literature* 37: 216–35.

Hall, Tom, Amanda Coffey, and Howard Williamson. 1999. "Self, Space and Place: Youth Identities and Citizenship." *British Journal of Sociology of Education* 20 (4): 501–13.

Haviland, Virginia. 1971. "Questions to an Artist Who Is Also an Author: A Conversation Between Maurice Sendak and Virginia Haviland." *The Quarterly Journal of the Library of Congress* 28 (4): 262–80.

Heller, Jason. 2016. "'Every Heart' Is a Doorway to Winning Fantasy." *National Public Radio*. April 9, 2016. https://www.npr.org/2016/04/09/471619427/every-heart-is-a-doorway-to-winning-fantasy.

Hentges, Sarah. 2018. *Girls on Fire: Transformative Heroines in Young Adult Dystopian Literature*. Jefferson, NC: McFarland & Company.

Hentoff, Nat. 1966. "Among the Wild Things: Maurice Sendak's Fantastic Imagination." *The New Yorker*. January 22, 1966. https://www.newyorker.com/magazine/1966/01/22/among-the-wild-things.

Holloway, Sarah L., Louise Holt, and Sarah Mills. 2019. "Questions of Agency: Capacity, Subjectivity, Spatiality and Temporality." *Progress in Human Geography* 43 (3): 458–77.

Honeyman, Susan. 2010. *Consuming Agency in Fairy Tales, Childlore, and Folkliterature*. New York, NY: Routledge.

Hood-Williams, John. 2001. "Power Relations in Children's Lives." In *Childhood in Europe: Approaches—Trends—Findings*, edited by Manuela Du Bois-Reymond, Heinz Sünker, and Heinz-Hermann Krüger, 91–116. New York, NY: Peter Lang.

James, Allison. 1993. *Childhood Identities: Self and Social Relationships in the Experience of the Child*. Edinburgh: Edinburgh University Press.

———. 2011. "To Be (Come) or Not to Be (Come): Understanding Children's Citizenship." *The ANNALS of the American Academy of Political and Social Science* 633 (1): 167–79.

James, Allison, Penny Curtis, and Joanna Birch. 2008. "Care and Control in the Construction of Children's Citizenship." In *Children and Citizenship*, edited by Antonella Invernizzi and Jane Williams, 85–96. Los Angeles, CA: SAGE.

James, Allison, and Adrian L. James. 2004. *Constructing Childhood: Theory, Policy and Social Practice*. Hampshire: Palgrave Macmillan.

James, Allison, Chris Jenks, and Alan Prout. 1998. *Theorizing Childhood*. Cambridge: Polity Press.

Jans, Marc. 2004. "Children As Citizens: Towards a Contemporary Notion of Child Participation." *Childhood* 11 (1): 27–44.

Jenkins, Henry. 1998. "Introduction: Childhood Innocence and Other Modern Myths." In *The Children's Culture Reader*, edited by Henry Jenkins, 1–37. New York, NY: New York University Press.

Jerome, Jim. 1985. "Great Goonies!" *People*. July 1, 1985. https://people.com/archive/cover-story-great-goonies-vol-24-no-1/.

Jones, Owain. 2009. "Approaching the Otherness of Childhood: Methodological Considerations." In *Doing Children's Geographies: Methodological Issues in Research with Young People*, edited by Lorraine van Blerk and Mike Kesby, 195–212. Oxfordshire: Routledge.

Kenneally, Stephen. 2016. "Hiding in Plain Sight: The Invisibility of Queer Fantasy." In *Gender and Sexuality in Contemporary Popular Fantasy: Beyond Boy Wizards and Kick-Ass Chicks*, edited by Jude Roberts and Esther MacCallum-Stewart, 8–20. Oxon: Routledge.

Kenny, Erin. 2019. "'Ship Wars' and the OTP: Narrating Desire, Literate Agency, and Emerging Sexualities in Fanfiction of *The 100*." In *Child and Youth Agency in Science Fiction: Travel, Technology, Time*, edited by Ingrid E. Castro and Jessica Clark, 181–205. Lanham, MD: Lexington Books.

Kitzinger, Jenny. 2015. "Who Are You Kidding? Children, Power and the Struggle Against Sexual Abuse." In *Constructing and Reconstructing Childhood: Contemporary Issues in the Sociological Study of Childhood* (classic ed.), edited by Allison James and Alan Prout, 145–66. Oxon: Routledge.

Kraftl, Peter. 2013. "Beyond 'Voice', Beyond 'Agency', Beyond 'Politics'? Hybrid Childhoods and Some Critical Reflections on Children's Emotional Geographies." *Emotion, Space and Society* 9 (1): 13–23.

Kuczynski, Leon, Lori Harach, and Silvia C. Bernardini. 1999. "Psychology's Child Meets Sociology's Child: Agency, Influence and Power in Parent-Child Relationships." In *Through the Eyes of the Child: Revisioning Children As Active Agents of Family Life*, edited by Constance L. Shehan, 21–52. Stamford, CT: JAI Press.

Kustatscher, Marlies, Kristina Konstantoni, and Akwugo Emejulu. 2018. "Hybridity, Hyphens, and Intersectionality: Relational Understandings of Children and Young People's Social Identities." In *Families, Intergenerationality, and Peer Group Relations*, edited by Samantha Punch and Robert M. Venderbeck, 475–92. Singapore: Springer.

Lauper, Cyndi. 1985. "The Goonies 'r' Good Enough," Parts I and II. Directed by Richard Donner. Music Video.

Lee, Nick. 1998. "Towards an Immature Sociology." *The Sociological Review* 46 (3): 458–82.
Lehtonen, Sanna. 2013. *Girls Transforming: Invisibility and Age-Shifting in Children's Fantasy Fiction Since the 1970s.* Jefferson, NC: McFarland & Company.
Leitch, Will. 2011. "Steven Spielberg Finally Admits the Walkie-Talkies Were a Mistake." *The Projector—Yahoo.com.* September 5, 2011. https://www.yahoo.com/entertainment/bp/steven-spielberg-finally-admits-walkie-talkies-were-mistake-142746809.html.
Leonard, Madeleine. 2007. "Trapped in Space? Children's Accounts of Risky Environments." *Children & Society* 21 (6): 432–45.
Liebel, Manfred. 2008. "Citizenship from Below: Children's Rights and Social Movements." In *Children and Citizenship*, edited by Antonella Invernizzi and Jane Williams, 32–43. Los Angeles, CA: SAGE.
Maslin, Janet. 1985. "Screen: 'The Goonies,' Written by Spielberg." *The New York Times.* June 7, 1985. https://www.nytimes.com/1985/06/07/movies/screen-the-goonies-written-by-spielberg.html.
Mathews, Richard. 2011. *Fantasy: The Liberation of Imagination* (paperback ed.). New York, NY: Routledge.
McGuire, Seanan. 2016. *Every Heart a Doorway.* New York, NY: Tor.com.
Moore, Deborah. 2014. "Interrupting Listening to Children: Researching with Children's Secret Places in Early Childhood Settings." *Australasian Journal of Early Childhood* 39 (2): 4–11.
Moss, Dorothy. 2010. "Memory, Space and Time: Researching Children's Lives." *Childhood* 17 (4): 530–44.
Musolf, Gil R. 1996. "Interactionism and the Child: Cahill, Corsaro, and Denzin on Childhood Socialization." *Symbolic Interaction* 19 (4): 303–21.
Nikolajeva, Maria. 2003. "Fairy Tale and Fantasy: From Archaic to Postmodern." *Marvels & Tales* 17 (1): 138–56.
Oswell, David. 2013. *The Agency of Children: From Family to Global Human Rights.* Cambridge: Cambridge University Press.
PBS. 2003. "American Masters: About Rod Serling." *Public Broadcasting Service.* https://www.pbs.org/wnet/americanmasters/rod-serling-about-rod-serling/702/.
Pluquailec, Jill. 2018. "Thinking and Doing Consent and Advocacy in Disabled Children's Childhood Research." In *The Palgrave Handbook of Disabled Children's Childhood Studies*, edited by Katherine Runswick-Cole, Tillie Curran, and Kirsty Liddiard, 213–28. London: Palgrave Macmillan.
Prout, Alan. 2000. "Childhood Bodies: Construction, Agency and Hybridity." In *The Body, Childhood and Society*, edited by Alan Prout, 1–18. Hampshire: Macmillan Press.
Pufall, Peter B., and Richard P. Unsworth. 2004. "Introduction: The Imperative and the Process for Rethinking Childhood." In *Rethinking Childhood*, edited by Peter B. Pufall and Richard P. Unsworth, 1–21. New Brunswick, NJ: Rutgers University Press.
Punch, Samantha. 2016. "Exploring Children's Agency Across Majority and Minority World Contexts." In *Reconceptualising Agency and Childhood: New Perspectives*

in Childhood Studies, edited by Florian Esser, Meike S. Baader, Tanja Betz, and Beatrice Hungerland, 183–96. Oxon: Routledge.

Qvortrup, Jens. 2008. "Macroanalysis of Childhood." In *Research with Children: Perspectives and Practices* (2nd ed.), edited by Pia Christensen and Allison James, 66–86. New York, NY: Routledge.

Rasmussen, Kim. 2004. "Places for Children—Children's Places." *Childhood* 11 (2): 155–73.

Renold, Emma, and Jessica Ringrose. 2008. "Regulation and Rupture: Mapping Tween and Teenage Girls' Resistance to the Heterosexual Matrix." *Feminist Theory* 9 (3): 313–38.

Roberts, Jude, and Esther MacCallum-Stewart. 2016. "Introduction." In *Gender and Sexuality in Contemporary Popular Fantasy: Beyond Boy Wizards and Kick-Ass Chicks*, edited by Jude Roberts and Esther MacCallum-Stewart, 1–7. Oxon: Routledge.

Shanahan, Suzanne. 2007. "Lost and Found: The Sociological Ambivalence Toward Childhood." *Annual Review of Sociology* 33: 407–28.

Sharkey, Patrick T. 2006. "Navigating Dangerous Streets: The Sources and Consequences of Street Efficacy." *American Sociological Review* 71 (5): 826–46.

Skelton, Tracey. 2000. "'Nothing to Do, Nowhere to Go?': Teenage Girls and 'Public' Space in the Rhondda Valleys, South Wales." In *Children's Geographies: Playing, Living, Learning*, edited by Sarah L. Holloway and Gill Valentine, 80–99. London: Routledge.

Spielberg, Steven. 1985. *The Goonies*. Directed by Richard Donner. DVD. USA: Amblin Entertainment, Warner Brothers Home Video.

Spillman, Rob. 2013. "Where the Wild Things Aren't: On the Banning of Sendak." *Pen America*. September 26, 2013. https://pen.org/where-the-wild-things-arent-on-the-banning-of-sendak/.

Spyrou, Spyros. 2016. "Researching Children's Silences: Exploring the Fullness of Voice in Childhood Research." *Childhood* 23 (1): 7–21.

Swauger, Melissa, Ingrid E. Castro, and Brent Harger. 2017. "The Continued Importance of Research with Children and Youth: The 'New' Sociology of Childhood 40 Years Later." In *Researching Children and Youth: Methodological Issues, Strategies, and Innovations—Sociological Studies of Children and Youth, Volume 22*, edited by Ingrid E. Castro, Melissa Swauger, and Brent Harger, 1–7. Bingley: Emerald.

Talley, Lee A. 2011. "Fantasies of Place and Childhood in Francesca Lia Block's *I Was a Teenage Fairy*." *Children's Literature* 39: 107–25.

TheJournal.ie. 2015. "*The Goonies* is 30 Years Old Today, Here's What the Stars Look Like Now." *Business Insider*. October 10, 2015. https://www.businessinsider.com/the-goonies-is-30-years-old-today-heres-what-the-stars-look-like-now-2015-10.

Uprichard, Emma. 2008. "Children As 'Being and Becomings': Children, Childhood and Temporality." *Children & Society* 22 (4): 303–13.

Valentine, Gill. 1996. "Angels and Devils: Moral Landscapes of Childhood." *Environment and Planning D: Society and Space* 14 (5): 581–99.

Willis, Jessica L. 2009. "Girls Reconstructing Gender: Agency, Hybridity and Transformations of 'Femininity.'" *Girlhood Studies* 2 (2): 96–118.

Wyness, Michael. 2006. *Childhood and Society: An Introduction to the Sociology of Childhood*. Hampshire: Palgrave Macmillan.
———. 2015. *Childhood*. Cambridge: Polity.
Zeiher, Helga. 2001. "Children's Islands in Space and Time: The Impact of Spatial Differentiation on Children's Ways of Shaping Social Life." In *Childhood in Europe: Approaches—Trends—Findings*, edited by Manuela Du Bois-Reymond, Heinz Sünker, and Heinz-Hermann Krüger, 138–59. New York, NY: Peter Lang.
———. 2003. "Shaping Daily Life in Urban Environments." In *Children in the City: Home, Neighbourhood and Community*, edited by Pia Christensen and Margaret O'Brien, 66–81. Oxon: Routledge.
Zipes, Jack. 1988. "The Changing Function of the Fairy Tale." *The Lion and the Unicorn* 12 (2): 7–31.

Dream/Good vs. Evil

Chapter 2

A Futile Rage against the Machine
The Triumph of The 5,000 Fingers of Dr. T

Peter W. Y. Lee

"The wonder musical of the future!" boasted the movie poster for *The 5,000 Fingers of Dr. T* (1953), a collaboration between independent producer Stanley Kramer, Columbia Pictures, and storyteller Theodor "Dr. Seuss" Geisel ("The 5,000 Fingers" 1952). The film, about a ten-year-old boy rebelling against his tyrannical piano teacher, was a fantasy decades in the making. Geisel drew from his own background as a children's book author, commercial illustrator, and recollections of a dictatorial piano educator from his youth (MacCann 1952). Kramer, a hot producer during Hollywood's postwar box office slump, had recently dazzled audiences with hard-hitting pictures like *The Men* (1950) and *High Noon* (1952), and had no qualms about challenging social conventions (Coe 1950). *The 5,000 Fingers of Dr. T* boasted a $1.6 million budget, cinematic magic of color and widescreen ("Wonderama") processes, and a child overthrowing an authoritarian regime in an elaborate fantasy, eliciting early comparisons to *The Wizard of Oz* (1939) (Kramer and Coffey 1997; Schallert 1952).

The 5,000 Fingers of Dr. T floundered at the box office. In part, the high costs associated with elaborate sets, glorious Technicolor, and studio reshoots made profit elusive ("5000 Fingers Puts Kramer" 1952). However, the film's failure rested within the celluloid social messaging. Contrary to the tagline, the picture was not "the future" but the present, with boy hero Bart Collins caught up in contemporary concerns surrounding boyhood and childrearing of the early Cold War. Dr. Seuss intended to criticize what historians later characterized as hallmarks of American Cold War containment: conformity, social mobility, and material consumerism deemed integral to the family unit's prosperity and wellbeing.

Unfortunately for producers, *The 5,000 Fingers of Dr. T* misfired as mass entertainment. Hoping to strike box office gold and appeal to the public,

Geisel, Kramer, and Columbia softened Bart Collins's fantasy and his agency. The film valorizes the nuclear family and gives Bart an active voice in shaping the Collins household. Bart, unhappy with his single mother forcing him to take private piano lessons from a demanding instructor, Dr. Terwilliker, and hopeful that a friendly but money-conscious plumber, Zabladowski, will become a permanent father figure in his life, falls asleep at the piano. In his slumber, Bart crafts a fantasy world wherein he and 499 other boys attend the "Happy Fingers Academy," an elite music academy ruled by the tyrannical Terwilliker. In his dream, Bart rescues his mother from Terwilliker's hypnotic spell, enlists Zabladowski as his new father, and liberates the boys. By overthrowing an allegorical fascist state, Bart gains spatial agency, which empowers him to display intergenerational agency, peer agency, and national agency. When Bart wakes up in the final scene, the film suggests that a close-knit family is in the works as Zabladowski begins to romance the boy's mother and Bart leaves his piano lessons to play outside. However, Bart's agency undermines the then societal purpose of idealized family togetherness: the socialization of boys as citizen-soldiers through disciplined maturation, with an emphasis on social mobility and consumerism. Critics, fickle audiences, and, indeed, the filmmakers were uncertain what to make of the final picture, leading to meager ticket sales.

The failure of *The 5,000 Fingers of Dr. T* shows the limits of childhood (especially boyhood) agency within the context of mass entertainment. A fantasy world springs from Bart's imagination and he is ultimately triumphant, but he fails to reconcile postwar expectations of childrearing practices in which children obediently followed their parents' footsteps while negotiating then-current countercultural arguments for individualism and self-expression. Through a boy's fantasy, the picture represents the tug-of-war between societal expectations for conformity and his attempts to assert his identity. While Bart overcomes what he envisions as abusive adult autocracy, the film's failure in the real world indicates that this Hollywood-Seussian vision of childhood agency never entirely escapes the 5,000 fingers of Dr. T.

A HAPPY FINGER METHOD

Author Theodor Geisel, whose tongue twisters, colorful characters, and deft artistry won acclaim for his children's books, had a long career in illustration and advertising under the pen name Dr. Seuss. Not simply a humorist, Geisel was an active progressive affiliated with leftist publishers such as Vanguard Press and PM, outlets that published studies on socialism and various labor movements during the interwar period (Mickenberg 2006). During the Great Depression, he critiqued American isolationism and unemployment (Smith

2011). When the United States entered World War II, Geisel helped craft the "Private Snafu" educational cartoon shorts for the armed services. After the war, he set his sights on Hollywood. He cowrote the screenplay for the Academy Award–winner *Design for Death* (1948), worked on the animated short "Gerald McBoing Boing" (1950), and then hoped to storm Tinseltown (Brady 1951).

Specifically, Geisel celebrated childhood freedoms against what he thought of as narrow-minded, misguided adults. During the war, he expressed alarm over fascist indoctrination tactics, in which Hitler Youth lusted for power through violence: "products of the worst educational crime in the entire history of the world" (Geisel quoted in Jenkins 2002, 195). Dr. Seuss's postwar books, such as *Horton Hears a Who* (1954), reflected a liberal stance on permissive child-rearing, in which kids freely voiced their concerns and explored the world around them, even if this position undercut prevailing social norms, as found in his pachyderm protagonist Horton. Geisel defined this type of agency, asserting adults should encourage children to think freely and creatively without grown-ups' interference: "Children are thwarted people. Their idea of tragedy is when some one [sic] says you *can't* do that" (Geisel quoted in Jenkins 2002, 196). Foreshadowing what theorists James and James (2004) call the creation of social spaces for kids to experiment and explore their environment, Dr. Seuss importantly situated youngsters in his stories agentically: they find their own way by the author and illustrator arming them with a sense of security and responsibility. *The 5,000 Fingers of Dr. T*'s storyline, in which the boy dreams up a fantasy realm, is literally the boy's subconscious mind come to life.

Geisel's framework of child agency collided against postwar American standards for raising children. Although debate circulated among politicians, social workers, and parents concerning the degree to which the U.S. government should regulate children's upbringing, an adult consensus developed that centered on combating communism, delinquency, and poverty (Holt 2014). Child experts of the age emphasized that this goal required parents to discipline children and carefully plan for their futures, especially careers for their sons. Educational films, such as *Benefits of Looking Ahead* (1952), featured scenarios wherein careless, lazy boys failed to prepare for adulthood and drifted through life, mired in poverty and loneliness (Kordas 2013). Parenting manuals and various advice columnists acknowledged the importance of individuality and independence for children (boys in particular) but framed these values in terms of growing up, landing a good job, and supporting a family. Boys should exercise their creativity and judgment-making skills, as Geisel advocated, but only within socially acceptable guidelines for growing up. Maturation was a top-down process, when children lived up to adult expectations.

Enter Dr. Terwilliker, the autocratic piano maestro who haunts young Bart Collins in *The 5,000 Fingers of Dr. T* and embodies such childrearing tensions. Geisel reworked this plot from his children's book, *The 500 Hats of Bartholomew Cubbins* (1938). The original story was a medieval tale about a king trying to reveal the head of a boy peasant who fails to doff his hat for His Majesty. The king has absolute power, controlling the land and people around him; the boy challenges this socially superior adult and the system that the king represents—authoritative law and dictated behavior for peasants who lack power. In the postwar update, Seuss fast-forwarded time, turning away from medieval kingship to a different sort of blind authority: the Almighty American Dollar.

Americans in the postwar environment were not just money-mad out of greed. Greenbacks brought economic security and symbolically bulwarked Americans against the past two decades of depression and war. The United States entered the 1950s as a prosperous superpower and, ideally, Americans built nest eggs via stable nuclear families, suburban housing, and advancing up the corporate ladder in steady white-collar careers. Many postwar parenting manuals, educational films, and childrearing guides were aimed at a middle-class audience as the de facto national standard, regardless of audiences' actual socioeconomic positionalities (Kordas 2013). These factors were intertwined; as leading child expert Dr. Benjamin Spock (1954) informed his millions of readers, "Your child imitates you!" explaining that a boy "is sopping up such qualities as bravery, determination, ambitiousness, chivalrousness, self-control, manly helpfulness—provided his father has these qualities in reasonable amounts." Here, the dad who employed these traits at home and on the job made his son more apt to succeed. Educator O. Spurgeon English (1951) encouraged this intergenerational link between adults and kids in the workplace through "expeditions": "More men should be willing to do this for the young in our society," wherein mentorships would train kids for jobs and stymie delinquency (162). Childhood values, such as teamwork and industriousness, supposedly prepped boys for adulthood as they imitated "proper" elders. In 1958, the guidebook *Blueprint for Teen-Age Living* lauded teenage individuality, but stressed conformity as essential to any organization: "We try to act in ways that are acceptable to them so that they will approve of us and include us in their activities" (Menniger 1958, 64). As for loners and "Beats," the manual assured readers that these youth "are usually unhappy people" (Menniger 1958, 65). The reason: nonconformists do "unusual things, wear off clothes, and make 'daring' remarks," but "are usually unsure of themselves" (Menniger 1958, 65). According to Menniger (1958), English (1951), and other childrearing experts of the 1950s, conformity and security mandated boys follow their fathers' rightly-placed footsteps.

Despite the prevalence of intergenerational conformity as the standard for child socialization, not every child wanted to be a figurative chip-off-the-old-block. Dr. Spock and Dr. Seuss expressed a preference for permissive child-raising, but such freedoms were potentially self-contradictory; the tension between independence from and obedience to social norms sowed the seeds for youth rebellion. In *The 5,000 Fingers of Dr. T*, Bart Collins rejects the social foundation of the postwar adult world, expressing his frustrations by combating a fantasy dictatorship. Geisel regarded fantasy "an extension of reality," albeit through the perspective of one individual (Geisel[i]). For the film, Geisel used fantasy as a mirror for how a boy saw himself, in which he played the role of freedom fighter to liberate boyhood from endless rote piano recitals. In a memo to Kramer, Geisel described Bart's spatial agency, stating, "The kid, psychologically, is in a box," which he must break out of to enjoy a carefree childhood (Jenkins 2002, 201). To do so, Bart takes on Dr. Terwilliker's authoritarian rule, his mother's misguided attempts to mold her son, the hired plumber's money-mad outlook on life, and the strict demands postwar America placed on childhood (Geisel[i]).

Bart's struggle to break free of this "psychological box" is clear in the opening scenes. After waking up from a nightmare wherein some men with nets pursue him, Bartholomew Collins finds himself sitting at a piano. The traditional testaments of boyhood—dog, baseball, and glove—sit neglected as Bart starts to play rote scales. The screenplay states Bart, "a lonely figure, is seated at the piano, suffering in silence" (Geisel[g]). With several of Dr. Terwilliker's finger exercise books before him, he "looks longingly at the ball glove" resting above the piano (Scott and Dr. Seuss 1952, 1). Already in these introductory shots, Bart is caught between social standards. As a "lonely" boy denied the joys of an outdoor sporting life with his dog and peers outside, he is vulnerable to becoming a frightful Beat; indeed, his forlorn expression indicates Bart already fulfills the "unhappy" requisite Menniger (1958) and other social guardians worried about. The immediate cause of his domestic confinement and misery is plain to see as he sits on the piano bench, slouched over and picking at the piano keys. All the while, Dr. Terwilliker's portrait peers at the boy from the music books, supervising his progress.

Originally, the film featured Terwilliker *only* appearing in the dream sequence, reducing the real piano teacher and instructor into an abstract force of childhood oppression. Bart's opening nightmare sequence, wherein yet-unseen Terwilliker's henchmen pursued the boy with nets, presumably to capture and contain him, suggested that Bart's fantasy formation already positioned the doctor as a symbol for childhood captivity and imprisonment. However, due to a disastrous sneak preview (see below), Kramer reshot the opening to make the film more linear, featuring Terwilliker as Bart's piano instructor. His real-life intrusion into Bart's personal life legitimates the boy's subsequent fantasy of childhood under assault, and it transforms Terwilliker's abstract symbol of adult expectations into a flesh-and-blood enemy who personally prevents Bart from leaving his home/prison/"box" to play outside with other boys.

Dr. Terwilliker's real-life presence threatens Bart not only by ruining the boy's afternoons but by serving as a makeshift father figure. The doctor certainly looks and acts odd, with flamboyant clothing and grandiose speech patterns, but he is not physically frightening. Indeed, in an early character note, Dr. Seuss stated that the doctor "looks no more vicious and harmful than Victor Moore," referring to the soft-spoken older actor who typically played warm-hearted fathers for children portrayed as cold, ungrateful brats (Geisel[a], 1). Nevertheless, Terwilliker displays a one-track mind as he tries to mold the boy into a pianist: "Why can't you dream about playing the piano?" he asks Bart, rhetorically attempting to control the boy's slumbering hours. The doctor's complaint that he cannot leave the room "for five minutes" without Bart falling asleep or goofing off renders Terwilliker a frustrated disciplinarian, teacher, and male role model. The pianist asserts a moral prerogative to keep Bart in check; the piano teacher blames the boy for being lazy, which, in turn, justifies the pianist's sternness (see Frankel 2017). Just as childrearing guides dispensed advice for parents to raise children "correctly," Terwilliker's music lesson books serve as a moral substitutive form of socialization for his students.

Young Bart certainly needed a father. Mr. Collins's death (he was presumably killed during World War II) left the boy under the care of a single mom. Mrs. Collins's widowhood made their family socially incomplete in the Cold War context, a family structure deemed detrimental to a boy's upbringing. In 1950, child psychologist Theodore Mead Newcomb warned parents that boys who lacked male role models were overly attached to their mothers, destined to become the pejorative "sissy," defined as meek, obedient, and passive. This view was not new; during the 1940s, social critics, notably Philip Wylie (1942), described the so-called decline of American life, with Wylie especially singling out "momism," in which doting, emasculated sons lacked virility as they clung to their mother's figurative apron strings. The result: a sissified, morally, mentally, and physically weak generation of men. This fear of sissification and its connotation of homosexuality lasted well into the 1950s. Dr. Spock (1957) also cautioned single mothers that their kids needed father figures: "The boy without a father particularly needs opportunity and encouragement to play with other boys" at a young age, and should "be mainly occupied with boyish pursuits" (577). If mom molded the son in her image, "getting him interested in clothes and interior decoration" and "other recreations she enjoys," she risked having him "grow up precocious, with feminine interests" (Spock 1957, 577–8). In Spock's (1957) mind, a single mom bent on forcing her child to live up to her standards and diverting him from "boyish pursuits," like Bart's neglected baseball and dog, could permanently emasculate him.

Mrs. Collins has good intentions; for her, good parenting includes prepping Bart to enter the workforce. An early draft of the screenplay finds Mrs. Collins explaining why she tortures her son: "give a child time, as I always say, and he'll eventually see things more clearly, outgrow his childish whims, and buckle down to good, solid work and when he grows older and discovers what a great social asset playing a piano is, well, he'll thank us then for having kept him at it" (Geisel[a], 2). This run-on sentence highlights her as a "good" parent: prepping her child for a career with him learning "social assets" to impress others and, in doing so, outgrowing his boyhood "whims." She embraces the use of piano lessons as a way to instill discipline and maturity in her son, and she regards Terwilliker as a makeshift father to guide Bart into manhood. As a singer and musician herself, Mrs. Collins corrects her son's mistakes as they sing along to Terwilliker's ditty, "Ten Happy Fingers." The song itself promotes the stripping of childhood individuality as each finger dances in complete control under a pianist's command. In a note, Geisel explained the "Happy Fingers Method" of brainwashing: "If your fingers are happy, your mind is relaxed. If your mind is relaxed, you have nothing to fear because the keys on the keyboard are your very good friends, and when you put your fingers down among friends, well, your fingers start enjoying themselves" (Geisel[a], 3). In the film, the Happy Fingers Method renders a happy mind as a complacent one, prioritizing conformity and obedience as measures of success, even if it placed people in figurative boxes.

Mrs. Collins means well by taking control of her son's development, but she fails to realize that by insisting her son obey her for his own good, she undermines their family unit. After all, Bart subconsciously associates piano lessons with men armed with nets and a loss of freedom. Mrs. Collins acknowledges that her son does not like playing the piano, dislikes his piano instructor, prefers playing trombone to the piano, and wants to play outside more than anything else, but swiftly dismisses his desires as childish and immature, prioritizing her own goals for his development. She negates the child's view and sacrifices her relationship with her son for the future, when she assumes he will eventually thank her for this excellent guidance.

However, the final version of the film juxtaposes Mrs. Collins's perspective by giving Bart a voice to refute his mother. When editing the film, the producers trimmed her dialogue to a simple admission that Bart "still hates it like poison." The finished movie excluded an extended speech in which she elaborated on her son's point of view during a phone conversation with another adult: "And beginning to hate me, too, I'm afraid. But he's going to learn that piano if it kills me. (Laughs). I know. I know. He'll outgrow

Figure 2.1 From Metronome to the Clock Stamp: Mrs. Collins (Mary Healy) teaches her son Bart (Tommy Rettig) that playing the piano is proper training for adulthood: *The 5,000 Fingers of Dr. T* (1953).

it. It's an age they all have to go through" (Scott and Dr. Seuss 1952, 3). Instead of dwelling on Mrs. Collins's perspective, the final cut hands the narration to Bart as he muses, "I think that Dr. Terwilliker has my mother hypnotized," indicating that she, too, adheres to the Happy Fingers method and the emphasis on moving up the social ladder. Bart disconnects from his mother in this statement; he follows her commands when he plays "Ten Happy Fingers," but he remains stoic in the shot, with a stone-faced expression as she smilingly sings along, giving her son loving looks. Bart rejects his mother's tenderness; he states, "I try to be everything she wants me to be [since Dad died]. But, boy, she's as hipped on the piano as Dr. Terwilliker." Bart believes her to be under the doctor's hypnotic influence, but he himself is not fooled. The boy regards the maestro as a gold-plated phony, in fact, a "double phony." Although Bart does not define the term, and his utterance in passing connotes the slur as a mere insult for his piano teacher, the boy suggests Terwilliker is neither a good father figure nor a caring teacher. Either way, Bart refuses Terwilliker as an appropriate role model, and he symbolically rejects his mother for her alliance to the pianist. This intergenerational disconnect connotes the slow disintegration of the family unit stemming from both mother and son, even as Mrs. Collins believes she is raising her son appropriately.[1]

For Bart, Terwilliker's supposedly "phony" act as a teacher and mentor for boys fools the adults. Geisel fashioned the doctor's portrayal with a hypnotism reminiscent of Adolf Hitler's bluster. Mr. Collins died in the fight against fascism, and Bart recreates the struggle in his fantasy, thereby forming a connection with his biological father in the grave rather than accepting Terwilliker as a teacher. Bart's fantasy world casts Terwilliker as a Hitler-wannabe and, by connotation, an anathema to the 1950s American middle-class household. The pianist's insistence on complete obedience, his brainwashing of boys who resist his methods, and even his hairstyle are reminiscent of the Third Reich's führer, and many of Geisel's notes in the scripts openly called for Terwilliker to mimic Hitler's mannerisms (Cohen 2004; Jenkins 2002).[2] An early screenplay described posters with Dr. T "in a Hitler-like dictator pose," while in another passage, Geisel instructed that Terwilliker "[fly] in a Hitlerian rage" (Geisel[a], 7 & 25). In his bid for freedom, Bart turns the doctor into a black-and-white caricature of evil. Doing so, Bart justifies his rejection of not only a tyrannical piano teacher but his disapproval of the process of socialization—consumerism and social mobility for maturing boys—that leads his mother to hire the pianist in the first place. Bart fantasizes about overthrowing the money-mad mindset of postwar America, paralleling obsessions of social conformity with fascism, both of which he regards as a threat to American individuality and boyhood.

IMAGING THE MACHINE

The "system" Bart rejects in his fantasy life was not without critics in the real world. Sociologists, notably William H. Whyte Jr. (1956), critiqued childrearing practices that encouraged boys to stifle their individuality and conform as they embarked on careers. Derogatory terms for this system, such as "the machine" or "the man in the gray flannel suit," as writer Sloan Wilson (1955) characterized the dull routine of cubicle life, permeated then-contemporary popular culture. Bart creates a parallel between Dr. Terwilliker's repetitive piano lessons with the monotony and single-mindedness of moving up the corporate ladder. Terwilliker plans to validate his system through public approval: "One month before I present all my pupils in a grand concert. And I'm not going to let one dreary little boy humiliate me, you understand?" Bart recognizes he is under enormous pressure. When he dozes off at the piano, he immediately envisions a giant piano, wherein he occupies one of five hundred seats, practicing Dr. Terwilliker's Ten Happy Fingers method. The script notes, "The music becomes the music of a hundred pianos, weirdly embellishing and embroidering the simple HAPPY FINGERS tune until its swelling to a tremendous, thunderous finale" (Scott and Dr. Seuss 1952, 10). Standing on a podium, baton at the ready, Terwilliker reiterates how his Happy Fingers Academy inculcates children's discipline and obedience, which Geisel observed during World War II, and Hitler also did when he indoctrinated children under fascism. By forcing children to replay the same composition, Terwilliker and his students will make beautiful music together, presumably until Bart and the occupants of the other 499 seats are just like their teacher.

Bart has other ideas. He does not question Terwilliker's motto that practice makes perfect, but the boy rejects mandates of absolute conformity from dictatorial adults. Instead, he believes in a well-rounded orchestra, with individual players contributing to the whole. In this vision, while the boys do play under a conductor, each musician has a unique role in the finished symphony. "I don't think the piano's my instrument," he begins, but Terwilliker quickly dismisses instruments other than the piano as inferior. The "scratchy violins, screechy piccolos," and "nauseating trumpets" have no place in his machine. The film later reveals that the doctor imprisons non-pianists in a dank dungeon, regarding them as failures. Underground and forgotten, these musicians morph into colorful subhumans, some literally attached to their instruments. While these captives (who are adults, not children) demonstrate spatial agency by staging an elaborate ballet, the prisoners have no voice aboveground in the posh Academy. Corsaro (2005) argues that children's fantasies are often impromptu, free from adult supervision or standards; however, while the entire Happy Fingers Academy springs from Bart's imagination, Terwilliker presides over the school with an iron will. The dungeon dance sequence is the only moment when the boy's imagination can run unfettered.[3] The captives, with their subhuman appearance and bionic musical attachments, engage in a choreographed frenzy far from Terwilliker's control, and serve as a visual metaphor for childhood chafing under adult expectations. Indeed, other than when Bart visits the dungeon, these non-pianists have no audience. As stated, Bart himself has an interest in the trombone, but his mother and Terwilliker dismiss the boy's preference because they believe the piano can open doors for him when he grows up. As the dungeon keeper notes, "Pretty soon there will be no other musicians in the world excepting for them what play the piano."[4] Terwilliker's machine becomes a self-perpetuating cycle of childhood conformity as the doctor preps his students to take over the world by piano. However, even under his tight "Hitlerian" control, a musical undercurrent subverts Terwilliker's rule, even if no one else is there to hear or see the children play.

Terwilliker has more grandiose ambitions for his students. He hopes to coopt Bart's fantasy, imposing adult standards on the child's spatial agency through a top-down intergenerational bond. He hopes to make a "Paderewski of you," a reference to Ignacy Jan Paderewski, a notable Polish composer and statesman, whom Bart and his 499 peers should mimic. Bart, of course, is ignorant of the musical canon ("Who?!"), but the pianist is undeterred. To further mold the boy to Academy standards, Terwilliker outfits him in a uniform consisting of an Official Terwilliker beanie: a blue cap with a yellow foam hand sticking out of the top, which acts as a reminder of the doctor's diabolical hold on his pupil's mind and fingers. Dr. T brags, "I will have 500 little boys. Five thousand little fingers. And they will be mine, all mine," as they devote their lives to practice. Bart calls his instructor's plan "crazy," but even if he is insane, Dr. T constructs his vision with adult society's tacit approval.

Terwilliker acts with parental sanction. In Bart's dream, Dr. T's right-hand woman is Bart's hypnotized mom, who enrolls her son as Terwilliker's first student. Befitting her status as a single parent, Bart envisions his mother as an ideal secretary, a career woman who will soon fail to recognize that she has a son. Dressed in half evening gown/half business suit, she coordinates Terwilliker's operation with the outside world. She informs parents that their sons will abandon boyish pursuits under the pianist's rigorous ministrations: "Your son will not be allowed to bring his baseball. Dr. Terwilliker does not believe in baseballs ... golf balls, basketballs or tennis balls, Ping-Pong balls, snowballs, croquet balls, or hockey pucks. Dr. Terwilliker believes only in the piano." The doctor's one-track mind forces boys to grow up under the strict discipline supposedly required of all pianists. Mrs. Collins reassures one anxious parent that Terwilliker's approach is the correct one: "The sole purpose of our endeavor is the musical benefit of American youth," whereby societal needs trump individual self-expression. Warming (2018) notes that as states globalize, they have an increasing interest in forming "future soldiers" to promote their interests in an increasingly competitive international arena (45). During the Cold War, the United States expanded its foreign policy agenda as the guardian of the free world, with children required to conform to adult expectations, or, as Mrs. Collins characterized it, projecting the "musical benefit of American youth" onto the world writ large. Once they enter the enclosed gates of the Happy Fingers Academy, boys of all ethnicities embark upon a maturation process that strips them of their "boyish whims" to promote the Cold War ideal as budding citizen-soldiers.

The students do not surrender their individuality easily. Most prospective students do not listen to Mrs. Collins reciting the list of banned items, bringing assorted sports equipment and toys to orientation. Mrs. Collins takes charge, ordering Terwilliker's soldiers to frisk the "long line of frightened boys carrying their luggage" (Scott and Dr. Seuss 1952, 77). The guards remove pistols, slingshots, comic books, frogs, and other reminders of carefree, idealized boyhood. In exchange for this loss of

Figure 2.2 Backed by security, Dr. Terwilliker (Hans Conried) prepares to conduct all the boys in the Happy Fingers Method: *The 5,000 Fingers of Dr. T* (1953).

identity, each child receives a standard-issue Happy Fingers beanie and an identification number. Relegated as mere cogs in the piano, these boys sit at their assigned seats, their numbered backs to the audience and their face buried in the scores and keys. The only face emerging from this technocratic hierarchy is the conductor standing on the podium, with the maestro as their master.[5]

OF DAD AND KIDS

While Terwilliker's machine threatens childhood, the film features a stronger theme than Bart battling a tyrannical teacher. As stated, Geisel characterized Terwilliker as "Hitlerian," tapping into 1950s patriotism and living memory of post–World War II. By depicting Terwilliker as unsavory, Geisel positioned Bart in need of finding an appropriate, alternate, father figure, a person he must redeem in the process of rebuilding his nuclear family. Since his mother is "hypnotized" under Terwilliker's program, Bart must find not only a good father but one who is a good husband for his mom.

By rejecting Terwilliker, Bart shuns the adult, Americanized capitalistic mindset. His father fantasy centers on Mr. Zabladowski, an independent contractor his mom hires to fix their home sink and who reprises his role as a plumber-for-hire on assignment at Bart's imagined Happy Fingers Academy. The boy taps Zabladowski as a potential mate for his mom to fulfill the image of the nuclear family as the national norm.[6] In part, Bart accepts that he *needs* a father figure in his life. As noted earlier, child experts like Dr. Spock worried about potential sissiness in boys raised by single mothers. The fear of emasculated boys itself was not new; the public associated effeminacy with homosexuality and delinquency. Bart himself is no sissy, as his one-boy war on the Happy Fingers Academy indicates. Bart plainly states that the "Hitlerian" Dr. Terwilliker is "the only enemy I got."

Bart's declaration that Terwilliker is his "only enemy" legitimatizes the boy's opposition to his mother's view of childhood maturation. Since the boy protagonist dislikes his piano teacher and playing the piano, he rejects his mother's beliefs that boyhood practice makes for a perfect manhood. Unfortunately for Bart, Zabladowski debuts in the film as an outsider on business, but one for whom Mrs. Collins has little patience. While Mrs. Collins fawns over the pianist who can mentor her son to a successful career, she has less esteem for the blue-collar workman eking out a living. When Zabladowski interferes with the piano lesson by taking Bart's side, suggesting that Mrs. Collins should consider her son's opposition to the piano more seriously, she reminds him to get back to work. Bart appreciates the plumber's support, foreshadowing future father-son bonding and creating a stronger contrast between the friendly plumber and the villainous piano teacher for the audience. However, Mrs. Collins does all she can to obstruct her boy from forming a real connection with a promising, self-chosen father figure. As a single mother, she tells Zabladowski that contradicting her "isn't helping me maintain discipline. It's not an easy thing to bring up a boy without a father." The hired man relents, and the observant Bart suspects the plumber yields not because his mom is right, but that, as a working man, Zabladowski is dependent on her business for his livelihood.

Deferring to a single mom regarding issues of boyhood demonstrates Zabladowski's priority is making money. The plumber is sympathetic to Bart, but, like other adults in the film, his career comes first. In a brief character sketch, "Who is Mr. Zabladowski?", Geisel described the plumber as a "warm, kindly immigrant plumber. A family man. He loves kids . . . . But he has learned that it is not economically sound to indulge in human relationships at random" (Geisel[j]). In short, "If you shoot your mouth off you're apt to get fired. If you get fired, it's tough to get money to live on" (Geisel[j]). As the plumber's name implies, Geisel originally intended to cast Zabladowski as an immigrant who assimilated to American capitalistic values of free enterprise. While his background does not appear on film save for the surname, Zabladowski's obsession with money dominates any notion of being a "family man" or loving kids. Geisel jotted down rough dialogue about earning income: "You have to keep working to bring in dough," "Life costs money," "I can't afford to get involved," "Anything—so long as you pay me," "I work where they pay me," and other blurbs stressing that cash trumps all (Geisel[j]). Dr. Seuss also penned lyrics to musical numbers meant for the film around the theme of capitalism: "About Money," "The Grindstone," "Count Me Out," "Freckle on a Poppy," and "I Will Not Get Involved," in which Zabladowki reiterated his desire to get paid rather than act on another's behalf (Scarpietta 1952).[7] As the latter song made clear: "This Earth has 10 trillion kinds/ of problems to be solved/ It is nothing new/ so let it stew/ I will not get involved!" (Scarpietta 1952). Although these songs were edited out of the finished film, it is notable that the songs' lyrics reflected concerns about sacrificing family togetherness in lieu of making a buck.

Zabladowski's money-madness was appropriate for postwar America, in which social mobility and family togetherness went hand in hand. According to the Cold War's version of the American Dream, the idealized white middle-class father worked so his kids could enjoy better lives than he did under twenty years of depression and war. This emphasis on upward mobility in some ways usurped the nuclear family while visions of "the good life" overtook the family unit. In one draft, Zabladowski spelled out the facts of life: "Terwilliger [an early name for the pianist] pays overtime. I pay off the mortgage. Terwilliger, mortgages, pianos. That's life.... Relax. Make the best of it" (Geisel[b], 19). In a handwritten note, Geisel clarified Zabladowski's line, adding, "Money is the stuff of life" (Geisel[b], 20). Bart's recreation of the plumber in his fantasy proves that the boy is aware of adult responsibilities; after all, a man has got to make a living. However, Bart rejects Zabladowski's criteria that money and the pursuit of luxury are benchmarks to judge an adult's or child's wellbeing or happiness (Bonvin and Stoecklin 2014). Bart believes in the nuclear family as a strength, but without the societal emphasis on class and mobility as end goals. His fantasy constructs Zabladowski as a means for Bart to rehabilitate him as a proper father, ultimately leading to their joint effort in the defeat of Terwilliker.

Bart knows reprogramming Zabladowski is crucial to defeating Terwilliker. He plans on rebuilding his nuclear family to exclude the diabolical pianist who, Bart imagines, schemes to marry his mother. At first, the boy tries to bond with Zabladowski on a pretend fishing trip, and the film's plot stops so the plumber and the boy can cast imaginary lines and reel in big-mouth bass. Zabladowski acts his part, correcting Bart's technique, and the two sing a duet, "Dream Stuff." The "dream" is manifold: Bart's desire for a dad, rescuing his mom, and even overlaying a fantasy about fishing within a fantasy. This dream, in which he asserts spatial and intergenerational agency to rehabilitate Zabladowski, is not strong enough. When the plumber confronts Terwilliker, the doctor counters Bart's pretend father-son getaway by presenting Zabladowski with cash, cigars, and other luxuries, all of which are (presumably) employee benefits at the Happy Fingers Academy. Zabladowki, Mrs. Collins, and Terwilliker cement an adult alliance by singing a song about getting together, while Bart rolls his eyes in disgust. Ironically, though this musical number comes from Bart's imagination, the boy is helpless even in his own mind as adults frolic and bask among the standards of postwar consumerism and moneymaking. Bart's imagined adults display their allegiance to social conformity (and, in doing so, rebel against their child creator) as the mad doctor lures Zabladowski with a bankroll and sundries as easily as he seduces Bart's mother.

Bart realizes that playing make-believe will not rehabilitate the adults' standpoints. He rejects the system entirely, subverting the saying that fathers (or any adults) "know best." Voicing his independence, Bart softly sings "Kid's Song," wherein he rebukes bigger, stronger adults for shoving "little kids around."[8] While the song refers to bullying, it also applies to close-minded adults like Zabladowski, foreshadowing what sociologists in the 1990s called a "new paradigm," in which children were, and continue to be, recognized as actors who shape and reflect their social contexts, rather than solely behave as "defective adults" (James, Jenks, and Prout 1998, 10). Bart concludes the song by singing that when he grows up, he will not be like those "bigger pound by pound," distancing himself from "bad" adult role models around him. One film critic for *Variety* singled out this song for coming "nearest to expressing childhood . . . touchingly done by young Rettig as he sings of rebellion against unthinking, dominating adults" (Brog 1953, 6). Indeed, composer Frederick Hollander, who put Seuss's lyrics to music, called the picture "an unusual child's opera for adults" (Beaufort 1953, 7). By blaming the lack of an intergenerational tie between kids and grownups on his elders, Bart makes the plumber ashamed for his part in the figurative lobotomy of 500 boys.

Nevertheless, Zabladowski finds change difficult. He apologizes for his earlier behavior and alliance with Terwilliker, claiming, "I don't like anyone who pushes anybody around." He also promises to believe Bart, saying, "People should always believe kids. They should even believe their lies." This statement affirms Bart's agency in toto; the fantasy is a "lie" in that the boy is dreaming the entire narrative, but for Bart and his imagined rendition of the plumber, acquiescence to children makes this lie a reality as the adult places the child's words above his own beliefs. However, even as Zabladowski gives lip service to Bart's worldview, he draws the line in surrendering overtime pay, a sum that equals roughly $20. Bart casually counters by offering $30, and Zabladowski changes sides, calling the boy "boss man." Knowing the plumber violates business contracts with the slightest incentive, Bart needs a more substantive connection to the plumber, something that carries more weight than money. Zabladowski promises not to betray his new employer, but the boy does not take any chances that Dr. T will entice the plumber with a counteroffer. To "seal this oath," Bart forces Zabladowski to swap blood by pricking their thumbs. This act, normally associated with youth's "blood brother" rituals, cements their bond and allows Bart to regard the man as a peer. Zabladowski plays the part; as a "boy," he cites the Scout Law from the Boy Scouts—to be trustworthy, loyal, helpful friendly, courteous, kind, obedient, cheerful, thrifty, brave, clean, and reverent. The film does not identify the oath on screen but, presumably, Boy Scouts (and their parents) in the audience would pick up on the plumber's vow to uphold the values of the organization publicly linked to responsibly guiding American boys through childhood to manhood (Honeck 2018). Postwar American advertisers and media encouraged fathers and sons to regard each other as "pals," even to the point of dressing in matching suits, an idea carried over from Scout masters and their troops (Cross 2004; Honeck 2018). Bart, however, accepts Zabladowski far more than a brother or pal, thus calling him "pop" and "my old man." Bart welcomes him into the Collins family and, by extension, offers his mom as Zabladowski's bride.[9]

Bart uses blood rather than money to reconstruct the nuclear family. LaRossa (1999) points out that in the early twentieth century, children were not passive when they perceived trouble in their families. LaRossa (1999) focuses on the interwar period, when children wrote to the blooming field of family experts (such as psychologists, medical doctors, social workers, and sociologists) for advice on how to approach family rifts and (re)construct what they considered appropriate formulations of home. These children proactively reinforced social norms regarding idealized, stable, middle-class family life, which certainly eluded many of them during the Great Depression and World War II. In the postwar environment, heavy societal and cultural emphasis on family togetherness projected the nuclear family as a national strength against totalitarianism and communism. In his attempts to rebuild the acceptable family unit, Bart reaffirms this national value by juxtaposing his recreated household against the authoritarian Happy Fingers Academy way.

The postwar American nuclear family projected strength and morality against communism, along with proscribing rigid gender roles that formulated children's behavior and character. For boys, this conditioning meant social mobility, preparing to enter the workforce (as Mrs. Collins prioritizes), and embracing the responsibilities of a citizen-soldier. Specifically, Bart unleashes his scientific knowhow in conjunction with social values of consumerism. As noted above, consumerism represented a postwar ideal for Americans as a bulwark against the propagandized fear of state ownership. The infamous 1959 "Kitchen Debate" between Vice President Richard Nixon and Soviet First Secretary Nikita Khrushchev highlighted the differences between American consumerism and Soviet communism, with Nixon gushing over how the individual right to purchase then-modern conveniences connotated a superior way of life.

As consumers, children fit within this materialist culture paradigm. Since the early 1900s, advertisers targeted children as purchasers, either with income of their own or as major influencers on family purchases, such as toys, food, clothing, and other brand name goods (Jacobson 2004). Proponents of child-oriented marketing argued that kid consumers acquired crucial skills like managing their budgets, assessing commodity quality, and learning the value of a dollar as they earned their money (Jacobson 2004). The early Cold War elevated the child consumer—expansion of the middle-class enabled children to emerge as a strong youth market (Cross 2004). This image of abundance and prosperity contrasted sharply with media accounts of Soviet life, wherein Russian children, living in squalor, yearned for the promise of capitalism and the American Way (Peacock 2014). Indeed, Terwilliker's demand for obedience bans the boys from bringing their prized possessions (meaningless trinkets to adults) into the Academy to ensure total focus while at school. Fittingly, when Bart prepares to go on the offensive, he empties his pockets of its many contents: marbles, peanuts, paper clips, string, washers, a yo-yo, checkers, a belt buckle, bubblegum, rings, a jackknife, a ping-pong ball, whistles, a spinning top, and other 1950s boyhood ephemera. From these assorted items, he builds a silencer that negates all sound.

As Bart innovates, Zabladowski stares in amazement. Since he views the boy's tools as junk, he is incredulous that these odds 'n' ends can produce the technological marvel Bart concocts.[10] The end result is more than a figment from Bart's imagination; rather, the newly built device represents a child's refusal to abide by a grownup's rationale, further strengthening Bart's spatial agency by shaping the world around him. Earlier, Bart's "Kid Song" branded adults who pushed their views on children as bullies, instead demanding for children's recognition and respect. Here, the fantasy allows the child to create something out of nothing, overriding Zabladowski's doubts and, notably, all adults' underestimation of children, their material culture, and childhood. Indeed, Bart's "silencer" can literally deny adults their voices, rendering them, and their views, completely mute.

At the same time, however, Bart's ingenuity reinforces Cold War expectations of boys as the inheritors of societal values. Bart especially taps into the American cultural motif of the boy inventor, in which technological prowess and progress propelled the United States forward as a world power (Miller and Van Riper 2012). While the boy inventor in the popular imagination was not new, the immediate postwar context elevated the image of the innovative child and junior scientist as proof of the superiority of the American Way over the Soviet Union (Onion 2016; Westfahl 2019). Such propaganda appeared in the form of education programs, such as President Eisenhower's 1953 Atoms for Peace program, patriotic history books like *Tom Edison: Young Inventor* (1947), and broad emphasis on science (or criticism concerning the lack thereof) in the classroom. Media prominently featured hero-scientists like television's *Captain Video and His Video Rangers* (1949–1955) and *Space Patrol* (1950–1955), assuaging fears in that children could harness the atom for peace and prosperity (Luciano and Coville 2012). Other contemporaneous screen children in films such as *The Decision of Christopher Blake* (1948), *Atomic City* (1952), *The Rocket Man* (1954), and *The Space Children* (1958) were optimistic, if not downright genius, in employing their knowhow of atomic power. In *The 5,000 Fingers of Dr. T*, Bart's determination drives the scene as he repeats, "It's gotta work! It just gotta!" With a father figure supporting him, Bart taps into the promise of science in the atomic age for children, just as the decade demanded.

Bart's silencer demonstrates children's agency in the negotiation of conflicting social expectations. While Bart rejects his father figure's drive for money and his mother's determination to instill discipline and maturity in him, the boy readily accepts consumerism and embraces material possessions when he turns inventor in the interest of national (and boyhood) security. In doing so, Bart appropriates material culture as a form of patriotism, thereby refuting those who bemoaned the American public's obsession with figuratively "keeping up with the Joneses." In the mid-1950s, critics singled out consumerism as an empty identity marker, coopting children's agency—in this case, how youth spent their money and how they enjoyed their free time. Specifically, psychologists and various childrearing experts believed "bad" forms of popular culture contributed to juvenile delinquency. Notably, a year after *The 5,000 Fingers of Dr. T*'s release, a comic book scare led to a Senate subcommittee investigation into how comic book publishers supposedly seduced innocent children and turned them into sex fiends and criminals (Hajdu 2008). Similarly, by 1957 the Soviet Union's *Sputnik* and *Sputnik II* launches prompted public concern regarding whether children spent too much time with frivolous luxuries like watching television, rather than studying and prepping for their roles as future citizen-soldiers (Mieczkowski 2013).

Bart's atomic-powered silencer preemptively negated such anxieties. In the film, the adults certainly want to curtail childhood freedoms, from Mrs. Collins hiring Terwilliker to tutor her son, to the Happy Fingers Academy banning sports and playthings in favor of discipline, to shots of Zabladowski's mystified face as Bart pulls assorted knickknacks from his pockets to construct his silencer. The reaction shots of Zabladowski's bewildered and impressed visage are indicative of the adult view that assorted bottle caps and dime-store toys cannot possibly construct an atomic weapon. Of course Bart succeeds since the movie privileges innovation and patriotism through consumerism. Just as Bart's father fought and died against fascism in World War II, the boy and his new figurative stepfather follow in his footsteps to do the same. Bart acts for a moral purpose, that is, saving boyhood and his mother from Terwilliker, connoting the decade's "correct" form of material consumerism while enabling him to form an intergenerational bond with a rehabilitated father figure.

Bart's atomic weapon also restores Zabladowski's sense of manhood. Historians and then-contemporary critics worried about so-called crises of masculinity, wherein sons and fathers lost a degree of manhood in the heightened "soft" consumerist lifestyle of 1950s suburban luxury (Cuordileone 2005; Osgerby 2001). Social commentators, notably Arthur Schlesinger, Jr., vigorously argued for a renewal of American male virility to thwart communism abroad and delinquency at home (Cuordileone 2005). This criticism renders Zabladowski's adherence to moneymaking problematic because he is susceptible to bribery and corruption; even when Bart seals their father-son bond in blood, he knows that the plumber initially agreed to help because Bart offered Zabladowski higher wages than Terwilliker. Thus, when Bart asserts agency as an innovative atomic scientist within the national imaginary, he restores Zabladowski's patriotism by encouraging him to assist in the father-son project. Zabladowski earlier stated he served four years in the army, and he now revives his inner warrior by participating in his figurative son's weapons project. Indeed, Zabladowski performs the final touches, testing the device and then cautioning Bart that the weapon is revolutionary: "If it starts smoking, get away from it—but fast!" Zabladowski's warnings are his last words to Bart as the boy departs to shut down Terwilliker's musical monstrosity. Aiding his son best he can, the father figure realizes he must let Bart go forward into the unknown.

In the end, Bart's device stops Dr. T as Terwilliker, bedecked in full military regalia and poised on his podium, prepares to unleash his Happy Fingers method on the world. With his students numbered and sporting the Academy beanie, the teacher relishes his students' obedience, his absolute control over their minds and bodies, and his imminent "date with destiny": "*Five thousand* little fingers! All playing together on *my* piano! Every finger obedient to the whim of me, the master! Every finger subservient to my lordly beck and call . . . . Every infinitesimal microscopic piece of tissue on those five thousand little fingers cringing and trembling and groveling before me!" However, on the downbeat, nothing plays. Bart assures the doctor that his weapon is operational and "very atomic!" An intimidated Terwilliker submits, begging his student not to silence him, and Bart arranges for all the boys' freedom. The boys immediately side with Bart, and this unified front serves as an affirmation of strength in numbers. That all the boys join Bart upholds peer agency, signifying Bart will not become an alienated, lonesome Beatnik (see Corsaro 2005). He projects boyhood on his own terms: individualism combined with peer strength, the ability to express knowledge that comes from living in childhood, and freedom from adult oversight. The kids collectively act as one while they celebrate with glee, tear up music scores, and drag Terwilliker to jail.

Bart cements his victory by taking Terwilliker's place leading the orchestra. Wielding a baton, he calls for order—the other kids comply, but Bart is no dictator. The script describes, "the five hundred boys cut loose with a spontaneous virtuoso rendition of Chopsticks," in which each lad uses his shared knowledge of "Chopsticks" to perform as one (Scott and Dr. Seuss 1952, 84). The boys create their own world where they have equal membership in making the rules (Corsaro 2005)—except there are no rules; each boy plays "Chopsticks" his own way, even jumping on the ivories, not bothering to harmonize with the next pianist, and all of them ignoring Bart waving the baton. This peer agency starts to fall apart as Bart forgets about his atomic silencer. Zabladowski previously gave warnings to run if he lost control of the weapon. The silencer starts to smoke, bubble, and sparkle, but Bart and the other boys, flushed with victory, forget the device as they wreak musical havoc.

Here, Bart's national, spatial, and intergenerational agency has limits. While he successfully overthrows a dictator, takes over the Academy, and rescues American boyhood from a tyrannical pianist, the boy's efforts clash with the adult knowledge needed to manage the atomic force he unleashes. Bart basks in his moral victory, but he lacks the discipline and maturity to responsibly run the Academy, as evidenced by quickly disregarding his father figure's parting words. The 500 boys enthusiastically express their musical selves without adult supervision, but this freedom comes at the price of self-control and restraint. The movie effectively negates all forms of child agency through the world's looming annihilation, caused by the child's own creation. Bart realizes his error and yells "No!" repeatedly—also his first lines that open the film—but his verbal missive cannot stop nuclear fission, even in a fantasy of his own making. The adult framework reasserts itself to curb chaos created by carefree children, somewhat justifying the prevalent strict childrearing practices of the 1950s, all for the child's own good (see Frankel 2017). As the kids flee, the Happy Fingers Academy vanishes under "a multicolored Bikini-like cloud" (Scott and Dr. Seuss 1952, 224).

Atomic obliteration wakes Bart from his fantasy and the movie concludes. However, the filmmakers had trouble bringing Bart back to reality. Geisel considered one ending to the film, wherein practice did make

Figure 2.3 Bart Collins (Tommy Rettig), the #1 piano student, subdues Dr. Terwilliker (Hans Conried) with the force of nuclear energy. Unfortunately, even in fantasy, adult intervention is presented as necessary since Bart cannot control the sheer power unleashed by his invention made from the bricolage of 1950s children's material culture: *The 5,000 Fingers of Dr. T* (1953).

perfection. In the first draft, Zabladowski suggested Bart take up the trombone, but Mrs. Collins refused: "You're *going* to learn that piano if I have to keep you at that keyboard *forever!*" (Geisel[c], 106–7).[11] A fadeout and adult voiceover proved her right, as an adult Bart brilliantly performed piano at symphony hall, perhaps not unlike Paderewski, while cries of "Bravo!" filled the soundtrack. The final shot depicted a gleeful Mrs. Collins and Zabladowski sitting in the audience, with the plumber declaring, "I told you to keep the kid at the piano!" (Geisel[c], 107). By eschewing boyish pursuits for piano practice, the adult Bart outgrew his childish fantasies for real-life success, just as his mother and instructor wanted. In this original coda, Bart's fantasy death was a moral wakeup call for him to shape up and do what grownups told him to do, allowing Dr. Terwilliker to triumph in the end.[12]

However, Geisel changed his mind. He discarded this ending because it "doesn't round out in a nice warm glow. The loose ends are not neatly tied up. It has no consummation of theme" (Geisel[i]). This original conclusion, while appropriate according to then-contemporary directives from child experts, parenting guides, and the general belief that parents in fact know best, did not pass as a good story. These "loose ends" and the lack of a "nice warm glow" connoted the "real" ending was a forced one. In the filmed finale, the lines between imagination and reality blur; Bart plays matchmaker, fulfilling the fantasy of turning Zabladowski into his stepfather. After prompting the plumber to agree that Mrs. Collins looks pretty, the boy forces Zabladowski to promise to take him fishing, suggesting the fantasy-within-a-fantasy scene will eventually come true. Presuming an appropriate father figure can now lead this nuclear family, Bart and his mother no longer need to subscribe to Terwilliker's strict standards. This family togetherness confirms Bart's capacity to mold his future wellbeing and happiness by figuratively denying the piano a place in the household (see Bonvin and Stoecklin 2014). Indeed, Terwilliker is not featured in the film's ending, connoting his banishment from the Collins's home. To reinforce the point, Bart shuts Dr. T out entirely. The script describes the action: "Bart, happily, runs back to the piano, turns the EXERCISES books around so that Terwlliker's face is hidden, picks up his ball and mitt [and] runs lickety-split down the street" (Scott and Dr. Seuss 1952, 236). With his dog beside him, baseball in hand, and Terwilliker figuratively blinded, Bart escapes his "box" and is set to enjoy childhood pursuits outdoors. He is sure to return to a promised two-parent household indoors, without their immediate pressure to grow up and conform to postwar capitalistic, social-climbing dictums.

AN UNHAPPY FILMMAKING METHOD

Bart Collins wins onscreen, but the film's fate was not as fortunate. After production wrapped, Geisel left Hollywood, calling the experience "the greatest 'down period'" of his career (Cohen 2004, 286). On paper, Geisel could unleash his imagination, but translating these drawings to a live-action studio set proved difficult. Some critics enjoyed the fantasy, but many more downplayed Bart's fantasy world, noting that it held little appeal other than for children (see "5,000 Fingers" 1953; Brog 1953; Crowther 1953; G.K. 1953; Horowitz 1953; R.L.K. 1953). To an extent, these adult critics legitimatized a child's unique perspective; by examining the technical qualities of filmmaking, they acknowledged Bart's creativity in shaping his surroundings, even if they ignored his agentic critique of adult social norms.

The studio also undermined Bart's message about standing up to tyranny. Geisel recalled certain storylines were "too hot to handle. The industry wants to please everyone and offend no one . . . . But don't quote that, or I'll get fired out of Hollywood" (Smith 2011, 157). Indeed, after a disastrous preview screening, producer Stanley Kramer excised much of Bart's criticism of adult material consumerism, leading to a second cut with a much shorter running time. Kramer also reshot the beginning scenes, bringing Terwilliker into the Collins's household as a private tutor and personal antagonist for Bart, rather than remaining as an abstract authoritarian and conformist figure for all children.

The producers' goal of selling tickets to family audiences further contradicted Bart's stance against social conformity through consumerism. Ancillary film campaigns existed, with the pressbook even (ironically) encouraging kids to join a Terwilliker club ("The 5,000 Fingers" 1952, 14). The film's merchandising tie-ins included toys, musical instruments, t-shirts, women's and children's beanies, and jewelry (Cohen 2004; "What the Showmen" 1953). This marketing bonanza, while tangential to the filmic text, indicates how Columbia Pictures advertised the film to audiences, including children. The studio invited kids and adults to collectively embrace mass consumerism, to the point of offering Happy Fingers Academy beanies for kids

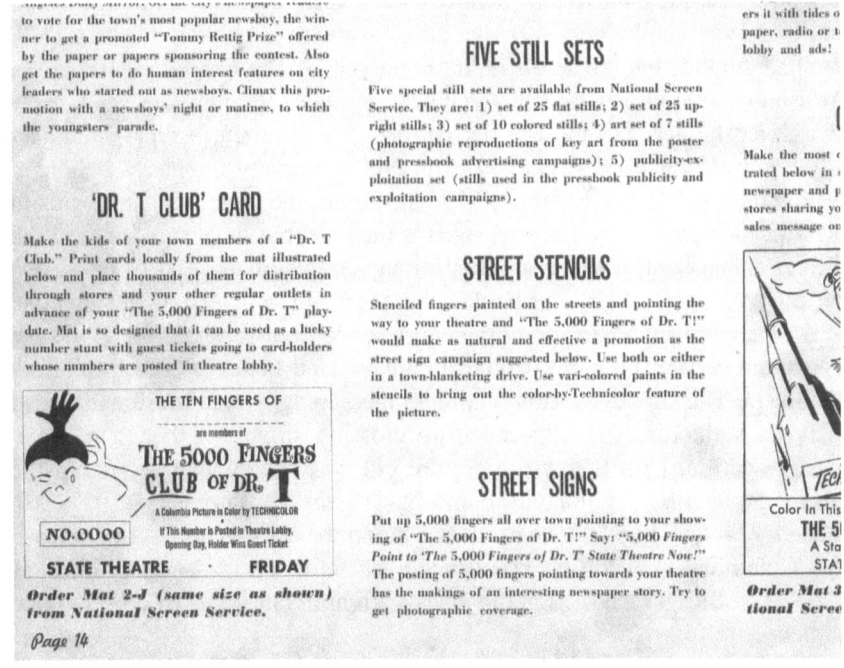

Figure 2.4 In this detail from the pressbook, Columbia Pictures hoped to profit from Bart's fantasy through consumerism and conformity—the very things Bart raged against. The studio's capitalistic efforts were unsuccessful. Above the Terwilliker fan club certificate: note the pitch stating child star Tommy Rettig was a "newsboy who made good" in the movies. Rettig supplemented his income as an actor by delivering newspapers, which presumably encouraged entrepreneurial newsboys to watch the movie.

to wear and extending opportunities for children to enroll in Terwilliker's club. This salesmanship coopted childhood peer agency, reducing children into commoditized fans who conformed under an adult/studio "club"—a parallel of the Happy Fingers Academy wherein each student wore matching caps. Bart himself was not above embracing material culture, as he used his pocket contents to construct an atomic device to vanquish a tyrant. But outside of Bart's fantasy (and outside the film), moviegoers also partook in consumerism as integral to the 1950s American Way. By purchasing a Happy Fingers Academy beanie, a child not only promoted the film but subscribed to the social conformity that Terwilliker symbolized and what Bart railed against.

Bart Collins's agency did not extend beyond his fantasy world. The film's lack of appeal for adults thwarted Bart's intergenerational agency, the film's merchandizing and advocacy for conformity subverted his national agency, and critics thought his spatial agency was unconvincing and made for poor cinema. One group, however, remained loyal to Bart: children. Exhibitors reported that kids liked the picture. One North Carolina exhibitor noted adults did not show up: "We played this on a single bill and did very well. We had the kids but the adults didn't come out" ("The Exhibitor" 1954a, 1). An Illinois exhibitor lauded the technical merits of the film, but the fantasy "was over the heads of most of our patrons. The children (we had an unusually high number for this one) liked it. Not as many walkouts as I thought there would be" ("The Exhibitor" 1954b, 1). So, the high number of kids in the audience enjoyed the movie, even if they did not understand it, and the theater manager proposed a solution for any confusion: the less of Dr. T, the better. "We were told by our booker that there are two versions for this one .... We were supposed to get the short version but received the long one. The short version probably would be appreciated better" ("The Exhibitor" 1954b, 1). The shorter version, with less messaging, would presumably lead to fewer walkouts. The film ended up grossing slightly higher than above average earnings for a first-run feature but was not enough to recoup the cost of production, let alone turn a profit ("Boxoffice Barometer" 1953, 26). Indeed, *The Los Angeles Times* noted a month before the film's June release that Columbia's hoped-for "box-office event is much in debate" (Schallert 1953, B7). Bart's imagination ran away with him, but he could not motivate audiences to follow.

Uneven box office attendance bore out the poor reviews. The film's premiere coincided with the end of the school year as kids left their personal Terwillikers behind for summer break. But, the opening was not successful: *Variety* noted, "With all schools going on summer vacation yesterday, film theatres are anticipating a sharp upbeat at matinees later this stanza" as families headed to air-conditioned theaters to escape the summer heat, but

The 5,000 Fingers of Dr. T was "somewhat of a disappointment" given such expectations ("B'way Strong" 1953, 13). As the film's run progressed, other theaters reported poor earnings despite its various promotions and product tie-ins ("'Bay' Thunderous" 1953; "Clips" 1953; "Product" 1953). In Los Angeles, Columbia Pictures reinforced adult expectations concerning "delinquents" and child welfare by eliciting child stars to endorse the picture, with proceeds heading to youth programs ("Junior Premiere" 1953, 10). Despite the film's critique against the evils of money, the producers, theater operators, retailers, marketers, and Geisel himself hoped for a box office bonanza. They were disappointed; *The 5,000 Fingers of Dr. T* grossed a paltry $250,000 (Kramer and Coffey 1997, 107).

CONCLUSION

Theodor Geisel had a history of embedding social messages in his writing. In the case of *The 5,000 Fingers of Dr. T*, however, he perhaps sensed that his alter persona Dr. Seuss had gone too far. On the cover of the second draft of his script, he wrote: "This is not a diatribe against parents who make boys practise [*sic*]. The theme is loneliness, anguish of childhood. Kid struggling to make his desires understood in a world peopled by and run by adults" (Geisel[d]). Geisel softened the blow against an obsessive devotion to practicing, either for the piano or for the workplace. The theme, he insisted, was an exploration of childhood self-expression and making kids heard over the din of Terwilliker's "Hitlerian" rage. Despite his intentions, Dr. Seuss's story did not unfold as planned. *The 5,000 Fingers of Dr. T*'s failure partly came from the Cold War context. Bart needed a father and a stable family life, but he rejected the underlying purpose of a strong father-son bond. The boy regarded family togetherness as fun: fishing was preferable to tickling the ivories. In doing so, he dismissed paternal responsibilities to make sure boys had regimented structure and could therefore grow up to successfully scale social and corporate adult ladders.

In 1958, Columbia gave Bart Collins another chance. The studio rereleased *The 5,000 Fingers of Dr. T*, retitling the picture *Crazy Music* to cash in on the rock 'n' roll craze popular among teenagers across the country (Gargiulo 2002, 90). Hollywood, discovering the teenage market, quickly churned out pictures like *Rock, Rock, Rock* (1956) and *Don't Knock the Rock* (1956), gave Elvis Presley a film career, and glorified clever teens making fools of dull and "square" adults. In its second life, *Crazy Music* failed (as it obviously did not feature rock 'n' roll), even if the titular "crazy music" centered on child rebellion, with which teenagers of the age could potentially identify. For Dr. Seuss, the unpleasant collaboration with Hollywood led him to return to children's books as his medium of choice. There, he could endow kids with agency, or the lack thereof, and let his imagination run wild.

ACKNOWLEDGMENTS

I thank the archivists and staff at the Geisel Library at the University of California, San Diego, the Charles E. Young Library at the University of California, Los Angeles, and the Margaret Herrick Library at the Academy of Motion Picture Arts and Sciences in Beverly Hills, California in making their special collections available for the completion of this chapter.

NOTES

1. One cut line detailed that Bart was not alone in this view. Zabladowski said, "Things are tough all over. They tell me, in practically every country in the world, from the suburbs of Stockholm to the heart of the Belgium Congo, mothers have got their children chained down to pianos" (Geisel[g], 2). Bart responded, "Day in, day out. Month after month" (Scott and Dr. Seuss 1952, 4).

2. Several drafts suggested Terwilliker simply wanted money. In one handwritten note, Geisel[h] described "Terwilliger's Racket" as a get-rich scheme: "get money before the jig is up." Part of this plot was to pay the hired staff in "pastoolas" rather than dollars. He kept the American tuition dollars for himself and doled out worthless tender (see Geisel[e], 44). Another script had Zabladowski calculating Terwilliker's profits per child for a nine-year Academy to be $3,437,000 net (see Geisel[d], 18).

3. Several critics singled out the underground concert as the best musical sequence in the film. Their performance is certainly more kinetic than Terwilliker's sedate "Ten Little Fingers."

4. Terwilliker has an electric fence surrounding the Academy to prevent escape. The doctor also installs a "Terwilligerizer" in the dungeon to "normalize" children. The machine transforms "small, disobedient boys," so after "a few nights being Terwilligerized, you will no longer fight against my piano" (Geisel[f], 84).

5. Geisel's[h] handwritten note explained the "idea isn't to give boy view of the piano—but that every seat is in full view of Dr. T—he can watch every boy every minute."

6. Fittingly, actors Peter Lynd Haynes and Mary Healy, playing Zabladowski and Mrs. Collins, were married in real life.

7. Columbia submitted the lyrics and script to the Production Code Administration, Hollywood's censorship agency, for approval. The censors passed the lyrics without comment. Another song, Mrs. Collins's "Many Questions Have No Answers," stated adults do not have all the answers.

8. "The Kid's Song" was originally titled "Boy's Song." Even though no girls appear in the finalized film (though very early screenplay drafts indicate Bart has an

older teenage sister), the filmmakers removed the song's gender-specific reference (Scarpietta 1952).

9. In an early screen draft, Zabladowski remained a conformist even while rebelling, citing plumbers' regulations dating back to 1907 just before assisting Bart, even if such ideas were outmoded. Terwilliker eventually captured them (see Geisel[e], 74).

10. See Clark and Castro (2019) for more on boys' technological innovation that arises from assembling "junk" material culture in 1980s child-friendly film.

11. In an early draft, Mrs. Collins described the social hierarchy of musicians: "A man who plays the piano has a great social asset," but if a musician became a trombone player, "nobody would would [*sic*] want you around at all" (Geisel[b], 3).

12. A different ending depicted Mrs. Collins rushing out to buy Bart a trombone and Bart ripping Terwilliker's photo in half, the pianist wiggling his eyebrows in protest (see Geisel[d], 65).

REFERENCES

"The 5,000 Fingers of Dr. T." 1952. Columbia Pictures, Pressbook. Author's Collection.

"5,000 Fingers of Dr. T." 1953. *Cue.* June 30, 1953. "The 5,000 Fingers of Dr. T [Col., 1952]," Motion Picture Association of America. Production Code Administration Records. Beverly Hills, CA: Margaret Herrick Library, Academy of Motion Picture Arts and Sciences.

"5,000 Fingers Puts Kramer in Multi Million Budget Bracket." 1952. *The Hollywood Reporter.* June 11, 1952. Core Collection Files. Beverly Hills, CA: Margaret Herrick Library, Academy of Motion Picture Arts and Sciences.

"'Bay' Thunderous 18G in Mild Hub." 1953. *Variety.* August 5, 1953: 11.

Beaufort, John. 1953. "Film Fantasy of Childhood at the Astor." *The Christian Science Monitor.* July 25, 1953: 7.

Bonvin, Jean-Michel, and Daniel Stoecklin. 2014. "Introduction." In *Children's Rights and the Capability Approach: Challenges and Prospects*, edited by Jean-Michel Bonvin and Daniel Stoecklin, 1–18. New York, NY: Springer.

"Boxoffice Barometer." 1953. *Boxoffice.* September 12, 1953: 26.

Brady, Thomas F. 1951. "Kramer Acquires Dr. Seuss Fantasy." *The New York Times.* April 28, 1951: 8.

Brog. 1953. "5,000 Fingers of Dr. T." *Variety.* June 17, 1953: 6 & 16.

"B'way Strong Despite Record Heat; 'Space' Smash 44G, 'Wet' Big $138,000, 'Dr. T.' Good 16G, 'Pickup' Fat 80G." 1953. *Variety.* June 24, 1953: 13.

Clark, Jessica, and Ingrid E. Castro. 2019. "Girl Zombies and Boy Wonders: The Future of Agency is Now!" In *Child and Youth Agency in Science Fiction: Travel, Technology, Time*, edited by Ingrid E. Castro and Jessica Clark, 1–21. Lanham, MD: Lexington Books.

"Clips from Film Review." 1953. *Variety.* July 15, 1953: 22.

Coe, Richard L. 1950. "Stanley Kramer Speaks His Mind." *The Washington Post.* September 12, 1950: B7.

Cohen, Charles D. 2004. *The Seuss, the Whole Seuss, and Nothing but the Seuss: A Visual Biography of Theodor Seuss Geisel.* New York, NY: Random House.

Corsaro, William A. 2005. "Collective Action and Agency in Young People's Peer Culture." In *Studies in Modern Childhood: Society, Agency, Culture*, edited by Jens Qvortrup, 231–47. New York, NY: Palgrave Macmillan.

Cross, Gary. 2004. *The Cute and the Cool: Wondrous Innocence and Modern American Children's Culture.* New York, NY: Oxford University Press.

Crowther, Bosley. 1953. "The Screen in Review." *The New York Times.* June 20, 1953: 8.

Cuordileone, K.A. 2005. *Manhood and American Political Culture in the Cold War.* New York, NY: Routledge.

Dr. Seuss. 1938. *The 500 Hats of Bartholomew Cubbins.* New York, NY: Vanguard Press.

Dr. Seuss, and Allan Scott. 1953. *The 5,000 Fingers of Dr. T.* Directed by Roy Rowland. Hollywood, CA: Columbia Pictures. 2017: Blu-Ray. Minnetonka, MN: Mill Creek Entertainment.

English, O. Spurgeon. 1951. *Fathers Are Parents, Too: A Constructive Guide to Successful Fatherhood.* New York, NY: Putnam.

"The Exhibitor Has His Say about Pictures." 1954a. *Boxoffice Bookin' Guide.* Supplement. January 9, 1954: 1–11.

———. 1954b. *Boxoffice Bookin' Guide.* Supplement. September 11, 1954: 1–12.

Frankel, Sam. 2017. *Negotiating Childhoods: Applying a Moral Filter to Children's Everyday Lives.* New York, NY: Palgrave Macmillan.

Gargiulo, Suzanne. 2002. *Hans Conried: A Biography; with a Filmography and a Listing of Radio, Television, Stage and Voice Work.* Jefferson, NC: McFarland & Company.

Geisel, Theodor[a]. "5,000 Fingers of Dr. T." "5,000 Fingers of Dr. T: Screenplay, Rough Notes." Box 7, Folder 13. Dr. Seuss Collection, 1919–2003 (MSS 0230). San Diego, CA: Mandeville Special Collections, Geisel Library, University of California.

———[b]. "New Opening. August 25, 1951." "5,000 Fingers of Dr. T: Screenplay, Rough Notes." Box 7, Folder 13. Dr. Seuss Collection, 1919–2003 (MSS 0230). San Diego, CA: Mandeville Special Collections, Geisel Library, University of California.

———[c]. "5,000 Fingers of Dr. T. August 31, 1951." "5,000 Fingers of Dr. T: Screenplay, Rough Notes." Box 7, Folder 13. Dr. Seuss Collection, 1919–2003 (MSS 0230). San Diego, CA: Mandeville Special Collections, Geisel Library, University of California.

———[d]. "5000 Fingers of Dr. T. (Screenplay)—Second Draft, August 14, 1951." "5,000 Fingers of Dr. T, 1951: Screenplay, Second Draft." Box 7, Folder 16. Dr. Seuss Collection, 1919–2003 (MSS 0230). San Diego, CA: Mandeville Special Collections, Geisel Library, University of California.

———[e]. "5,000 Fingers of Dr. T (Screenplay)—Second Draft, August 14, 1951." "5,000 Fingers of Dr. T, 1951: Screenplay, Second Draft, Unannotated." Box

7, Folder 18. Dr. Seuss Collection, 1919–2003 (MSS 0230). San Diego, CA: Mandeville Special Collections, Geisel Library, University of California.

———[f]. "5,000 Fingers of Dr. T (Screenplay)—Revised Second Draft, September 26, 1951." "5,000 Fingers of Dr. T, 1951: Screenplay, Revised Second Draft." Box 8, Folder 3. Dr. Seuss Collection, 1919–2003 (MSS 0230). San Diego, CA: Mandeville Special Collections, Geisel Library, University of California.

———[g]. "5,000 Fingers of Dr. T (Screenplay), Final Draft, January 30, 1952." "5,000 Fingers of Dr. T, 1952: Screenplay, Final Draft." Box 8, Folder 4. Dr. Seuss Collection, 1919–2003 (MSS 0230). San Diego, CA: Mandeville Special Collections, Geisel Library, University of California.

———[h]. "Are Ideas Kept Alive?" "5,000 Fingers of Dr. T: Screenplay, Rough Notes." Box 7, Folder 13. Dr. Seuss Collection, 1919–2003 (MSS 0230). San Diego, CA: Mandeville Special Collections, Geisel Library, University of California.

———[i]. "Some Notes by the Professor." "5,000 Fingers of Dr. T: Screenplay, First Draft." Box 7, Folder 14. Dr. Seuss Collection, 1919–2003 (MSS 0230). San Diego, CA: Mandeville Special Collections, Geisel Library, University of California.

———[j]. "Who is Zabladowski?" "5,000 Fingers of Dr. T, 1951: Screenplay, Second Draft." Box 7, Folder 16. Dr. Seuss Collection, 1919–2003 (MSS 0230). San Diego, CA: Mandeville Special Collections, Geisel Library, University of California.

G.K. 1953. "Whimsy and Music Blend in Fantasy." *The Los Angeles Times*. October 1, 1953: B11.

Hajdu, David. 2008. *The Ten-Cent Plague: The Great Comic-Book Scare and How It Changed America*. New York, NY: Farrar, Straus and Giroux.

Holt, Marilyn I. 2014. *Cold War Kids: Politics and Childhood in Postwar America, 1945–1960*. Lawrence, KS: University Press of Kansas.

Honeck, Mischa. 2018. *Our Frontier Is the World: The Boys Scouts in the Age of American Ascendancy*. Ithaca, NY: Cornell University Press.

Horowitz, Murray. 1953. "Review: The 5,000 Fingers of Dr. T." *The Motion Picture Daily*. June 16, 1953: 2.

Jacobson, Lisa. 2004. *Raising Consumers: Children and the American Mass Market in the Early Twentieth Century*. New York, NY: Columbia University Press.

James, Allison, and Adrian L. James. 2004. *Constructing Childhood: Theory, Policy and Social Practice*. New York, NY: Palgrave Macmillan.

James, Allison, Chris Jenks, and Alan Prout. 1998. *Theorizing Childhood*. Cambridge: Polity Press.

Jenkins, Henry. 2002. "'No Matter How Small': The Democratic Imagination of Dr. Seuss." In *Hop on Pop: The Politics and Pleasure of Popular Culture*, edited by Henry Jenkins, Tara McPherson, and Jane Shattuc, 187–208. Durham, NC: Duke University Press.

"Junior Premiere." 1953. *Variety*. October 28, 1953: 10.

Kordas, Anne M. 2013. *The Politics of Childhood in Cold War America*. New York, NY: Routledge.

Kramer, Stanley, and Thomas M. Coffey. 1997. *A Mad, Mad, Mad, Mad World: A Life in Hollywood.* New York, NY: Harcourt Brace and Company.

LaRossa, Ralph. 1999. "A Call from a Child: Help Seeking Behavior Among Early Twentieth Century American Youth." In *Through the Eyes of the Child: Re-Visioning Children As Active Agents of Family Life*, edited by Constance L. Shehan, 157–76. Bingley: Emerald.

Luciano, Patrick, and Gary Coville. 2012. "Shooting for the Stars: Captain Video, the Rocket Rangers, and America's Conquest of Space." In *1950s "Rocketman" TV Series and Their Fans: Cadets, Rangers, and Junior Space Men*, edited by Cynthia J. Miller and A. Bowdoin Van Riper, 97–114. New York, NY: Palgrave Macmillan.

MacCann, Richard D. 1952. "Ted Geisel's Tale of Boys at the Piano." *The Christian Science Monitor.* April 22, 1952: 7.

Menniger, William C. 1958. *Blueprint for Teen-Age Living.* New York, NY: Sterling Publishing Co.

Mickenberg, Julia L. 2006. *Learning from the Left: Children's Literature, the Cold War, and Radical Politics in the United States.* New York, NY: Oxford University Press.

Mieczkowski, Yanek. 2013. *Eisenhower's Sputnik Moment: The Race for Space and World Prestige.* Ithaca, NY: Cornell University Press.

Miller, Cynthia J., and A. Bowdoin Van Riper. 2012. "Introduction." In *1950s "Rocketman" TV Series and Their Fans: Cadets, Rangers, and Junior Space Men*, edited by Cynthia J. Miller and A. Bowdoin Van Riper, 1–16. New York, NY: Palgrave Macmillan.

Newcomb, Theodore M. 1950. *Social Psychology.* New York, NY: Dryden Press.

Onion, Rebecca. 2016. *Innocent Experiments: Childhood and the Culture of Popular Science in the United States.* Chapel Hill, NC: The University of North Carolina Press.

Osgerby, Bill. 2001. *Playboys in Paradise: Masculinity, Youth, and Leisure-Style in Modern America.* New York, NY: Berg Publishers.

Peacock, Margaret. 2014. *Innocent Weapons: The Soviet and American Politics of Childhood in the Cold War.* Chapel Hill, NC: The University of North Carolina Press.

"Product, Weather, Shriners Up B.O. On B'way; 'Wagon' Rolling to 171G, 'Moon' $51,500 for 2, 'Sea' $13,500." 1953. *Variety.* July 15, 1953: 11.

R.L.K. 1953. "With Teacher Like This, Who Would Want to Play a Piano?" *The Washington Post.* July 23, 1953: 28.

Scarpietta, Maria. 1952. "Letter to J.I. Breen." January 11, 1952. "The 5,000 Fingers of Dr. T [Col., 1952]," Motion Picture Association of America. Production Code Administration Records. Beverly Hills, CA: Margaret Herrick Library, Academy of Motion Picture Arts and Sciences.

Schallert, Edwin. 1952. "Hayes, Healy Return for Film—Together." *The Los Angeles Times.* March 23, 1952: D1.

———. 1953. "Hayes, Healy Starring Deal on Way; 'Phantom Ape' Put On 3D Slate." *The Los Angeles Times.* May 1, 1953: B7.

Scott, Allan, and Dr. Seuss. 1952. "The 5,000 Fingers of Dr. T." "Final Shooting Script, February 2, 1952." Box 6. Stanley Kramer Papers (Collection 161). Los Angeles, CA: Department of Special Collections, Charles E. Young Research Library, University of California.

Smith, Caroline M. 2011. *Dr. Seuss: The Cat Behind the Hat—The Art of Dr. Seuss*. Kansas City, MO: Andrews McMeel Publishing.

Spock, Benjamin. 1954. "Your Child Imitates You!" *Washington Post*. July 18, 1954: AW7.

———. 1957. *The Common Sense Book of Baby and Child Care*. New York, NY: Duell, Sloan, and Pearce.

Warming, Hanne. 2018. "Children's Citizenship in Globalised Societies." In *Theorising Childhood: Citizenship, Rights and Participation*, edited by Claudio Baraldi and Tom Cockburn, 29–52. New York, NY: Palgrave Macmillan.

Westfahl, Gary. 2019. "Afterword: The Children of Wonder." In *Child and Youth Agency in Science Fiction: Travel, Technology, Time*, edited by Ingrid E. Castro and Jessica Clark, 273–81. Lanham, MD: Lexington Books.

"What the Showmen Are Doing." 1953. *The Independent Exhibitors Film Bulletin*. April 20, 1953: 18 & 20.

Whyte Jr., William H. 1956. *The Organization Man*. New York, NY: Simon and Schuster.

Wilson, Sloan. 1955. *The Man in the Gray Flannel Suit*. New York, NY: Simon and Schuster.

Wylie, Philip. 1942. *Generation of Vipers*. New York, NY: Farrar & Rinehart.

Imagination/Transformation

Chapter 3

Developing Children's Agency through Play with Imaginary Companions

Kostas Magos and Sophia Kremmydiotou

CHILDREN AS AGENTS

According to views of the "new" sociology of childhood, children are not passive subjects but active agents in their worlds (see Corsaro 2005; Mayall 2002). Children make decisions about things that concern them and reflect on their own and others' views and attitudes. Similarly, Theobald, Danby, and Ailwood (2011) underscore that children are active decision-makers and active participants who make sense of their lives. The role of children as agents is often not accepted by adults. Corsaro (2005) explains the distinction between children's lives, namely, the marked difference between what children experience and feel and adults' ideas about what children's realities and lives look like. Thomayer (2017) finds this distinction points out that it may never be possible for adults to completely see and understand children's points of view from children's perspectives. James, Jenks, and Prout (1998) write that childhood is "an independent place with its own folklore, rituals, rules and normative constraints . . . within a system that is unfamiliar to adults" (29). Such primary rituals associated with childhood are found in the processes of children's play.

Children's right to play is one of the basic rights referred to in the United Nations Convention on the Rights of the Child (UNCRC). According to the UNCRC's play policy, choice is characteristic of play. As Kapasi and Gleave (2009) explain, children value freedom from structure, making choices, and having time for themselves during play. In this framework, children become agents of their play and with playmates; as a result, they "benefit from the unique opportunities that play allows for their learning and development, socialization, and imaginative capabilities" (Wood 2014, 4).

A common type of play is pretend play. According to von Benzon (2015), play is synonymous with pretense, particularly for young children. Young children engage real or imaginary friends in their pretend play and often share these play scenarios with adults (Canning 2013). According to Galyer and Evans (2001), pretense is a healthy and developmentally valuable part of children's play. Corsaro (1993) writes that through role-playing, which is the most common type of pretend play, "children actively appropriate information from the adult world to create stable and coherent interactive routines in the peer culture" (72). Thus, pretend play is a stepping stone or tool for young children to become agents of their lives and cultures. One of the most common types of pretend play, particularly for young children, is play with imaginary companions.

IMAGINARY COMPANIONS

During early childhood, many children form companionships with imaginary friends, who serve important roles in children's lives and daily routines (Hart and Zellars 2006; Motoshima et al. 2014; Singer and Singer 1990). Although it is not common among *all* preschool children, the creation of imaginary companions is a fairly usual phenomenon in children and often a healthy expression of their imaginations (Gleason 2004a). Some children continue to keep their imaginary friends even when they are in their first years of primary school (Roby and Kidd 2008; Taylor and Carlson 1997; Taylor et al. 2004). Pearson and colleagues (2001) asked a sample of 1,800 children between five and twelve years old about imaginary friends. Their research findings show that more than 46 percent of them currently have or had a type of imaginary friend in the past (Pearson et al. 2001).

In order to qualify as imaginary, the friend must meet certain conditions, such as being involved in long periods of interaction with the child and forming an important part of the child's life and everyday routine (Taylor, Cartwright, and Carlson 1993). Imaginary friends can be described as imaginary characters: usually either people or cuddly toys (Bouldin and Pratt 1999; Gleason 2004a). Bouldin (2006) contributes a further note to the nature of imaginary friends, affirming that they are lively imaginary characters, people, or animals, and although they do not actually exist, children pretend and act as if these friends are corporeal. Children create emotional relationships with their imaginary friends; thus, in this way, they cease to be merely thoughts in the minds of children (Taylor, Cartwright, and Carlson 1993; Taylor and Mannering 2007). When the imaginary friend is a special toy, such as a stuffed animal or something else, Harris (2000) states the item is a "personified object," calling the process of having this type of imaginary friend "personification." Nieuwenhuys (2011) offers characteristic examples of this process in the case of teddy bears, mentioning three stories that take place in different parts of the world and concluding, "as children engage with the objects that surround them, they interpret them, invest them with meaning and bring them to life" (417). Moriguchi and Shinohara (2012) link the concept of imaginary friends to that of imaginary agents, explaining that these friends are characters to which children themselves attribute both biological and psychological characteristics. In addition, children think these characters personify elements of reality. In Moriguchi and Shinohara's (2012) study, children were introduced to an invisible agent and an invisible stone. During their play, children assigned biological properties, as well as feelings, to the agent but not to the stone. The researchers found that the tendency to allot such properties was stronger in children with imaginary companions than for those without them.

In addition to cuddly toys, the development of a consumerist culture for children's products gives children the ability to choose imaginary friends from a large selection of toys designed for or addressed to them. Dolls, stuffed animals, superheroes, Playmobil figures, etc. commonly function in the role of imaginary friends. Some researchers do regard cuddly toys and dolls as imaginary friends, but only on the condition that children treat them as if they have specific personalities and names and interact with them by including them in their everyday lives (see Singer and Singer 1990; Taylor 1999).

In fact, there are really only two main categories of imaginary friends: invisible friends (who are often the same age as the child) and objects children bring to life, such as stuffed animals (Gleason et al. 1997). Some children engage in the creation of entire fantasy worlds that are completely different from their usual, conventional ones (Singer and Singer 1990). These particular worlds are known as paracosms (MacKeith 1984) and bring to mind the term "heterotopias," which Foucault (1997) identified as other spaces created through play. However, in order to be included in the category of imaginary friends, certain criteria must be met, such as the fact that children must know that these worlds are figments of their imaginations. The paracosm should also monopolize the interests of children for a long period of time and be of paramount importance to children, who must have the desire to preserve these worlds in time (Singer and Singer 1990). In these imaginary worlds (which may encompass entire cities), there are often special people and special species of flowers and trees and a special language people use to communicate with one another (Hoff 2005; Singer and Singer 1990).

Of particular importance to the present research is the fact that children's imaginary friends, irrespective of the category they belong to, should have specific names, ages, genders, and appearances (Singer and Singer 1990;

Taylor 1999). Taylor and Carlson (2000) find that parents' religious and cultural perceptions of children's imaginary friends influence and determine the types of imaginary friends children create. Children's play and children's relationships are deeply influenced by the social and cultural environment within which they grow; thus, the choice, role, and function of imaginary companions will also be affected by those very same social and cultural constructions (Corsaro 2005).

Research on imaginary friends occasionally contradicts itself. Girls are more likely to create imaginary friends than boys (Fritz 2015). Other studies prove that while girls may create imaginary friends, boys primarily like to pretend to be animals, people, or objects, such as planes or machines (Carlson and Taylor 2005). Research by Gleason, Sebanc, and Hartup (2000) shows that firstborn children and only children are most likely to create imaginary friends, perhaps due to the lack of peer company in their real-world families. Also, according to Bouldin and Pratt (1999) and Gleason (2004a), some children with imaginary friends display a lack of social and communicative skills, which could be attributed to the time children devote to playing with imaginary friends instead of looking for or forming real ones. Contrary to this negative view, Taylor (1999) and Singer and Singer (1990) highlight that children with imaginary friends are often particularly sociable and extroverted, and are equally friendly with both imaginary and real friends. The creation of imaginary friends is a phenomenon within "normative" childhood, but it can also help children face personal difficulties or social problems in their lives. In particular, young children who feel lonely, isolated, or neglected by the people around them, especially their peers, may be more likely to create imaginary friends (Seeman, Widrow, and Yesavage 1984). Children also potentially increase their self-confidence by creating imaginary friends (Fritz 2015).

Some parents do not realize that their children create imaginary friends whom they treat like real people or animals with distinct personalities (Wigger, Paxson, and Ryan 2013). Parents do not play a decisive role in whether or not their children create imaginary friends (Taylor and Carlson 2000). Although some parents view children's creation of imaginary friends positively, because they believe that the process cultivates imagination and signals heightened intelligence, the majority of parents do not support or want their children to form such friendships (Gleason and Kalpidou 2014; Taylor 1999). The reason for their reluctance is that the process of creating and playing with imaginary friends is out of parents' and other adults' social and familial constructions. As most adults cannot easily comprehend why and how children create imaginary companions, and also cannot control the process of imaginary friendship formation, they often choose to reject and/or ask children to relinquish such companionships. Also, it is possible that some parents wonder whether the existence of imaginary, predominantly invisible, friends constitutes a "normal" characteristic of their children's development. Considering that the creation and interaction with imaginary friends belongs to what Leonard (2015) calls "micro-childhoods," namely pastimes and habits found in children's everyday personal lives, some parents and other adults might feel that children's communication with imaginary friends is an unknown and mostly incomprehensible world for them. However, as Leonard (2015) notes, children and adults do not live in separate worlds; they merely share the same places from different generational locations. Research shows that despite their parents' objections, many young children choose to have one or more imaginary companions, friends who occupy significant roles in their everyday lives (Taylor and Carlson 2000). This process indicates the willingness of young children to be agents in the framework of their play and, more generally, in their lived experiences.

IMAGINARY COMPANIONS AND CHILDREN'S AGENCY DEVELOPMENT

The circumstance of creating imaginary friends is dynamically linked to children's imaginations. According to Bouldin (2006), there are five dimensions of childhood imagination: imaginary friends, dreams, daydreams, frightening thoughts, and pretend play. Bouldin (2006) finds that the formation of imaginary friends is linked to an inherent predisposition in children to engage with their imaginations. Children with imaginary friends have vivid dreams and daydreams, and the games they play together often differ from children without imaginary friends (Taylor, Cartwright, and Carlson 1993). Additionally, children with imaginary friends are usually more willing to discuss their fantasies, daydreams, and dreams; they are also more involved in pretend play involving imaginary activities (Bouldin 2006; Bouldin and Pratt 2002).

According to Paige, Meins, and Fernyhough (2014), children who participate in imaginary friendships benefit from these relationships in a variety of ways. They gain better understanding of information, practice their listening and observation skills, and better perceive and accept others' opinions. The creation of imaginary friends can improve children's relationships with their peers by enabling them to initially practice their communication skills with imaginary friends and then, later on, with peers (Gleason 2004a; Gleason, Jarudi, and Cheek 2003). Also, imaginary friends provide children the opportunity to practice social recognition and develop the process of taking on different social roles. These activities help children achieve deeper understanding of themselves and their personalities, supply motives to make decisions and reflect on them, and offer opportunities to manage their peer relationships without adult intervention (Gleason 2004a; Gleason, Jarudi, and Cheek 2003). In this way, imaginary friends have a mediating role in the creation of peer cultures. As Corsaro (2005) theorizes, through interpretive reproduction children transform information they take from the world of adults when creating their own peer cultures. The presence of imaginary companions could constitute a stage in the development of such transformations.

According to Harris (2000), imaginary friends can be "inner mentors" who help with children's identity formation. Harris (2000) writes that imaginary companions support primary dimensions of children's personalities and needs through building self-esteem and self-regulation, while imaginary friends also provide comfort or substitute company. Taken together, these advances greatly enhance children's quality of life. Majors (2013) finds that imaginary companions help children approach the real world, support cognitive, social, and emotional development, enable children to respond to events in their lives, and develop deeper senses of the self.

According to Hart and Zellars (2006), imaginary friends function as indicators and sources of wisdom, provide consolation and guidance, and cultivate innate abilities of good sense in children. In addition, they find that imaginary friends heighten children's self-expression, communication skills, and emotional development. In the process of having and communicating with imaginary friends, children gain experiences of interaction with and recognition of important situations and individuals, psychosocial stress levels of children are frequently reduced, and they gain tools to deal with various problems or difficulties (Hart and Zellars 2006).

Children with imaginary friends tend to be more academically gifted and have a predisposition to creative thinking (Nagera 1969; Singer and Singer 1990). Research indicates that the creation of imaginary friends has positive effects on the development of social, cognitive, emotional, and communication abilities (Giménez-Dasí, Pons, and Bender 2016). Ultimately, creating and interacting with imaginary friends showcases the efforts of young children to understand and interpret the world that surrounds them. These friends are not simply a stop on the path to growing up; importantly, they indicate children's capabilities to agentically attribute their own meanings to their surroundings, creating their own bridges of interaction.

IMAGINARY FRIENDS AS CULTURAL OBJECTS

Visible imaginary friends like cuddly toys and dolls constitute a form of cultural object, as long as they function and acquire meaning in specific familial and social (and consequently cultural) contexts within which children live and grow. According to the sociocultural approach, everything can constitute a "cultural object" as long as it exists in a specific cultural context and its use and function are directly related to that context (Vygotsky 2016). Hennig and Kirova (2012) stress that there are no culturally neutral objects and, as a consequence, every object that is dear to a child simultaneously carries some sort of cultural message and a cultural way of using the object. Thus, stuffed animals and dolls are found to be, on an international scale, the most usual form of imaginary friends. How each child shapes the relationship of his/her imaginary friendship with the object, as well as the form of interaction that he/she creates with the object, is dictated by the cultural context within which the child lives. We believe it would be particularly interesting to further study the relationships children growing in different cultural contexts have with their imaginary friends and to highlight similarities and differences between locales. The prospect of a child presenting and sharing his/her imaginary friends with children living in other parts of the world could constitute a path to developing intercultural communication and empathy.

According to Wood (2009), objects have many interconnecting dimensions and values; as a result, the study of an object should consider physical, cultural, and personal dimensions. Transferring Wood's (2009) stance to the case of imaginary friends, we can focus on three different dimensions of children's interactions with their imaginary friends, all connected to experience. The first concerns putting experience into context and giving it meaning, as this element is created both in the child's relationship with the imaginary friend and immediate others who might interfere in the relationship, like older members of the child's family. The second dimension concerns the ability of imaginary friends to create experiences, which gradually shape the child's personality and life. If the child is living in the period of early childhood, as is usually the case with children who have imaginary friends, experiences interacting with imaginary friends are important to shaping the child's character and personality. Finally, the third dimension refers to the development of an "experiential transaction" (Wood 2009, 155) between the child and the imaginary friend, including the child's ability to comprehend both outer and inner meanings of the object that functions as an imaginary friend. Outer meanings are related to the usual material and functional dimensions of the object, while inner meanings focus on the deeper significance of the relationship between the object and its owner. If, for example, the object that a child chooses as an imaginary friend is a present from a loved one, the relationship with the imaginary friend is potentially a projection of the child's relationship with the giver, and vice versa. If the object is inherited or passed down from person to person, additional meanings take root; as Pahl (2012) explains, "every object tells a story" directly or indirectly related to the life of the present owner, but also past owners (303).

In such context, an imaginary friend may constitute what Hoskins (1998) calls a "biographical object," referring to an object directly connected to cultural or other identities of the owner, which contribute to the creation of his/her personal identity dimensions. Biographical objects that are loved and important to the lives of owners are found among all people, irrespective of racial, national, cultural, religious, professional, social, temporal, or other identity descriptors (Hoskins 1998). They are found all over the world and throughout time and mark people's need to create life references that are connected to particular material objects, but also to the people who are connected to those objects. With this approach, we find that material imaginary friends like cuddly toys, dolls, Playmobil figures, etc. constitute one of the first types of biographical objects found in the lives of children. As they grow up, children replace these first meaningful items with other favorite objects that mark out elements of young people's popular material culture, like clothing, jewelry, technical gadgets, musical instruments, and sporting and band paraphernalia.

A CASE STUDY

The purpose of the following case study research was to explore children's play with their imaginary friends and its contribution to children's agency. In particular, this research sought to uncover the sorts of imaginary friends that children create, the types of games they usually play with them, and the influence of such play on and through children's agency. There were eight children who participated in the research: four girls and four boys ranging from four to nine years old. The researchers also spoke with these children's mothers—it was necessary to conduct interviews with parents because, as Taylor and colleagues (2013) and Gleason (2004b) find, children sometimes invent imaginary friends in response to researchers asking them about the subject. Moreover, it is also common for children to describe real friends rather than imaginary ones, so parents' interview contributions are crucial since their corroboration with children's answers increases the validity of research on imaginary friends.

Our 2017 case study took place in Athens, Greece. A case study helps researchers better approach a particular situation and thereby gain a more general picture and understanding of the subjects they are studying (Yin 1994). In the present case study, data collection techniques included semi-structured interviews with children and their mothers, as well as participatory observation during children's play with imaginary friends. All names of children in this study are pseudonyms that were selected by the researchers.

A child's plastic play phone was used in the research, a technique that has been implemented in a variety of research projects with children and their imaginary friends (see Taylor, Cartwright, and Carlson 1993; Taylor and Mannering 2007; Taylor et al. 2013). Compared to other techniques, such as representing the imaginary friend in a drawing, contacting him/her with the use of a plastic phone was considered best, as it gave the child a productive role and created an imaginary context similar to real activities common in the child's everyday life. In our study, children were asked to call their imaginary friends and invite them to the place where the research was being conducted. This imaginary encounter was the subject of participatory observation by the researchers.

RESEARCH FINDINGS

Forms of Imaginary Friends

In the sample of eight children, two created invisible imaginary friends; two formed a paracosm as well as invisible imaginary friends; one had two dolls as imaginary friends; two used cuddly toys as imaginary friends; and one child had a Playmobil figure as his friend, which also fit into the doll category. The specifics of the children's imaginary friends and play are as follows:

- Maria had an invisible friend named Angeliki the Strawberry Lady and created an imaginary city called Strawberryland.
- Elli formed an imaginary country and an imaginary friend who lived there: "I have a country called Houseland [the word *Spitakia* in Greek] and I also have another friend called Aeolia."
- Kostis constructed an imaginary friend who was an invisible crocodile without a specific name.
- Elsa's imaginary friend was invisible: "My imaginary friend is called Philondat." She acknowledged, "Philondat is totally imaginary."
- Eleni had two imaginary friends, two baby dolls named Lucia and Lydia. When Eleni was asked whether she had an imaginary friend, she immediately replied, "Yes, Lucia and Lydia, they are dolls."
- Alex had the imaginary friend Mr. No One, a Playmobil figure.
- Angel had an imaginary friend, a toy puppy called Gagakis, who also functioned as his older brother Andreas's imaginary friend. Choosing a common imaginary friend potentially reflected the means of everyday communication and interaction between two brothers in the same family.

Imaginary Friends' Features

As previously stated, children typically choose to form imaginary friends that belong to the same gender as themselves, so the gender of the child determines the gender of the imaginary friend. In our case study, out of the eight children, seven imaginary friends had the same gender as them. Only Elsa reversed this trend, as she is a girl and her friend was a boy called Philondat.

Although we assumed that imaginary friends would be the same age as the children, this did not prove to be the case. In this sample, two children said they did not know the age of their imaginary friends, two said that their imaginary friends were the same age as them, two said they were younger, and two said that their friends were older. We believe it is possible that the difference in ages of imaginary friends to that of the children who created them is connected to the desired age of nonexistent brothers/sisters or potential real friends whom the children would like to have in their lives.

Imaginary Friends: Appearance and Personality

Many imaginary friends had specific outward features; for example, blonde hair and blue eyes, or brown hair and black eyes, or more unusual colors because the friends existed solely in the children's imaginations. The imaginary friends' hair and eye colors and clothing were determined by the wishes of the children themselves; for example, one friend had blonde hair because the child wanted to have blonde hair. Eleni's and Alex's imaginary friends, who were dolls and a Playmobil figure, respectively, had white skin, the same as the skin color of the children. Clothes were related to the friends' gender, age, and the children's preferences or beliefs. Sometimes, features of outward appearance corresponded to real people in the children's lives, but this correlation was not always the case. There were instances when physical features were drawn from the realms of fantasy. Personality traits of imaginary friends varied: they were described as quiet, good, mischievous, or beautiful. A wide range of imaginary friend personalities existed that aligned with the imaginations or wishes of the children. Children offered the following descriptions of their imaginary friends:

- Usually she wears trousers and tops. She does not wear skirts, because they have a gym at school and they run . . . . She's mischievous; she plays jokes on her sister. (Maria)
- I would call him naughty. He has taught me to smoke. (Kostis)
- She has brown eyes and black hair. She wears colorful dresses . . . . She does naughty silly things with her cousins. (Elli)

Of the sample of eight children, three parents were unable to give any details about imaginary friends' appearances. Thus, five parents knew details about friends' physical appearances: four mentioned stuffed animals, toys, and dolls, so it was easier for them to provide information and a description of their child's friend. For example, Alex's mother stated: "Yes, it is a Playmobil soldier, with a shield, a helmet, and a sword." However, only Elli's mother had information about her child's friend and the imaginary country set up for the friend: "The country is called 'Houseland' [*Spitikia*] and they speak a language called 'Houselanguage' [*spitika*]; my daughter's name is Aeolia in this country. My daughter's alter ego, let's say, is always up to some form of mischief, always something. Well, she says 'Mommy eat the food' and replies, 'Shall I eat it with my mouth or with my nose?'" Elli's mother added other information about her child's friend regarding her character: "Aeolia is something like Pippi Longstocking, who was in fashion in my time, but I have not said anything about her but it was what my generation knew, about Pippi Longstocking who did bizarre things, was scruffy, dirty, but clever all in one."

Relationships between Children and Imaginary Friends

Relationships with imaginary friends may sometimes be peaceful and sometimes confrontational, mirroring relationships of children and their friends in the real world. Eleni, who had two imaginary friends, dolls named Lukia and Lydia, stated that her imaginary friends "are sometimes not very good children," adding, "sometimes they argue and I tell them off." Eleni was trying to ease tensions between her imaginary friends, putting herself in the role of mediator, placing her in the position of having to calm the friends and negotiate their conflicts. Eleni's mother confirmed that there were sometimes tensions between Eleni and her imaginary friends, but in general they played well together. In particular, Eleni's mother noted, "They play peacefully, though it has happened that I have not understood why she tells me she's quarreled with Lukia." Unlike Eleni's mother, Angel's mother seemed to ignore interactions between Angel and his imaginary friend. She said that the imaginary friend and Angel "have no dialogue." This view contradicts the child's own words, who explained that he "tells Gagakis off because he is being naughty."

Of particular interest was an observation of Andreas's game with his imaginary friend. While playing, his imaginary friend Gagakis suffered an accident and Andreas explained his friend needed an operation to get well; otherwise, the imaginary friend would stay in a wheelchair for half a year. The cost of surgery was high, but Andreas made the agentic decision to spend all his money to save his imaginary friend, showing how much he cared for and loved him. Andreas said, "What shall we do, either we leave him or we pay, and he'll get well quickly but we have to give all that money. I don't know, I spent it all on the airplane wing. I made the decision that we'd do it." The imaginary incident that Andreas described shows young children's desire to function as caregivers and their abilities to respond to difficult family situations, which include accidents or chronic health conditions of family members (real or imaginary). Wihstutz (2011) connects children's agency to the desires and abilities of children, whom she identifies as "caring" children, to look after, help, or support vulnerable members of their families. Related, Leonard (2015) recognizes children's roles as active supporters to mothers abused by their partners, exemplifying children's agency in contrast to the traditional figuration of children as family victims.

Playing with Imaginary Friends

Using the play phone to call their imaginary friends, all the children pretended to actually talk to them. Eleni, Angel, and Alex were terse, just saying "Hello" and "How are you" to their friends. Elli was talkative on the phone, as were some other children, and she used her imagination in the process because while she was trying to call her friend, she stated the mobile phone did not have a signal. This process was repeated a few times until she managed to get a signal, make the call, and wake her friend up. She provided specifics of the phone interaction: "There is no signal. . . . I think he is still asleep. . . . I can't hear anything, just snoring." This version of a phone call to a friend was not expected and thus struck us as particularly interesting. Maria, Elsa, Kostis, and Andreas were also talkative and descriptive; calls to their friends were, we imagine, similar to speaking with real-life friends. In particular, phone conversations contained the necessary waiting time for the child to listen to their imaginary friends' points of view; the children gave their friends opportunities to respond and construct dialogue exchanges. When Alex was asked to chat with his imaginary friend, Mr. No One, he asked, "Mr. No One, are you coming? The battle is starting!" Kostis used real dialogue with his friend the crocodile: "Yes, crocodile, can you come to my house?" (waits a few seconds for his friend to answer), "Lovely, come to play, come on." And Andreas developed realistic dialogue with his friend Gagakis: "Hey Gagakis, how are you?" (waits a few seconds for his friend to answer), "Do you want to come over here to meet someone? Okay. Ciao." What is particularly interesting in the latter exchange is that Andreas included the researchers in the context of dialogue with his imaginary friend since he proposed his imaginary friend Gagakis meet with us as a group.

Decision-Making/Mutual Assistance

Maria said that all decisions about games with her imaginary friend are made by the friend, but, if necessary, they discuss the games. Kostis said that he makes the decisions, but together with his friend they decide what is right and wrong and ultimately everything works out fine between them. He also said that his friend never gets angry and they help each other. As to who decides what and when to play, Elli stated, "Philondat decides more quickly than me." The obvious reason for this answer might be the fact that Philondat is older than Elli. Elli said the two discuss what and when to play, but she decides what is wrong because, "I usually think I am older," which shows how she functions somewhat like a big sister in the friend relationship. Eleni asserted that all of her decisions are made by one of her two imaginary friends, but primarily Lucia. Angel stressed that he decides what is right and wrong to do, but his friend is the one who stops playing when things do not work out between them. Similar to Kostis, Angel said that his friend never gets angry and they help each other. Andreas said that he makes decisions about everything, and his friend is the one who usually stops playing when he does not agree with Andreas's views.

Game Scenarios with Imaginary Friends

Children typically engage with their imaginary friends by playing a variety of games. Some are movement games, while other games are inspired by everyday life (such as cooking, eating, and walking to swing sets). The choices of children's games with their imaginary friends point to their preferences, inclinations, and favorite activities. In our research, a wide range of games was uncovered, as each child's play preferences were unique. The frequent phenomenon of symbolic and pretend or make-believe play is considered to be a main feature of children's lives at these young ages; as such, most children we spoke to participated in fantasized activities with their imaginary friends.

More specifically, Maria pretended she was in a supermarket with her friend buying spaghetti and sauce to cook. Later, they went to various shops, pretending they were long-haired ladies buying dresses. Kostis pretended to drink coffee in a cafeteria with his friend. He was taken to the café by the friend in his car—although the initial plan was to go by bike, Kostis's bike tire had a puncture. They ordered coffee, ate croissants, and smoked. Elli played doctor and her friend was one of the patients. At the hospital, she treated children and gave babies vaccines, and medicine was dispensed when necessary. At some point, her friend arrived in the surgery ward and the child treated him. Elli also pretended to go swimming in the sea with her friend; they walked to the beach and found a lounge chair to sit on. They swam, dove, got their hair wet, and played together in the sea; then they got out of the water and ordered a glass of juice with a straw to cool off. Afterward, a pajama party was organized, in which Elli and her friend played music to celebrate her birthday the next day, had a pillow fight, watched a film, and ate popcorn. Later, they slept, whence Elli pretended to snore, and then they woke up. As soon as she woke up, she made breakfast and watched some TV. Finally, Elli and her friend went for a walk to shops to buy clothes and shoes. Eleni cooked: she baked two different puddings for her friends, fed them, wiped their faces, and washed their bowls. Then she decided to take them to play on swings. Angel was involved in pretend play, trying to find a hidden treasure with his friend. Specifically, they had a map leading to treasure on Skeleton Island, a location quite difficult to pinpoint as there were a variety of traps on the road leading to the treasure. Alex grappled with Playmobil and ships since his imaginary friend was a Playmobil figure. Alex helped his friend in a quest since they belonged to the same group: both were knights and developed a type of alliance against bad pirates. The aim was for the knights to recapture their castle, which the pirates had infiltrated. Finally, Andreas and his friend had an airplane for carrying those injured in war to nearby hospitals. At some point, however, the plane suffered engine failure and Andreas's friend got injured and needed help. After his friend was brought to the nearest hospital, the doctor said he needed surgery in order to get better quickly; otherwise, he would have to stay in a wheelchair for a while. Despite the high cost of surgery, Andreas decided to move forward with the procedure to make his friend well.

The children creatively played with their imaginary friends in such scenarios, indicating the richness of their imaginations and highlighting the children's ability and desire to utilize their toys in various aspects beyond their original purposes. Toy instructions are nearly always delineated for children's usage by way of adult manufacturers' suggestions, beliefs, or, often, warnings. The fact that the children in our study modified the traditional, and often singular, way of using toys in order to set their own play goals and fit the content of game contexts, which they themselves designed and realized, demonstrates children's ability to function as active change agents in fantasy play with imaginary friends.

DISCUSSION AND CONCLUSIONS

Our study found that imaginary friends of the children fell into three main categories: invisible characters, cuddly toys or dolls, or paracosms that encompassed where imaginary friends lived. Children developed a special relationship with their imaginary friends, who played leading roles in their lives. In particular, they were part of their families and everyday worlds—they slept, chatted, and played together. Most imaginary friends were good, while some were viewed as antagonistic, given they were sometimes aggressive and did not treat the children well. Most of the imaginary friends had similar features to the children in regard to their appearances and behaviors. Also, nearly all imaginary friends were the same gender as their creators, except in the case of a girl who opted for a boy as her imaginary friend. Four of the eight friends were mischievous, described as either joke-tellers or naughty when playing.

Our research found that games with imaginary friends varied and were usually emplaced in the realm of make-believe. Pretend play characterized and dominated imaginary friend/child interaction in this age group. The children were primarily involved in pretend play that represented scenes from real life, such as eating food, shopping at the supermarket, swimming in the sea, or drinking coffee at a café. However, conventional play contrasted with fantasy play: some children who engaged in pretend play deviated from activities found in the everyday, such as seeking treasure, rescuing the war-wounded via aircraft, or waging war between pirates, knights, and police officers.

Observations of children's play with their imaginary friends revealed much variety in children's choices, decisions, and attitudes, pinpointing children's desires to be agents in their real and fantasy lives (and, in many cases, the lives of their imaginary friends). Maria indicated that her imaginary female friend did not wear skirts, which perhaps emerged from her own desire not to wear skirts. In this way, the child may be expressing her agentic resistance to her family's or culture's belief that "you are a girl and you must wear skirts," a dominant view in many Greek families. Respectively, Kostis's explanation that his imaginary friend taught him how to smoke is perhaps linked to parental advice regarding the profile of the "good child," one that many children do not like and do not want to accept. The enforcement of the "good child model," one that is created by adults, is a common attitude found in all of Greece (not merely in certain families), which often culturally suppresses children. As Leonard (2015) claims, when children contest parental urging and advice, they prove that they are not "sponges" and that they have the ability to act independently. Leonard (2015) also supports the conclusion that the alternative way—compared to predetermined instructions issued by adults—children creatively interact with their toys constitutes additional proof of children's agency.

Elli envisioned an imaginary friend who, according to her mother, resembled Pippi Longstocking (a literary character often characterized as a "tomboy"). This characterization reflects Elli's personal desires and agentic resistance to the model of a "prim girl," a gendered construction found in dominant social messages and cultural standards created by adults in Greece.

The fact that Elli created her own language to communicate with her imaginary friend reflects Elli's desire for independence; we also see her methods of resistance through the use of a "mystical" language incomprehensible to her family members. Challenging adults' views and attitudes is commonly found in older children, who sometimes decide to rebel against rules set forth by their families and schools; youth do so by behaving in ways deemed unacceptable by the social or cultural majority (Willis 1977). Younger children, however, choose different routes of reaction or reflection that may be less overt though no less meaningful. Pretend play with imaginary friends is one such alternative path to younger children agentically expressing their views, desires, and choices. To note, Leonard (2015) and Castro (2017) explain that children's agency does not always signify children's resistance to adults. Even if children agree with their parents' beliefs and follow their instructions and advice, this similitude does not mean they cannot function as active agents in their own lives or within their families.

According to Majors (2013), sometimes play with imaginary friends allows children to explore different dimensions of self that may be unexpressed prior to the moment of exchange between friends. The fact that Eleni pursued, using pretend play, effective strategies of conflict resolution between her two imaginary friends may reflect the desire to explore and vocalize her "angry self" (which she does not or cannot easily express) through fantasy, or perhaps indicates Eleni's need to search out new ways of managing conflicts between herself and others. Relatedly, Majors (2013) refers to the case of John, a friendly and even-tempered child, who in his interactions with his imaginary friend "was able to experience and release angry feelings in a way that was beneficial to him," which was "preferable to bottling up his anger" (56).

The relationship between the brothers Alex and Andreas and their imaginary friend, a stuffed dog, perhaps revealed their desire to have a real pet, a common wish held by many children with which adults often do not agree (due to parental concerns regarding cost, time required for care, allergies, judgment of children's capacities for responsibility, etc.). Majors (2013) underscores that the choice of a pet as an imaginary friend shows children's need for fulfilling the wish to have a pet. Importantly, Morrow (1998) states that young children's caring for pets and the deep feelings that often accompany these close relationships reveal a unique dimension of children's agency.

Gleason, Sebanc, and Hartup's (2000) discussion of relationships between children and imaginary friends points out that children who have invisible imaginary friends interact more with them than those children who befriend stuffed animals or dolls. However, in our study, children who had stuffed animals or dolls as friends were not limited in their caring roles or in their fantasy game constructions (rescuing war-wounded, treasure hunting, etc.).

Our research does not align with those of Gleason and colleagues (1997), who stress that children with cuddly toys as imaginary friends are more engaged with role-playing and make-believe than those with invisible friends. Instead, our study finds that regardless of the type of imaginary friend, all children participated in pretend fantasy and role-playing with their friends.

Research conducted by Gleason, Sebanc, and Hartup (2000) found that relationships created between children and their imaginary friends are generally characterized as deeply friendly and social. Majors (2013) observed that "children spoke positively about their imaginary companions. They valued the entertainment, game playing and friendship elements of interactions with imaginary companions" (56). This positive interaction between children and their imaginary friends was reflected in our research since the majority of children, irrespective of their type of imaginary friend, developed friendly and emotionally positive relationships with friends, factors which, in a few cases, were ignored or discounted by parents.

Parents do not necessarily have a particularly important role in the formation of children's imaginary friends (Taylor and Carlson 2000). However, some parents may influence the creation of imaginary friends if they too had such friends during childhood. In our study, two mothers admitted they had imaginary friends in their own childhoods and wanted their children to have the same. According to Gleason and Kalpidou (2014), some parents hold positive outlooks regarding their children creating imaginary friends because they link this phenomenon with the development of children's imagination. This view seemed to be held by the majority of mothers in our research, who said they were happy that their children created imaginary friends. Most of them spoke about children's imaginations, but they did not link play with imaginary friends to the manifestation of children's agency.

The realm of "playing with imaginary friends" and its influence in the development of children's agency is a highly interesting and open field of research, wherein scientific approaches from the fields of psychology, sociology, education, and childhood studies intersect. Present and future research will likely uncover many more dimensions found in children's play with their imaginary friends to hopefully reveal elements and features of fantasy relationships that serve key roles in the wider development and expression of children's agency.

REFERENCES

Bouldin, Paula. 2006. "An Investigation of the Fantasy Predisposition and Fantasy Style of Children with Imaginary Companions." *The Journal of Genetic Psychology* 167 (1): 17–29.

Bouldin, Paula, and Chris Pratt. 1999. "Characteristics of Preschool and School-Age Children with Imaginary Companions." *The Journal of Genetic Psychology* 160 (4): 397–410.

———. 2002. "A Systematic Assessment of the Specific Fears, Anxiety Level, and Temperament of Children with Imaginary Companions." *Australian Journal of Psychology* 54 (2): 79–85.

Canning, Natalie. 2013. "'Where's the Bear? Over There!'—Creative Thinking and Imagination in Den Making." *Early Child Development and Care* 183 (8): 1042–53.

Carlson, Stephanie M., and Marjorie Taylor. 2005. "Imaginary Companions and Impersonated Characters: Sex Differences in Children's Fantasy Play." *Merrill-Palmer Quarterly* 51 (1): 93–118.

Castro, Ingrid E. 2017. "Contextualizing Agency in High-Structure Environments: Children's Participation in Parent Interviews." In *Researching Children and Youth: Methodological Issues, Strategies, and Innovations—Sociological Studies of Children and Youth, Volume 22*, edited by Ingrid E. Castro, Melissa Swauger, and Brent Harger, 149–73. Bingley: Emerald.

Corsaro, William A. 1993. "Interpretive Reproduction in Children's Role Play." *Childhood* 1 (2): 64–74.

———. 2005. *The Sociology of Childhood* (2nd ed.). Thousand Oaks, CA: Pine Forge Press.

Foucault, Michel. 1997. "Of Other Spaces: Utopias and Heterotopias." In *Rethinking Architecture: A Reader in Cultural Theory*, edited by Neil Leach, 350–6. New York, NY: Routledge.

Fritz, Gregory K. 2015. "Imaginary Friends." *The Brown University Child and Adolescent Behavior Letter* 31 (5): 8.

Galyer, Karma T., and Ian M. Evans. 2001. "Pretend Play and the Development of Emotional Regulation in Preschool Children." *Early Child Development and Care* 166 (1): 93–108.

Giménez-Dasí, Marta, Francisco Pons, and Patrick K. Bender. 2016. "Imaginary Companions, Theory of Mind and Emotion Understanding in Young Children." *European Early Childhood Education Research Journal* 24 (2): 186–97.

Gleason, Tracy R. 2004a. "Imaginary Companions and Peer Acceptance." *International Journal of Behavioral Development* 28 (3): 204–9.

———. 2004b. "Imaginary Companions: An Evaluation of Parents as Reporters." *Infant and Child Development* 13 (3): 199–215.

Gleason, Tracy R., Raceel N. Jarudi, and Jonathan M. Cheek. 2003. "Imagination, Personality, and Imaginary Companions." *Social Behavior and Personality* 31 (7): 721–37.

Gleason, Tracy R., and Maria Kalpidou. 2014. "Imaginary Companions and Young Children's Coping and Competence." *Social Development* 23 (4): 820–39.

Gleason, Tracy R., Anne M. Sebanc, and Willard W. Hartup. 2000. "Imaginary Companions of Preschool Children." *Developmental Psychology* 36 (4): 419–28.

Gleason, Tracy R., Anne M. Sebanc, Jennifer McGinley, and Willard W. Hartup. 1997. *Invisible Friends and Personified Objects: Qualitative Differences in*

Relationships with Imaginary Companions. Washington, DC: Paper presented at the Biennial Meeting of the Society for Research in Child Development. https://files.eric.ed.gov/fulltext/ED419629.pdf.
Harris, Paul L. 2000. *The Work of the Imagination*. Oxford: Wiley-Blackwell.
Hart, Tobin, and Erin E. Zellars. 2006. "When Imaginary Companions Are Sources of Wisdom." *Encounter: Education for Meaning and Social Justice* 19 (1): 6–15.
Hennig, Kelly, and Anna Kirova. 2012. "The Role of Cultural Artefacts in Play As Tools to Mediate Learning in an Intercultural Preschool Programme." *Contemporary Issues in Early Childhood* 13 (3): 226–41.
Hoff, Eva V. 2005. "Imaginary Companions, Creativity, and Self-Image in Middle Childhood." *Creativity Research Journal* 17 (2–3): 167–80.
Hoskins, Janet. 1998. *Biographical Objects: How Things Tell the Stories of People's Lives*. New York, NY: Routledge.
James, Allison, Chris Jenks, and Alan Prout. 1998. *Theorizing Childhood*. Cambridge: Polity Press.
Kapasi, Haki, and Josie Gleave. 2009. *Because It's Freedom: Children's Views on Their Time to Play*. London: Play England.
Leonard, Madeleine. 2015. *The Sociology of Children, Childhood and Generation*. London: SAGE.
MacKeith, Stephan A. 1984. "Paracosms and the Development of Fantasy in Childhood." *Ambit Magazine* 96: 50–4.
Majors, Karen. 2013. "Children's Perceptions of Their Imaginary Companions and the Purposes They Serve: An Exploratory Study in the United Kingdom." *Childhood* 20 (4): 550–65.
Mayall, Berry. 2002. *Towards a Sociology for Childhood: Thinking from Children's Lives*. Berkshire: Open University Press.
Moriguchi, Yusuke, and Ikuko Shinohara. 2012. "My Neighbor: Children's Perception of Agency in Interaction with an Imaginary Agent." *PLoS One* 7 (9). https://doi.org/10.1371/journal.pone.0044463.
Morrow, Virginia. 1998. "My Animals and Other Family: Children's Perspectives on Their Relationships with Companion Animals." *Anthrozoös: A Multidisciplinary Journal of the Interactions of People and Animals* 11 (4): 218–26.
Motoshima, Yuko, Ikuko Shinohara, Naoya Todo, and Yusuke Moriguchi. 2014. "Parental Behaviour and Children's Creation of Imaginary Companions: A Longitudinal Study." *European Journal of Developmental Psychology* 11 (6): 716–27.
Nagera, Humberto. 1969. "The Imaginary Companion: Its Significance for Ego Development and Conflict Solution." *The Psychoanalytic Study of the Child* 24 (1): 165–96.
Nieuwenhuys, Olga. 2011. "Can the Teddy Bear Speak?" *Childhood* 18 (4): 411–8.
Pahl, Kate. 2012. "Every Object Tells a Story: International Stories and Objects in the Homes of Pakistani Heritage Families in South Yorkshire, UK." *Home Cultures: The Journal of Architecture, Design, and Domestic Space* 9 (3): 303–27.

Paige, Davis E., Elizabeth Meins, and Charles Fernyhough. 2014. "Children with Imaginary Companions Focus on Mental Characteristics When Describing Their Real-Life Friends." *Infant and Child Development* 23 (6): 622–33.

Pearson, D., H. Rouse, S. Doswell, C. Ainsworth, O. Dawson, K. Simms, L. Edwards, and J. Faulconbridge. 2001. "Prevalence of Imaginary Companions in a Normal Child Population." *Child: Care, Health and Development* 27 (1): 13–22.

Roby, Anna C., and Evan Kidd. 2008. "The Referential Communication Skills of Children with Imaginary Companions." *Developmental Science* 11 (4): 531–40.

Seeman, Kenneth, Leslie Widrow, and Jerome Yesavage. 1984. "Fantasized Companions and Suicidal Depressions: Two Case Reports." *The American Journal of Psychotherapy* 38 (4): 541–57.

Singer, Dorothy G., and Jerome L. Singer. 1990. *The House of Make-Believe: Children's Play and the Developing Imagination*. Cambridge, MA: Harvard University Press.

Taylor, Marjorie. 1999. *Imaginary Companions and the Children Who Create Them*. Oxford: Oxford University Press.

Taylor, Marjorie, and Stephanie M. Carlson. 1997. "The Relation Between Individual Differences in Fantasy and Theory of Mind." *Child Development* 68 (3): 436–55.

———. 2000. "The Influence of Religious Beliefs on Parental Attitudes About Children's Fantasy Behavior." In *Imagining the Impossible: Magical, Scientific, and Religious Thinking in Children*, edited by Karl S. Rosengren, Carl N. Johnson, and Paul L. Harris, 247–68. Cambridge: Cambridge University Press.

Taylor, Marjorie, Stephanie M. Carlson, Bayta L. Maring, Lynn Gerow, and Carolyn M. Charley. 2004. "The Characteristics and Correlates of Fantasy in School-Age Children: Imaginary Companions, Impersonation, and Social Understanding." *Developmental Psychology* 40 (6): 1173–87.

Taylor, Marjorie, Bridget S. Cartwright, and Stephanie M. Carlson. 1993. "A Developmental Investigation of Children's Imaginary Companions." *Developmental Psychology* 29 (2): 276–85.

Taylor, Marjorie, and Anne M. Mannering. 2007. "Of Hobbes and Harvey: The Imaginary Companions Created by Children and Adults." In *Play and Development: Evolutionary, Sociocultural, and Functional Perspectives*, edited by Artin Gönkü and Suzanne Gaskins, 227–45. New York, NY: Laurence Erlbaum Associates.

Taylor, Marjorie, Alison B. Sachet, Bayta L. Maring, and Anne M. Mannering. 2013. "The Assessment of Elaborated Role Play in Young Children: Invisible Friends, Personified Objects, and Pretend Identities." *Social Development* 22 (1): 75–93.

Theobald, Maryanne, Susan Danby, and Jo Ailwood. 2011. "Child Participation in the Early Years: Challenges for Education." *Australasian Journal of Early Childhood* 36 (3): 19–26.

Thomayer, Claudia. 2017. *"Teachers' Perception of Children's Agency in Early Childhood Education."* Master's Thesis: University of Jyväskylä.

von Benzon, Nadia. 2015. "'I Fell Out of a Tree and Broke My Neck': Acknowledging Fantasy in Children's Research Contributions." *Children's Geographies* 13 (3): 330–42.

Vygotsky, L. S. 2016. "Play and Its Role in the Mental Development of the Child." *International Research in Early Childhood Education* 7 (2): 3–25.

Wigger, J. Bradley, Katrina Paxson, and Lacey Ryan. 2013. "What Do Invisible Friends Know? Imaginary Companions, God, and Theory of Mind." *The International Journal for the Psychology of Religion* 23 (1): 2–14.

Wihstutz, Anne. 2011. "Working Vulnerability: Agency of Caring Children and Children's Rights." *Childhood* 18 (4): 447–59.

Willis, Paul. 1977. *Learning to Labor: How Working Class Kids Get Working Class Jobs*. New York, NY: Columbia University Press.

Wood, Elizabeth. 2009. "Saving Childhood in Everyday Objects." *Childhood in the Past: An International Journal* 2 (1): 151–62.

Wood, Elizabeth A. 2014. "Free Choice and Free Play in Early Childhood Education: Troubling the Discourse." *International Journal of Early Years Education* 22 (1): 4–18.

Yin, Robert K. 1994. *Case Study Research: Design and Methods* (2nd ed.). Thousand Oaks, CA: SAGE.

Heroism/Supernatural

Chapter 4

Arcadia Is in the Hands of Teenagers

Team Power in Guillermo del Toro's Trollhunters

Tara Moore

In the last few decades, children's and young adult (YA) fiction authors have been creating protagonists bursting with agency, but scholarship of children's literature has not kept up. According to Flynn (2016), the discussion of agency is "far less common in children's literature studies than in childhood studies" (249). Literary analysis has a part to play in the widening world of childhood studies, though. Duane (2013) states that studies of childhood should consider texts that "both influence and occlude the lives of actual young people" (4). Just as 1990s princess movies spawned an influential commodity culture and princess fascination, so too could portrayals of active, noble children and their loyal friendships motivate real children's behaviors. To be clear from the start, this is not a readership study.[1] I am, what Vallone (2013) calls, a "book person" tracking "images and representations of children or children's culture" (244). Rather than chronicle children's responses to scenes of agency, this chapter examines cultural portrayals of children's agency in one television series that casts the "chosen one" fairy tale into a modern, team-based fantasy narrative.

Trollhunters (2016–2018), created by Guillermo del Toro and hosted on Netflix, blends delightful, child-empowered fantasy with a double-life storyline. Here, Jim Lake, a fifteen-year-old latchkey child, is selected by magical powers to be the next defender of a peaceful society of trolls living in caverns beneath his hometown of Arcadia Oaks, California.[2] After claiming the Amulet of Daylight—the talisman of the trollhunter ostensibly created long ago by Arthurian legend's sorcerer Merlin—Jim is slowly initiated into the secret troll world and grows into the power that will make him a fully confident and self-sacrificing trollhunter. Along the way, he aligns with a team of companions who join him and, moreover, protect him in his battles.

Netflix produced three seasons of *Trollhunters* as part of del Toro's larger vision for this storyworld.[3] In the first season, Jim Lake Jr. and Toby Domzalski (Jim's best friend) learn that the Amulet of Daylight chooses Jim to be the next trollhunter.[4] As Jim wrestles with accepting his destiny, two trolls (Blinky and AAARRRGGHH!!!) arrive to offer mentorship and support in Jim's transition, and a trollhunter team forms. The band initially includes a few helpful trolls and some human teens: Jim, Toby, and Jim's girlfriend, Claire. The company later expands to involve the youths' parents and several troll allies. The team fights against a cast of magical antagonists; as they defeat one, another more powerful villain emerges. To increase Jim's magical abilities in battle, the team conducts mini-quests to collect stones that enhance Jim's trollhunter armor. The trollhunters try to prevent evil trolls from escaping the prison dimension because these malicious trolls would decimate the peaceful trolls and, eventually, eat humans and destroy human society living aboveground in Arcadia. Along the way, Jim becomes trapped in the prison dimension and his team rescues him. The evil trolls escape too, and they reawaken their supreme leader and Merlin's sworn enemy, Morgana le Fey. Together, the villains attempt to bring eternal night and troll rule to Earth's surface. Initially, when the conflicts have lower stakes, Jim struggles to maintain his role as a high school student. Over time, the threats increase and his sacrifices become more extreme. Finally,

Figure 4.1 Jim's troll mentors Blinky and AAARRRGGHH!!! offer Jim guidance in the way of the Trollhunter, but they also accept the wisdom of Jim's perspective: "Win Lose or Draal"—*Trollhunters* (2016).

Jim forfeits his human identity to become a troll so that he can defeat the enemies' final onslaught.

The presentation of children's fierce power and strategic planning in *Trollhunters* provides ample fodder for a conversation about how children's entertainment adapts ideas of child agency. Since the 1970s, sociologists have created a new space for seeing the child as agent (James 2011). Children's authors also present this restructuring of childhood, primarily in children's fantasy writing. The fantasy quest has a penchant for characterizing the child as social agent in imaginative ways. The child's fantasy quest became an established part of children's literature in the 1990s (built upon the fantasy novels of Tamora Pierce, J.K. Rowling, and Garth Nix), with an enormous blossoming of this theme in the early 2000s. Sociological interest in children as agentic beings coincides with this growth in marketable fantasy texts of the empowered, untethered child. Like children in *The Giver* (1993), the Harry Potter series (1997–2007), and *The City of Ember* (2003), questing children serve as agents of change for their societies. Rather than socialized to blindly accept adult authority and rule, literary children frequently use quests to rework society and shape it to fit their needs.

As self-guided, questing entities, child protagonists of such stories embody my driving definition of agency: "the capability of individuals to both shape their own lives, and to influence their social contexts" (Baraldi and Ieverse 2014, 46). Literature has not always afforded child characters' agentic mobility. As a result, Meeusen (2017) surmises that child audiences are enculturated into a paradigm that "often limits their agency" (126). As such, child viewers are prevented from seeing agency modeled by people who look, act, and think like them; however, recent children's fantasy plots move away from such limitations. *Trollhunters* proves to be an excellent narrative example of agentic children that is marketed to both children and parents.

The *Trollhunters* story design supports multigenerational viewing. Buckingham (1994) finds that parents delimit their children's television viewing and children then actively work to circumvent such regulations. *Trollhunters* remains, at all times, highly aware of its matrix of cultural references and storytelling genres, appealing to both middle-school audiences and adults/parents. While the preteen viewer may not recognize older literary and film references—"To Catch a Changeling," "Claire and Present Danger"— parents surely do.[5] Adults may also recognize moments that clearly pay homage to previous science fiction stories like *Lost* (2004–2010), *Stranger Things* (2016–present), and the *Star Wars* franchise, as well as 1980s movies that middle grade viewers are unlikely to know.[6] *Trollhunters* christens one episode "Hero with a Thousand Faces" to send a message not only about the internal plot of that episode (a spell creates multiple clones of the protagonist) but also about the nature of this narrative. The title of the episode, as well as the series as a whole, references the quest story as theorized by Campbell (2008) and Vogler (2007).

These clever messages may engage adult viewers, but they also emphasize what Meeusen (2017) refers to as a "strong adult authorial presence" (129). Children may cheer for a little gnome that Jim befriends, but they may not understand the reference when Toby names their new gnome pal "Chomsky."[7] At one point, Blinky, Jim's troll mentor, uses the word "Faustian" and then explains the idea since the other characters and, assumedly, child audience members do not know what this term means. To some extent, maintaining subtext of adult references undercuts the presentation of the postmodern agentic child because, at times, the series stresses neoliberal adult cultural connections and promotes adult knowledge over that of child viewers.

del Toro's story rolled out during a dearth of clever, cross-generational television shows that are rated TV-Y7, which makes the few television shows that do fall into this category particularly valuable for a joint watching experience.[8] Parents may bond with their children over quality television, but this project is especially challenging when shows for school-age children are created in such a way that adults might find them uncomfortably fast-paced, plot-poor, or obnoxious in both design and sound editing. *Trollhunters* attempts to solve such deficits by offering solid story arcs, careful, adult-friendly artwork and pacing, and enough action and ethical conflict to fascinate children, all while utilizing pop culture references to engage adults.

One important aspect of this joint viewership is the intergenerational popularity of some children's and YA fiction. According to a 2012 *Publisher's Weekly* study, 55 percent of YA fiction is purchased by adults, and 78 percent of those adults say they make the purchase for themselves. Such numbers attest to the startling prevalence of the "reading down" trend—adults consuming YA literature ostensibly marketed to and written for children and teens. "Reading down" has been recognized as a trend since the Harry Potter series but it is also influenced by the popularity of children's culture, as evidenced by voracious, adult participation-driven fandoms created for content initially shelved in the children's section of bookstores and libraries.

Both children and their parents might enjoy *Trollhunters*' structural similarities to the Harry Potter novels. While there is some debate over the actual level of child agency depicted in those novels (see Mendlesohn 2005), J.K. Rowling's series promotes the postmodern child protagonist. Chappell (2008) states that Rowling's series positions postmodern child characters "unrealistically and unproblematically" in positions of authority (281). However, these depictions might be "preparing young readers to critically engage with power structures in their lives and become architects of their own agency" (Chappell 2008, 282). Positively, main characters Harry, Hermione, and Ron resist "the domination imposed on them by wizarding society, forming a pattern for contemporary children to follow" (Chappell 2008, 284). Rowling's children learn they cannot fully trust adult society to right its own inequalities, and they believe the welfare of magical society rests, to some degree, on their shoulders.[9] These iconic children make decisions in spite of adult expectations, based on their own moral decisions regarding how society ought to be structured.

TEENS AMONG TROLLS

Like the Harry Potter novels, *Trollhunters* offers children (and their parents) a portal narrative, an imaginary nexus between the twenty-first century and a magical world. The human trollhunters repeatedly use portals to enter troll worlds, found either underground beneath their city or in an alternate dimension. Campbell (2010) argues that portals do more than simply move characters to new worlds; these deeply symbolic locations also "reflect the conditions of the author's time and place" (6). The creators of *Trollhunters* use this brand of symbolism to explore the challenges of being a teenager burdened by ethical choices and responsibilities in society.

Trollhunters episodes depict how challenges faced by the team in the troll world parallel their lives at Arcadia Oaks High. For example, a troll bullies and threatens Jim, so that troll becomes a mythical translation of the high school bully. The presence of such metaphors corresponds to Campbell's (2010) claim that it is not important if fantasy is believable, but it does matter if fantasy elements are realistic—if the stories articulate and transform power dynamics in the real world. In *Trollhunters*, fantasy is used to explore challenges facing teenagers. For example, Jim experiences the burden of dual responsibilities. While he grows as the trollhunter, his supernatural responsibilities inhibit his ability to succeed in regard to what middle-class culture expects of a teenage boy who appears free of work responsibilities.[10] Jim's balancing act between demanding school responsibilities and exciting, magical power directly addresses the challenges of middle-class teen life. By creating magical parallels for American teenage conflicts (school tests, bullies, and adult expectations), the series transforms everyday challenges into epic, symbolic battles.

The fact that Jim maintains his place in the cycle of high school rites of passage—the school play, gym class, the spring formal—keeps him rooted in his identity as an adolescent. As a warrior and protector of trolls and humankind, Jim is clearly not the passive child Castro (2016) finds in some of Steven Spielberg's films. Nor is he the child forced to grow up too soon. Yes, Jim's burdens are heavy, but he is still a teen, not an emotionally hardened or jaded adult. Jim's exploration of romance is the most visible sign of his inexperience. He worries about kissing Claire in the school play even as he contemplates a fight to the death in the underworld arena. Later, he agonizes over asking her to a dance, a concern that seems on par with fighting the new villain who invades Arcadia Oaks. As he makes difficult choices and battles enemies who try to kill him, Jim demonstrates resiliency and agency that is communal in nature and, thus, societally influential.

AN UPDATED HELLMOUTH

Trollhunters resurrects the idea that a child warrior must balance the pretense of a normal teenage life with duties demanded from a specially selected monster killer. For example, Jim rushes from magical task to theater practice, recognizing that he is not successfully balancing both. This male, twenty-first-century recasting of the eponymous hero from *Buffy the Vampire Slayer* (1997–2003) plays to a younger audience. In both projects, teens collaborate with magical entities and protect nonviolent innocents in their communities. Just as Buffy works to control what dangers might spill out of the Hellmouth below Sunnydale, California, Jim must manage his own dangerous interdimensional portal—also in California—that could release evil trolls bent on world domination. There is not much difference between *Buffy*'s season one "big bad" vampire nemesis (The Master) and various villains the trollhunters face. Both series contain an underground portal into an uncanny dimension, and both heroes are children of single mothers.[11] Fans of Joss Whedon's series will no doubt unearth many similarities in the unfolding plot elements of *Trollhunters*.

As is the case with *Buffy*, the high school in *Trollhunters* becomes a battleground. In *Trollhunters*, a troll, Strickler, becomes principal, wielding institutional power over Jim, just as Principle Snyder brings pressure in seasons two and three of *Buffy*. In both narratives, the teens' frustration is fully justified since malicious principals intentionally work to thwart them in and out of school. Yet another hostile principal crops up in a recent fantasy/horror teen narrative—this time, in the first season of the Netflix series *Chilling Adventures of Sabrina* (2018–present). Sabrina's misogynistic but fully mundane principal Mr. Hawthorne becomes a focal antagonist in the young witch's coming of age story. This arrangement of an enemy empowered with adult authority highlights teenage angst directed at unsympathetic, controlling adults. The principals in *Trollhunters* and *Buffy* have insider knowledge about the magical threat to their towns but do not use their positions as educators and leaders to mentor the teen protagonists. Instead, adults' knowledge looms ominously over the teens, representing another seemingly insurmountable injustice against which the teens must struggle. The agentic teen heroes eventually triumph over their evil principals, making the teens' victories far more satisfying for the viewer.

Buffy and Jim feel the burden of being "the chosen one," but they also enjoy enhanced powers that come with their magical destinies. As Campbell (2010) points out, "magic equals power" (11), and Jim is clearly portrayed as a magical teen. The show frequently depicts how the Amulet of Daylight arms him—lifting him off the ground, materializing the pieces of his knight-like armor, assembling it on his body while a blue light glows to highlight magical properties of transformation. Seeing a child selected and empowered for a special destiny seems to be a central mission of the story, and the armoring scenes remind viewers of Jim's secret authority in the magical world, one that adults in his society cannot match or control.

TROLLHUNTING IN AN ADULT-FREE ZONE

Since the show's narrative permits only teens to know and interact with trolls, it emphasizes the liminal nature of teenagers. They are able to move between two worlds—Trollmarket and Arcadia Oaks, the magical and the mundane. They are the only human characters capable enough to grasp the enormity of the magical world and its demands. More symbolically, these locations represent the transition point between the magical realm of childhood knowledge and the mundane world of future adulthood.

Unlike *Buffy*'s Sunnydale, most human adults are not aware of the dangers that broil beneath Arcadia Oaks. This fact is significant, given Meeusen's (2017) claims regarding comic and film adaptations: these portrayals "reinforce adult-child power dynamics that place adults in power over children, a tradition in children's literature created in part by the unique situation of adults writing for children" (126). In opposition, *Trollhunters* frames adults as the demographic in need of protection and nurturance from and by children. Consider the naming of the town—Arcadia—a symbol of "the pastoral idyll, an innocent world" (Sidney 1977, 36). The innocence at risk belongs to the adults, not the children.[12] del Toro's series depicts teens as those who are in the unique position of being able to provide wisdom and security to all.

I want to pause to consider how this series upends demographic norms found in past narratives, the types that attribute greater power to white adult hegemony. Here, Claire Nuñez, Jim's girlfriend and fellow trollhunter, brings some diversity to the human teens' peer group. While Toby and Jim are white, Claire comes from a Spanish-speaking family, and her mother is a councilwoman in Arcadia. Claire's mother sets the example that women and ethnic minorities can occupy influential positions in society. Claire's role on the team presents girls as a powerful force, both physically and strategically.

According to Eder, Evans, and Parker (1995), children challenge adult gender roles and actively construct their own expectations of gender roles. When girls are seen as objects, they tend to lose sense of their agency, and they learn to associate worth to physical appearance (Eder, Evans, and Parker 1995). *Trollhunters* subverts this depressing element of high school life. In this series, peer groups do not focus on girls' appearances, but on their hobbies, friend groups, and, eventually, their access to magical powers. The teen peer group in *Trollhunters* supports non-limiting gender roles; they promote Jim's resistance to active battle in some circumstances (in the face of "traditional masculine behavior" such as aggressive competition), and they likewise support Claire's punk guitar interests (Eder, Evans, and Parker 1995, 157). The series empowers Claire as a warrior in her own right; she is not limited by her gender any more than her peer group is limited by the age of its members.

Since the teens are all sixteen-year-olds residing with their middle-class parents or guardians, they initially struggle to live up to their families' deterministic presumptions about childhood. Barbara Lake, Jim's mother, feels she should be doing more to care for her child, but the demands of a career and single motherhood restrict her until she starts to see the cracks caused by Jim's double life. Like Buffy's mom Joyce, Barbara later learns that her child is a demon hunter. Eventually, Barbara attempts to control Jim's behavior. Her new priorities are clearly based on the American perception that parents are responsible for their children and that the success of children in society directly reflects on parents (Corsaro 2002). By the time Barbara renews her efforts to shape Jim's behavior, his dual loyalties to himself and his trollhunter identity force him to reject her role as his protector. The mother/son relationship appears solid and loving at first, but only because Barbara invests so little time in Jim's welfare, trusting him to raise himself. Her insensitivity to his complicated life becomes most evident when she presents Jim with a food processor as a birthday present (he wanted a Vespa) and when she does not notice trolls and changelings entering her house on a regular basis.[13] Barbara fails to see Jim for who he truly is and how he labors to balance the burdens of his two worlds, an adult blindness that aligns with ethnocentric adult assumptions about childhood—that children lack "specific and coherent meaning structure" (Bohm 2005, 9). Since viewers witness Jim struggle with his dueling responsibilities, they have a clearer picture of how seriously he takes his roles compared to Jim's mother. The audience also sees that Jim can creatively navigate through and around adult-controlled institutions, all while demonstrating wisdom and sensitive insight (which is often deemed insignificant by adults) that should elevate the worlds of children to the same level of respect society confers on the worlds of adults (Castro 2017). Since viewers are privy to both of Jim's identities, they see him as an agent negotiating the meanings of his complex responsibilities.

The teens work to maintain their secret mission to allow (in part) for balancing both the excitement in their lives as trollhunters and expectations their society places on them to be "mundane" high school students. This pretense becomes increasingly difficult to manage as the series continues, and the children go to greater lengths to hide their dual identities from their parents. In the show's final season, the children choose to reveal their identities as trollhunters to their parents. Jim's mother begins to guess at the truth, and she asserts that the parents of all of the teens be made aware of the struggles their children are facing. In this final season, Barbara no longer seeks to protect and control Jim. In what feels like an enormous pivot for her character, she focuses on supporting him in his magical role without insisting that he conform to her idea of how a child should live. With this step, the parents of the teens transition into minor members of the trollhunter team. They remain relatively useless as fighters or strategists, but they reclaim their role as supporters of their children, even when their struggles fall outside the realm of expected high school conflicts. When the parents choose to support the team's trollhunting endeavors, they accept their children as adept, authoritative agents within their society. They move beyond evaluating their children's voices as insignificant, small, and unauthoritative to recognizing the specialized experience their children can and do express (Castro 2017; Wyness 2006).

The team works to hide the troll world from the adult-run society of Arcadia, represented by teachers and a policeman. In keeping with Corsaro's (1992, 2005) research on peer cultures and interpretive reproduction, the teens creatively appropriate knowledge from adults—adult expectations of safety and normalcy—and they use this knowledge to inform priorities and motivations within their peer group. The teenagers wish to protect adults from knowledge that may overwhelm them, but they also recognize that their choice will protect trolls from human meddling. The decision to guard the secrets of trollhunting (for responsible reasons) highlights the show's children as "moral interpreters of the worlds they engage with, capable of participating in shared decisions on important topics" (Mayall 1994, 8). By giving children power to protect adult society, the series mocks the commonly held belief that children are invisible actors who lack abilities to impact society, partly due to their purported status as "semi-citizens" (Esser et al. 2016, 3). Mayall (2002) posits that adults tend to downgrade children's moral agency, but her findings demonstrate that children are moral agents able to manage the complexities of ethical dilemmas. In *Trollhunters*, the course of the plot validates the children's moral choices, and, when their secret is finally revealed, the children take charge with a commanding role over their parents and other adults in their town. The children's moral authority aligns with Chappell's (2008) assessment of why Rowling's wizarding children operate in defiance of adults: "adults cannot address certain issues because they have been subsumed by the ideologies and institutions that are the source of danger and injustice" (282). The trollhunter teens accept the dual realities they inhabit, but they do not trust adults to accept the existence of a magical world. Castro (2016) defines altruistic agency as "a child's thoughts, expressions, and actions enacted for the express benefit of others instead of merely oneself" (124). Castro's (2016) study specifically investigates the gendering of altruistic agency, so it is relevant to mention that both Claire and Jim altruistically act on behalf of their team as well as the larger Arcadia Oaks society.

Corsaro (2005) explains that children actively participate in society, a fact that is overlooked since children are "marginalized" due to their "subordinate" positioning (6). The *Trollhunters* series develops an ironic plot: children protect adult society so that it can continue to be ignorant of magical threats to its safety. Adult-held assumptions about power hierarchies undermine the deterministic model of socialization, ascribing the child the limited power of a novice. In that scenario, the child is a relatively powerless entity who must learn how to navigate and later take charge of society after reaching adulthood. In *Trollhunters*, however, the continuation of society is placed in the "charge" of children since the "adult-run" society aboveground will crumble if the children fail in their mission to maintain order in the magical world. In addition to stemming the human society of Arcadia Oaks from gaining awareness of the trolls, the children also actively engage in revising the rules of troll society. Human children teach the trolls to reevaluate execution as a punishment for certain crimes, they advise a tribe of Floridian trolls to consider appointing a female leader for the first time, and they force the council of trollhunters to acknowledge that Jim does not need to perform as a lone trollhunter, but can instead work with a team.

Corsaro (2002) explains that children "creatively take information from the adult world to produce their own unique childhood cultures" (4). Symbolically, the troll world underneath Arcadia Oaks is one of those childhood cultures. The audience accesses this magical world through the teens' experiences and peer cultures. At the same time, the teens must negotiate expectations stemming from the adult world—their parents' homes and their teachers' school. Children participate simultaneously in the adult world and the world of their peers (Corsaro 2002), and this series exemplifies children's dual natures by setting up a world accessible only to the children (the trolls' underground world). While the adults of Arcadia Oaks erect Rasmussen's (2004) concept of "places for children"—places created by adults and designated by them to be "best" for children—the teens claim additional "children's spaces" in Trollmarket. Rasmussen (2004) outlines necessary routes children take to move between the "institutional triangle," defined as adult-approved spaces of school, home, and recreational facility (157). In *Trollhunters*, the children access their secret troll world while on the way to school; they deviate from the adult-sanctioned path to the institution and detour through an unapproved spaced, in this case a dry floodwater canal. Adults would see this canal space as unusable and possibly dangerous, but it is in this unauthorized, liminal space that the teens find the Amulet of Daylight and later the entrance to Trollmarket.[14] The children in Rasmussen's (2004) research experience their special children's places "as a world" (161); the Netflix series takes this concept further, creating a fully realized world as a children's place. Trollmarket has politics, an economy, and connections to further worlds through various magical tunnels. The richness of the children's world in *Trollhunters* represents the vibrancy that can be found in children's places and their imaginations. Rasmussen (2004) stresses that recognizing and honoring children's places can help researchers acknowledge children as "social and cultural actors who create places" (171). del Toro's secret magical world, one that only teens can access, serves as a fictional representation of how children take an agentic role in shaping their own, adult-free, spaces.

Furthermore, in this magical space the trolls accept the teens' authority. Troll culture rejects adult hegemony and allows for child agency. The trolls initially distrust Jim because he is human, but they quickly learn to trust his leadership and they look to him and the team for salvation from evil forces. Eventually, even the surface world (the one ostensibly run by adults) comes to accept the teens' authority. During the series climax, the morally agentic children reveal their trollhunter identities and command their parents and teachers by relaying battle plans. The narrative floods the world above with the trolls' battle and trolls themselves, bringing the children's authority and experiences from their children's place into the adult realm aboveground. The series conclusion offers a particularly satisfying depiction of child competency and expert authority despite earlier adult skepticism.

ENSEMBLE WORK AND PEER CULTURE IN TROLLHUNTING STRATEGY

Not only must the teens negotiate a complex web of roles in two different worlds but they must also work to develop their peer culture, which becomes their main tool for succeeding within their various roles. Corsaro (1992) defines peer culture as "a stable set of activities or routines, artifacts, values, and concerns that children produce and share in interactions with peers" (162). In *Trollhunters*, the teens work together to negotiate their shared values and move ahead to take action based on said values. Their peer culture does not come together haphazardly; instead, the teens are particularly self-aware as they debate and revise power structure among themselves. This team is not developing and rehearsing social skills; instead, they apply the type of "competent meaning-making" Wyness (2006) finds possible in children's culture (168). The teens' peer culture is elevated by how it is labeled in the series: the children are trollhunters, and their shared values determine how they work together on a team.

A running conflict for the arc of the second part of season one develops around Jim's reliance on his team. Jim learns that none of the past trollhunters used a team, and troll authorities criticize his choice to recruit and employ friends in his duties as a trollhunter. Eventually, Jim convinces the authorities that his company of trollhunters is advantageous—toward the end of season one, the spokesperson for the trollhunter council finally acquiesces: "You were right. You are stronger together." This change is particularly important because the trollhunter council has centuries of wisdom and serves as the ultimate institutional voice in the troll realm, yet they come to officially accept morally driven, meaning-making lessons championed by the teens (see Frankel 2017). Teen characters in the show shift smoothly from "individual" to "team orientation" (Adler and Adler 1998, 112). The teenagers recognize the expectations team members carry in their families and at their school. They accept their team's mission—protecting trolls and humans—and they also work together to achieve members' personal goals of pleasing parents and carrying out family and school responsibilities.

Most importantly, the narrative distinctly argues that any success Jim has as the official trollhunter comes from his choice to partner with friends. According to Adler and Adler (1998), peer culture shapes how children make sense of the world and is influenced not just by friend groups, but also by other similar-aged children. Jim and his team are buffeted by their peer group at school—found in the class bully who exhibits aggressive masculinity and Claire's friends who make demands on her time and influence romantic expectations between the teens. Children work within their peer group hierarchy to wield power and establish dominance if they are able to do so (Adler and Adler 1998). The trollhunter team becomes a refuge for otherwise outcast teens, but they resist applying their power over trolls onto their classmates. Toby and Jim seem relatively complacent about their role as outcasts at the start of the series, but becoming trollhunters gives the boys access to a whole new society with the trolls of Trollmarket. Eventually, their troll-driven lives envelop Claire, too, and later more teens from school join the fringes of their growing trollhunters' network.

The name of the series—the plural *Trollhunters*—seems grammatically incorrect until an episode in the middle of the first season when Jim officially rebrands his team in the face of enemies who thought they lured him alone into danger: "Not trollhunter. Trollhunters!" The linguistic switch emphasizes a major theme in the series—Jim's reliance on his comrades. Jim christens his team "trollhunters" to mark them with equal status. According to

Rosette and Tost (2010), male leadership is associated with assertive, agentic power, while female leadership is associated with communal characteristics; for example, being sympathetic and "relationship-oriented" (222). Although the trollhunter team is led by Jim, he depends on a communitarian style of leadership.

The team learns to recognize and rely on each other's skills. If audiences fail to mark out this trend, the series highlights it with lines like that voiced by Claire: "It was a team effort." Similarly, when Jim's troll mentor Blinky says, "Another victory for our trollhunter," Jim retorts with "Trollhunters. Come on guys, it's a team effort." Each season builds upon the cooperative efforts of the team, but their interwoven reliance becomes especially clear in each season's finale. For example, in the climactic conclusion to season one, the team struggles to destroy the main antagonist, the deadly, powerful Angor Rot. The mechanics of how the team bests Angor Rot are important because, in the moment of climactic battle, the "staging" pointedly emphasizes the importance of ensemble work. Claire uses her portal-creating weapon to send Toby into a strategic position. Toby distracts the villain, and then Jim swoops in with a magical weapon that finally paralyzes Angor Rot. Toby follows through with his own swing, smashing the villain to pieces (which constitutes death for a troll). The team works together in one smooth choreographed motion to achieve their shared goal, and the expression of their peer structure—the interwoven nature of their collaboration in combat—underscores shared power found in their horizontal peer group that is articulated throughout the season. A similarly collaborative staging brings about total victory in the series finale. With Jim wounded and unable to continue in the final battle, the team coordinates a group attack on their last antagonist, Morgana le Fey, and finally removes her from the human dimension.

Comparisons can be made between *Trollhunters*' season finales and the contortions required to ensure Harry Potter's lone confrontations with his adult nemesis, Voldemort, that occur at the end of most Rowling's novels. Chappell (2008) identifies these finale scenes as a break from peer collaborations found earlier in each of the Potter novels. In contrast, *Trollhunters* arranges communal battles. This expression of social agency does not happen automatically with the formation of the team. While Jim is initially invested in the idea of a trollhunters team, his friends need some convincing. In the middle of the first season, Jim is still trying to brand the team. Nonetheless, his human friends Toby and Claire feel like sidekicks. After Toby fails in a mission, he begs Claire not to tell Jim: "He'll think I'm useless." Instead of reassuring him, Claire expresses her own insecurity: "We *are* useless." As they succeed in missions, Jim's friends slowly get on board with the nonhierarchical team structure. When other members of the team are injured on their missions, Jim temporarily abandons his communal philosophy and tries to strike out as a lone hero in order to protect them from further harm. The series sends messages—expressed through who does what to complete team goals—that Jim's lone wolf act will always result in failure, and reliance on his social group will consistently bring about victory. The fact that the children debate, test, and eventually accept the idea of a collaborative team structure shines a bright light on the horizontal collaboration that can characterize children's peer cultures.

While the team of trollhunters works to minimize hierarchy in their peer group, they focus on utilizing each other's skills to overcome obstacles. Their power as a peer group is contrasted to adult power and, especially, evil antagonists' powers. Three different antagonists face the team, one per season, with each serving as a dictator ordering around nameless, sometimes identical, henchmen in a clearly hierarchical social arrangement. The teens' horizontal structure contrasts with their magical enemies' power dynamic; moreover, the teens are aware that teamwork is necessary to overcome limitations placed on them by adults who do not acknowledge their agency. The teens' awareness of one another's needs and strengths falls in line with the notion of social agency, wherein children connect with others and build agentic pathways through their relationships (Clark and Castro 2019). del Toro's storyworld exemplifies Clark's (2019) assessment that "agency is not solely an individual endeavor" (143). Overcoming imposing villains is the highest expression of the trollhunter teens' agency, and so it is meaningful that the

Figure 4.2 Toby, Jim, and Claire establish a nonhierarchical team structure as they strategize how to solve problems and take on obstacles: "Party Monster"—*Trollhunters* (2016).

series depicts success reliant on peer joint efforts. While adults work in strict top-down hierarchies (i.e., teacher/student or dictator/henchmen), the teens develop and foster their fluid, horizontal peer culture to achieve important societal goals for the good of all humans.

The powerful children depicted in *Trollhunters* may represent a satisfying fantasy for children in the viewing audience (see Castro 2005). Here, child peer networks working toward collective goals upend adult assumptions about the naissance, incompetence, and silence of child agency and hold a dominant position over adults and their usually foregrounded culture. The show's children serve as authorities in their community—first secretly, then openly in the series conclusion when the battle leaks into public spaces of Arcadia. Since adults cannot or do not recognize children's agency for much of the series, the teens turn to each other for validation and support, constructing a collaborative, empathetic peer structure, one that becomes more versatile as it grows to include more teenagers outside their core friend peer group.

Eder, Evans, and Parker (1995) associate societal aggressiveness with the training young people receive in aggressive competition, made all the more powerful in certain violent, hierarchical team sports. The trollhunters' violent duties—slaughtering enemies—do not lead to the outcomes Eder, Evans, and Parker (1995) observe; instead, the trollhunters remain altruistic, even self-sacrificing, in the face of danger and death. Such an outcome may be wish fulfillment on the part of the adult creators of the series. The teen protagonists approach their roles with great responsibility, emotional balance, and logic, even while confronting teen bullies and, later, troll enemies.

The trollhunters' clearest moments of agency are expressed through mythopoeic combat scenes that have little similarity to current news reports of child soldiers in real-life armed conflicts. According to Wyness (2006), protectionist mindsets find certain children to be vulnerable beings who may be, at most, pawns in the hands of warlords. Denov and Gervais (2007) work to highlight the agency and cultural capability of girls who survive as combatants, sex-slaves, and commanders in adult-orchestrated conflicts like the rebel Revolutionary United Front (RUF) of Sierra Leone. In *Trollhunters*, only one girl participates as a trollhunter/warrior, and Claire does not encounter the same traditional patriarchal oppression and gender-based vulnerability faced by girls in actual armed conflicts. Nonetheless, the image of an empowered warrior girl who finds her weapon and wields power against dark, oppressive forces represents a potent fantasy image in this day of fictional girl fighters. Starting with Xena in *Xena the Warrior Princess* (1995—2001) and Buffy and expanding to the current crop of twenty-first-century girl warriors marketed after the popularity of *The Hunger Games* (2008), YA media culture has found a thread with which audiences are enthralled. *Trollhunters*' target audience is younger than readers consuming stories like *The Hunger Games*, *Divergent* (2011), *Enclave* (2011), and *Red Queen* (2015), but characters like Claire prepare these consumers for warrior girls who proliferate in the current YA literature market.

Claire's staff-wielding skills bring back memories of *Buffy the Vampire Slayer*—no doubt, similarities between that television series and *Trollhunters* stand out in my current analysis. Not only do both shows feature mentors who surround themselves with books, both series explore their characters' double lives, the liminal nature of teens, and the development of a growing peer network of empowered children navigating under the radar of adult institutions that partially control them. While *Buffy* demonstrates the effectiveness (and trials and tribulations) of a violent female hero as feminist argument, *Trollhunters* establishes a different claim about children as heroes and wielders of agency—the importance of peer groups. Like Jim, Buffy works within an ensemble group knit together to achieve collaborative ends. However, the fundamental feminist efforts motivating her narrative means that Buffy, as "the chosen one," often stands alone against the enemy, similar to those arguments made about Harry Potter. While some seasons end with collaborative combat, Buffy's agency is often asserted through her fighting skills and im/moral decisions. In *Trollhunters*, however, feminist rhetoric is less prevalent. Jim is not proving the potentiality of his gender. Instead, his openness to low-structure peer relationships downplays masculinized heroics, wherein carefully orchestrated social and collaborative agency is necessary to defeat the series' villains.

Adult-held perceptions of children as vulnerable beings do impact the trollhunting team, though the children ultimately demonstrate agency via

Figure 4.3 Claire learns to wield the Shadow Staff, which creates portals, and she frequently uses it to save her friends: "Grand Theft Otto"—*Trollhunters* (2017).

strategic encounters with enemies. The teen trollhunters are not plagued by realistic, psychological effects of battle. Instead, the series depicts child warfare as an empowering activity, a place where and time when teens establish their collective authority over the less flexible, highly structured adult society. Allowing young consumers to delight in detailed depictions of warfare—especially gun-free warfare—is a common feature in twenty-first-century media (Moore 2018). As critics continue to deconstruct presentations of powerful children, researchers will need to process the trope of the child warrior and chart its role in training children to see themselves as powerful, collaborative beings.

NOTES

1. Any accurate readership/audience study would be greatly hampered by the nature of Netflix's streaming service and the company's well-documented secrecy. Netflix does not release the numbers of viewers watching its shows; instead, it treats this information as a guarded secret. What media analysts do know is that Netflix had 104 million paying subscribers as of late 2017, and more than half of these viewers lived outside the United States (Koblin 2017).

2. A "latchkey child" has little adult supervision. The term comes from the idea that the child unlocks the door to enter an empty house after school. See Castro (2005, 2016) for discussion of 1980s films, children's agency, and home alone narratives related to the emergence of latchkey children in middle-class America.

3. del Toro is known for creating gothic, horned monsters in *Hellboy* (2004) and *Pan's Labyrinth* (2006). The latter, a dark film created for an adult audience, centers on a girl's painful experience during Francoist Spain. In *Trollhunters*, del Toro (and other makers of the series) toned down the gothic horror he usually employs to make the story palatable for a middle school audience (ages eight to twelve years old).

4. To clarify a confusing point of nomenclature, a "trollhunter" works to protect peaceful trolls by hunting down the evil trolls that eat humans and threaten to expose the secret of all trolls' existence to an otherwise ignorant mankind. Trollhunters have always been trolls themselves until the magical force of Merlin's amulet selects Jim.

5. "To Catch a Changeling" is a play on the Alfred Hitchcock film, *To Catch a Thief* (1955). "Claire and Present Danger" references *Clear and Present Danger* (1989), a Jack Ryan novel by Tom Clancy.

6. The episode "Grand Theft Otto" is a reference to the video game franchise Grand Theft Auto, and the episode includes a training video staged and filtered to look just like the Others' training film found on the island in the television series *Lost* (2004–2010). *Trollhunters* seasons one and two came out alongside *Stranger Things*, with the second season of *Trollhunters* offering shots suggesting that the Darklands are Arcadia Oaks' own Upside Down. Finally, 1980s references in the show include titles and parallel storylines that hint at *The Breakfast Club* (1985) and *Adventures in Babysitting* (1987).

7. Humans cannot understand gnome language, so when Toby takes a gnome home to live with him, he names the tiny creature Chomsky, a reference to Noam Chomsky, the famous linguist and cognitive scientist.

8. "TV-Y7" is an age-appropriate rating designed by the American Federal Communication Commission (FCC). Programming in this category is deemed appropriate for children ages seven and up.

9. In the Harry Potter series, Headmaster Dumbledore withholds central facts from Harry, even though this secret knowledge is intimately tied to Harry's past, his identity, and his life and death destiny. The novels' plots contain an element of detective fiction because the children cannot rely on adult authorities to tell them what they need to know about dangerous mysteries at their school or why they should trust some teachers but not others. The teachers and adults possess this knowledge, but they mete out crumbs of this information to the children, who then resort to eavesdropping, spying, and thought-theft to fill in the gaps.

10. For example, "It's about Time" plays on the idea that Jim does not have the time he needs to succeed at both his trollhunter and his teenage lives. While a steady theme in the series, this particular episode provides Jim with a time-freezing device, allowing him to ponder what he would do with limitless time.

11. Similarities in theme, setting, and conflict between *Buffy the Vampire Slayer* and *Trollhunters* are hard to ignore. A teenager befriends some magical creatures but battles others who feed on humans but only come out at night. In Arcadia Oaks, these rogue trolls use the sewers, just like Joss Whedon's vampires did, to access vulnerable parts of the city as they target Jim.

12. See Castro's (2019) similar argument that posthuman children set the structure found in their lives, not adults.

13. Changelings are trolls who have been altered so they can take on human forms. In *Buffy*, Joyce, too, is impossibly obtuse regarding the presence of vampires in her town and home.

14. Similar to adultist views of "messy" children's places discussed in Rasmussen's (2004) work.

REFERENCES

Adler, Patricia A., and Peter Adler. 1998. *Peer Power: Preadolescent Power and Identity*. New Brunswick, NJ: Rutgers University Press.

Baraldi, Claudio, and Vittorio Ieverse. 2014. "Observing Children's Capabilities as Agency." In *Children's Rights and the Capability Approach: Challenges and Prospects*, edited by Daniel Stoecklin and Jean-Michel Bonvin, 43–65. Dordrecht: Springer.

Blaas, Rodrigo, Guillermo del Toro, and Marc Guggenheim. 2016–2018. *Trollhunters*. Streaming: Netflix. USA: Dreamworks Animation Television.

Bohm, David. 2005. *Childhood*. New York, NY: Routledge.

Buckingham, David. 1994. "Television and the Definition of Childhood." In *Children's Childhoods: Observed and Experienced*, edited by Berry Mayall, 79–96. London: The Falmer Press.

Campbell, Joseph. 2008. *The Hero with a Thousand Faces* (3rd ed.). Novato, CA: New World Library.

Campbell, Lori M. 2010. *Portals of Power: Magical Agency and Transformation in Literary Fantasy*. Jefferson, NC: McFarland & Co.

Castro, Ingrid E. 2005. "Children's Agency and Cinema's New Fairy Tale." In *Sociological Studies of Children and Youth, Volume 11*, edited by David A. Kinney and Katherine B. Rosier, 215–37. Amsterdam: Elsevier.

———. 2016. "Children, Innocence, and Agency in the Films of Steven Spielberg." In *Children in the Films of Steven Spielberg*, edited by Adrian Schober and Debbie Olson, 121–40. Lanham, MD: Lexington Books.

———. 2017. "Contextualizing Agency in High-Structure Environments: Children's Participation in Parent Interviews." In *Researching Children and Youth: Methodological Issues, Strategies, and Innovations—Sociological Studies of Children and Youth, Volume 22*, edited by Ingrid E. Castro, Melissa Swauger, and Brent Harger, 149–73. Bingley: Emerald.

———. 2019. "The *Emergence* of Agency After Bionuclear War: Posthuman Child—Animal Possibilities." In *Child and Youth Agency in Science Fiction: Travel, Technology, Time*, edited by Ingrid E. Castro and Jessica Clark, 251–72. Lanham, MD: Lexington Books.

Chappell, Drew. 2008. "Sneaking Out After Dark: Resistance, Agency, and the Postmodern Child in JK Rowling's Harry Potter Series." *Children's Literature in Education* 39 (4): 281–93.

Clark, Jessica. 2019. "'Speddies' with Spray Paints: Intersections of Agency, Childhood, and Disability in Award-Winning Young Adult Fiction." In *Representing Agency in Popular Culture: Children and Youth on Page, Screen, and In Between*, edited by Ingrid E. Castro and Jessica Clark, 133–56. Lanham, MD: Lexington Books.

Clark, Jessica, and Ingrid E. Castro. 2019. "Introduction: Zuzu's Petals and Scout's Mockingbirds: The Legacy of Children's Agency in Popular Culture." In *Representing Agency in Popular Culture: Children and Youth on Page, Screen, and In Between*, edited by Ingrid E. Castro and Jessica Clark, ix–xxxi. Lanham, MD: Lexington Books.

Corsaro, William A. 1992. "Interpretive Reproduction in Children's Peer Cultures." *Social Psychology Quarterly* 55 (2): 160–77.

———. 2002. *We're Friends, Right?: Inside Kids' Culture*. Washington, DC: Joseph Henry Press.

———. 2005. *The Sociology of Childhood* (2nd ed.). London: Pine Forge Press.

Denov, Myriam, and Christine Gervais. 2007. "Negotiating (In)Security: Agency, Resistance, and Resourcefulness Among Girls Formerly Associated with Sierra Leone's Revolutionary United Front." *Signs: Journal of Women in Culture and Society* 32 (4): 885–910.

Duane, Anna M. 2013. "Introduction: The Children's Table: Childhood Studies and the Humanities." In *The Children's Table: Childhood Studies and the Humanities*, edited by Anna M. Duane, 1–14. Athens, GA: University of Georgia Press.

Eder, Donna, Catherine C. Evans, and Stephen Parker. 1995. *School Talk: Gender and Adolescent Culture*. New Brunswick, NJ: Rutgers University Press.

Esser, Florian, Meike S. Baader, Tanja Betz, and Beatrice Hungerland. 2016. "Reconceptualising Agency and Childhood: An Introduction." In *Reconceptualising Agency and Childhood: New Perspectives in Childhood Studies*, edited by Florian Esser, Meike S. Baader, Tanja Betz, and Beatrice Hungerland, 1–16. New York, NY: Routledge.

Flynn, Richard. 2016. "Introduction: Disputing the Role of Agency in Children's Literature and Culture." *Jeuness: Young People, Texts, Cultures* 8 (1): 248–53.

Frankel, Sam. 2017. *Negotiating Childhoods: Applying a Moral Filter to Children's Everyday Lives*. Hampshire: Palgrave Macmillan.

James, Allison. 2011. "Agency." In *The Palgrave Handbook of Childhood Studies* (paperback ed.), edited by Jens Qvortrup, William A. Corsaro, and Michael-Sebastian Honig, 34–45. New York, NY: Palgrave Macmillan.

Koblin, John. 2017. "How Many People Watch Netflix? Nielson Tries to Solve Mystery." *The New York Times*. October 18, 2017. https://www.nytimes.com/2017/10/18/business/media/nielsen-netflix-viewers.html.

Mayall, Berry. 1994. "Introduction." In *Children's Childhoods: Observed and Experienced*, edited by Berry Mayall, 1–12. London: The Falmer Press.

———. 2002. *Towards a Sociology for Childhood*. Berkshire: Open University Press.

Meeusen, Meghann. 2017. "Framing Agency: Comics Adaptations of *Coraline* and *City of Ember*." In *Graphic Novels for Children and Young Adults: A Collection of Critical Essays*, edited by Michelle A. Abate and Gwen A. Tarbox, 126–38. Jackson, MS: University Press of Mississippi.

Mendlesohn, Farah. 2005. *Diana Wynne Jones: Children's Literature and the Fantastic Tradition*. New York, NY: Routledge.

Moore, Tara. 2018. "Violent Girls: Power, Predation, and the Use of Weapons in Young Adult Narratives." In *Handmaids, Tributes, and Carers: Dystopian Females' Roles and Goals*, edited by Myrna Santos, 114–30. Newcastle Upon Tyne: Cambridge Scholars Publishing.

Publisher's Weekly. 2012. "New Study: 55% of YA Books Bought by Adults." *Publisher's Weekly*. September 13, 2012. https://www.publishersweekly.com/pw/by-topic/childrens/childrens-industry-news/article/53937-new-study-55-of-ya-books-bought-by-adults.html.

Rasmussen, Kim. 2004. "Places for Children—Children's Places." *Childhood* 11 (2): 155–73.

Rosette, Ashleigh S., and Leigh P. Tost. 2010. "Agentic Women and Communal Leadership: How Role Prescriptions Confer Advantage to Top Women Leaders." *Journal of Applied Psychology* 95 (2): 221–35.

Sidney, Sir Philip. 1977. *The Countess of Pembroke's Arcadia (The Old Arcadia)*. London: Penguin Books.

Vallone, Lynne. 2013. "Doing Childhood Studies: The View from Within." In *The Children's Table: Childhood Studies and the Humanities*, edited by Anna M. Duane, 238–54. Athens, GA: University of Georgia Press.

Vogler, Christopher. 2007. *The Writers Journey: Mythic Structure for Writers* (3rd ed.). Studio City, CA: Michael Wiese Productions.

Wyness, Michael. 2006. *Childhood and Society*. New York, NY: Palgrave Macmillan.

Magic/Journey

Chapter 5

The Boy Who Lives

Agentic Locations of Friendship Identity, Peer Culture, and Interpretive Reproduction in Harry Potter

Ingrid E. Castro

INTRODUCTION: "NEW" SOCIOLOGY OF CHILDHOOD, CHILDREN'S GEOGRAPHIES

One cannot help but think of friendship when reflecting on the story of Harry Potter. Through seven years of acclimation, participation, and exploration, his best friends Ron Weasley and Hermione Granger, and occasionally other various-aged peers he interacts with, serve as Harry's support system within Hogwarts and beyond the boundaries of his school. In addition to friendship and peer culture, J.K. Rowling's Harry Potter series intertwines themes of space, place, and identity, providing the reader with an intricately woven fantasy tale of belongingness. An analysis that brings these elements together requires combining theories from the "new" sociology of childhood with the children's geographies framework to arrive at innovative considerations of friendship and peer culture as represented in children's fantasy literature.

In order to understand why there was, and continues to be, a call for a "new" sociology of childhood, one must understand what the "old" sociology of childhood encompassed. First, the "old" sociology of childhood embraced early developmental psychology models. These constructivist models of development, like those of Jean Piaget, have since been criticized by "new" sociology of childhood scholars for not bearing in mind the important interpersonal relationships children have with others, particularly peers, as well as disapproval that these early models were primarily concerned with children's developmental movement toward "adult competence" and future adulthood (Corsaro 2015, 16). Second, and related, "new" sociology of childhood scholars criticize the "old" sociology's focus on socialization processes of passive children growing into adulthood instead of finding value in children's own social worlds and their active roles within childhood. The socialization perspective failed "to recognize children's competence to interpret the social world and act on it" (Matthews 2007, 327). Third, the "old" sociology of childhood, for all its good intentions, did not tend to work directly with children. This misstep led to the realization that children were "oddly absent" from sociological research on children and childhood (Shanahan 2007, 410). Primarily, sociologists situated in the "old" sociology of childhood either spoke for children or were satisfied with recollections of childhood by adults, neither of which enabled true inquiry into the everyday realities of what it means to be a child and the specificities of living within and navigating through multiple childhoods.

In contrast, "new" sociology of childhood scholars believe children are active, not passive, participants in society, and their positions in society are in constant threat of marginalization due to adults infantilizing and silencing them. "New" sociology theorists recognize that children actively construct their own environments, wherein they are "not only affected by but also affect social structures and relationships" (Matthews 2007, 323). Due to criticism that "old" sociology of childhood scholars homogenized children through a belief in shared experiences of childhood as a static and universal truth, "new" scholars understand "children experience childhood differently depending on many factors" (Matthews 2007, 327). These factors include historical, political, geographical, cultural, technological, familial, and/or social variances (Buckingham 2000; Shanahan 2007). In fact, fluctuations associated with each of these elements lead to dissimilar outcomes for individual children or peer culture groups, wherein they experience alternate versions of childhood in a particular time and a particular space. Additionally, "new" sociology of childhood scholars are dedicated to putting children first in their research, crafting creative participant-driven methodologies that foreground research *with* children instead of *on* children (see Swauger, Castro, and Harger 2017).

Moving from sociologists accepting that childhood is a "social space" (Shanahan 2007, 420), similarly, theorists and researchers who work in children's geographies believe children's unique places and spaces in the physical and social world were ignored in the past in lieu of an overarching attention paid to adult-constructed and adult-occupied public and private spaces. As Blundell (2016) states, work in children's geographies is, at its heart, based on "the conviction that the incorporation of spatialized ways of seeing enhances our insight into the way that childhood as an ideal shapes and constrains the institutionalized realities that enframe children's lives" (11). Particularly, questions of children's locations and their negotiation of access to and meaning-making of places are central to children's geographies inquiry (Halldén 2003).

Works by scholars Sarah L. Holloway and Gill Valentine are often called upon when theorizing children's geographies. Their writings draw on the "new" sociology of childhood as a springboard for contextualizing the importance of locating children within place, time, and identity. They challenge that these three elements must shape our modern understandings of children and childhood as socially constructed (Holloway and Valentine 2000a). In addition, they contend that by integrating "new" sociology of childhood research with children's geographies theories, we can "illustrate the ways in which children's identities and lives are made and (re)made" through a focus on children's everyday spaces (Holloway and Valentine 2000a, 18, 2000b). These spaces include places such as homes, schools, and playgrounds, with special attention paid to children's social locations and relationships found within.[1] Modern children's geographers also examine places that are everyday for some, but not all, children; for example, hospitals ("sick" children) and streets ("homeless" children).

Finally, current children's geographies work extends (seemingly unbeknownst to many of the researchers) from sociologist Bill Corsaro's interpretive reproduction theories. Children's geography scholars argue that in recognizing space is socially produced, it can also be socially altered through children's "agency, actions or perspectives" (Hackett, Procter, and Seymour 2015, 4; Satta, 2015). Corsaro's contributions to the field of the "new" sociology of childhood are vast, but he is perhaps best known for theories pertaining to children's interpretive reproduction. He views children's cultural membership as a reproductive, not linear, process, explaining:

> ...children do not simply imitate or internalize the world around them. They strive to interpret or make sense of their culture and to participate in it. In attempting to make sense of the adult world, children come to collectively produce their own peer worlds and cultures. . . .This is made up of three types of collective action: (a) children's creative appropriation of information and knowledge from the adult world; (b) children's production and participation in a series of peer cultures; and (c) children's contribution to the reproduction and extension of the adult culture. (Corsaro 2015, 23 & 41)

Within the process of interpretive reproduction, children take in the world and messages around them, and may or may not directly reproduce them. If they do reproduce adult thoughts, actions, ideologies, or structures, it is because children agentically choose to do so, not passively accepting these bases as true or total. Children may also adopt messages from adult society and selectively reproduce them in an altered manner within peer groups that align with their own beliefs, which is, in effect, interpretive reproduction.

For the present study on the Harry Potter book series, the adult culture is the magical community, whereby magical adults run the Ministry of Magic, Hogwarts, all shops in Diagon Alley and the Village of Hogsmeade, and, in more insular spaces, witches and wizards monitor children's (mis)use of magic in non-muggle and muggle homes alike.[2] As will be argued, the children of the magical community form their own peer cultures within which they may, or may not, agentically appropriate, reproduce, or uphold ideologies, rules, and values of the adult magical world. In many cases, children in the series create new ways of thinking within their peer cultures, acting in accordance with their views of what is morally right, certainly true, and/ or desperately needed. Through these interpretive reproduction processes, intrinsically linked to their agency, Harry and his friends build identities within the magical community, formulated through their place at Hogwarts and the social spaces of Gryffindor House.

THE ISLANDING OF HARRY POTTER

Surrey
Little Whinging
4 Privet Drive
The Cupboard Under the Stairs

When first introduced, ten-year-old Harry Potter is a non-entity at 4 Privet Drive: "The room held no sign at all that another boy lived in the house" (Year 1, 18).[3] With an aunt and uncle who give all their love and attention to their son, Harry spends most of his time alone, either whiling away "long hours in his cupboard" or "as much time as possible out of the house, wandering around" (Year 1, 29 & 31). Harry is expected to be at once invisible yet visible while functioning as cook and maid to the Dursley's: Aunt Petunia, Uncle Vernon, and cousin Dudley. For children like Harry, time alone is imposed by adults, defined through the social relations in the home, and usually not voluntarily chosen (Christensen, James, and Jenks 2000). Other than his small, restrictive family, Harry is not connected to the outside world: "At school, Harry had no one" and "He had no friends, no other relatives" (Year 1, 30 & 34). As such, Harry is a socially islanded child since the minimal relationships he has with his family are detached—Harry does not look like them, talk like them, think like them, or dream like them.

Harry is living on the island of 4 Privet Drive, and on an even smaller island (in fact, the smallest household island) of the cupboard under the stairs in his relatives' home. Not only is Harry isolated physically from other places and spaces in the muggle world but, more importantly, he is isolated socially from other children in his neighborhood and school. With a brutish, larger-than-life cousin whose gang terrorizes other children, no one dares cross the imaginary line to befriend Harry Potter, a child "small and skinny for his age" who looks even more so dressed in his cousin Dudley's enormous hand-me-down cast-offs (Year 1, 20). While "no man is an island," Harry experiences his early childhood as such, a child living on an island of his relatives' making.

The concept of islanded children was first, briefly, introduced by Danish sociologist and childhood scholar Jens Qvortrup in 1994. He explains, "it may provocatively be suggested that children's institutionalization is adults' way of confining them in particular 'islands' and buildings, and thus a way of marginalizing or excluding childhood from adult society" (Qvortrup 1994, 9). Following, German sociologist and childhood scholar Helga Zeiher expanded theories on the islanding of children, believing children are forced to live on a variety of islands during childhood, shuttled from island to island by adults, never to experience the more public spaces in between. She asks, "Where do children live in such a landscape of islands?" and "How do children live in and move around such landscapes of islands?" (Zeiher 2001, 147, 2003, 66). Her concern is that as children exist in islanded childhoods, children's spaces are insularized from the spaces of adults and detrimentally separated from other children's spaces (Gillis 2008). As is evident in the Harry Potter series, the islanding of Harry indeed keeps him away from other neighborhood children (he has no direct relationship with any other child except for Dudley) and, later in the series, his lonely summer isolations on Privet Drive leave him, at times, believing he is forsaken by the wizarding world.

One must ask why children are placed on ever-smaller islands as history rolls on, relegated to a diminished capacity to connect with other children socially and physically. The overarching push toward keeping places safe for children results in heightened structural limitations, hyper-protectionism, and surveillance of children by adults (Swauger, Castro, and Harger 2017). In this process, adults make "judgements about the balance between risk and protection, freedom and safety" (Elsey 2011, 112). Tellingly, Gillis (2008) explains that islands are "thought of as places ideal for children. They are deemed safe places for preserving childish innocence" (318). As such, I and other theorists argue that protectionist discourses and agency-constricting hyper-structure disadvantage children, leaving them world-naïve through a process that dangerously romanticizes characterizations of childhood as innocent (see Castro 2016). The attribution of childhood innocence is often equated with children's simplicity, harmlessness, and passivity (Castro

2016). Related, children who are placed on "extreme islands" (the smallest and most cut off from others) are viewed twofold: "they are perceived as the epitome of innocence and goodness; on the other hand, they can stand for that which is uncivilized, even savage" (Gillis 2008, 327). Undoubtedly, this dichotomy is evident in the characterizations of Harry and cousin Dudley. Harry is frequently labeled as an ungrateful and abnormal delinquent by his extended family, at one point told by Aunt Marge (Uncle Vernon's sister) that he is "rotten on the *inside*" and likened to bad puppy produced from a "bitch" dog (Year 3, 25). Solidifying this offender status, Harry's family maintains a public façade that he attends "St. Brutis's Secure Center for Incurably Criminal Boys" rather than admit he goes to Hogwarts School of Witchcraft and Wizardry (Year 3, 19). Dudley, in contrast, is branded as precious and dear, a boy who can do no wrong in adults' eyes even though he is a greedy bully with no sense of self-control. Valentine (1996) finds that parents "voicing concerns about their own children's 'innocence' and safety (angels), are simultaneously articulating fears about other people's children as 'dangerous', 'out of control', and lacking respect for 'natural' adult authority (devils)" (596). Each fiercely guarded by his aunt and uncle or his parents (toward different ends), throughout the course of the Harry Potter series Dudley is infantilized and glorified with utmost protection, while Harry is demonized and punished, also with utmost protection.

An interesting quandary arises from the push to island children: someone must monitor these islands and the children stuck on them. Adults find it more and more difficult to manage children's islands, as the ritual "requires the investment of large amounts of time and energy, not to mention money, all to the purpose of creating and maintaining islanded worlds capable of sustaining the desired image of childhood" (Gillis 2008, 318). We certainly find this condition true in the islanding of Harry Potter. In the beginning of Harry's story, *Harry Potter and the Sorcerer's Stone* (1997), Uncle Vernon puts great effort into the process of keeping Harry away from his Hogwarts letter and magical destiny. On the arrival of his first letter, Uncle Vernon's face turns from "red to green" and "within seconds it was the grayish white of old porridge," while his Aunt Petunia "looked as though she might faint. She clutched her throat and made a choking noise" (Year 1, 35). Uncle Vernon follows these physical distresses from this letter's arrival (and hundreds more thereafter) by moving Harry into Dudley's second bedroom, staying home from work, nailing the mail slot shut, boarding up cracks in the house, moving out of the house, and finally settling the family on "what looked like a large rock way out at sea" (Year 1, 43). This last location is obviously the literal attempt to island Harry: by placing him on an island in the middle of the ocean, Uncle Vernon wrongly assumes the magical world cannot reach Harry and he (and the rest of the Dursley family) will forever be protected from the world of magic. These efforts to island Harry do not stop once he completes his first year of school; for example, in *Harry Potter and the Chamber of Secrets* (1999) Uncle Vernon pays someone to put bars on Harry's bedroom window and installs a cat-flap on the bedroom door for the delivery of sub-par meals, all to prevent Harry from returning to school, definitively turning his bedroom island into a prison island. As Rowling writes, "They let Harry out to use the bathroom morning and evening. Otherwise, he was locked in his room around the clock" (Year 2, 22).

Even though Harry develops meaningful friendships, immerses himself in peer culture, and closely identifies with Hogwarts throughout the series, at different points Harry continues to feel the effects of being marooned from the wizarding world while relegated to his summertime Privet Drive island. Harry is kept from the material culture of the magical world by the Durselys, as "their general wish of keeping Harry as miserable as possible, coupled with their fear of his powers, had led them to lock his school trunk in the cupboard under the stairs every summer" (Year 4, 23–4). Socially, beginning with *Chamber of Secrets*, Harry is back with his family, "being treated like a dog that had rolled in something smelly," wondering several times over why his peers from school do not contact him, believing "maybe he *didn't* have any friends at Hogwarts" (Year 2, 5 & 10). Later in the series (*Harry Potter and the Order of the Phoenix*, 2003), Harry is once again left without meaningful word from his friends Ron and Hermione, leading him to accuse them of purposely keeping information from him and excluding him from their peer culture: "So how come I have to stay at the Dursleys' while you two get to join in everything that's going on here?... YOU'VE STILL BEEN TOGETHER! ME, I'VE BEEN STUCK AT THE DURSLEYS' FOR A MONTH!... BUT WHY SHOULD I KNOW WHAT'S GOING ON? WHY SHOULD ANYONE BOTHER TO TELL ME WHAT'S BEEN HAPPENING?" (Year 5, 65–6). In the above examples, efforts associated with protectionism lead to the social islanding of Harry Potter. In the first instance, Dobby the house elf steals all of Harry's correspondence in the hope Harry will not want to return to school if he believes his friends forget him, all in the name of Dobby's steadfast mantra, "Harry Potter must stay where he is safe" (Year 2, 16). In the second example, Ron and Hermione explain to Harry that Headmaster Dumbledore believes he is "safest with the Muggles" (Year 5, 63).

At the end of *Order of the Phoenix*, the true reason for Harry's islanding becomes clear—it is through his mother's life sacrifice and bloodline, also found in Aunt Petunia, that Harry is sheltered from Voldemort and his crew of Death Eaters.[4] While this connection is the ultimate, and perhaps most excusable, reason for islanding children, it still comes down to the base reason of protectionism. Even though Dumbledore admits, "I knew I was condemning you to ten dark and difficult years" and Harry contends, Aunt Petunia "doesn't love me.... She doesn't give a damn" (Year 5, 835–6), the result is the same—Harry is isolated from his socially supportive community, extended family, and peer culture.[5] Due to such issues associated with islanding, researchers argue that we need to remove children from these overly protected spaces, and instead consider children "as valuable and active contributors to societies within which they live . . . [with] the capacity to participate meaningfully" (Moore, McArthur, and Noble-Carr 2008, 78). And so, we turn to the joy Harry experiences each time he is allowed to leave the Privet Drive island, whereby he learns the meaning of participating in friendships and peer culture and is allotted both the space and the people to do so meaningfully and agentically.

THE TRAIN TO SOMEWHERE, THE SORT TO SOMETHING, THE SCHOOL TO SOMEONE

Once Harry is informed of his family's legacy by Hogwarts gamekeeper/gentle giant Hagrid, his world opens exponentially. In Diagon Alley, he learns he is wealthy by magical standards and receives the first of many momentous gifts, a birthday present from Hagrid, his owl Hedwig—"his companion, his one great link with the magical world whenever he had been forced to return to the Dursleys" (Year 7, 67). He purchases books, cauldron, and robes, and, through much trial and error, he is chosen worthy by his wand, later described after seven years of challenges as one that "survived so much" (Year 7, 349). As he finds himself at the Hogwart's Express, Platform Nine and Three-Quarters, he crosses the barrier between the muggle and magical world, finally able to start building friendships and a peer culture, not knowing "what he was going to—but it had to be better than what he was leaving behind" (Year 1, 98).

On their first train ride together, there are several exchanges between Ron Weasley and Harry that are indicative of meaningful friendship development. One important central theme resounding in children's friendships and peer cultures is the value they place on sharing (Corsaro and Eder 1990). Harry clearly recognizes the significance of finally having the space and opportunity to share with another child. While offering his cornucopia of food and sweets to Ron, Harry thinks about how he "never had anything to share before or, indeed, anyone to share it with. It was a nice feeling" (Year 1, 102). Beyond the physical aspects of this first sharing encounter, Harry also shares his story and background with Ron in the effort to make Ron feel better about the Weasley's poverty. After an embarrassed Ron explains to Harry that all his Hogwarts items are hand-me-downs, Harry connects with Ron on a deep level of experiential social sharing: "Harry didn't think there was anything wrong with not being able to afford an owl. After all, he's never had any money in his life until a month ago, and he told Ron so, all about having to wear Dudley's old clothes and never getting proper birthday presents. This seemed to cheer Ron up" (Year 1, 100). In this exchange, it is clear Ron and Harry are "sharing their understanding, as children, of their social worlds" (Mayall 2008, 122).

A second, just as central element of children's friendship and peer culture is solidarity. Solidarity emerges from being friends with other children, serving integrative functions in the requirement for meaningful friendship and peer group cohesion between children (Adler and Adler 1998; Corsaro 2015). Ron and Harry's friendship is cemented when they together face, for the first time, Harry's peer nemesis Draco Malfoy and Draco's cronies on the Hogwarts Express (all soon to be assigned to Slytherin House). When Draco insults Ron's family and threatens Harry's life, the two stand up to the three, ready in the fight to defend their joint honors. In her extensive research on youth friendships, Niobe Way (2006) finds that mutual protection from physical fights and emotional harm is a prerequisite for male children's close friendships.[6] I argue Ron's never-wavering support of Harry in the ongoing feud with Draco is at the heart of Harry and Ron's friendship. Ron is always quick to defend Harry and others in their close peer culture from Draco's litany of xenophobic insults, regardless of outcome (for example, Ron throwing up slugs after the curse he directs at Malfoy, in defense of Hermione, backfires in *Chamber of Secrets*). He also defends Harry when members of their extended peer culture doubt Harry's sanity and/or truth-telling (for example, Ron threatening fellow Gryffindor, roommate, and cohort member Seamus Finnigan with detention in *Order of the Phoenix*).

And so, Harry and Ron establish the seeds of a peer culture that grow through their sorting into Gryffindor House and the eventual addition of Hermione Granger. Also introduced on the train, Harry and Ron initially find Hermione to be a know-it-all, rule-loving, goody-two-shoes who is quick to tell them in all manner how they are going wrong, whether it be in classes, hallways, or Gryffindor's common room. Much has been written by scholars on the Sorting Ceremony in the Harry Potter books, but it is notable just how much the four Hogwarts Houses dictate children's peer cultures. Professor McGonagall, Head of Gryffindor House, explains: "The Sorting is a very important ceremony because, while you are here, your house will be something like your family within Hogwarts. You will have classes with the rest of your house, sleep in your house dormitory, and spend free time in your house common room" (Year 1, 114). Harry's close friendships and extended peer cultures are formed because of Gryffindor House; Gryffindors are described throughout the series as being brave, bold, and daring.[7] Given that House members have traits recognized by the Sorting Hat as indicative of belonging, children's peer culture at Hogwarts is, to a certain degree, organized for and placed on children as soon as they arrive at school. These ties that bind are made evident by the fact that while Harry has a loose affinity for children who are members of other Houses, he does not consider any of them close friends or part of his inner peer group culture (with the exception of Luna Lovegood, an outlier whose utmost importance I discuss later in this chapter).

The third element of peer culture formation is the ability to put trust in one's friends, as this component encompasses the other two integral friendship areas of sharing and solidarity. Specifically, children value being able to trust friends, reflecting their ability to share confidences with a few individuals they feel solidarity with compared to their larger extended peer groups (Adler and Adler 1998; Musolf 1996). While Harry and Ron do not initially trust Hermione, given her characterization as more informant than comrade, they eventually solidify their friendship group and intimate peer culture after sharing in an adventure that requires the combination of all their agentic efforts and skills—battling a troll in a girls' bathroom. In the span of a few pages, Hermione transforms from someone who, according to Ron, is "a nightmare" with no friends because "no one can stand her" to becoming an integral part of their close-knit peer group: "from that moment on, Hermione Granger became their friend. There are some things you can't share without liking each other" (Year 1, 172 & 179). The mutual trust Harry, Ron, and Hermione build throughout the series grows in importance as Harry's destiny becomes apparent. At times, the trust between them is underscored by Dumbledore, who later in the series very clearly delineates the difference between Ron and Hermione and the rest of Harry's larger peer group or extended family: "Yes, I think Mr. Weasley and Miss Granger have proved themselves trustworthy. But Harry, I am going to ask you to ask them not to repeat any of this to anybody else" (Year 6, 215).

In tandem, their friendship bonds are tested at different points in the Harry Potter series, with both Hermione and Ron breaking trust within their close peer group. There are three clear examples of trust fracture in the series, one perpetrated by Hermione and the other two by Ron. In the first instance, Hermione breaches Ron and Harry's trust when she informs Professor McGonagall that Harry receives a broom from an unknown benefactor for Christmas. While her motives are good, Ron views the ramifications of her "running to McGonagall" as "nothing less than criminal damage" (Year 3, 232–3). This feud between Ron and Hermione is fueled throughout *Harry Potter and the Prisoner of Azkaban* (1999) by the ongoing war between Ron's rat and Hermione's cat, but at the heart of the problem is Ron's conviction that the "base of intimacy and trust" in their close friendship was not "held in confidence" (Adler and Adler 1998, 116).

In contrast, Ron breaks trust with Harry at two points in the series, to such a degree that Harry is led to think quite negatively about Ron's moral character. In both instances, the fissures that infiltrate the peer group are due to Ron's betrayal, jealousy, and distrust, resulting from disloyalty and unreliability (Asher, Guerry, and McDonald 2014; Way 2006). In the first example, Ron is unwilling to accept that Harry did not enter the Triwizard Tournament on his own accord.[8] Ron sees Harry's act as base treason to their friendship: "It's okay, you know, you can tell me the truth . . . . If you don't want everyone else to know, fine, but I don't know why you're bothering to lie, you didn't get into trouble" (Year 4, 287). Even though Hermione attempts to explain to Harry that Ron's reaction sprouts from jealousy since, "it's always you who gets all the attention, you know it is . . . you're his best friend, and you're really famous—he's always shunted to one side whenever people see you, and he puts up with it, and he never mentions it, but I suppose this is just one time too many" (Year 4, 289–90), the friendship is not repaired and the peer group is not reunited until after Harry faces off against a dragon in *Harry Potter and the Goblet of Fire* (2000).

In the second, lengthier, and altogether more serious feud, Ron elects to abandon Harry and Hermione while the trio is on the hunt for Voldemort's horcruxes in the final volume, *Harry Potter and the Deathly Hallows* (2007).[9] In this instance, Harry and Hermione are physically separated from Ron when he leaves them to return to the bosom of his family. On their journey, jealousy, misunderstanding, and blame mount between the group, until Ron finally accuses Harry of not knowing what he is doing, not having a plan, and not caring about the Weasley family. When it appears the two are going to draw wands against each other, Hermione places a protective shield between them: "Harry and Ron glared from either side of the transparent barrier as though they were seeing each other clearly for the first time. Harry felt a corrosive hatred toward Ron: Something had broken between them" (Year 7, 309). Their friendship bonds are indeed reconstituted once Ron saves Harry's life, faces the heteromasculinist core of his jealousy, and destroys a horcrux;[10] it is important to note that this deep fissure reflects the emotional vulnerability boys can have with one another in friendships (Way 2011).

Interestingly, Harry never betrays the trust of Ron or Hermione, but one could argue that while Harry shares many confidences with them, they do not do so in kind. This lack of exchange does not mean, however, that trust issues do not fall on the shoulders of Harry, causing interruptions to their friendship group or influencing the larger Hogwarts collective peer culture. On the local level, Harry is often burdened by the belief that he cannot trust himself. Due to the psychic and physical links he shares with Voldemort (evidenced by his forehead's lighting scar), at times Harry is sure he is a danger to his friends and school peers. Addressing whether status markers affect peer group solidarity versus peer group differentiation, Murray Milner (2004) finds: "It is much easier to change an insignia on your label then a brand on your forehead" (207).[11] Similarly, Allison James (2013) notes that children's "external marks of personhood cannot be separated out from experiences of selfhood" (13). Given the sticky connection between physical (body) marks of difference and social (identity) marks of difference,

Harry removes himself from his close friendship group to "save" them. For example, Harry isolates himself from his friends in Grimmauld Place when he believes he inhabits the snake that nearly kills Ron's father.[12] In this case and many others, Harry employs moral agency, willing to physically and socially island himself from others, making sacrifices for what he believes is the greater good of his friends, school, and extended family/magical community: "He would have to leave Grimmauld Place straightaway .... He would spend Christmas ... without the others, which would keep them safe .... A leaden sensation was settling in the pit of his stomach. He had no alternative. He was going to have to return to Privet Drive, cut himself off from other wizards entirely" (Year 5, 494). The emotionality of his self-imposed distrust (and resultant self-islanding) haunts Harry throughout the series. Harry is aware, very early on, that his expressions "of strong negative emotions must be temporally and spatially constrained" away from his friends, peers, and extended family (Christensen, James, and Jenks 2000, 150).[13]

On the broader level, sometimes the larger school peer group joins in this islanding, removing Harry from their collectivity when the lightning brand reminds students of his connection to Voldemort. This mark of difference serves as a fissure between Harry and his peers at Hogwarts and the wider magical world, who frequently use Harry as a "cultural scapegoat" (James 1993, 154). James (1993) states that, among children, "traits which strongly mark a person as being unique—[are] none the less still culturally patterned and shaped" (151). Here, children at Hogwarts reflect interpretive reproduction in their peer groups—mirroring a belief that the lightening scar is dangerously important because the larger, adult-led, magical culture makes it so. In *Chamber of Secrets*, for example, Harry is suspected of being the Heir of Slytherin due to his ability to speak Parseltongue (he can converse with snakes), "the mark of a Dark wizard" (Year 2, 199). Children who are marked by difference may isolate themselves or be made to feel excluded in their peer group culture because of labeling and stigmatization (Aitken 2001; James 1993). In *Chamber of Secrets*, the label of the "Heir of Slytherin" only dissolves when a member of his close peer group, Hermione, is attacked by the snake monster living in the bowels of Hogwarts. With this case, as all others listed above, trust-based vulnerability emerges from one specific thread that binds Harry's peer group culture together at Hogwarts, and that is the meaning and value of secrecy.

SPACES OF SECRECY, PLACES OF RESISTANCE

Just as secrets abound in the Harry Potter books, so do they infiltrate children's peer groups in the real world. Time and again, research with children finds that secrets serve as the test that enables friendships to form, the glue that holds them together, and the risk that tears them apart. Perhaps the reason J.K. Rowling places such value on secrets in the Harry Potter series is because childhood is "represented as a secret and protected world" to and by adults (James 1993, 89). Harry's close friendships are all-encompassed and all-consumed by his secrets, items that create "a reality of trust" and function as "social currency," indicators of the closeness of their bonds and the intimacy shared between friends (Merten 1999, 132; Milner 2004). The clearest example of the linkage between friendship and secrecy in Harry's peer culture occurs in Grimmauld Place. In *Order of the Phoenix*, Harry's godfather, Sirius Black, decides he will allow Harry access to Order secrets (an adult-occupied social and militarized space), while Ron's mother forbids all other children in the home from hearing the information. They are incensed since this kind of selectivity displayed by adults goes against the desire of children to have fair access to information, preventing them from agentically, impactfully, and collectively contributing to society (Hill 2006). As such, Ron protests his mother's decision in the following exchange:

"Harry'll tell me and Hermione everything you say anyway!" said Ron hotly.
  "Won't—won't you?" he added uncertainly, meeting Harry's eyes.
For a split second, Harry considered telling Ron that he wouldn't tell him a
  single word, that he could try a taste of being kept in the dark and see how
  he liked it. But the nasty impulse vanished as they looked at each other.
"'Course I will," Harry said. Ron and Hermione beamed. (Year 5, 91)

The secrets Harry, Ron, and Hermione attempt to keep hold of or gain access to grow in complexity as they age (see Way 2006). The secrets of the Order are controlled so tightly by adults that the children must agentically resort to using a variety of "highly innovative access strategies" to break through adults' attempts to keep information from them, as the territory of "too young" that Mrs. Weasley socially maps out for the children is not an area they "wish to occupy" (Corsaro 1992, 172; Gillis 2008, 327). They throw Dungbombs at the door and use Extendable Ears (invented by the Weasley twins) to eavesdrop on adult conversations—efforts to retrieve information, however surreptitiously gained, that encompass the adult Order's secrets. Therefore, Harry's peer group employs children's material culture and capital to agentically negotiate through the constraints and conditions placed upon them, utilizing interpretive reproduction to take, reject, or adapt to roles set forth by adults (see Corsaro 2015; Zeiher 2003). In consequence, these efforts vary throughout the Harry Potter series, depending on how much adults tell the children and how much they still want to know.

The aura of secrecy surrounding Harry's peer group culture is further presented through children's material culture and children's places of resistance. Items related to the importance of secrecy in Harry's peer group begin to arrive during his first year at Hogwarts. For Christmas, he receives an Invisibility Cloak from an anonymous source.[14] In the final book, this cloak is revealed to be an extremely rare and powerful wizarding cultural artifact—one of three Deathly Hallows—with Dumbledore explaining, "the true magic of which, of course, is that it can be used to protect and shield others as well as its owner" (Year 7, 716).[15] Harry, Ron, and Hermione put this cloak to much use over the years, prowling around Hogwarts at night to a variety of ends, including emotionally supporting Hagrid, investigating suspicious activity in their school, and solving a host of problems and mysteries. The second artifact that assists Harry's peer group in their secret explorations of the school, and later their ability to monitor the school for infiltrators, is the Marauder's Map. Ron's older twin brothers and fellow Gryffindors give Harry the map because they believe his need for it is far greater than theirs—they are aware of the heightened adult protectionism that is frequently foisted on Harry by various magical adults and Ministry officials. A highly valued item covertly appropriated from a file kept by the school's cantankerous caretaker, the brothers state, "This little beauty's taught us more than all the teachers in this school" (Year 3, 192). With the combination of this secret map, the cloak, and his agentic spirit, Harry avoids the watchful eyes of (and Secrecy Sensors/Probity Probes employed by) adults at the school.[16] Thus, he circumvents rules set forth by magical adults in power, each holding a thinly veiled agenda to continue the islanding of Harry Potter.

Most interesting, this valuable map is the truest piece of children's material culture and children's geographies product that can exist since it was made by children; many years prior, Harry's father and his peer group created it when they were students at Hogwarts, all members of Gryffindor House. In this item of children's material culture, we find Harry, his close friends, and his extended Gryffindor peer group (and those who came before them) shape their roles as individuals and as a united culture, creating new ways of enacting agency in socially altered spaces (see Corsaro 2015; Frønes 1994; James and James 2004). What the map gave previous generations, and subsequently allots Harry and his close friends, is an agentic, specialized, and secret spatial knowledge of the school and all those inhabiting it (see Christensen and Prout 2003). Just as the Invisibility Cloak is meant to be used, in *Deathly Hallows* Harry puts the Marauder's Map to its final magical purpose—Harry frequently looks at the map to assure himself that his close and extended peer group members are safe and protected at Hogwarts while he is on the hunt for horcruxes. The Marauder's Map, then, serves as a symbol of growth for Harry, his friendships, and his peer culture. As Christensen and Prout (2003) explain, "children map their experiences and memories of growing up on to spaces .... Their changing mobility in and between these different spaces and their bodily experience of them was important to how they saw themselves for achieving independence, competence and maturity and to how they formed and sustained their social relations with peers" (140). Therefore, children's material culture is physically, socially, and emotionally connected to their identity formation in and out of friendship, while items such as the Invisibility Cloak and the Marauder's Map serve to solidify elements of secrecy and interpretive reproduction, inspiring agency in children's peer cultures at Hogwarts.[17]

The spaces of shared secrecy between Harry, Ron, and Hermione are many. Using the Invisibility Cloak and the Marauder's Map, they explore the castle and grounds of Hogwarts with little to no ramifications afterward (though many times they are nearly caught and/or punished for being out of bed at night). Perhaps most central to Hogwarts students' bonding rituals, formulated through secret sharing, are the spaces they occupy while doing so. Each of these spaces is "everyday" for children in boarding school: classrooms, dormitories, and grounds. On many occasions, the friends take advantage of the din in practice-based classes, time in between classes, bustle during meals, or empty common spaces to share information and make plans. The following excerpt (among many in the series) from *Harry Potter and the Half-Blood Prince* (2005) exemplifies the intensity of the friends' secrets as well as their peer culture's growing magical abilities to agentically keep secrets from being overheard by adults and out-of-peer-circle students. While in one of their louder practice-based classes, "Harry told Ron and Hermione everything that had happened during next morning's Charm's lesson (having first cast the *Muffliato* spell upon those nearest them)" (Year 6, 513). Rendering recipients temporarily deaf, the *Muffliato* spell is, once again, an example of children's material culture passed down over generations—in this case, appropriated by Harry from his used Potions book, a spell created by Professor Snape while he was a student at Hogwarts.[18] In addition, with this spell the friends are able to alter the physical and social space of the classroom to match their needs, reflecting that children's peer cultures and the adult-run spaces in which they reside are not "forever fixed, solidified in place, but open to change" (Holloway and Valentine 2000b, 773).

The least fixed and most changeable space at Hogwarts, used many times by Harry and his larger peer culture network, is the Room of Requirement. The room, a secret to all who do not know it exists, does not even appear on the Marauder's Map, which I believe implies that Harry's father and his peer group never found it during their vast exploration of Hogwarts and its grounds.[19] The location of and instructions for entry into the secret Room of Requirement are provided to Harry by Dobby in *Order of the Phoenix*, solving an issue Harry and his peers contend with throughout Year 5 and others—that childhood "is that status of personhood which is by definition often in the wrong place" (James, Jenks, and Prout 1998, 37). Harry and his peer network adapt the Room of Requirement to fit their culture's needs, agentically converting it into a new space for their own uses (see Leverett 2011). This room becomes particularly meaningful to Harry, as he appropriates the space to resist dictums handed down by the Ministry of Magic via the detested Professor/Headmistress Umbridge in *Order of the Phoenix*. Forming Dumbledore's Army (the D.A.) at the urging of Hermione, Harry converts the room into a training ground to teach his peers from Gryffindor (as well as select students from other years and Hogwarts Houses) how to protect themselves from and fight against the Dark Arts. When children actively and agentically construct their surroundings, "they make their own meanings about these localities through their own practices and discussions. Their practices may make new meanings, different from those of older generations and specific to children's own emplaced knowledge that is also situated in time" (Christensen and Prout 2003, 152).

Interpretive reproduction and agency abound in the creation of the D.A. The group comes together in resistance to adult rules, they have their first meeting in the Hog's Head (an "adult" dive bar in Hogsmeade), and they hold secret group meetings throughout Year Five. Harry and his friends and allies embark on this organizing mission even though they are banned from doing so by Umbridge and the Ministry of Magic via Educational Decree Number Twenty-Four: "All Student Organizations, Societies, Teams, Groups, and Clubs are henceforth disbanded" (Year 5, 351). The D.A. is extremely significant given that its formation is the one clear instance, prior to *Deathly Hallows*, when various students from three of the four Hogwarts Houses unite for a cause, supporting one another in a peer-based learning environment for the common good of the whole. In fact, the structure of the D.A. as a secret club is indicative of the interrelationship between interpretive reproduction, agency, and the importance of sharing secrets for children: "Sharing secrets involves activities ranging from verbal whispering to the writing and passing of notes, the establishment of secret clubs, and the production of complex texts and artifacts. The whispering talk and control of space marks the fact that members of a secret club are part of an exclusive group" (Corsaro 2015, 235).[20]

Hermione's role in secretly organizing members and coordinating meetings of the D.A. clearly reflects interpretive reproduction of adult rules and customs for subversive and agentic use in children's peer culture. Under the watchful eye of Umbridge, Hermione devises "a very clever method of communicating the time and date of the next meeting to all the members . . . because it would look so suspicious if people from different Houses were seen crossing the Great Hall to talk to each other too often" (Year 5, 398). By using fake coins and a Protean Charm, she enables Harry to alter the date and time on his coin, which changes the time and date for meetings on all other D.A. peer members' coins. In this informational exchange, the coins warm when updated, which reminds Harry of "The Death Eaters' scars. Voldemort touches one of them, and all their scars burn, and they know they've got to join him," to which Hermione responds, "That *is* where I got the idea from" (Year 5, 399). So, Hermione utilizes interpretive reproduction, appropriating adult maladaptive culture from Voldemort and his dreaded followers. In doing so, she creates altogether better moralistic, supportive, and educational agentic uses of similar magic within her own youth peer culture's resistance to the ruling adult establishment and threats stemming from Voldemort's return. Hermione's coins, Harry's lessons, and the meetings students (those deemed trustworthy) attend contribute to a very strong D.A. peer group identity that is agentically formed around their self-made "local laws of belonging" (Hearst 2004, 251).

As Harry's knowledge of the Room of Requirement and how it works expands, enabling him to further create and define the space, he builds meaningful relationships affiliated with the room, the D.A., and his expanding peer culture (see Rasmussen 2004). Moreover, the Room of Requirement becomes different things to different people, depending on need or desire. Harry experiences students joining together there as a powerful emotion, his first kiss there as a protected emotion, and the group getting caught by Umbridge there as a terrifying emotion. The Room of Requirement later serves the growing D.A. peer culture in *Deathly Hallows*, transforming into a refuge/hideout/dormitory space for all children who need it in response to their agentic efforts to resist and confront Voldemort's abusive Death Eaters, who are now running Hogwarts:

> He did not recognize the room at all. It was enormous, and looked rather like the interior of a particularly sumptuous tree house, or perhaps a gigantic ship's cabin. Multicolored hammocks were strung from the ceiling and from a balcony that ran around the dark wood-paneled and windowless walls, which were covered in bright tapestry hangings . . . . There were bulging bookcases, a few broomsticks propped against the walls, and in the corner, a large wooden-cased wireless. (Year 7, 577)

Harry's longtime roommate Neville Longbottom takes control of the space in *Deathly Hallows*, and quiet, forgetful, clumsy, ineffectual Neville transforms just as much as the Room of Requirement does. In Harry's absence, Neville becomes the leader of the D.A., uses Hermione's coins to communicate with youth D.A. and adult Order of the Phoenix members, and gains the respect of all by agentically standing up to the Death Eaters and, later, Voldemort himself. Importantly, Neville learns the room cannot be entered by Death Eaters/Hogwarts faculty members as long as a student remains inside—a Room of Requirement secret Harry never discovered.[21]

In this way, the Room of Requirement is an interactive and liminal childhood space and, therefore, in need of protection by children (see Corsaro 2015). By providing an interactive peer culture space, the Room of Requirement is fragile since, "children's places do not last forever" (Musolf 1996; Rasmussen 2004, 166). Ultimately, the Room of Requirement is destroyed by Fiendfyre: called forth by one of Draco's Slytherin sidekicks, the dangerous, cursed fire reflects this fragility—not only of the room but of childhood itself. For the room at that specific point in time is filled with the material culture of past generations of Hogwart's students—a towering city ("*the place where everything is hidden*," Year 7, 627), walls piled high with questionable ephemera and oddments centuries of children did not wish to be caught with in their school's hallowed halls. Adding to the metaphor, while not caused by the fire, on the very next page of the book one of the Weasley twins dies in the battle to save Hogwarts. The devastating loss of Fred is enough to make Harry lose all optimism in his fight against Voldemort: "The world had ended, so why had the battle not ceased, the castle fallen silent in horror, and every combatant laid down their arms? Harry's mind was in a free fall, spinning out of control" (Year 7, 638). When he sees a hundred Dementors approaching and cannot find the strength to protect Ron, Hermione, or D.A. peers, it is Luna Lovegood who is the catalyst to summon his hope/Patronus (a protective spirit animal) in *Deathly Hallows*:

"That's right," said Luna encouragingly, as if they were back in the Room of Requirement and this was simply spell practice for the D.A. "That's right, Harry . . . come on, think of something happy . . . ."
"Something happy?" he said, his voice cracked.
"We're all still here," she whispered, "we're still fighting. Come on, now . . . ."
There was a silver spark, then a wavering light, and then, with the greatest effort it had ever cost him, the stag burst from the end of Harry's wand. (Year 7, 649)

CONTEXTUALIZING FRIENDSHIP: LUNA LOVEGOOD

Of all Harry's friends and members of his close or extended peer culture, Luna is Harry's touchstone, the singular person who can ignite his light when no one or nothing else can. Cockrell (2002) states that Voldemort is "Harry's shadow side, his dark twin" (20); if this is the case, then Luna Lovegood is Harry's bright side, his light twin.[22] Luna is the only close friend Harry makes after being at Hogwarts for several years—a member of Ravenclaw House, and a year younger than him, Harry fittingly meets Luna for the first time on the Hogwarts Express. Like Harry, Luna is marked in her appearance throughout the series, though most of these indicators are by her own design: wearing brightly colored dress robes, earrings made of radishes, and a butterbeer cap necklace; carrying around Gurdyroots; and storing her wand behind her ear. She also strongly believes in many things that are "unproven" to exist by most witches and wizards: Crumple-Horned Snorkacks, Blibbering Humdingers, Nargles, Heliopaths, Wrackspurts, and Gulping Plimpies. Just as Luna is known around Hogwarts as "Loony" Lovegood, earlier in the summer of *Order of the Phoenix* (not coincidentally, the same year he meets Luna), Hermione informs Harry that the wizarding newspaper *The Daily Prophet* keeps "slipping in snide comments about you. If some far-fetched story appears they say something like 'a tale worthy of Harry Potter' .... They want wizards on the street to think you're just some stupid boy who's a bit of a joke, who tells ridiculous tall stories" (Year 5, 74).

For these reasons, both Harry and Luna are marked out as heterogeneous and contradictory by the majority of the students and their peer cultures at Hogwarts, giving Harry and Luna a "sense of shared social positioning and experience" (Mayall 2002, 123; Mortier 2002). The affinity between Harry and Luna is rooted in their inability to completely blend into Hogwart's peer cultures since cultural and communal belonging are critically linked to children's understandings of belongingness (Hearst 2004). Luna's unique gift to believe in what others do not or cannot initially draws Harry and Luna together: by witnessing death, they both see winged Thestrals pulling the Hogwarts carriages. Since neither Ron nor Hermione see these skeletal creatures, as they never experienced death and thus do not suffer from "dark marks" on their psyches, Harry clings to Luna's ability to see the unseen:

"Can't . . . can't you see them?"
"See what?"
Can't you see what's pulling the carriages?"
Ron looked seriously alarmed now.
"Are you feeling all right, Harry?"
. . .
"It's all right," said a dreamy voice from beside Harry as Ron vanished into the coach's dark interior. "You're not going mad or anything. I can see them too."
"Can you?" said Harry desperately, turning to Luna. He could see the bat-winged horses reflected in her wide, silvery eyes.
"Oh yes," said Luna, "I've been able to see them ever since my first day here. They've always pulled the carriages. Don't worry. You're just as sane as I am." (Year 5, 198–9)

Luna validates Harry multiple times throughout the series in ways that are closely bound to their shared feelings and experiences inside and outside of Hogwarts. Through their authenticity and honest self-disclosure, Harry and Luna build a sophisticated relationship based on the foundations of validation and emotional support—core elements of friendship for children (Asher, Guerry, and McDonald 2014). The significance of mirroring is highlighted in psychological research on friendships, and I suggest Harry and Luna are important relational mirrors to one another. For, just as Harry sees "the bat-winged horses reflected in her wide, silvery eyes," Lillian Rubin (1985) explains in her classic treatise on friendship:

> We learn much about ourselves in our relationships with friends—learning that comes partly at least from who they are, how they respond to us, *what we see reflected in their eyes*. For friends become for us a mirror on the self; and what we see there, whether it pleasures or pains us, helps to affirm those parts of self we like and respect and to change those whose reflection brings us discomfort. (Rubin 1985, 40–1, italics added)

In the relational mirroring that grows between them through the latter parts of the series, Luna and Harry develop "greater self-knowledge through a process of mutual reflection," a source of compassion and acceptance, support and unspoken trust, and understanding and mutual intimacy (Corsaro and Eder 1990, 207).

Later in *Order of the Phoenix*, Luna joins Harry on the doomed quest to save his Godfather Sirius at the Ministry of Magic. She is the one who suggests using the Thestrals "to overcome the spatial distances involved" (Zeiher 2003, 68) in getting the children to the Ministry from Hogwarts. This agentic solution enables their peer group to have "far more contact with different sections of society" than most other adults (Olwig and Gulløv 2003, 8), as the Department of Mysteries with its "fabled" Hall of Prophecy remains rumor/tall tale to the greater adult magical community.[23] The fact that both Harry and Luna can hear voices behind the veil in the dais room at the Department of Mysteries furthers the bond between the two, as pragmatic Hermione, in particular, denies the existence of any voices "in there" (Year 5, 774). Both Hermione and Ron have a very hard time accepting Luna into the peer culture they share with Harry. Hermione is described by Luna's father as "painfully limited. Narrow. Close-minded" (Year 7, 410). In clear evidence of her character deficiencies, when discussing Luna, Hermione tells Harry, "you can do better than her" since, "apparently she'll only believe in things as long as there's no proof at all" (Year 5, 262). Ron, for the greater part of the series, continues to call Luna "Loony," skeptical of the friendship Harry and Luna form. So, just as Harry represents the same to his peers at Hogwarts and the larger magical community, in Luna, Harry finds a friend who embodies "the knowable and unknowable, the familiar and the strange, the close and the distance" (Jones 2009, 197).

Harry is inconsolable after Sirius's death, and yet his connection with Luna grows when he discovers that Luna's mother died a few years prior and that Luna is bullied by her fellow Ravenclaws. As both his parents were killed by Voldemort and Harry is tormented ad nauseam by his cousin Dudley, Draco Malfoy, and Draco's Slytherin allies, Luna's experiences harken back to his own. Due to these convergences, Harry and Luna are considered "among society's most vulnerable members," with similar stories of being friendless children attempting later in life to make friends (Ennew 2005, 128; James 1993). By connecting with her (he "found that for some reason he did not mind Luna talking about Sirius"), discussing the bullying ("'How come people hide your stuff?' . . . 'I think they think I'm a bit odd, you know. Some people call me "Loony" Lovegood, actually' . . . 'That's no reason for them to take your things'") and the potential of the voices behind the veil ("'They were just lurking out of sight, that's all. You heard them' . . . . Harry did not know what to say, or to think. Luna believed so many extraordinary things"), Harry discovers "the terrible weight in his stomach seemed to have lessened slightly" (Year 5, 862–4). Luna places Harry in a pivotal position of creating a friendship with her that "cuts to the heart of the multidirectionality of friendships and their recursive, rather than single, parallel, or dual influences in children's lives" (Deegan 1996, 13). In Luna, Harry finally has a friend with whom peer connection, cultural acceptance, and the personal importance of the relationship are clearly not unidirectional.

In all Harry's other friendships, connections are created, in great part, by shared experiences commonly starting school together as Gryffindors. Luna, however, is a friend he individually and agentically chooses, ignoring the incredulous questioning of others in his close circle. This friendship with Luna reflects Harry's growing interactional competence in making friends, showing he is "increasingly capable of taking the role of the other, developing the 'looking-glass self,' and competently aligning [his] actions with others" (Adler and Adler 1998, 10). When his elf-friend Dobby is killed in *Deathly Hallows* Harry is devastated, unable to express his loss in words. While Harry digs the grave and sets the gravestone, he cannot bring himself to say anything but "Good-bye Dobby" at the small, makeshift funeral (Year 7, 480). Luna is the one who closes Dobby's eyes and she is the person who speaks of Dobby's "good and brave" character, thanking him for saving them from Death Eaters—in these words, Harry finds solace in Luna, who "said it all for him" (Year 7, 480).

The emotions Harry and Luna share in their friendship are deeply rooted not just in sorrow, but equally in mirth. Luna, more than any other character in the Harry Potter series, lightens Harry's mood and, significantly, she is the only one who engenders his joyous laughter. In *Half-Blood Prince*, Harry invites Luna to accompany him to a party (one he is desperate to avoid) without consciously recognizing why. Once Luna tells tale to adult partygoers of the Aurors' Rotfang Conspiracy, a plan to "bring down the Ministry of Magic from within using a combination of Dark Magic and gum disease," Harry nearly chokes on his drink from laughing and he realizes, "Really, it had been worth bringing Luna just for this" (Year 6, p. 320).[24] Indeed, she displays "one of the most valuable skills in children's peer culture—the ability to make people laugh" (Eder, Evans, and Parker 1995, 169). Related, Luna's gift of providing levity in a variety of seemingly dire situations ultimately brings Ron to wholeheartedly accept her as part of their friendship group, for her contribution to their peer culture through laughter is what Ron admires most about Luna.

Luna and Harry's connection is indicative of friendship being "the key to children's meaning-making," wherein their relationship is characterized by clear commitment to one another and high levels of emotional investment (James 1993; Wyness 2006, 174). This bond between the two is highlighted several times in *Deathly Hallows*—in addition to her pivotal role at Dobby's funeral, earlier in the book Luna immediately sees through Harry's complete body-transforming Polyjuice Potion disguise. When Harry wonders how she does it, Luna states it is "just your expression" (Year 7, 140). And, prior to the final battle at Hogwarts, Harry shields Luna with his Invisibility Cloak; notably, she is the only other friend, outside of Ron and Hermione, who receives this honor in the whole of the series.[25] Harry's friendship to Luna is meaningful, and he knows it because Luna tells him in various ways. In *Half-Blood Prince*, she is excited to get the party invitation from him, exclaiming, "I'd love to go with you as friends! . . . Nobody's ever asked me to a party before, as a friend!" (Year 6, 311). In *Deathly Hallows*, when Harry, Hermione, and Ron visit the home Luna shares with her father, Harry sees that "Luna had decorated her bedroom ceiling with five beautifully painted faces: Harry, Ron, Hermione, Ginny [Ron's sister], and Neville . . . there was a certain magic about them . . . Harry thought they breathed" (Year 7, 417). On closer inspection, he sees there are words surrounding the mural "repeated a thousand times in golden ink: friends . . . friends . . . friends . . . " (Year 7, 417). After seeing her artwork, "Harry felt a great rush of affection for Luna" (Year 7, 417). The important close, meaningful friendship connection Luna makes with Gryffindor peers at Hogwarts is pointedly evident in this bedroom mural, given no Ravenclaws are depicted.[26] In Luna, Harry can finally "distinguish the experience of being friends from that of having friends" (James 1993, 209). Because Luna can see through him, see inside him, reach the depths of his despair and the heights of his glee, Harry realizes that being Luna's friend is just as important to him as having Luna as a friend, something I am not quite sure he comes to terms with in his friendships with Ron and Hermione.

HOGWARTS, A LARGE CHILDREN'S ISLAND?

Concluding my examination of the Harry Potter series, I am faced with the complicated question of whether or not Hogwarts School of Witchcraft and Wizardry is presented as a large children's island, and, if so, how this islanding impacts agentic expression for the students enrolled. Large children's islands are locations constituted by special opportunities, where children may seek out and nurture social connections, particularly friendships (Zeiher 2001). At the same time, "Classic children's literature is frequently structured around a geography or location that separates events from the wider, everyday and (implicitly adult) world. The staging of stories on island locations allows an unfolding of events that are largely untroubled by external affairs and that enfold place and narrative as a unified whole" (Blundell 2016, 18). If children's literature purposely islands children to highlight the importance of their friendships, agency, and peer cultures, then Hogwarts is certainly a good place to do so. However, contrary to Blundell's (2016) assertion, Harry and his friends frequently contend with "troubling external affairs" radiating out from the adult world, and the teachers of Hogwarts are, in the main, supportive of peer culture strategies that are agentically and creatively employed by children in resistance to adult oppression.

Teachers will relax school rule enforcement if they recognize the creativity and agency of children's peer cultures (Corsaro 1992). Nowhere in the Harry Potter series is this exchange clearer than in *Order of the Phoenix* when Harry gives an interview that, when published, is banned by Professor Umbridge with threats of school removal by Educational Decree Number Twenty-Seven ("Any student found in possession of the magazine *The Quibbler* will be expelled," Year 5, 581). The agentic children of Hogwarts creatively appropriate magic through the process of interpretive reproduction in pursuit of reading the article and gaining knowledge: "students were several steps ahead of her. The pages carrying Harry's interview had been bewitched to resemble extracts from textbooks if anyone but themselves read it, or else wiped magically blank until they wanted to peruse it again. Soon it seemed that every single person in the school had read it" (Year 5, 581–2). Harry receives small token gifts from Hogwarts teachers who appreciate the efforts he and his friends put forth in getting the true story of Voldemort's return out to the wider magical community. Though forbidden to discuss it per Educational Decree Number Twenty-Six ("Teachers are hereby banned from giving students any information that is not strictly related to the subjects they are paid to teach," Year 5, 551), Harry is awarded extra points, given candy, and told he will live a long, reproductive life by various teachers at Hogwarts in response to the article. So, children find help and support in their agency from adults and the larger Hogwarts structure when they present a collective front as students, in many cases efforts forged "in overt opposition to the power of adults" (Mayall 2008, 122).

Therefore, there is salient generational interplay between children's peer cultures fighting against adult rules and adults working with, or at least not prohibiting, attempts by children to find spaces to meaningfully participate, with children enacting agency through negotiation, compromise, and reasoning with those very same adults (Castro 2017, 2019). Dumbledore leads this charge at Hogwarts with the oft-repeated series statement, "Help will always be given at Hogwarts to those who ask for it" (Year 2, 264). While Harry believes his secrets and experiences at Hogwarts are his own, it is revealed that is not exactly true—nearly all of Harry's secrets only remain thus to children outside his close peer culture and to some, but not all, adults. As Dumbledore informs Harry, "I have watched you more closely than you can have imagined . . . . I have watched you struggling under more burdens than any student who has ever passed through this school" (Year 5, 839). For as much as Dumbledore endeavors to enshroud Harry with a blanket of protectionism in "the real world," he views Harry's childhood at Hogwarts "as a protected social space" to test his agency and navigate his vulnerabilities, as well as "a training camp for adulthood" (Shanahan 2007, 422).

After all, Hogwarts is, ultimately, a school to educate future adult wizards and witches. While schools are "children's spaces," they are also "associative spaces" where children and adults work together, forming "understandings and assumptions premised on a sharing of the same (cultural and physical) space" (Hall, Coffey, and Williamson 1999, 509; Petrie 2011, 132). Issues surrounding belongingness, citizenship, participation, and shared identity at Hogwarts are presented in the "spirit of democracy and dialogue, with children being seen as strong, powerful and competent, in a joint enterprise with the adults, but also respected as children with their own distinct culture and interests" (Hall, Coffey, and Williamson 1999; Petrie 2011, 132). This democracy of collaboration exists alongside children's efforts to agentically transform information appropriated from adults through interpretive reproduction. The fruits of this process can address concerns, fears, ambiguities, and conflicts in peer cultures—feelings that often arise from children's experiences in adult-structured environments (Corsaro 2015; Corsaro and Eder 1990). Taken together, I do believe Hogwarts is a large children's island, though, as discussed earlier, the islanding of children can only occur with the explicit participation of adults in power. So, Harry's school may be a children's island, but the teachers of Hogwarts willingly interact, corroborate, and, at times, directly dialogue with the insulated and protectionist construction of its halls, classrooms, dormitories, and grounds.[27] Occasionally, Hogwarts teachers and staff acknowledge they do not have as much discursive power as the larger body of children housed within—students and friends who agentically utilize interpretive reproduction within their peer cultures for better social and relational futures in the wizarding world.

Having friends at school allows children to manage rules of teachers, negotiate school agendas, and help one another enjoy their time there (Mayall 2000). Since friendship is "one of the great equalizers" at school, these relationships provide an overarching feeling of safety within children's peer cultures (Adler and Adler 1998, 156). Berry Mayall (2002) states that the reason the Harry Potter series is so popular with children is because they "identify strongly with children's agency as a social group, and enjoy stories which give power of independent action to children, in contradistinction to much of ordinary life where they are subject to adult authority" (30). J.K. Rowling's series depicts Harry and his peers gaining great insight and authority from lived experiences during specific moments in time while at Hogwarts and beyond (see Castro 2005). Utilizing interpretive reproduction to negotiate imbalances of power inside and outside of Hogwarts, Harry, Hermione, Ron, Luna, Neville, and a host of other students make sense of their worlds and discover that children's islands are navigable, changeable, and escapable. The peer cultures that grow give birth to feelings of belongingness and shared agentic participation, transforming Harry Potter from "The Boy Who Lived" into, accompanied by his friends, "The Boy Who Lives."

NOTES

1. Zeiher (2003) and Rasmussen (2004) refer to these three locations as the "institutional triangle" commonly found in children's lives.

2. The Ministry of Magic is the political entity that oversees all magical people, places, and things associated with wizardry in Great Britain. Diagon Alley and the Village of Hogsmeade are shopping districts frequented by wizards, witches, and advanced students for their magical needs and wants. A muggle is a non-magical person.

3. For the remainder of this chapter, quotes will be referenced by Harry Potter's school year in the J.K. Rowling series instead of author name and publication date for clarity and sense of time progression in the lives of youth in the series.

4. This blood protection is presumably also found in cousin Dudley, perhaps why Harry and Dudley easily survive the alleyway Dementor attack in Little Whinging in *Order of the Phoenix*. Dementors are dangerous entities who guard the wizard prison but eventually join the ranks of Voldemort. Voldemort is a powerful

dark wizard who killed Harry's mother, father, and countless others. He tried to kill Harry as a baby but the killing curse backfired, which sent Voldemort into hiding for many years to heal, leaving Harry with the lightning scar on his forehead. Voldemort returns to magical society in Year 1, eventually rejoined by his loyal band of witch and wizard followers called Death Eaters, leading to vast death and destruction throughout the series.

5. In the series, Harry discovers the existence of and forms a bond with his Godfather Sirius Black; Harry also comes to closely align with Ron's family, spending much time at the Weasley home, the Burrow, located outside Ottery St. Catchpole. Ron's parents think of Harry as one of their own, evident by Mrs. Weasley proclaiming in front of Harry's peers and various adults (including Sirius) that he is "as good as" her son (Year 5, 90). Interestingly, Hermione Granger's home locale is never indicated in the books, and during school breaks she often travels with her parents or is invited to stay at the Burrow. At the same time, the fact that her home residence is never revealed, and she travels much more than Harry or Ron, reveals three things: (1) both of her parents are dentists, so we can assume the Grangers are a much wealthier family than the Weasleys or the Dursleys; (2) Hermione is perhaps the most liminal of the trio, given her opportunities to travel with ease; and (3) not giving Hermione a home address perhaps contributes to the gendered message discrepancies Rowling constructs between Hermione and Harry/Ron (see note 10 for more).

6. In their examination of home and family themes in the Harry Potter series, Kornfeld and Prothro (2003) note the relationship between Harry, Hermione, and Ron is based on the same "protective factors" found in resilient family units (194).

7. The Houses of Hogwarts represent various personality traits of students: Ravenclaw for intellect, reason, and wit (characterized as the smartest students); Slytherin for ambition, cunning, and resourcefulness (known to produce many evil witches and wizards); and Hufflepuff for hard work, loyalty, and patience (often thought of as the leftover students).

8. The Triwizard Tournament is comprised of three tasks set to Champions from three international magic schools, including Hogwarts. Through adult deception, Harry is entered into the tournament without his knowledge or consent. Though not meeting the age requirement (he is fourteen years old, and the minimum age is seventeen), Harry wins the Triwizard Tournament, but at great cost—a second Hogwarts Champion from Hufflepuff is killed by Voldemort in the process. Interestingly, many of my friends who are parents delay reading *Goblet of Fire* to their children or try to stop their children from reading *Goblet of Fire* for as long as possible under the guise of protectionism, as they "hear" or "know" the Year 4 book is very dark and scary compared to the previous three novels.

9. The bulk of Year 6 is spent searching for information about Voldemort, culminating in the discovery that Voldemort severed his soul into multiple parts, each housed within a horcrux. Year 7, Harry, Hermione, and Ron search for the horcruxes with the intent to destroy them all, as Voldemort cannot be killed if any of his horcruxes remain.

10. In this book passage, it is revealed that Ron always suspected Harry and Hermione had unexpressed romantic feelings toward each other, but Harry explains

that he loves her like a sister. Unfortunately, while Rowling depicts, in detail, Harry and Ron destroying horcruxes, Hermione destroying a horcrux is merely, and quite briefly, described to Harry by Ron in the last installment. Since the only scenes detailed outside of Harry's immediate physical or psychic viewpoint are those of adults (always via the first chapter of a book installment when this tool is used by Rowling), and Hermione destroys the horcrux with only Ron as a witness, this missing scene is explained as far as the narrative structure of the series goes. Regrettably, in the instance of horcruxes, the reader therefore gets very clearly depicted messages regarding boys' agency in action against evil and for freedom, but does not receive the same message about girls.

11. While Murray Milner (2004) was not speaking at all of Harry Potter in his study of peer cultures and identity in school, this theory exactly reflects Harry's place and peer point-of-perspective at Hogwarts.

12. Grimmauld Place is Sirius's childhood home and headquarters of the Order of the Phoenix. Since Sirius's immediate relatives are all dead, he has no children, and Harry is Sirius's only godchild, Harry inherits Grimmauld Place and the rest of his godfather's vast assets after Sirius is killed.

13. Harry also hides his emotions from his family of origin, but primarily to protect his own interests instead of the Dursleys.

14. Belonging to his late father, the Invisibility Cloak gift-giver is later revealed to be Dumbledore, providing a good example of how children's agency can work in consort with adult cooperation or intervention (see Castro 2017 and 2019 for more on generationalism and agency).

15. The Deathly Hallows include the Invisibility Cloak, the Resurrection Stone (can bring back an echoic spirit of anyone dead), and the Elder Wand/Wand of Destiny/Deathstick (the most powerful wand known to exist). Harry comes to possess all three in the last book, making him "Master of Death." As the cloak has been passed down through his family, beginning with its original owner, for untold generations, he chooses to keep the Invisibility Cloak and discards the other two Hallows.

16. Chappell (2008) states that the Marauder's Map, Invisibility Cloak, and Room of Requirement allow the students of Hogwarts to resist "control imposed over their bodies" (287).

17. Children's material culture and secret-keeping are linked when considering real-world children's peer cultures. For example, agentic creativity found in note-passing, the secret folding of notes, and alternative coded language is enacted by children to communicate secretly, especially in schools—these are children's peer material culture products symbolizing the creativity that can be found in their close friendships built on trust and group belongingness.

18. One area I wonder about across the Harry Potter series is the invention of magical spells or the creation of artifacts. A previous generation of students, which encompassed Harry's father and his school friends (Sirius Black, Remus Lupin, and Peter Pettigrew/Wormtail) and Professor Snape, were quite adept at inventing their own magic when they attended Hogwarts. While Ron's twin brothers create new magic, Harry, Ron, and Hermione, however, do not seem to do so throughout the series. That said, Hermione's Protean Charm and other magical solutions Harry and his friends

enact display their abilities to interpretively reproduce existing magic. Therefore, one could argue Harry's peer group is more agentically adept at understanding the relational magic found in sharing and trust in comparison to generations that came before them at Hogwarts. This deficit, of course, is clearly evident in Dumbledore's early friendship with Voldemort's evil wizard predecessor Grindelwald, a relationship in part based on greed and power instead of sharing and compassion, as well as the fissure that occurred between Harry's father and his school peer group post-graduation. Each friend deeply mistrusting one another during the "dark times," changing the Potter's "Secret Keeper" from Sirius to Wormtail, Wormtail turning into a Death Eater, and Wormtail releasing the Potter's location to Voldemort together as one ultimately caused the deaths of Harry's parents. In Year 3, when Harry learns of the truth regarding the person who betrayed his parents, Sirius clearly recognizes this connection because while he did not divulge the information to Voldemort, he states that he does not deny that he killed Harry's parents (indirectly through his participation in the above furtive actions, based on the mistrust/misplaced trust of friends, of course).

19. Fans of Harry Potter agree on the possibility of this take on the relationship between the room and the creation of the map, though it is also believed the room is unplottable (Harry Potter Wiki, n.d.).

20. Relatedly, in his hallmark study of youth peer cultures, Milner (2004) states, "Sharing secrets with someone is a sign of intimacy and trust. Conversely, those not let in on the secret are kept at a distance. Often secrets involve some kind of deviance. The most obvious example is the secrets that adolescents do not want parents, teachers, and other adults to know" (70). Milner (2004) goes on to explain that "Secrets also divide teenagers; they should be shared with friends and members of your clique or crowd ... keeping secret information about the time and locale of social events is a key means of status differentiation. On the other hand, breaking a confidence is a form of disrespect, and frequently is associated with rejection and exclusion" (70). In evidence of this process, one less-liked member of the D.A. (Marietta, a Ravenclaw) breaks the peer-established rules of the group and informs Umbridge of the time and location of their next meeting, leading to the capture of Harry, Ron, Hermione, Neville, Ginny, and Luna outside of the Room of Requirement. As a result of breeching her peer group bond and oath, Marietta is cursed with a "horribly disfigured" face through "a series of close-set purple pustules that had spread across her nose and cheeks to form the word 'SNEAK'" (Year 5, 565). Rowling is sure to mention in the following book that the "odd formation of pimples [was] still etched across her face" (Year 6, 142)—a permanent memory of the cost of going against peer group culture and breaking children's trust.

21. Even though Rowling depicts Draco and his cronies entering the room when Harry, Ron, and Hermione are in there during the series finale, the narrative also explains that Neville understands the room better than anyone; thus, Neville is able to give the room explicit instructions to keep out unwanted Voldemort supporters.

22. Cockrell (2002) goes on to note that J.K. Rowling has "a good deal of fun with names" (23). We certainly see the meaning in the name Rowling bestows on Luna Lovegood: she is love, she is good, and she is the light of the moon and stars to the dark shadow of Voldemort.

23. Lending to this air of secrecy in the larger magical world, ministry officials who work at the Department of Mysteries are called "Unspeakables"; no one (even those who work for other departments at the Ministry) knowing exactly what they do.

24. Aurors are dark wizard catchers who work for the Ministry.

25. That said, there is a very brief moment when Neville, perhaps, goes under the Invisibility Cloak with Harry while on the Hogwarts Express to try and spy on Draco and the Slytherins; however, the effort immediately "came to nothing" due to the overcrowded and raucous nature of the train (Year 6, 142). Outside of Harry's peer group/Hogwarts, Griphook the goblin is hidden under the Invisibility Cloak with Harry when Harry, Hermione, Ron, and Griphook break into Gringotts bank at Diagon Alley to steal one of Voldemort's horcruxes from a Death Eater's vault.

26. In addition, the author notes their unique closeness in the names of Harry's future children. In the documentary *J.K. Rowling: A Year in the Life* (2007), which follows Rowling's progress to publication of the final book *Deathly Hallows*, she reveals that Harry's daughter is named Lily Luna. Lily for his mother, and Luna for Harry's "dear friend." Of Harry's three children, the name Luna is the only first or middle name given for a significant person in Harry's life who is not a dead elder (his other children are James Sirius—James for his father, Sirius for his godfather, and Albus Severus—Albus for Dumbledore, Severus for Snape).

27. The adults of Hogwarts shape the structures of the school—and occasionally attempt to limit the agency of its students—by giving orders to paintings, ghosts, armor, the entrance door, etc. As Chappell (2008) similarly points out, even though students at the school have freedom, the teachers simultaneously restrict children's uses of magic and confine them from certain areas of Hogwarts.

REFERENCES

Adler, Patricia A., and Peter Adler. 1998. *Peer Power: Preadolescent Culture and Identity*. New Brunswick, NJ: Rutgers University Press.

Aitken, Stuart C. 2001. *Geographies of Young People: The Morally Contested Spaces of Identity*. London: Routledge.

Asher, Steven R., Whitney B. Guerry, and Kristina L. McDonald. 2014. "Children As Friends." In *The SAGE Handbook of Child Research*, edited by Gary B. Melon, Asher Ben-Arieh, Judith Cashmore, Gail S. Goodman, and Natalie K. Worley, 169–94. Thousand Oaks, CA: SAGE.

Blundell, David. 2016. *Rethinking Children's Spaces and Places*. London: Bloomsbury.

Buckingham, David. 2000. *After the Death of Childhood: Growing Up in the Age of Electronic Media*. Cambridge: Polity Press.

Castro, Ingrid E. 2005. "Children's Agency and Cinema's New Fairy Tale." In *Sociological Studies of Children and Youth, Volume 11*, edited by David A. Kinney and Katherine B. Rosier, 215–37. Amsterdam: Elsevier.

———. 2016. "Children, Innocence, and Agency in the Films of Steven Spielberg." In *Children in the Films of Steven Spielberg*, edited by Adrian Schober and Debbie Olson, 121–40. Lanham, MD: Lexington Books.

———. 2017. "Contextualizing Agency in High-Structure Environments: Children's Participation in Parent Interviews." In *Researching Children and Youth: Methodological Issues, Strategies, and Innovations—Sociological Studies of Children and Youth, Volume 22*, edited by Ingrid E. Castro, Melissa Swauger, and Brent Harger, 149–73. Bingley: Emerald.

———. 2019. "The Spirit and the Witch: Hayao Miyazaki's Agentic Girls and Their (Intra)Independent Genderational Childhoods." In *Representing Agency in Popular Culture: Children and Youth on Page, Screen, and In Between*, edited by Ingrid E. Castro and Jessica Clark, 255–82. Lanham, MD: Lexington Books.

Chappell, Drew. 2008. "Sneaking Out After Dark: Resistance, Agency, and the Postmodern Child in JK Rowling's Harry Potter Series." *Children's Literature in Education* 39 (4): 281–93.

Christensen, Pia, Allison James, and Chris Jenks. 2000. "Home and Movement: Children Constructing 'Family Time.'" In *Children's Geographies: Playing, Living, Learning*, edited by Sarah L. Holloway and Gill Valentine, 139–55. London: Routledge.

Christensen, Pia, and Alan Prout. 2003. "Children, Place, Space and Generation." In *Childhood in Generational Perspective*, edited by Berry Mayall and Helga Zeiher, 133–54. London: Institute of Education, University of London.

Cockrell, Amanda. 2002. "Harry Potter and the Secret Password: Finding Our Way in the Magical Genre." In *The Ivory Tower and Harry Potter: Perspectives on a Literary Phenomenon*, edited by Lana A. Whited, 15–26. Columbia, MO: University of Missouri Press.

Corsaro, William A. 1992. Interpretive Reproduction in Children's Peer Cultures. *Social Psychology Quarterly* 55 (2): 160–77.

———. 2015. *The Sociology of Childhood* (4th ed.). Thousand Oaks, CA: SAGE.

Corsaro, William A., and Donna Eder. 1990. "Children's Peer Cultures." *Annual Review of Sociology* 16: 197–220.

Deegan, James G. 1996. *Children's Friendships in Culturally Diverse Classrooms*. London: The Falmer Press.

Eder, Donna, Catherine C. Evans, and Stephen Parker. 1995. *School Talk: Gender and Adolescent Culture*. New Brunswick, NJ: Rutgers University Press.

Elsey, Susan. 2011. "Out of the Way: Children, Young People and Outdoor Spaces." In *Children and Young People's Spaces: Developing Practice*, edited by Pam Foley and Stephen Leverett, 102–15. Hampshire: Palgrave Macmillan.

Ennew, Judith. 2005. "Prisoners of Childhood: Orphans and Economic Dependency." In *Studies in Modern Childhood: Society, Agency, Culture*, edited by Jens Qvortrup, 128–46. Hampshire: Palgrave Macmillan.

Frønes, Ivar. 1994. "Dimensions of Childhood." In *Childhood Matters: Social Theory, Practice and Politics*, edited by Jens Qvortrup, Marjatta Bardy, Giovanni Sgritta, and Helmut Wintersberger, 145–64. Aldershot: Avebury.

Gillis, John R. 2008. "Epilogue: The Islanding of Children—Reshaping the Mythical Landscapes of Childhood." In *Designing Modern Childhoods: History, Space, and the Material Culture of Children*, edited by Marta Gutman and Ning de Coninck-Smith, 316–30. New Brunswick, NJ: Rutgers University Press.

Hackett, Abigail, Lisa Procter, and Julie Seymour. 2015. "Introduction: Spatial Perspectives and Childhood Studies." In *Children's Spatialities: Embodiment, Emotion and Agency*, edited by Abigail Hackett, Lisa Procter, and Julie Seymour, 1–17. Hampshire: Palgrave Macmillan.

Hall, Tom, Amanda Coffey, and Howard Williamson. 1999. "Self, Space and Place: Youth Identities and Citizenship." *British Journal of Sociology of Education* 20 (4): 501–13.

Halldén, Gunilla. 2003. "Children's Views of Family, Home and House." In *Children in the City: Home, Neighbourhood and Community*, edited by Pia Christensen and Margaret O'Brien, 29–45. Oxon: Routledge.

Harry Potter Wiki. n.d. "Room of Requirement." https://harrypotter.fandom.com/wiki/Room_of_Requirement.

Hearst, Alice. 2004. "Recognizing the Roots: Children's Identity Rights." In *Rethinking Childhood*, edited by Peter B. Pufall and Richard P. Unsworth, 244–61. New Brunswick, NJ: Rutgers University Press.

Hill, Malcolm. 2006. "Children's Voices on Ways of Having a Voice: Children's and Young People's Perspectives on Methods Used in Research and Consultation." *Childhood* 13 (1): 69–89.

Holloway, Sarah L., and Gill Valentine. 2000a. "Children's Geographies and the New Social Studies of Childhood." In *Children's Geographies: Playing, Living, Learning*, edited by Sarah L. Holloway and Gill Valentine, 1–26. London: Routledge.

———. 2000b. "Spatiality and the New Social Studies of Childhood." *Sociology* 34 (4): 763–83.

James, Allison. 1993. *Childhood Identities: Self and Social Relationships in the Experience of the Child*. Edinburgh: Edinburgh University Press.

———. 2013. *Socialising Children*. Hampshire: Palgrave Macmillan.

James, Allison, and Adrian L. James. 2004. *Constructing Childhood: Theory, Policy and Social Practice*. Hampshire: Palgrave Macmillan.

James, Allison, Chris Jenks, and Alan Prout. 1998. *Theorizing Childhood*. Cambridge: Polity Press.

Jones, Owain. 2009. "Approaching the Otherness of Childhood: Methodological Considerations." In *Doing Children's Geographies: Methodological Issues in Research with Young People*, edited by Lorraine van Blerk and Mike Kesby, 195–212. Oxfordshire: Routledge.

Kornfeld, John, and Laurie Prothro. 2003. "Comedy, Conflict, and Community: Home and Family in Harry Potter." In *Critical Perspectives on Harry Potter*, edited by Elizabeth E. Heilman, 187–202. New York, NY: Routledge.

Leverett, Stephen. 2011. "Children's Spaces." In *Children and Young People's Spaces: Developing Practice*, edited by Pam Foley and Stephen Leverett, 9–24. Hampshire: Palgrave Macmillan.

Matthews, Sarah H. 2007. "A Window on the 'New' Sociology of Childhood." *Sociology Compass* 1 (1): 322–34.

Mayall, Berry. 2000. "The Sociology of Childhood in Relation to Children's Rights." *The International Journal of Children's Rights* 8 (3): 243–59.

———. 2002. *Towards a Sociology for Childhood: Thinking from Children's Lives*. Berkshire: Open University Press.

———. 2008. "Conversations with Children: Working with Generational Issues." In *Research with Children: Perspectives and Practices* (2nd ed.), edited by Pia Christensen and Allison James, 109–23. New York, NY: Routledge.

Merten, Don E. 1999. "Enculturation Into Secrecy Among Junior High School Girls." *Journal of Contemporary Ethnography* 28 (2): 107–37.

Milner Jr., Murray. 2004. *Freaks, Geeks, and Cool Kids: American Teenagers, Schools, and the Culture of Consumption*. New York, NY: Routledge.

Moore, Tim, Morag McArthur, and Debbie Noble-Carr. 2008. "Little Voices and Big Ideas: Lessons Learned from Children about Research." *International Journal of Qualitative Methods* 7 (2): 77–91.

Mortier, Freddy. 2002. "The Meaning of Individualization for Children's Citizenship." In *Childhood and Children's Culture*, edited by Flemming Mouritsen and Jens Qvortrup, 79–102. Odense: University Press of Southern Denmark.

Musolf, Gil R. 1996. "Interactionism and the Child: Cahill, Corsaro, and Denzin on Childhood Socialization." *Symbolic Interaction* 19 (4): 303–21.

Olwig, Karen F., and Eva Gulløv. 2003. "Towards an Anthropology of Children and Place." In *Children's Places: Cross-Cultural Perspectives*, edited by Karen F. Olwig and Eva Gulløv, 1–19. London: Routledge.

Petrie, Pat. 2011. "Children's Associative Spaces and Social Pedagogy." In *Children and Young People's Spaces: Developing Practice*, edited by Pam Foley and Stephen Leverett, 131–44. Hampshire: Palgrave Macmillan.

Qvortrup, Jens. 1994. "Childhood Matters: An Introduction." In *Childhood Matters: Social Theory, Practice and Politics*, edited by Jens Qvortrup, Marjatta Bardy, Giovanni Sgritta, and Helmut Wintersberger, 1–24. Aldershot: Avebury.

Rasmussen, Kim. 2004. "Places for Children—Children's Places." *Childhood* 11 (2): 155–73.

Rowling, J.K. 1997. *Harry Potter and the Sorcerer's Stone*. Year 1. New York, NY: Scholastic Press.

———. 1999a. *Harry Potter and the Chamber of Secrets*. Year 2. New York, NY: Scholastic Inc.

———. 1999b. *Harry Potter and the Prisoner of Azkaban*. Year 3. New York, NY: Scholastic Inc.

———. 2000. *Harry Potter and the Goblet of Fire*. Year 4. New York, NY: Scholastic Press.

———. 2003. *Harry Potter and the Order of the Phoenix*. Year 5. New York, NY: Scholastic Press.

———. 2005. *Harry Potter and the Half-Blood Prince*. Year 6. New York, NY: Scholastic Inc.

———. 2007. *Harry Potter and the Deathly Hallows*. Year 7. New York, NY: Scholastic Inc.
Rubin, Lillian B. 1985. *Just Friends: The Role of Friendship in Our Lives*. New York, NY: Harper & Row.
Runcie, James. 2007. *J.K. Rowling: A Year in the Life*. Documentary. Streaming: YouTube. UK: IWC Media, RDF Television.
Satta, Caterina. 2015. "A Proper Place for a Proper Childhood? Children's Spatiality in a Play Centre." In *Children's Spatialities: Embodiment, Emotion and Agency*, edited by Abigail Hackett, Lisa Procter, and Julie Seymour, 178–97. Hampshire: Palgrave Macmillan.
Shanahan, Suzanne. 2007. "Lost and Found: The Sociological Ambivalence Toward Childhood." *Annual Review of Sociology* 33: 407–28.
Swauger, Melissa, Ingrid E. Castro, and Brent Harger. 2017. "The Continued Importance of Research with Children and Youth: The 'New' Sociology of Childhood 40 Years Later." In *Researching Children and Youth: Methodological Issues, Strategies, and Innovations—Sociological Studies of Children and Youth, Volume 22*, edited by Ingrid E. Castro, Melissa Swauger, and Brent Harger, 1–7. Bingley: Emerald.
Valentine, Gill. 1996. "Angels and Devils: Moral Landscapes of Childhood." *Environment and Planning D: Society and Space* 14 (5): 581–99.
Way, Niobe. 2006. "The Cultural Practice of Close Friendships Among Urban Adolescents in the United States." In *Peer Relationships in Cultural Context*, edited by Xinyin Chen, Doran C. French, and Barry H. Schneider, 403–25. New York, NY: Cambridge University Press.
———. 2011. *Deep Secrets: Boys' Friendships and the Crisis of Connection*. Cambridge, MA: Harvard University Press.
Wyness, Michael. 2006. *Childhood and Society: An Introduction to the Sociology of Childhood*. Hampshire: Palgrave Macmillan.
Zeiher, Helga. 2001. "Children's Islands in Space and Time: The Impact of Spatial Differentiation on Children's Ways of Shaping Social Life." In *Childhood in Europe: Approaches—Trends—Findings*, edited by Manuela Du Bois-Reymond, Heinz Sünker, and Heinz-Hermann Krüger, 138–59. New York, NY: Peter Lang.
———. 2003. "Shaping Daily Life in Urban Environments." In *Children in the City: Home, Neighbourhood and Community*, edited by Pia Christensen and Margaret O'Brien, 66–81. Oxon: Routledge.

Mythology/Quest

Chapter 6

All in the Family

The Agency of Demigods and Godlings in the Mythic World of Rick Riordan

Michele D. Castleman

Rick Riordan's five myth-based, fantasy series for middle-grade children have sold well over thirty million copies worldwide and been translated into thirty-seven languages (Lodge 2011).[1] Whether Percy Jackson, Annabeth Chase, Jason Grace, or the god Apollo are on quests to fulfill prophecies to protect the Greek and Roman gods; whether siblings Sadie and Carter Kane host Egyptian gods in their bodies in the hopes of preventing chaos from overtaking the world; or whether Magnus Chase seeks a mythical object of a Norse god, all adventures Riordan's young protagonists undertake are intrinsically connected to agency and family. Many protagonists' statuses within Riordan's mythic world allow them to explore their own agency while also working to empower and save others within their families and beyond, indicating they have "the capacity to do things" (Oswell 2013, 42). Related to the environments traversed on such quests, Tsushima and Burke (1999) define agency "as a person's ability to achieve internalized goal states represented in identity standards despite changing or opposing environmental conditions" (173). Not only do Riordan's young protagonists achieve their goals but, in most cases (given their powerful status and connections to the gods), they also influence environmental conditions for other demigods and the mortal world. The protagonists' choices and interactions with their family members draw attention to their cultural and gender identities. As these teens seek to satisfy their own needs and desires and explore their growing powers and autonomy, they also find themselves in conflict with societal expectations and prophesied actions they are expected to fulfill. Diverse representations among Riordan's protagonists point to the intersectionality of childhood and the complex relationship between the agency of youth and the wider social structures they navigate.

The premises of Percy Jackson and the Olympians, Heroes of Olympus, and Magnus Chase series feature quests of children born from a Greek, Roman, or Norse god in mythology. Each child of a god, usually referred to as a demigod, makes choices and acts in response to his or her immortal parent's status and authority. These choices impact immediate family and larger mythic and mortal worlds within each book series. The Kane Chronicles, in contrast, is the story of siblings descended from Egyptian pharaohs. Carter and Sadie Kane are simultaneously magicians, mortals, and "godlings" who can serve as hosts to two Egyptian gods, Horus and Isis (respectively), in the mortal realm. Also deviating from the focus on young demigods as protagonists, The Trials of Apollo series is unique among Riordan's work: this series focuses upon the Greek god Apollo, aged 4,612. In the series, Zeus, king of the Greek gods and father to Apollo, casts Apollo down into the mortal realm to live as a mortal and to serve twelve-year-old demigod Meg McCaffrey. Forced by magic to obey Meg's commands, Apollo now has the appearance of Lester Papadopoulos, "a dorky, curly-haired teen" who interacts with demigods from the Percy Jackson and the Olympians and Heroes of Olympus storylines (Riordan 2016b, 6). Apollo, as an adult living in a teen body, functions as an example of the "new" sociology of childhood's central tenet that "childhood is a social construction" (Oswell 2013, 10). Despite living for over four millennia, Zeus still holds authority over Apollo and Apollo is nascent in his earth experiences, learning how to interact with mortals and demigods, including his own children. Research on the agency of children within families occasionally, and unfortunately, prioritizes the adult perspective: "Some researchers, while acknowledging that agency is present in parent-child relationships and practiced by both, nonetheless suggest that adults have the upper hand" (Leonard 2016, 69). Just as Zeus has authority over Apollo, Riordan's protagonists face similar power imbalances with their parents, as well as reader-relatable problems in the mortal world.

DIAGNOSIS: DEMIGOD

Demigod protagonists like those presented in Percy Jackson and the Olympians, Heroes of Olympus, and Magnus Chase series face difficulties in their mortal world. Some of these problems hail from gifts endowed from their immortal parents. All demigods exhibit symptoms of dyslexia and attention deficit hyperactivity disorder (ADHD). Annabeth Chase, daughter of the Greek goddess Athena, explains this fact to Percy Jackson soon after he learns he is the son of a god in *Percy Jackson and the Olympians: The Lightning Thief* (2005):

> The letters float off the page when you read right? That's because your mind is hardwired for ancient Greek. And the AHDH—you're impulsive, can't sit still in the classroom. That's your battlefield reflexes. In a real fight, they'd keep you alive. As for the attention problems, that's because you see too much, Percy, not too little. Your senses are better than a regular mortal's. (Riordan 2005, 88)

Riordan notes that his choice to present dyslexia and ADHD as empowering was intentional while he crafted the Percy Jackson and the Olympians series, stating, "In the story, Percy Jackson discovers that being different can be a source of strength—and a mark of greatness. Being academically hopeless does not mean you are a hopeless person. Percy was my way of honoring all the children I've taught who have ADHD and dyslexia" (Riordan 2008, vii–viii). Some readers may feel valued and encouraged reading about powerful protagonists diagnosed with dyslexia and ADHD, demonstrating how these popular fantasy series contribute to newly nuanced and more positive interpretations of these diagnoses. Christensen (2000) asserts that vulnerability associated with children operates through the "construction of the way in which children perceive themselves and are perceived by others. It is embedded in cultural understandings of the child as a social person, of the child's body and conceptions of health and illness" (57). Riordan's many series provide an empowering understanding of dyslexia and ADHD diagnoses. For Percy and the other protagonists, attributes of ADHD and dyslexia as symptoms tied to their familial connection to an ancient god or goddess is one way children's bodies are "experienced, managed and understood socially. The body is both a direct source of agency and can be drawn on as a source of agency and power in social interaction" (Fingerson 2009, 226).

STATUS: MULTICULTURAL

In their study of child autonomy in children's literature, Kelen and Sundmark (2017) assert that "children of Zeus and Hera exercising power throughout the Olympian pantheon" is a historical example of children's powers and the capacity to rule (2). Riordan's protagonists have special mythical power and status as the children of gods or as gods themselves. In *The Heroes of Olympus: The Lost Hero* (2010), the Roman goddess Juno reflects upon demigods' special status and her jealousy toward other gods who produce such special children, stating, "You demigods can span both worlds. I think this helps your godly parents—even Jupiter, curse him—to understand the mortal world better than I" (Riordan 2010a, 545). The demigods serve as a bridge between the mortal world and that of myth, creating change in both worlds through their choices and actions.

Riordan's five series reflect societal and mythical ideologies associated with authority. Nodelman and Reimer (2003) note the power of ideologies within children's books, stating children's literature represents "an effort by adults to colonize children" (97). Myth is also a colonizing force, since it reflects unique usage of language.[2] Bruce Lincoln (1999) examines the terms "myth" and "mythos" across time and text, exploring how at various points myths are connected to both truth and falsehoods. He concludes his study by asserting that myth has special weight, as it is "ideology in narrative form" (Lincoln 1999, 207). Csapo (2005) also notes that myth can be defined as "a narrative which is considered socially important, and is told in such a way as to allow the entire social collective to share a sense of this importance" (9). Thus, narratives classified as myth are associated with the construct of authority, presenting a particular view of the world. Myths have "special status" in society, and are particularly important to religion:

> For those who believe in them, [myths] are true—not symbolically true or allegorically true, but absolutely true, a factual accounting of the nature of the world as it is. For readers who accept their truth, furthermore, myths tell them how to live, what to believe, and how to behave. In other words, "myth" is the name given to stories that express religious truth by those who happen not to believe they are true. (Nodelman and Reimer 2003, 324)

Whether myth is regarded as truth depends upon the storyteller's outlook, the recipients of the tale, and consumers' beliefs. Feldt (2016) further connects the potential association between truth, ideology, and religion to position religious texts that are housed in the fantasy genre: "Religious texts can thus be understood as fantasy narratives with specific pragmatic determinants. The decisive differences between fantasy fiction and religious narratives lie, I argue, in the realm of pragmatics, in the special status and authority that religious groups ascribe to religious narratives via their use, not in text-internal features" (555). Reader interpretation and audience response determine the significance of a text and whether it is classified as myth, religion, or fantasy.

Although Riordan's many series are widely accepted as fantasy, the inclusion of characters from traditional myth, who are associated with both truth and fiction, adds a connection to the past and an air of authority to each novel. The protagonists' interactions with both their mortal and immortal family members provide a complex view of child agency, in which protagonists find their voices and advocate for other youths' voices to be heard. Alanen (1988) notes that, within scholarship, "the term 'family' covers a wide range of material arrangements, sets of relationships and ideologies" (62). Likewise, Riordan's novels importantly provide representation of diverse family structures. All of Riordan's five myth-based series are set within a single fantastic world wherein the gods of Egyptian, Greek, Norse, and Roman myths exist and interact with mortals. Discussing the Percy Jackson and the Olympians series, Riordan (2008) acknowledges, "We are still creating myths all the time. My books, among other things, explore the myth of America as the beacon of civilization, the myth of New York, and the myth of the American teenager" (ix). Riordan's series present child-parent relationships in variable ways that connect to young readers' lived experiences. Jensen (2009) writes that by the turn of the twenty-first century, children were likely to "be born outside marriage, to experience family shifts, to have few siblings, and to live either in a dual-earner or a one-parent family" (142).

In *The Lightning Thief*, the first of Riordan's myth-based novels, twelve-year-old Percy, raised by his mother, learns that his biological father is the Greek god of the sea, Poseidon. This family structure—Riordan's protagonists are usually raised by a mortal parent with little knowledge of or interaction with their immortal noncustodial parent—normalizes readers' experiences in single-parent households. Single-parent households are further nuanced when paired with various family structures as more books are added and more series written, including: being adopted into a same-sex household, having stepparents and stepsiblings, living with grandparents, being orphaned, having half-siblings, and developing self-created families with peers. In the cases of Magnus Chase and Meg McCaffrey, they are storied as homeless at the onset of *Magnus Chase and the Gods of Asgard: The Sword of Summer* (2015) and *The Trials of Apollo: The Dark Prophecy* (2017). Glauser (1997) describes how homelessness is an unstable situation for children; while many do not live on the street consistently or permanently, they are often unsuccessful in finding more stable residencies.

Portraying varied family structures is an important aspect of children's publishing:

> What is read by children influences the development of their values and beliefs. Authors and publishers provide powerful validation for what makes us the same and different. For this reason they must be sensitive to representing the complex realities of life rather than settling for simplified exaggerations and stereotypes. The results of this study underscore the importance of accurately reflecting the range of family structures that exist. (Despain et al. 2015, 333)

Riordan also works to include varied racial and ethnic representations of family structures among his five middle grade series: Jason Grace and his sister Thalia grow up separately, but they represent a bicultural experience since their mother had Thalia with the Greek aspect of the lightning god, Zeus, and Jason hails from the Roman aspect of the same god, Jupiter. In the Kane Chronicles, siblings are from a multiethnic family, but Carter phenotypically presents black while his sister Sadie "passes" as white. In one novel from the series, *The Kane Chronicles: The Red Pyramid* (2010), Carter describes seeing his sister for the first time in months, noting, "You would never guess she's my sister. First of all, she'd been living in England so long, she has a British accent. Second, she takes after our mom, who was white, so Sadie's skin is much lighter than mine" (Riordan 2010b, 120). In the Kane Chronicles series, Carter occasionally reflects on the racial discrimination he encounters that his sister does not due to phenotype. Carter's experiences hint at the need for focus on intersectionality and adaptability when considering childhood, family, and social structures since children's "social life is organized around . . . powerful systems, such as class and ethnicity" (Leonard 2016, 120).

All Riordan's young protagonists go on quests with little adult oversight, navigating the world of monsters with near-complete autonomy. These journeys are comparable to the "world of travelers" that some children experience when traveling alone between homes of separated parents (Jensen 2009, 151). Protagonists' journeys and accompanying fears of being targeted by monsters since they are demigods speak to youth's "challenges and uncertainties in moving between homes" (Jensen 2009, 151). In "depictions of children who have to fend for themselves in places without adults, some of them will soon adopt adult-like qualities" (Kelen and Sundmark 2017, 7). Various responsibilities of Riordan's young protagonists serve to demonstrate that roles of children and adults are positionally and socially constructed, with young protagonists adapting to uncertain circumstances.

Leonard (2016) acknowledges the adaptability of children, stating, "the changing demography of the family has resulted in children being confronted with a plurality of increasingly complex living arrangements and indeed adjusting to more than one family type during their childhood" (72). Award-winning books can allow audiences to witness positive and negative family change, functioning as important pedagogical tools to "help students understand and adapt" (Despain et al. 2015, 332). Novels and other mass media texts can expose children and teens "to a much larger cultural world" (Fingerson 2009, 220). Hengst (2009) also notes that "media and commercial culture can no longer be viewed as something separable from society, social change, cultural work and the conduct of lives. They affect relationships, the framing of events, and the construction of individual and collective identities" (203). With these important influences in mind, examining how Riordan's myth-based series frame and present the family provides insight into how main protagonists create space for other young characters to be heard and feel safe within their families and beyond.

PROTECTING FUTURE FAMILY MEMBERS

Not only do Riordan's protagonists lean upon the voices of past authority, they then adopt that authority to speak for the welfare of others to improve familial circumstances for their future siblings. The central conflict that threatens the world in Riordan's five Percy Jackson novels is a family affair: Kronos, who Zeus defeated in the creation of the world, conspires to return to power. That destructive, all-devouring god is aided by many monsters, lesser gods, and a number of demigods. In *Percy Jackson and the Olympians: The Last Olympian* (2009), the final novel in the series, some children of less powerful gods reveal why they and their immortal parents fight for Kronos. The character Ethan Nakamura is a son of Nemesis[3]—Ethan fights and dies on Kronos's side of the war, hoping that his mother will be allotted a central place among the gods. He gasps the dying words, "'Deserve better . . . . If they just . . . had thrones'" (Riordan 2009, 328). He wants his mother to have a voice and to hold power among the gods. Ethan's plea speaks to a larger trend in encouraging democratic relationships within family structures. Leonard (2016) notes that recent research and snapshots of "some aspects of family life [suggest] that traditional parent-child relationships within the family based on authoritarianism are weakening and being replaced by more democratic relationships" (73).

Hearing Ethan's plea and knowing how it felt to remain unclaimed by his own father at the war's end, Percy stands before the twelve most powerful Olympian gods and advocates for those who rebelled with Kronos against the ruling class, declaring:

> Kronos couldn't have risen if it hadn't been for a lot of demigods who felt abandoned by their parents . . . .They felt angry, resentful, and unloved, and they had a good reason . . . . No more undetermined children . . . . I want you to promise to claim your children—all your demigod children by the time they turn thirteen. They won't be left out in the world on their own at the mercy of monsters. I want them claimed and brought to camp so they can be trained right, and survive . . . . No unclaimed demigods . . . anymore, wondering who their parents are. (Riordan 2009, 353)

Percy makes these requests for the gods' children (mortal demigods like him), characters with whom young readers are most likely to empathize. In Percy's demands of Zeus, young demigods will from then on be sent to Camp Half-Blood to be welcomed, given homes, provided with protection, and trained to defend themselves.[4] Jensen (2009) notes that "children, as a rule, have modest influence" when impacting adult structures and as actors within pluralized family forms (153). However, affording young protagonists "speaking rights" within families can lead to "a broader narrative of the modernisation of the family" (Oswell 2013, 104). Such "attribution of voice to children comes with demands as well as rights," elements that are connected to various political structures at work within families and larger institutional and governmental organizations (Oswell 2013, 106). Fairness is a common concern in children's accounts of participation within their families, wherein "the home and the family are a place for negotiations" (Bjerke 2011, 96).

In her work on children's agency displayed during high-structure parent interviews taking place within the home, Ingrid E. Castro (2017) notes that children employ a variety of agency routes while negotiating their representation and voice in adults', and their families', narratives. In my chapter's case, the gods *do* listen as Percy expands upon his request at the end of *The Last Olympian*, wishing, "You've got to stop trying to get rid of powerful demigods. We're going to train them and accept them instead. All children of the gods will be welcome and treated with respect" (Riordan 2009, 353–4). Percy agentically argues for a safe, peer-based space for demigod children to live.[5] Employing young protagonists' agentic voices to create safe homes for demigod children also contributes to an underlying textual message of inclusion, equity, and diversity.

POWER, BODIES, AND GENDER IN MAGNUS CHASE

Fingerson (2009) argues third-wave feminism allows for increased "media prevalence and more open talk about body and sexuality" (221).[6] In Riordan's novels, young protagonists' changing and gendered bodies impact family dynamics. Most notably, *Magnus Chase and the Gods of Asgard: The Hammer of Thor* (2016) introduces the character of Alex Fierro, who is the child of the Norse god Loki and identifies as genderfluid.[7] Zamani-Gallahar (2017) discusses gender and genderfluidity, noting, "As gender denotes a socially constructed concept, gender identity comprises a spectrum of how individuals identify that is multidimensional and not linear, but rather a continuum of maleness, femaleness, and gender identities not bounded by the twofold of male or female" (91).

The Hammer of Thor received a children's Stonewall Award, an award established in 2012 to recognize books of exceptional merit in the presentation of gay, lesbian, bisexual, and transgender experiences (American Library Association 2019). In his Stonewall acceptance speech, Riordan expressed the importance of including characters such as Alex in his books:

As important as it is to offer authentic voices and empower authors and role models from within LGBTQ community, it is also important that LGBTQ kids see themselves reflected and valued in the larger world of mass media, including my books. I know this because my non-heteronormative readers tell me so. They actively lobby to see characters like themselves in my books. They like the universe I've created. They want to be part of it. They deserve that opportunity. (RickRiordan.com 2017)

Riordan's comments parallel Zamani-Gallaher's (2017) argument that "self-defined identity is important to many minoritized, marginalized groups in terms of establishing their collective identity on their own terms" (91). In addition, the god Loki can be interpreted to represent a transgender experience—being Alex's mother and another demigod's father: the Magnus Chase series asserts that transgendered and genderfluid individuals always had a presence within myth and thus are now found in the modern literary/fantasy worlds Riordan creates.

Alex has the power to shapeshift. She asserts that this power, inherited from Loki, is separate from her genderfluidity. She informs Magnus, who is the son of Norse god Frey, the ruler of peace and fertility, rain, and sunshine, "I can *look* like whatever or whoever I want. But my actual gender? No. I can't change it at will. It's truly fluid, in the sense that I don't control it. Most of the time, I identify as female, but sometimes I have very *male* days. And please don't ask me how I know which I am on which days" (Riordan 2016a, 272). Though Alex's comments do not present gender as a socially constructed concept, Alex explains that she lacks control over her gender and seeks to be regarded as "normal." Related, children's "bodies are not static, but constantly change and shift through processes such as aging, puberty or illness. This is particularly true for children whose bodies change even more dramatically and quickly than those of adults. When something changes about our physical bodies, it changes the way we interact with others" (Fingerson 2009, 217). As Alex shifts, she is aware of how others respond to how she changes, which then continues to impact how she changes, importantly and agentically embedded with her peers.

Zamani-Gallaher (2017) comments that transgender and gender non-conforming persons "who have a sense of agency to be themselves face gender-role conflict in terms of negative consequences" (92). Focusing more specifically on children's experiences, The 2015 National School Climate Survey addresses specific challenges school-aged LGBTQ children face (Kosciw et al. 2016). They note 43.3 percent of LGBTQ students surveyed feel "unsafe at school" because of their gender expression (Kosciw et al. 2016, xvi). The study also finds that LGBTQ students have lower self-esteem and higher rates of depression (see also Castro and Sujak 2014). Alex experiences a rift in her relationship with her mortal father due to his inability to regard Alex's gender fluidity as "normal." Her experience serves as a small hint to the larger difficulties genderfluid characters and real-world people can potentially face in unsupportive environments.

Alex's ability to shapeshift becomes central to the exploration of power dynamics between child and parent.[8] Alex's half-sister, Samirah al-Abbas, or Sam, is also a daughter of Loki. In her case, Loki is Sam's father. Sam cautions Alex against using their shapeshifting abilities, worrying that using it allows Loki to have a measure of control over them. She cautions that Alex "doesn't realize how dangerous it is to rely on Loki's power. You can't give him any more of a hold than he already has" (Riordan 2016a, 94–5). Sam seeks freedom from her father by ignoring the power she inherited from him. Alex, in contrast, views using shapeshifting as an avenue to gain independence from Loki and seeks to teach Sam to do the same, knowing it will be a necessary skill to defeat the god. Speaking to an underlying need for children to be adaptable while calling on peer learning and support, Alex informs Magnus:

> You have to be *comfortable* changing. All the time. You have to make Loki's power *your* power . . . . Clay can be shaped and reshaped, over and over, but if it gets too dry, if it sets . . . then there's only so much you can do with it. When it gets to that point, you'd better be sure it's in the shape you want it to have forever . . . if [Sam] won't let me teach her how I resist Loki, if she won't at least try—then the next time we face him, we're all dead. (Riordan 2016a, 448)

Shapeshifting serves as an important way for Alex to define and represent herself in conflict with her mother Loki, even though it is a skill she also inherited from the god. In addition, her relationship with Sam is built on children's agentic negotiation and compromise within intra-family communication and relationships (Castro 2017).

Expanding on the complicated power dynamics within this family, Alex and Sam's identities are constrained by Loki's ability to physically control his children with verbal commands. For example, while attempting to keep an artifact away from Loki, Sam "grabbed her spear and lunged toward her father," only to have him respond by snapping his fingers, saying, "No, dear"; "Instantly, Sam's legs buckled. She collapsed sideways on the floor and lay immobile, her eyes half-closed" (Riordan 2016a, 131). Loki asserts complete control over Sam physically, serving as a representation of abusive child-parent relationships. Mason and Falloon (2001) explain that children identify "abuse as the use of power to control children. This control is exercised through physical actions, emotional constraints and boundary-setting which devalues and excludes younger people from adult, or mainstream society"

(111). Loki's power does not extend to control Alex's emotional and mental desires, however. In a later fight, Loki once again commands Sam to freeze. She physically does as she is told, but "her teeth clenched with effort. Her eyes burned with rage. She let loose a guttural howl . . . but couldn't seem to break Loki's command" (Riordan 2016a, 417). With Alex's help and instruction, Sam learns to resist Loki's commands in practicing her shapeshifting, finally gaining control over her own powers. During the demigods' climactic battle with Loki in *Magnus Chase and the Gods of Asgard: The Ship of the Dead* (2017), the god attempts to control his children once more:

> "Alex! Samirah!" Loki tried for a confident smile. "Come on my dears. You *know* I love you! Don't be difficult. Kill your friends for me and all will be forgiven."
> Alex adjusted her shaggy green fur cloak over her sweater vest. "Sorry, Mom. I'm afraid I gotta say no."
> Loki dashed toward Samirah, who pushed him back at spear point. (Riordan 2017a, 375)

Loki emotionally manipulates Alex and Sam by mentioning his love for them while he also tries to physically control them. The use of emotional manipulation adds a new dimension to his abusive parenting, one that is designed to create pleasure. Foucault (1977) spoke to the complicated reasons why power is difficult to disobey, noting, "What makes power hold good, what makes it accepted, is simply the fact that it doesn't only weigh on us a force that says no, but that it traverses and produces things, it induces pleasure, forms knowledge" (119). Loki's attempts to manipulate his children to obey him prove ineffective since both teens gain comfort and confidence in their shapeshifting powers; hence, they can resist him by working together as a peer/sibling team. Alex and Sam's growing ability to defy Loki's commands serves as a powerful metaphor for youth taking traits or skills inherited or learned from parents and reclaiming them, using those competences for their own empowerment. Alex and Sam become powerful in their own bodies, agentically resisting not only a parent's will but that of a god.

POSITION: BEING A FATHER AND A SON IN THE TRIALS OF APOLLO

In contrast with Alex and Sam rebelling against an abusive father, Riordan's The Trials of Apollo series provides a different perspective on a father's flawed relationship with his children. This series is unique among Riordan's works: instead of a young demigod as the protagonist, the books focus on the god Apollo who is being punished by his father, Zeus. Zeus forces Apollo to take on the appearance of a teenager and live in the mortal world, serving a demigod and daughter of Demeter (Greek goddess of harvest and sacred law) named Meg McCaffrey. In addition to this role, Apollo previously fathered several of the demigods with whom he interacts while on quests with Meg. Henceforth, he must face the reality that he has been neglectful to his children.

Apollo's experiences as both father and son are positional in that a change in one position—whether that of the parent or child—effects a change in the other position (see Alanen 2009). Mayall (2009) notes that socialization "extends across a life" (181); Apollo demonstrates that as a god, as a father, and as a son he can learn and negotiate the social order within his family and beyond. In the novel *The Trials of Apollo: The Hidden Oracle* (2016), Apollo reflects on how he is a neglectful parent. He notes, "These demigods were my protectors and my family, but for the present I could not think of myself as their father. A father should do more—a father should give more to his children than he takes. I have to admit that this was a novel idea for me" (Riordan 2016b, 117). The acknowledgment that his children protect him and not vice versa embodies a reverse positional change of parent-child relationships' common characterization. Apollo admitting to past mistakes and his efforts to improve and grow contribute to making him a more likable and relatable character. Apollo's efforts to reestablish contact with his children speaks to the political attention given to "strengthening the linkages between children and their fathers after break-up" (Jensen 2009, 150). In the book's sequel, *The Dark Prophecy*, Apollo jokes about forgiveness, telling Lityerses (a son of King Midas), "I believe in [second chances]. And third and fourth chances. But I only forgive each person once a millennium, so don't mess up for the next thousand years" (Riordan 2017b, 398).[9] Although stated with humor, this assertion could apply to Apollo as well. Instead of vilifying all absentee parents, Apollo's take on the adage "to err is human" allows for readers to consider Apollo's perspective as a father and as a son and get an inside view into the integrally positional and generational nature of parent-child relationships.

Apollo's experience of living for thousands of years also serves to promote LGBTQ-inclusivity and establishes that LGBTQ relationships have always existed. Not only does he support that one of his daughters, Georgina, is being raised by a lesbian couple but he is also supportive of his son Will's relationship with Nico di Angelo, another male demigod.[10] Apollo reflects upon his own lovers once he sees Will and Nico together: "Perhaps some of you are wondering how I felt seeing him [Will, his son] with a boyfriend rather than a girlfriend. If that's the case, please. We gods are not hung up about such things. I myself have had . . . let's see, thirty-three mortal girlfriends and eleven mortal boyfriends? I've lost count"

(Riordan 2016b, 94). This normalization of sexual fluidity is lent power with the voice of a god asserting that boundaryless love is normal now and has been for millennia.

BREAKING CHAINS: PATTERNS AND PROPHECY

The Kane Chronicles: The Red Pyramid includes insights about sacrifice and autonomy within families. As godlings, two siblings are chosen as hosts for Egyptian gods in order to prevent chaos from reigning the mortal world. Carter hears the voice of the falcon god Horus in his head, while his sister Sadie is chosen by the goddess Isis. Throughout *The Red Pyramid*, the siblings resist the gods' influence on their behaviors, fearing that giving the gods control over their bodies signifies loss of their own autonomy. Carter compares the experience to being "possessed" and fears he cannot trust Horus. He asks, "How can I be sure you wouldn't get me killed and just move on to some other host? How can I be sure you're not influencing my thoughts right now?" (Riordan 2010b, 220). Eventually, Carter realizes his and Horus's motives are the same, and they work together as a team instead of Carter losing total bodily control to Horus. During a fight scene, when Carter battles the god Set, he realizes the union between himself and Horus will save Sadie. He narrates:

> The falcon god and I had been wrestling with each other for days as he tried to take control of my body. But *neither* of us could be in control. That was the answer.... We had to act in unison, trust each other completely, or we were both dead.... I understood his power, his memories, and his fears.... And he saw my mind—everything, even the stuff I wasn't proud of.... He did not control me. I did not use him for power. We acted as one. (Riordan 2010b, 457)

This marriage of motivation and power serves to unite the young protagonists with the gods, granting Sadie's and Carter's choices and actions more authority in their battles. Carter's feelings of wrestling with the god for control of his body speak to the larger discussion of children's bodies within agency scholarship. Fingerson (2009) notes that even with individual action, "there is a tension between attributing action to an individual's own power and desires versus the constraints of society, or structure, on that individual's actions" (217). Horus's initial effort to control Carter serves as a constraining structural attempt to repeat patterns of his existence in previous body hosts. Carter's individuality and agency allow for both Horus and Carter to grow and change. Iskandar, a powerful magician who guides the Kane siblings, informs Carter that the gods prefer to have human hosts because "only humans have creativity, the power to change history rather than simply repeat it" (Riordan

2010b, 179). Hope is associated with the young protagonists because they represent both the future and the opportunity to make new and better choices.

Similar assertions about mortals, godlings, and demigods' power to innovate and end destructive cycles are scattered among the series.[11] In *The Hidden Oracle*, Apollo expresses frustration with the potential fate of repeating his ancient patterns, and he is comforted by a mortal girl, Rachel Dare, who has prophetic gifts: "Things can turn out differently, Apollo. That's the nice thing about being human. We only have one life, but we can choose what kind of story it's going to be," to which Apollo thinks, "perhaps human persistence was an asset. They never seemed to give up hope. Every so often they *did* manage to surprise me" (Riordan 2016b, 348–9). Assertions like this one emphasize the value of protagonists' choices, efforts to change their worlds, and hopes for better futures. "Choosing the kind of story" Apollo can have implies that agency is not only enacted through choice but also found in the interpretation of experiences.

The breaking of patterns in the effort to improve the worlds of the gods and mortals usually overlaps with protagonists' motivations among Riordan's series; however, in a few instances characters' desires are at odds with the larger goal of saving the world. In *The Red Pyramid*, Carter and Sadie's goal is to be reunited with their father. Anubis, the god of funerals, asks Sadie whether she is willing to lose her father if it means "saving the world" (Riordan 2010b, 364). Sadie thinks about how to answer: "Of course I knew the 'right' answer. The heroine is supposed to refuse to sacrifice her father. Then she boldly goes off and saves her dad *and* the world, right? But what if it really was one or the other? The whole world was an awfully large place . . . everyone I'd ever known. What would my dad say if I chose him instead?" (Riordan 2010b, 364). Sadie acknowledges the expected arc of many fantasy novels, connecting her choices to a predictable narrative or script in which she would save both the world and her father. This reflection on fate versus choice parallels the story metaphor Rachel presents to Apollo.

Eventually, when faced with the actual choice of whether to save her father or the world, Sadie's father informs her it is her job to restore order instead of trying to save him. He tells her, "One of my hardest jobs as a father, one of my greatest duties, was to realize that my own dreams, my own goals and wishes, are secondary to my children's. Your mother and I have set the stage. But it is your stage" (Riordan 2010b, 472). Her father's declaration serves as a call for Sadie to make the "right" choice with her father's approval. With this call to child action and autonomy, combined with family obligation and negotiation, Sadie allows her will to merge with that of the goddess Isis. During this process, she describes seeing the pattern of the goddess' life "repeating itself over and over again through the ages, through a thousand different hosts," recalling the assertion that while the gods have power, "humans have creativity, the power to change history" (Riordan 2010b, 474). Once again, a child's agency is framed as the solution to repeating problems. Sadie's humanity, when combined with the powers of Isis, allows for Sadie and Isis to make new choices together that Isis cannot make alone. Sadie and Carter's alteration to the patterns of history ideologically serve as a call for children to use knowledge gained from past patterns to make new and better choices than those found in previous generations.

Such foci emphasize the presentation of children serving as the hope for better societal futures. Radhiah Chowdhury (2006) questions why the world so often depends on children and youth to save it within children's fantasy novels. Referring to such characters as "child messiahs," she notes, "Aside from the fact that the child reader of children's fantasy will be able to empathise with a child protagonist, the child also embodies the future of any society. Although it may be that adults aid the Child Messiah during his or her quest, the pivotal action must come from the children themselves" (Chowdhury 2006, 107). Demigods and other protagonists in Riordan's works face potential restriction of their agency as they concomitantly provide such hope for the future through prophecy. Riordan incorporates prophecies into many of his series, including Percy Jackson and the Olympians, The Heroes of Olympus, the Trials of Apollo, and Magnus Chase and the Gods of Asgard. Each raises the question: "To what extent do protagonists have free will, or are they fated to complete prophesied tasks?" Chowdhury (2006) views young protagonists who have destinies to save the world as doomed. She further details the outlined path of child messiahs:

> It is the ultimate irony that the Child Messiah is not permitted to be childlike, and must forego the essence of the "child" identity in order to fulfill the messianic destiny. In this they have no choice—the idea of the "fated" or prophesized Child Messiah removes agency from the child. Their heroic destiny is literally forced upon them. While it is possible to say they could choose to ignore their destiny, destiny has a habit of catching up to its victims. (Chowdhury 2006, 108)

Positioning free will and fate as dichotomous, Chowdhury (2006) emphasizes fate will always win, though it is possible to read the experiences of Riordan's protagonists as more nuanced and agentic.

Other scholars express more optimism about young protagonists who face a certain destiny or prophecy within fantasy narratives. In examining J.K. Rowling's Harry Potter series, Pond (2010) asserts fate and freewill work concurrently.[12] She builds upon the work of Friedrich Nietzsche, stating, "free will is attained within the limits of personal fate. By accepting and loving a personal fate, each individual embraces her destiny, calling it hers and living fully within the limitations that she has now freely and purposefully chosen" (Pond 2010,

196). Applying this balance between free will and fate to the Percy Jackson and the Olympians quintet, Percy potentially has a role in a great prophecy to prevent Kronos from rising once Percy turns sixteen years old.[13] The wording of this prophecy is unclear as to who might fulfill it beyond the central role of a sixteen-year-old child of Zeus, Hades, or Poseidon. Throughout the series, both Thalia Grace and Nico di Angelo (children of Zeus and Hades, respectively) are introduced as other contenders for this prophecy's fulfillment. Early in the series, Chiron, the centaur and trainer of heroes at Camp Half-Blood, specifically elects not to tell Percy of this great prophecy to allow him to make choices for himself. However, choices that all three youth demigods make eventually position Percy to be the one who completes the prophecy.

In the third book of the series, *Percy Jackson and the Olympians: The Titan's Curse* (2007), Thalia, who is the oldest among the potential prophesied demigods and is about to turn sixteen, chooses to become the new lieutenant of Artemis's Hunters, making her immortal. She tells her father, "I will not turn sixteen tomorrow. I will never turn sixteen. I won't let the prophecy be mine. I stand with my sister Artemis" (Riordan 2007, 292). By taking on this role of leadership among Artemis's Hunters, Thalia asserts agency in the face of prophesied fate.

Just as Thalia chooses a loophole to avoid prophesied fate, Percy intentionally chooses fate so as to prevent Nico from being considered for the prophecy. He does so in order to protect Nico and his family. As with Pond's (2010) assertions about the Harry Potter series, Percy similarly exerts his free will to commit to a fate articulated through a vague and ancient prophecy. Percy employs agency, taking on great responsibility to ensure the safety of his peers in both mortal and mythic worlds. Continuing exploration of fate and free will in another series, Magnus Chase's *The Ship of the Dead* ends by drawing attention to the balance protagonists must strike between destiny and choice. Magnus reflects on how as an einherji (one of the chosen soldiers to serve in Odin's eternal army) he is "destined to die. The world will end. The big pictures cannot be changed. But in the meantime, as Loki once said, we can choose to alter the details. That's how we take control of our destiny" (Riordan 2017a, 410). The focus on altering details, on doing what is right within the individual moment to have greater positive impact on the most amount of people proves true for all Riordan's protagonists: small individual choices accumulate, ripple, and impact larger worlds.

CONCLUSION

Among each of Riordan's myth-based series, protagonists assert their agency and respond to their families in multifaceted ways. Riordan's five myth-based series provide varied representations of family and offer empowering interpretations of ADHD and dyslexia diagnoses. A choice Percy makes at the conclusion of the Percy Jackson and the Olympians quintet provides a sense of safety and family to all peer demigods that extends into the premises of the Heroes of Olympus and Trials of Apollo series. Sadie and Carter break the unending cycles of restriction gods made in the past to lead them into new directions for the future, with their tales demonstrating the intersectionality of race, gender, and childhood. The Norse god Loki is one of several representations of an abusive parent. He can exert complete control over his children, Sam and Alex, robbing them of free will, and it is only through agentically and interpretively using a skill they inherited from Loki that they can break free from their parent's control. The Trials of Apollo explores the positional relationships of being a son and an absentee father. The Apollo books also contribute to a multifaceted and LGBTQ-inclusive view of families, children, and power. In all series, Riordan explores youth agency within family dynamics and in relation to many dimensions of present-day American culture. The protagonists assert their agency with attention to familial relationships, but experience consequences that impact broader mythic and mortal worlds within each story. The characters demonstrate agency in the effort to claim voice within their varied and inclusive family structures and the wider social realms they regularly navigate. The mythos of child autonomy is a powerful one in Riordan's works; these books are chockfull of young characters who are trusted to save the world through rebellion, negotiation, and communion to ensure the safety of their families, friends, and countless others.

NOTES

1. "Middle grade" generally refers to books intended for readers between the ages of eight and twelve (Maughan 2018).
2. See Csapo (2005) for exploration of how "myth" is defined.
3. Nemesis is the goddess of revenge.
4. Camp Half-Blood is a demigod training facility fictionally located on Long Island, New York.
5. Similarly, Magnus and his love interest Alex establish a safe place for homeless teens to stay as long as they need at the conclusion of *The Ship of the Dead*.
6. Unlike some others, Fingerson (2009) believes this stage is the current wave, which prioritizes "women's rights to sexual pleasure and women's rights to use and display their bodies as they choose" (221).
7. Loki is a Norse god who is known to be a cunning trickster who can shapeshift and change his sex from male to female. When applying gender pronouns to Alex, I use "she" because in the novels Alex expresses a general preference to be perceived

as female; in fact, in *The Hammer of Thor*, Alex dismisses the use of plural or non-gendered pronouns (see Riordan 2016a).

8. Alex asserts that her shapeshifting ability and her genderfluidity are separate aspects of her identity and are unrelated.

9. Lityerses and Apollo additionally bond over how they are "sons of overbearing fathers," how they have been "misled and burdened by bad choices," and how they are talented in their own unique ways (Riordan 2017b, 398).

10. Apollo experiences shame for not remembering whether he fathered young Georgina, who is being raised by Josephine and Emmie.

11. Juno expresses a similar sentiment in *The Lost Hero*.

12. Pond (2010) asserts the inclusion of fate contributes to the mythic and heroic dimensions of the Harry Potter fantasy series.

13. There are many other prophecies realized among Riordan's series that impact young characters' choices. The prophecies I focus on in this chapter are "Great Prophecies" that are fulfilled over multiple books in a single series.

REFERENCES

Alanen, Leena. 1988. "Rethinking Childhood." *Acta Sociologica* 31 (1): 53–67.

———. 2009. "Generational Order." In *The Palgrave Handbook of Childhood Studies*, edited by Jens Qvortrup, William A. Corsaro, and Michael-Sebastian Honig, 159–74. New York, NY: Palgrave Macmillan.

American Library Association. 2019. "Stonewall Book Awards History." *GLBTRT*. http://www.ala.org/rt/glbtrt/award/stonewall/honored.

Bjerke, Håvard. 2011. "'It's the Way They Do It': Expressions of Agency in Child-Adult Relations at Home and School." *Children & Society* 25 (2): 93–103.

Castro, Ingrid E. 2017. "Contextualizing Agency in High-Structure Environments: Children's Participation in Parent Interviews." In *Researching Children and Youth: Methodological Issues, Strategies, and Innovations—Sociological Studies of Children and Youth, Volume 22*, edited by Ingrid E. Castro, Melissa Swauger, and Brent Harger, 149–73. Bingley: Emerald.

Castro, Ingrid E., and Mark C. Sujak. 2014. "'Why Can't We Learn About This?' Sexual Minority Students Navigate the Official and Hidden Curricular Spaces of High School." *Education and Urban Society* 46 (4): 450–73.

Chowdhury, Radhiah. 2006. "A Chosen Sacrifice: The Doomed Destiny of the Child Messiah in Late Twentieth-Century Children's Fantasy." *Papers: Explorations into Children's Literature* 16 (2): 107–11.

Christensen, Pia H. 2000. "Childhood and the Cultural Constitution of Vulnerable Bodies." In *The Body, Childhood and Society*, edited by Alan Prout, 38–59. New York, NY: St. Martin's Press.

Csapo, Eric. 2005. *Theories of Mythology*. Malden, MA: Blackwell Publishing.

Despain, Shannon M., Michael O. Tunnell, Brad Wilcox, and Timothy G. Morrison. 2015. "Investigating Shifts in Diverse Family Structures in Newbery Award and

Honor Books Utilizing U.S. Census Data, 1930–2010." *Literacy Research and Instruction* 54 (4): 316–40.
Feldt, Laura. 2016. "Contemporary Fantasy Fiction and Representations of Religion: Playing with Reality, Myth and Magic in *His Dark Materials* and *Harry Potter*." *Religion* 46 (4): 550–74.
Fingerson, Laura. 2009. "Children's Bodies." In *The Palgrave Handbook of Childhood Studies*, edited by Jens Qvortrup, William A. Corsaro, and Michael-Sebastian Honig, 217–27. New York, NY: Palgrave Macmillan.
Foucault, Michel. 1977. "Truth and Power." In *Power/Knowledge: Selected Interviews and Other Writings 1972–1977*, edited by Colin Gordon, 109–33. New York, NY: Pantheon Books.
Glauser, Benno. 1997. "Street Children: Deconstructing a Construct." In *Constructing and Reconstructing Childhood: Contemporary Issues in the Sociological Study of Childhood* (2nd ed.), edited by Allison James and Allen Prout, 145–64. Oxon: Routledge.
Hengst, Heinz. 2009. "Collective Identities." In *The Palgrave Handbook of Childhood Studies*, edited by Jens Qvortrup, William A. Corsaro, and Michael-Sebastian Honig, 202–14. New York, NY: Palgrave Macmillan.
Jensen, An-Magritt. 2009. "Pluralization of Family Forms." In *The Palgrave Handbook of Childhood Studies*, edited by Jens Qvortrup, William A. Corsaro, and Michael-Sebastian Honig, 140–55. New York, NY: Palgrave Macmillan.
Kelen, Christopher, and Björn Sundmark. 2017. "Where Children Rule: An Introduction." In *Child Autonomy and Child Governance in Children's Literature: Where Children Rule*, edited by Christopher Kelen and Björn Sundmark, 1–15. New York, NY: Routledge.
Kosciw, Joseph G., Emily A. Greytak, Noreen M. Giga, Christian Villenas, and David J. Danischewski. 2016. *The 2015 National School Climate Survey: The Experiences of Lesbian, Gay, Bisexual, Transgender, and Queer Youth in Our Nation's Schools*. New York, NY: GLSEN.
Leonard, Madeleine. 2016. *The Sociology of Children, Childhood and Generation*. Los Angeles, CA: SAGE.
Lincoln, Bruce. 1999. *Theorizing Myth: Narrative, Ideology, and Scholarship*. Chicago, IL: The University of Chicago Press.
Lodge, Sally. 2011. "First Printing of Three Million for New Percy Jackson Book." *Publishers Weekly*. August 18, 2011. https://www.publishersweekly.com/pw/by-topic/childrens/childrens-book-news/article/48404-first-printing-of-three-million-for-new-percy-jackson-book.html.
Mason, Jan, and Jan Falloon. 2001. "Some Sydney Children Define Abuse: Implications for Agency in Childhood." In *Conceptualizing Child-Adult Relations*, edited by Leena Alanen and Berry Mayall, 99–113. New York, NY: RoutledgeFalmer.
Maughan, Shannon. 2018. "Navigating Middle Grade Books." *Publishers Weekly*. April 13, 2018. https://www.publishersweekly.com/pw/by-topic/childrens/childrens-industry-news/article/76625-navigating-middle-grade.html.

Mayall, Berry. 2009. "Generational Relations at Family Level." In *The Palgrave Handbook of Childhood Studies*, edited by Jens Qvortrup, William A. Corsaro, and Michael-Sebastian Honig, 175–87. New York, NY: Palgrave Macmillan.

Nodelman, Perry, and Mavis Reimer. 2003. *The Pleasures of Children's Literature* (3rd ed.). Boston, MA: Allyn and Bacon.

Oswell, David. 2013. *The Agency of Children: From Family to Global Human Rights*. New York, NY: Cambridge University Press.

Pond, Julia. 2010. "A Story of the Exceptional: Fate and Freewill in the Harry Potter Series." *Children's Literature* 38: 181–206.

RickRiordan.com. 2017. "The Stonewall Award." *RickRiordan.com*. June 26, 2017. http://rickriordan.com/2017/06/the-stonewall-award/.

Riordan, Rick. 2005. *Percy Jackson and the Olympians: The Lightning Thief*. New York, NY: Hyperion.

———. 2007. *Percy Jackson and the Olympians: The Titan's Curse*. New York, NY: Hyperion.

———. 2008. "Introduction." In *Demigods and Monsters*, edited by Rick Riordan and Leah Wilson, v–x. Dallas, TX: Benbella Books.

———. 2009. *Percy Jackson and the Olympians: The Last Olympian*. New York, NY: Hyperion.

———. 2010a. *The Heroes of Olympus: The Lost Hero*. New York, NY: Hyperion.

———. 2010b. *The Kane Chronicles: The Red Pyramid*. New York, NY: Hyperion.

———. 2015. *Magnus Chase and the Gods of Asgard: The Sword of Summer*. New York, NY: Disney Hyperion.

———. 2016a. *Magnus Chase and the Gods of Asgard: The Hammer of Thor*. New York, NY: Disney Hyperion.

———. 2016b. *The Trials of Apollo: The Hidden Oracle*. New York, NY: Disney Hyperion.

———. 2017a. *Magnus Chase and the Gods of Asgard: The Ship of the Dead*. New York, NY: Disney Hyperion.

———. 2017b. *The Trials of Apollo: The Dark Prophecy*. New York, NY: Disney Hyperion.

Tsushima, Teresa, and Peter J. Burke. 1999. "Levels, Agency, and Control in the Parent Identity." *Social Psychology Quarterly* 62 (2): 173–89.

Zamani-Gallaher, Eboni M. 2017. "Conflating Gender and Identity: The Need for Gender-Fluid Programming in Community Colleges." In *New Directions for Community Colleges: Constructions of Gender 179*, edited by Pamela L. Eddy, 89–99. San Francisco, CA: Jossey-Bass.

Conflict/Justice

Chapter 7

Young People's Agency in Online Fan Spaces

Parinita Shetty

FANTASY AND CHILDREN'S LITERATURE

Both fantasy and children's literature have a history of marginalization in mainstream literature. Fantasy is often labeled childish and escapist. This accusation overlooks the fact that alternative worlds can be used to better understand the real world by providing readers with an outside perspective (Hunt and Lenz 2001). Fantasy frequently analyzes socioeconomic and political aspects of real life and calls into question the social norms of the everyday world, therein exposing inadequate parts of reality. Fantasy illuminates and challenges reality, opens up new possibilities, and explores complex moral dilemmas (Lynn 2005). Fantasy also highlights the hidden and unsavory parts of culture and allows readers to reconsider norms taken for granted in society (Jackson 1981).

Fantasy in children's literature is particularly empowering. In the real world, adult social structures often prevent young people from wholly exercising their agency, but in fantasy, groups of young people frequently resist adult authority and oppressive structures (Lynn 2005). Fantasy questions current assumptions of society and presents social, economic, political, and cultural values that might not necessarily mirror those of adult world structures, but may find currency in young people's worlds (Lurie 1990). Fantasy demonstrates that evil exists but also emphasizes the importance of hope, optimism, and making active choices to change current circumstances (Johansen 2005; Reynolds 2007). Fantasy, in children's literature, has the potential to raise a population of critical and compassionate thinkers—children who value social justice, believe in the importance of choices, and express their agency in different ways by challenging the status quo and questioning why established norms and structures are slow to change.

Fantasy offers a roadmap on how to deal with complex real-world problems (Johansen 2005). Examples of child protagonists fighting powers much bigger than themselves demonstrate that successful struggles are possible, providing opportunities for readers to reflect on how they engage with the world. This empowerment, in turn, is sometimes transferred to the real world. Young activists—inspired by the stories they read growing up—fight against real-world adult injustices; for example, a sign at the 2018 March For Our Lives protest that advocated for gun control in the United States declared, "We grew up on Harry Potter. Of course we're fighting back" (McNair 2018).

As well-meaning as writers of children's fantasy literature may be when offering their readers alternative perspectives to how the world works, it is still a genre largely controlled by adults. Most young people lack access to the structure of the publishing world that controls the literature they read. Traditionally—and controversially—adults oversee the processes of writing, producing, and promoting literature for young people, deciding what is considered suitable for various age groups. However, "children have always been producers of stories, riddles, verse, jokes and other materials (including novels, poems, plays and other more obviously literary creations)" (Reynolds 2011, 34). The difference between children's creations and adult-produced texts is that young people do not have broad access to the technical and financial resources necessary to produce their texts in a way that legitimizes them, wherein their works are rarely printed or produced and distributed for widespread consumption—not without adult intervention, at any rate.

AGENCY AND THE DIGITAL WORLD

The internet offers young people a space to communicate their ideas with both peers and adults, expands their social networks, and exposes them to alternative perspectives (boyd 2007; Katz 1996). boyd (2007) claims the internet is an empowering space for young people since they can participate in virtual environments that are not monitored by adults in their lives, even while the virtual world is present in adult-regulated spaces like homes and schools. Online spaces allow young people to circumvent adult concerns and controls over what information and cultures children have access to (Katz 1996). However, many adults curtail young people's access to online public platforms to protect them from potential risks. Studies suggest that, yes, youth who actively engage in online activities encounter more risks, but they are also afforded more opportunities (Cabello-Hutt, Cabello, and Claro 2018; Livingstone and Helsper 2010). Technological censorship disempowers young people and prevents them from exercising their agency in learning to navigate a wide range of online encounters and experiences (boyd 2007; Jenkins 1998; Katz 1996).

Digital technology lowers barriers to creation and enables readers to become writers with little technical expertise (Jenkins 2006a). Everyday citizens, including young people, have always produced their own versions of texts, commentaries, and stories; what has changed in the twenty-first century is the capacity to disseminate their texts to an international audience (Jenkins 1998). The internet allows an increasing number of young people unprecedented access to information and affords the ability to contribute to their own digital and literacy cultures; however, not everyone is an equally active participant in digital spaces. Ito and colleagues' (2008) investigation of young people's usages of new media technologies suggests that young people participate in two types of online communities: friendship-driven and interest-driven. This chapter examines interest-driven fan communities of two children's literature fantasy texts. Fan activities range from more passive "hanging out," wherein fans are spectators; more active "messing around," wherein fans occasionally tinker with technologies and tools to create and share texts; and the most active "geeking out," wherein fans actively produce and share media, culture, and knowledge (Ito et al. 2008). In interest-driven fan spaces, young people and adults frequently work side by side and learn from each other, thereby complicating traditional notions of authority and status.

In comparison to adults, fan texts written by young people are a more authentic form of children's literature. Fan texts are a way for marginalized populations to push against the dominant culture (Derecho 2006; Thomas 2011). In this context, young people's fan texts respond to adult-authored source texts. Young people in fan communities shape and simultaneously contribute to their own cultures within and outside of adult-controlled structures. Black's (2009) investigation of young fans proposes youth draw on various sources to write about issues that concern or interest them. Fans "employ creative agency as they create fan fiction texts that are relevant to their own lives" (Black 2009, 76). Consequently, while my chapter acknowledges the importance of the source texts as catalysts, I consider fan writing that is produced in online communities as the primary texts for analysis. Fan texts are "the entirety of stories and critical commentary written in a fandom" in response to the source text (Busse and Hellekson 2006, 7). A fandom or fan community refers to the collective entity of people who produce and consume fan texts, and the burgeoning field of fan studies charts the development and growth of creative and critical fan reactions to popular media (Busse and Hellekson 2006). This chapter explores how young people express multiple forms of agency through participation in online fan communities, wherein they actively interact with children's literature texts and with each other.

Social media websites are making it progressively easier for young people to participate in fan communities, either by reading and sharing texts other fans produce or by creating texts themselves. This exchange allows young people to access multiple interpretations and foster attitudes that help them articulate, negotiate, and reformulate their own readings. In fan spaces, young people exercise their agency in ways that James and James (2012) describe: fans appropriate their favorite fictional worlds and characters, and create texts that emphasize their own ideas and views on topics that matter to them. Members of fan communities do not always passively receive the author's intended meaning. Fans employ the fictional framework to create their own interpretations, reflecting on social, economic, political, and moral structures of the societies they inhabit. Thus, young fans actively participate in the creation of their own cultures (see Corsaro 2015; Mayall 2002). Online fan communities act as peer groups by providing an important context for young people to develop understandings of social and cultural practices (James and James 2012). Young fans' agency in such spaces can both reproduce social norms or disrupt them (valentine 2011). Fan spaces are not always progressive and can reproduce conservative norms inherent within both the fictional text and the world writ large.

Mayall (2002) argues that adult structures marginalize young people who are, for many childhood scholars, considered a societal minority group. Adult dismissals of young people's agency contribute to this minority status. To an extent, fan communities counter such imbalanced power hierarchies since young people and adults inhabit and construct fan spaces together. Fan communities challenge established social structures that do not take young people's voices seriously. As valentine (2011) argues, while children have agency, established adult-centric social structures need to be reorganized so as to enable children's participation and agency; henceforth, fan communities contribute to such reorganization. Fan communities are a form of peer culture as described by Corsaro (2009), whereby young fans collectively produce their own cultures. According to Corsaro (2009), children's peer cultures are not entirely separate from adult cultures. These cultures are interlinked and young people participate in peer as well as adult cultures. In fan spaces, young fans do not merely imitate or directly appropriate adult-authored texts. Rather, young people engage in interpretive reproduction by creatively appropriating and reinventing source texts to produce their own cultures (Corsaro 2009, 2015). Fan texts transform source texts in ways that address young people's own concerns. Fans do not just passively internalize social and cultural messages inherent in source texts and broader society, but actively negotiate and construct meaning by creating and sharing fan texts. Thus, young people interpret adult-authored texts, worlds, and cultures by using information and knowledge appropriated from the adult space to create and participate in their own peer cultures. Furthermore, this process of interpretive reproduction also enables young people to contribute to and extend adult cultures (Corsaro 2015).

Fan spaces demonstrate the importance of collective and communal activity. Works by Jeffrey (2012), Castro (2017, 2019), and Clark and Castro (2019) challenge the understanding of agency as an independent, individualized, and autonomous process. These scholars argue that young people's agency is social and emerges through relationships with peers *and* with adults; online fan spaces demonstrate such social agency. In fan communities, young people are involved in interdependent relationships across generations. Fans engage in acts of complex and collective meaning-making, so that knowledge is co-constructed through their rereadings of the source texts and their interactions with one another (Jenkins 2013). Fandoms encourage new ideas through critical readings of favorite texts, creation of new social structures, and mounting new modes of cultural production (Jenkins et al. 2009). In this way, social agency becomes an alternative source of power for young people and represents a qualitative difference in how youth make sense of cultural, social, and political experiences.

Frankel (2012) and Mayall (2002) point out that adults seldom respect young people's moral agency or acknowledge the countless moral issues youth encounter in their daily lives. Books and fan communities act as unexpected routes to negotiating, articulating, and shaping moral agency. In this context, young people express moral agency through a fictional framework that nevertheless draws on their own experiences and beliefs. Just as with children's books written by adults, fan texts also reflect writers' ideologies and influence readers through exposure to ideas and beliefs valued by those who pen them (Reynolds 2011). As found in several examples of fantasy in children's literature,[1] engagement with fan texts—both as readers and writers—can encourage young people "to think independently and from as informed a position as possible about issues such as justice, freedom, right and wrong, and what it means to behave well" (Reynolds 2011, 92).

The internet allows young people greater access to information than in previous decades and the opportunity to network with people from different backgrounds, thereby gaining further access and insight to diverse perspectives (Dresang 1999; Jenkins 2013). The resultant exposure to multiple interpretations within fan texts can challenge, expand, and reformulate perspectives. Youth interpretations counter dominant ways of viewing the world as they deliberate over issues that matter to them (Coker 2012). Fan communities allow young people to interpret their beloved texts in ways that place their perspectives, hopes, fears, and beliefs at the forefront (The Janissary Collective 2014). To note, young people are able to handle nuances and complexities that are found in books far more than adults recognize (Dresang

1999). In this process, young readers construct and negotiate meanings from novels and stories that adult authors did not necessarily intend to convey, with readers using fan texts to better articulate their interpretations through fan fiction or user commentary (Coker 2012; Rosenblatt 1978).

I recognize that not all young people are able to participate in online fan communities. This participation gap—wherein many populations lack access to technology (hardware, software, and/or internet access) or do not hold the necessary skills to contribute to online discussions based on their educational, geographical, social, cultural, and economic backgrounds—excludes many voices from digital spaces (Jenkins 2006b). This schism in social, cultural, educational, and monetary capital dictates that many young people have unequal access to information, skills, and opportunities; they face challenges in learning to recognize how media shape perceptions of the world; and they do not have experience navigating the ethical challenges of being responsible creators and promoters of media in online community spaces (Jenkins et al. 2009).

THE FANS OF FANTASY

I acknowledge my identity as both scholar and fan to signify that these identities play an important role in my research (see Busse and Hellekson 2006). As a former writer of Harry Potter fanfiction, reading about how participation in fan communities shapes and changes attitudes resonates with me deeply. The benefits of participating in fan communities remain with me as an adult, and I identify as a fan of several diverse media texts. In this chapter, I examine the fandoms of the Harry Potter series by J.K. Rowling (1997–2007) and the Percy Jackson series by Rick Riordan (2005–2009). I use these texts and fandoms because being a relative "insider" leads to a more comprehensive and contextual analysis (Duffet 2013). I am familiar with the culture, common themes, practices, and norms of the source texts, as well as the fan communities creating Potter and Jackson fan fiction and commentary.

The Harry Potter series follows the adventures of young wizard Harry Potter, his friendships, his time as a student at Hogwarts School of Witchcraft and Wizardry, and his struggles against a dark wizard, Voldemort. While originally written for children, it garnered a large adult readership, in part due to the complex themes it addresses within the mode of fantasy. A recent study suggests that reading Harry Potter books leads to increased empathy toward the LGBTQ community and refugees (Stetka 2014). Vezzali and colleagues (2015) find that fantasy is a good tool to change attitudes since, as Stetka (2014) asserts, "the genre typically doesn't feature actual populations" and thus allows people to discuss sensitive issues under the guise of fiction. The five books in the Percy Jackson and the Olympians series began Riordan's irreverent mythological adventures featuring demigods living in the twenty-first century. The series focused on Greek mythology, followed by other series featuring Roman, Egyptian, and Norse mythologies. Over the years, Riordan's books became increasingly inclusive in the diversity of characters portrayed within. Percy Jackson's attention deficit hyperactivity disorder (ADHD) and dyslexia are inspired by Riordan's oldest son who holds these diagnoses too (Adams 2016). Riordan's other books include characters who are homeless, deaf and mute, homosexual, bisexual and gender fluid, and belong to various ethnic and religious backgrounds (Berlatsky 2014). His range of characters is a welcome inclusion of diverse perspectives that are not as prevalent in popular, mainstream books for children. This expansion of representation is a conscious choice by Riordan, who wants children with a multiplicity of identities to recognize themselves in his books (Books-A-Million 2017).

For the current study, I analyze the fan pages *Pottermore: More Than An Insider* (PMTAI) and *Fans of Percy Jackson* (FOPJ). I studied fan communities on Facebook in June 2017. Over a two-week period, the pages contained 296 texts—27 in *FOPJ* and 269 in *PMTAI*. My analysis examines texts posted in the pages, as well as conversations in the comments sections of the original posts. Facebook allows for multimodal fan texts—posts include diverse media such as YouTube, screenshots from Tumblr and Twitter, GIFs, and comics. The pages have adult gatekeepers since Facebook page administrators control the content posted, even while they actively encourage fan contributions. Additionally, fans need an internet connection, a Facebook account, and the skills to create content and navigate online communities. At the same time, Facebook pages are reasonably open to young people and adults, and it is relatively easy to find pages for fandoms of interest.

I believe that a significant proportion of the participants were teenagers and young adults based on the themes and linguistic styles I observed within the fan communities. Nevertheless, I am making a research assumption since it is sometimes difficult to gauge the age and social background of fans when employing online participant observation, or, to use the colloquial term, "lurking." I did not interfere directly in the community, nor did I gather any demographic or identifiable data from the fans. As Standlee (2017) notes, since conversations occurred in the virtual public space of Facebook fan pages, I treat my observations just as offline researchers treat their observations in semi-public spaces. Getting consent from participants in such public spaces is largely impractical and often impossible (Standlee 2017).

"I KNEW A BOY WHO MADE ALL THE WRONG CHOICES": AGENCY WITHIN THE FANDOM AND THE FICTIONAL UNIVERSE

An investigation of fan communities and agency contributes to research that studies how young people exercise agency in a wide range of contexts (valentine 2011).[2] Young people do not always engage in open resistance to exhibit their agency (Jeffrey 2012). The fans I observed identify strongly with the fictional world, including characters, events, and their respective fan community. Fans use this deep emotional attachment with the source text to exercise their agency in innovative and resourceful ways. Fans are aware of the important role their debates and discussions play in helping the fictional world thrive beyond the books. A fan clearly articulates this sentiment: "If it weren't for us, the Magical World would have ended with the books. We're the ones who kept it alive" (PMTAI 2017b).[3]

Fans are equally self-assured of their right to express their own ideas and views about the fictional world and its characters. A fan demonstrates this confidence by reassuring a fellow member who "ships" Draco/Harry and Snape/Hermione that the products of her imagination are just as valid as those more popularly accepted within the fandom and canon.[4] Jeffrey (2012) observes that irreverence and humor are characteristic of young people's interactions as they navigate the social world. Among solemn discussions and debates, fan communities also feature playful and irreverent texts and comments. Participation in the digital age does not just mean access to adult-approved serious information and culture, but also recreational and social activities that act as gateways to active participation in cultural production (Ito et al. 2008).

The communities provide members "a space to gather, talk, imagine, debate, and engage with each other . . . it [is] a space where other kinds of conversations emerge" (Jenkins et al. 2016, 108). Fans examine multiple forms of agency performed by the fictional characters when scrutinizing both source and fan texts in great detail. A *PMTAI* fan text analyzes the different choices and associated consequences of Tom Riddle,[5] Severus Snape, and Draco Malfoy throughout their fictional lives. This analysis leads to thoughtful discussions about characters' motivations, what their lives commonly share or how they diverge, and their ultimate fates. The comments deliberate over themes of privilege, violence, abuse, neglect, bullying, prejudice, regret, and redemption. Fans are thus able to identify and debate complex subjects and make justifications for characters' behaviors. In other instances, fans analyze textual gaps to explore characters' feelings not explicitly found in the source text by using reasoned examinations of information that was provided in series canon. After considering a brief conversation in *Harry Potter and The Prisoner of Azkaban* (1999) between Professor Remus Lupin and Harry,[6] a poster concludes that Lupin's actions signify a highly empathetic and responsible guardian—"the adultiest adult who has ever adulted," who "would have been such a great father" (PMTAI 2017c). In another instance, fans criticize Headmaster Albus Dumbledore for not providing the teenage protagonists with clear guidance or enough information and leaving them to largely fend for themselves.[7] Fans are able to recognize and appreciate the hallmarks of good fictional role models. Members draw on experiences from their own lives as they discuss the pros and cons of Ron Weasley and Hermione Granger's relationship.[8] Some fans believe Ron's behavior toward Hermione constitutes emotional abuse, while others defend Ron's conduct as a product of immaturity and insecurity that dissipates as he grows older. A few fans are aghast that such an incompatible couple date in the first place, while others believe their hasty courtship and marriage sets unrealistic expectations for young readers: "Seriously, how many people get married with (and not divorce) their first serious relationship?!" (PMTAI 2017d).

In *PMTAI*, a fan theory about Harry's rage in *Harry Potter and the Order of the Phoenix* (2003) leads to considerations of trauma, emotional abuse, torture, lack of counseling, and the government's and media's constant criticism of him. One fan identifies post-traumatic stress disorder (PTSD) symptoms in Harry's behaviors, thereby drawing connections between real and fictional worlds. Fans hone their emotional intelligence as they navigate fictional expressions of agency and publicly question information posted by others. Engaging in debates and discussions about fictional elements can promote the following skills: analytic, conceptual, empathetic, emotional, and critical thinking. Thus, fan texts and interactions with fellow members in fan communities encourage young people to question taken-for-granted assumptions, including adult norms and values, through acts of interpretive reproduction and social agency (Corsaro 2009).

"RICK RIORDAN BUT EVERY TIME HE PUBLISHES A NEW BOOK IT GETS GAYER": REPRESENTATIONS OF GENDER AND SEXUALITY

Young people's agency can reproduce social norms or disrupt them (valentine 2011); as such, fan communities I observed reflect examples of both progressive and conservative practices.[9] An *FOPJ* fan text normalizes homosexuality by featuring Nico di Angelo, a canonical gay character, casually revealing his sexual orientation.[10] A fan declares she is gay too, to which another fan responds supportively by slightly adapting the original fan text. Fans also celebrate LGBTQ Pride Month by creating fan art featuring Nico and his boyfriend Will Solace wearing rainbow heart patches.[11] These representations reflect a subtle political statement about inclusivity that mirrors sexual inclusivity displayed in the series canon. The sharing of such perspectives in fan spaces, which may not be as acceptable or welcome in everyone's private social networks, encourages members to articulate their feelings and find support, empathy, and like-minded peers within unexpected contexts.

Similarly, a fan in *FOPJ* explores textual gaps in Rick Riordan's fictional world, wherein the Hunters of Artemis achieve immortality and become members of the group by swearing off men.[12] The fan points out that this practice does not signify renouncing romance or sex: "10/10 think they're all lesbians" (FOPJ 2017b). As another fan hints, later in the series Riordan addresses sexuality in the Hunters of Artemis, when two Hunters are forced to leave the sisterhood after they fall in love with each other. Connectedly, *PMTAI* fans employ Harry Potter as a "form of cultural currency [to] carry [their] messages," thereby using the text's "power as a shared reference point within the fan community" to promote individualized narratives and beliefs (Jenkins 2015, 217). A fan text features a photograph of a T-shirt with the quote: "If Harry Potter taught us anything—It's that no one should live in a closet" (PMTAI 2017e).

By referring to Harry's young childhood spent living in a cupboard under the stairs, the fan playfully repurposes the source text to express solidarity with the LGBTQ community and, perhaps, to represent one's own identity. Additionally, this text leads to debates surrounding implicit morality in the series. While one poster (PMTAI 2017f) believes the Potter books have "bigger morals" than the fan text implies, others insist that the text fittingly celebrates series themes of "having people accept one another," "love is what matters regardless of gender," and "Love overcome everything" (PMTAI 2017g, 2017h). Fans apply lessons they glean from the source text to their lives beyond the fictional context; however, fan spaces are not always progressive. One fan protests a Sirius Black/Remus Lupin "ship" as "gay fantasies about characters," calling on fans to "be normal and leave it the way it is" (PMTAI 2017i). He supplements his comment with a photo of Hitler and Nazis containing the words, "Absolutely Degenerate." Nevertheless, another fan is quick to challenge the bigotry: "Dunno wot u mean by 'normal' cause gay is normal too" (PMTAI 2017j).

Investigations of young people's agency reveal how their interactions with others influence decisions, relationships, and norms (Mayall 2002). Online fan communities allow young people to access diverse perspectives. Young fans encounter people both similar and dissimilar to them beyond those they know in their offline lives (boyd 2007). Fans negotiate character representations and perceptions by scrutinizing fictional attitudes and actions and sharing their perspectives with others. In turn, these opinions offer refreshing perspectives to other members within the community. *FOPJ* features two somewhat sexualized illustrations of Annabeth Chase.[13] The caption "Annabae Chase"[14] implies that while the character is otherwise known for her intelligence, the fan argues that Annabeth is also physically attractive. The fan suggests that intelligence and physical appeal do not need to be separate identities, somewhat countering mainstream portrayals of smart versus good-looking youth. In *PMTAI*, a fan engages in a detailed and sympathetic analysis of Fleur Delacour,[15] which causes another fan to appreciate the character in a whole new light. During a discussion of Ginny Weasley,[16] one fan complains that the film version does a disservice to the character by making her too feminine, as opposed to her fearless character portrayed in the books. To this opinion, a Potter fan points out, "You can be a badass and be feminine, it's not mutually exclusive" (PMTAI 2017k). This response and others demonstrate nuanced understandings of the characters and indicators of femininity/masculinity. A fan video shared in *PMTAI* titled "The Fantastic Masculinity of Newt Scamander" subjects the eponymous character to a detailed analysis. Newt is the protagonist of the Harry Potter spinoff film *Fantastic Beasts and Where to Find Them* (2016). The video entry concludes that emotional and empathetic Newt offers a positive representation of masculinity in mainstream culture—otherwise populated with brash and violent fantasy heroes—and thereby provides an excellent alternative to everyday male protagonists.[17] This analysis demonstrates a fan's ability to question taken-for-granted aspects of culture by turning his gaze toward alternate popular media narratives. His perspective enables other fans to call for more examples of sensitive, humble, and vulnerable fantasy heroes who counteract traditional gender roles.

"BUT HOGWARTS DIDN'T CHARGE TUITION": NEGOTIATIONS OF COMPLEX ISSUES

Castro (2005) notes that youth representations in popular media both reflect and shape how children and young people are perceived by adults and by each other.[18] Traditionally, these representations have presented young people either as wholly innocent beings in need of protection from the evils of the world or as willful rebels who need to be tamed by adults, lest they become corrupting influences on others (Castro 2016). In both cases, young people are not often seen as agents in their own right capable of making their own decisions and dealing with the consequences of their choices. Fantasy narratives in books and films increasingly depict complex and nuanced portrayals of young people from diverse backgrounds. Characters in fantasy worlds grapple with issues of oppression, differing political ideologies, economic and social injustices, imbalanced power structures, and moral conflicts. Such explicit and implicit representations prompt deeper exploration of text characters, events, and themes by young fans. While adults may consider youth too ignorant or ill-equipped to discuss such topics, young people draw on their own lived multiplicity of experiences, encounters with fictional characters and events, and real-world beliefs to engage with these elements. Online fan communities offer the space for young fans to actively participate in multiplatform culture by negotiating and critiquing others' perspectives while sophisticatedly expressing their own.

In *PMTAI*, Harry Potter fans discuss the plight of creatures in the wizarding world who are considered to be of a lower class than witches and wizards. The conversation includes deliberations about the oppression of house elves—most are indentured servants to rich and powerful families—and an underestimation of giants and half-giants based on their non-pureblood status.[19] A conversation about the lack of educational options for wizarding children before they arrive at Hogwarts leads to discussion surrounding prejudice and stigmas faced by people who are different, albeit framed in the context of the fictional world; in this instance, Lupin's lycanthropy.[20] Interactions with other members allow fans to gain personal and theoretical distance from the source text in order to critique it and question implicit assumptions. This exploration of the lives and circumstances of peoples and cultures who are otherized and underserved in the source text offers an alternative viewpoint for members to consider. Conversations about discrimination and prejudice display awareness among fans about themes of oppression within fictional worlds, and the discussion of Lupin and others like him who are considered uneducable or unemployable in the Potter series highlight similar situations found in the real world.

Young people share space with adults in online fan communities, constructing interpretations and opinions collectively. In such contexts, young people and adults access and negotiate each other's perspectives to better understand different viewpoints (see Castro 2017, 2019; James and James 2012). A *PMTAI* fan text ponders the economic and emotional fears of contemporary millennials if they might encounter a Boggart—a creature that manifests into the worst fear of the person it meets. The original fan text and subsequent discussion suggests issues that many millennials grapple with, such as abandonment, poverty, student loans, and the steep price of education. Fan communities offer members opportunities to reflect on dominant views and social practices in the fictional world and potentially encourage them to consider real-world limitations. In a conversation about the cost of education at Hogwarts, one fan cannot conceive of how an educational institution can function without charging tuition. This incredulity implies the fan has not encountered a free educational system in the real world. Other fans offer alternative situations based on real-life examples, suggesting that taxes and the magical government fund the education system of Hogwarts, as reflected in many real-world societies (for example, over twenty countries in the world currently offer free higher education). Fans pool their creative resources and combine their skills in this exercise of social agency and knowledge-sharing. James, Jenks, and Prout (1998) argue that children are social actors who both shape and are shaped by their circumstances. Reflecting this fact, young fans' opinions are shaped by the texts they read; at the same time, the fan texts they create and share in fandom spaces shape others' beliefs.

In fan spaces, young fans do not merely imitate or directly appropriate adult-authored texts. Rather, young people engage in interpretive reproduction whereby they creatively appropriate source texts to produce their own culture in the form of fan texts and transform the source texts in ways that address their own concerns (see Corsaro 2009, 2015). Mayall (2002) argues that young people's experiences can be better understood if their viewpoints are included in adult conceptualizations of childhood and youth. Fan communities offer an unconventional avenue to young people's expressed perspectives about a range of issues, including social in/justice and mental health. *FOPJ* features a fan art album of illustrated characters from the Percy Jackson series, supplemented by inspirational quotes. A fan responds gratefully, stating that the album offers comfort and hope during a difficult time. The fan admits to struggling with depression, feelings that were compounded after ending a close friendship. In the previously mentioned PMTAI text that describes fears of millennials, a fan uses the opportunity to describe his own fears. He provides an in-depth explanation of how his anxiety makes him feel and suggests that having a Boggart would be a great way to help others understand how anxiety works, particularly for people who do not experience feelings of constant stress and self-doubt or do not understand depressive disorders. In another instance, a comic illustrates a person battling soul-sucking Dementors by summoning a Patronus in the form of a bed.[21] In response, a fan remarks that since Dementors are supposed to represent depression, the weapon of choice (i.e., the bed) is accurate—therein suggesting she has personal experience with depression.[22] Another fan's response reads, "I wish it were that easy" (PMTAI 2017m), implying he has first-hand experience with depression and that the disorder does not have as simple a solution as the comic suggests.

Additionally, fans use fictional characters to negotiate real-world political issues and adapt ideas and texts to their own causes. For example, in *FOPJ* a text features Percy Jackson's Calypso—an immortal sorceress from Greek mythology imprisoned on an island away from civilization for thousands of years. In the illustration, Calypso stands with a protest group and angrily holds up a sign that declares, "I did not leave my island for this" (FOPJ 2017c). The caption accompanying the illustration exclaims, "Fight for those rights Calypso! Get em'! [chants] EQUAL PAY!!!! EQUAL PAY!!!!" The post implies that Calypso does not appreciate gaining freedom after millennia only to arrive in a world where women are not paid the same as men. Another fan text features a photograph of a real-world protest with a person holding up a sign that proclaims, "Dumbledore wouldn't let this happen." While the context of the protest is not apparent, the sign demonstrates that fans use fictional contexts to engage with real-world social and political issues in their social activism.

In another example of a political statement, a fan text declares: "We need more leaders like Kingsley instead of all the Fudges we have at the moment."[23] This text draws responses from fans in the United States, United Kingdom, Australia, and Pakistan who discuss real-life political counterparts in their respective countries. In the case of the United States, fans debate which political leader deserves the mantle of Kingsley—Barack Obama, Hillary Clinton, or Donald Trump. Varying international responses indicate different political allegiances and worldviews of fans. Fan texts authored by young people also have the potential to contest norms taken for granted by the adult world (see James and James 2012). Fan texts act as an informal yet important way for young fans to understand and comment on the political worlds in which they live. As Jenkins and colleagues (2016) observe, the fictional status of texts allows fans to communicate with each other in a more heterogeneous sphere, wherein they are able "to avoid the exclusiveness and violence" that are often found in ideological discussions (112). Furthermore, discussions centered around fictional worlds can "help challenge one-sided convictions people hold about the real world" (Jenkins et al. 2016, 134). The communities offer a space for fans to go beyond real-life contexts, places where they may be surrounded by people who echo similar political and cultural beliefs.

Another fan text exploring complex issues praises different fictional texts and the morals they instill, dismissing the idea that religion is the singular guide for ethical behavior. The fan's assertion that people do not need religion to be a good person leads to debates about religion. One fan finds the implication disrespectful: "Some people find all of this in religion" (PMTAI 2017n). Another fan responds by maintaining that there are other ways to acquire values besides religion and emphasizes that people without religion are not devoid of moral values. A third fan joins the debate by pointing out that unlike religion, fandom has not caused wars around the world. The original poster responds by emphatically dismissing the claim that "terrorists/warmongers are actually religious and representative of their religion" (PMTAI 2017n). Fan communities offer a space to discuss topics people might not otherwise be comfortable discussing in public. This sophisticated debate about a potentially contentious issue from diverse viewpoints demonstrates that young people are willing and able to talk about a range of issues adults might consider inappropriate for youth to discuss. Young people can and do participate meaningfully in debates about complex topics—topics adults might consider too uninteresting or problematic for young people to explore. James, Jenks, and Prout (1998) suggest that children's minority status can confront, rather than reinforce, imbalanced power relations between children and adults. Fan communities challenge those established social structures that do not take young people's voices seriously. Fan texts can also explain dominant ideologies that concern young people's interests and viewpoints. These communities allow fans to explore perspectives that might have previously been considered "improper for them to encounter or too complicated for them to understand" (Dresang 1999, 24). By expanding notions of what are considered acceptable topics for young people, fan texts "reflect real life more accurately and authentically—even if not always more pleasantly" (Dresang 1999, 176).

"I THINK ITS A HUMAN RIGHTS THING": FAN EXPLORATIONS OF MORAL AGENCY

Mayall (2002) argues that through their relationships with peers and adults, children "demonstrate that they have well established moral abilities, recognition of others' points of view, empathy and willingness to give time to others' problems" (176–7).[24] Young people are moral agents who develop working knowledge of moral concepts based on their encounters. As they grow older and face new situations, they expand and sometimes refine or reframe their moral conceptualizations. This process sees young people sharing encounters with adults as they develop their moral agency (Frankel 2012; Mayall 2002). In fan spaces, these new situations and experiences arise in the form of fictional events and characters, accompanied by deliberations over fictional moral issues. Fans also consider story or character elements left unaddressed or inadequately explained by the author. In *PMTAI*, fans discuss Voldemort's conception under the non-consensual influence of a love potion (placed on his biological father) and subsequent childhood raised in a muggle orphanage after his mother died in childbirth. Fans analyze the reasons behind why Voldemort grows up to be an evil wizard and conclude that if he had been raised by his mother with love and care, rather than with the perceived neglect he faced at the orphanage, the Second Wizarding War may have been prevented. Fans of the text are able to ascertain parental and emotional guidance needed in childhood and are further able to empathize with Voldemort, whose childhood emotional and magical needs were not met.

Another fan in *PMTAI* conducts a thought experiment, wherein he ponders whether Israeli wizards of Jewish ancestry who survive the Holocaust and emigrate to Israel after World War II fall prey to the anti-muggle-born propaganda distributed during the Second Wizarding War. The fan examines textual gaps to draw connections between real-world and fictional oppression, prejudice, and propaganda to wonder how persecution manifests in different contexts. In another instance, a fan's suggestion about using a magical method of mindreading to make wizarding criminal proceedings found in Harry Potter more efficient leads to conversations about ethics, autonomy, consent, the protection of criminals' human rights and privacy, and the government's complicity in maintaining an aura of justice while perpetuating a repressive environment. Another fan text prompts answers about what fans would do if they were in charge of the British wizarding world. Following, insightful responses from posters explore issues such as hiring better educators in Hogwarts; fostering interschool international cooperation; setting up orphanages for magical children to prevent childhood abuse and neglect; and reforming the prison system by ridding it of Dementors to make it a more humane correctional facility. Such issues or suggestions are not explicitly mentioned in the source text, revealing the fans' detailed consideration and identification of important aspects left unexplored in the fictional world of Harry Potter. By commenting on the texts within their online community, fans are able to engage "in larger conversations that impact the culture" (Jenkins 2013, xxxviii). Fan communities offer young people a space to describe and discuss difficult topics. These topics may not necessarily impact fans' lives, but they *do* influence conversations and considerations about oppression and justice.

One fan analyzes the complexity and contradictions inherent in Draco Malfoy's character by comparing him to reformed Nazis who recognized the atrocities they were a part of and then worked against former allies in the pursuit of justice. While expressing her own agency when investigating the text, the fan also navigates agency found in both real-life social actors and fictional characters:

> I always thought there was a lot of aspects of the "pure bloods" in Harry Potter series coincided with Nazism in WW2 and I feel like by the end of the series Draco represented members of the Nazi Party who recognized the atrocities they had been convinced to commit and tried in their own way to aid the resistance. Draco was a very complex character that was easy for everyone to write off as the villain but I think if you examine deeper you can see how Draco was a product of his environment and might not have been so villainous if he was in a different situation. (PMTAI 2017p)

In *PMTAI*, a fan responds to a text cataloging the various character deaths in Harry Potter by using Lavender Brown's death[25] as a fictional comparison to discuss how countless innocent young people are often victims in wars that are started by those who are older and more powerful. The fan's emphatic anti-war message uses a fictional example to emphasize their real-world beliefs. "A 17 year old girl who never hurt a fly got mauled and murdered by a savage werewolf!! All because of a damn war that she didn't even fully understand. Why does no one talk about it?? Do we need a stronger example from the fictional world that wars are bad for everyone no matter what side you choose?" (PMTAI 2017q).

CONCLUSION

While other fan scholars have legitimized fan texts as worthy of study, I suggest that fan communities can play a role in empowering fans—particularly young people interacting with children's literature. Participation in online fan communities beyond the direct control of adults contributes to this process. Thanks to advances in technology, demographics of fans are shifting to include younger people who previously did not have access to global fan communities. Not only are young people capable citizens of the digital world but "the empowering function and disseminating power of online spaces and social media" also provides them the potential to shape digital culture (Jenkins, Ito, and boyd 2016; O'Neill 2015, 17).

Fan spaces offer several indirect and unexpected opportunities for young people to voice perspectives on issues that matter to them. These communities allow young people to shape and contribute to their own cultures, as well as access the ideas and views of others from their generation with diverse ideological and environmental backgrounds. This exposure to diverse perspectives can, in turn, help shape their own ideas about the world—both fictional and real. Young people have the potential to resist, transform, and redefine adult norms (Jenkins, Ito, and boyd 2016). Young people are uniquely positioned to effect social change, and digital citizenship provides a space to shape society and culture, despite youth's potential lack of economic and institutional power and resources (Jenkins, Ito, and boyd 2016). Fandom remains constantly in flux and responds to the historical, social, political, and cultural contexts of the time fan texts are produced (Busse and Hellekson 2006). Subsequently, the norms and principles that fans value are diverse and constantly evolving. By using virtual space and fictional worlds as testing grounds for their ideas, online fan communities can, thus, offer spaces for young people to construct and debate their understandings of the world.

Jon Katz (1996) acknowledges that young people's educational, cultural, and social agendas are different to that of previous generations. He insists that these agendas should not be dismissed; rather, young people should be able to write against norms they do not agree with, in turn creating new norms and values (Katz 1996). Fan communities display young people's agendas in forms that may not be taken seriously by adults; however, as examples in this chapter show, fans use a wide range of methods to articulate their responses to real-world issues. Rather than ignoring how young people use popular culture to understand and address real-world limitations, adults should embrace these new forms of citizenship. Lister (2007) argues that citizenship promotes the practice of active and participatory agency and enables people to be agents. In fan communities, young people consistently negotiate and construct their own cultural citizenries. Fans express their agency by appropriating adult-authored texts and transforming them to reflect their own perspectives in the course of cultural and interpretive reproduction (see Corsaro 2015; James, Jenks, and Prout 1998). These processes demonstrate active and collaborative construction of meaning-making through exchanges with other fans. Young fans interact and communicate with peers and adults, negotiate public virtual spaces that host fan communities, and use fan texts to articulate experiences that are important to them.

According to Lister (2007), citizenship is an active and participatory process that enables young people to exercise their rights as agents. A view of young people as active citizens goes against the perception that young people are ignorant or uninterested in political, social, cultural, economic, and moral practices. Young people negotiate complex topics and voice their perspectives in innovative ways (see Castro 2017). Adults frequently exclude young people from citizenship due to a perceived lack of competency and capacity; however, one should be mindful that political and social participation varies in expression and appearance. As Lister (2007) suggests, participation among young people may take on atypical forms that do not match adult notions of agency and citizenship. That said, young people's practices are worthy of recognition and respect, equal to "normative" adult templates of participation.

In fan communities, agency and cultural citizenship are not shaped or enabled by outside authority, but negotiated by young people based on shared interests. Fan activism emerges from fan cultures and uses fictional elements from popular texts to understand and address real-world issues (Jenkins et al. 2016). This form of activism offers an alternative to adult practices and can serve as an entry point to civic and political engagement in the real world, particularly for those young people who may not have otherwise identified themselves as civically minded or politically agentic. Debates and discussions surrounding fictional fantasy worlds and parallels found in the real world allow fans to imagine alternatives to social, political, or economic injustices. Jenkins, Ito, and boyd (2016) call this process "connected civics," wherein young people analyze cultural products for social and political themes relevant to the real world and use digital and social media to share their interpretations. The Harry Potter Alliance[26] popularized the term "cultural acupuncture" to describe the playful and imaginative process of using fictional content worlds (characters, settings, events, and themes) to address real-world issues (Slack 2010). This nonprofit organization respects young fans' emotional investment with popular media and harnesses their culture to encourage political and civic participation (Jenkins 2015). Kahne, Lee, and Feezell's (2013) study suggests that young people's participation in non-political, interest-driven online activities acts as a gateway to engaging in civic and political action in their offline lives.

As my chapter demonstrates, young people express their agency within fandoms and use fictional contexts to discuss issues impacting the larger world. Thus, young people's agency and citizenship may take on unexpected forms after reading and engaging with fantasy texts. Young people play an active role in shaping their own cultures *and* adult cultures. Adults may misjudge young people's interest in and methods of active political and social participation; however, here I reveal numerous inventive ways young people shape their own and others' worlds in online fan spaces. Their practices may not exactly mirror adult notions of participation, but this discrepancy requires an expansion of adult norms rather than outright dismissal of youth interpretations and resultant textual and on-the-ground activisms.

NOTES

1. Some examples include the Harry Potter series by J.K. Rowling, The Chronicles of Narnia series by C.S. Lewis (1950–1956), *Matilda* by Roald Dahl (1988), *The Graveyard Book* by Neil Gaiman (2008), the His Dark Materials series by Philip Pullman (1995–2000), *The Wee Free Men* by Terry Pratchett (2003), and The Bartimaeus Sequence series by Jonathan Stroud (2003–2010).

2. Quote for this section subheading from PMTAI (2017a).

3. All fan text extracts are direct quotes, retaining original spelling, grammar, capitalization, punctuation, and sentence structure.

4. "Ship" is a modern abbreviation for relationship. In fan communities, "shipping" refers to a fan's preferred romantic pairing of fictional characters. These "ships" may or may not be romantically linked in series canons (see Kenny 2019 for more on the history of "shipping" and youths "shipping" their favorite characters online). Draco Malfoy is Harry Potter's rival throughout their time together at school and is often portrayed as an antagonist. Severus Snape is a professor of Potions at Hogwarts—he is frequently belligerent toward Harry and his friends. He used to be a member of Voldemort's gang of dark witches and wizards. Later in the series, it is revealed that he was in love with Lily Potter, Harry's mother, whose murder by Voldemort causes Snape to switch loyalties to school Headmaster Albus Dumbledore. Dumbledore is widely thought to be one of the wisest and most powerful wizards in the world. He is also one of Harry's most important sources of guidance and counsel. Hermione

Granger is one of Harry's two best friends. She is well-known for being extremely intelligent.

5. Voldemort's original name is Tom Riddle, a name he shares with his father. He eventually gives up this moniker and proclaims himself to be Lord Voldemort.

6. Remus Lupin was briefly a professor of Defense Against the Dark Arts at Hogwarts during Harry's third year at the school. He was best friends with Harry's father, James Potter, and Harry's godfather, Sirius Black, prior to their deaths.

7. This fan criticism aligns with Castro's (2019) theories on how children's agency can exist intraindependently, reflecting cooperation between children and adults.

8. Ron Weasley is Harry's other best friend. He is occasionally wracked by feelings of inadequacy and jealousy, which temporarily affect relationships with Harry and Hermione at different times throughout the series. He and Hermione begin a romantic relationship toward the end of the series and eventually marry. See Kenny (2019) for more regarding Rowling's post-series reflections on Hermione and Ron's relationship and marriage.

9. Quote for this section subheading from FOPJ (2017a).

10. Nico di Angelo is a Greek demigod—the son of Hades, god of the dead. He was ashamed of his crush on Percy Jackson and kept it a secret, but eventually he comes out to Percy and Annabeth in Riordan's *The Blood of Olympus* (2014).

11. Will Solace is a Greek demigod—the son of Apollo, god of healing. He and Nico begin a romantic relationship between the events of the last book in the Percy Jackson and the Heroes of Olympus series and the first book in Rick Riordan's The Trials of Apollo series. The LGBTQ community uses the rainbow as a symbol to represent diversity of various gender, sexual, racial, and generational identities.

12. The Hunters of Artemis are a group of young girls who are loyal to Artemis, maiden goddess of the hunt. They swear off the company of men in exchange for immortality and the chance to hunt monsters with the goddess.

13. Annabeth Chase is one of the primary protagonists in the Percy Jackson series. She is a Greek demigod—daughter of Athena, the goddess of wisdom—and is known in the series for her intelligence. She is one of Percy's best friends and they eventually become romantic.

14. Bae is an acronym for Before Anyone Else. The term has been popularized by teens and young adults on social media and is used to refer to someone of romantic interest or someone attractive (Moreau 2019).

15. Fleur Delacour is a French witch, first introduced in *Harry Potter and the Goblet of Fire* (2000), who arrives at Hogwarts to participate in an interschool competition. She eventually marries Bill Weasley, Ron's eldest brother. Her beauty has special powers, given she is the daughter of a Veela, who are semi-human magical creatures.

16. Ginny Weasley is Ron's sister and present during many of Harry's battles against Voldemort. She was possessed by Voldemort in *Harry Potter and the Chamber of Secrets* (1998). She begins a romantic relationship with Harry and they eventually marry.

17. According to the video, examples of film characters with positive masculine traits include Thor from *Thor: The Dark World* (2013), Star-Lord/Peter Quill from *The Guardians of the Galaxy* (2014), and Captain Kirk in *Star Trek Beyond* (2016).

18. Quote for this section subheading from PMTAI (2017l).

19. Pure-blood refers to those people who descend from witches and wizards, as opposed to others who may have one or two non-magical parents. In the Harry Potter series, a muggle is a human, someone who does not have any magical ability and muggle-born refers to a witch or wizard whose parents are muggles but the child has magical abilities. Someone who is born to magical parents but has no magical ability is termed a squib.

20. Remus Lupin is revealed to be a werewolf at the end of *Harry Potter and the Prisoner of Azkaban*. He was bitten as a child and continues to experience great societal prejudice from the wizarding world due to his werewolf condition, wherein he is unwelcomed and feared in the magical world, making it very difficult for him to secure stable employment or housing, thus leaving him poor.

21. Dementors guard the wizarding prison Azkaban. They feed on happiness and cause feelings of despair among humans they encounter. They are also used to punish the worst of crimes by sucking out the soul of the perpetrator. A Patronus, resulting from an incantation, guards witches and wizards against Dementors. To cast it, the witch or wizard must invoke their happiest memories. When the spell is successfully cast, it takes on the form of an animal (specific to each person) to guard the witch or wizard.

22. Rowling recognizes the connection between depression and Dementors (see Treneman 2000).

23. Kingsley Shacklebolt is an important member of the resistance against Voldemort. He is a dark wizard hunter (Auror) and eventually appointed Minister of Magic at the end of the series, as he is viewed as an extremely capable, yet easygoing, leader. Cornelius Fudge was a previous Minister of Magic who did not initially believe Harry or Dumbledore's claims that Voldemort had returned from the dead. He used the government and media to tarnish Harry and Dumbledore's characters and criticized them for spreading fear among the wizarding population. Fudge was forced to resign once the wizarding community discovered Voldemort had, in fact, returned.

24. Quote for this section subheading from PMTAI (2017o).

25. Lavender Brown is Harry's classmate in school. She was briefly in a romantic relationship with Ron Weasley. Lavender's death is hotly contested in Harry Potter fandom since she is only described as injured and unconscious, but not dead, in the last book of the series.

26. Founded in 2005, The Harry Potter Alliance is primarily run by Harry Potter fans and works for equality, human rights, and literacy around the globe.

REFERENCES

Adams, Tim. 2016. "Rick Riordan: 'I'm Hardly the First to Modernise Greek Myths.'" *The Guardian*. April 24, 2016. https://www.theguardian.com/books/2016/apr/24/rick-riordan-percy-jackson-the-hiddle-oracle-interview.

Berlatsky, Noah. 2014. "Young Adult Fiction Doesn't Need to Be a 'Gateway' to the Classics." *The Atlantic*. October 27, 2014. https://www.theatlantic.com/national/

archive/2014/10/young-adult-fiction-doesnt-need-to-be-a-gateway-to-the-classics/381959/.
Black, Rebecca W. 2009. "Online Fan Fiction and Critical Media Literacy." *Journal of Computing in Teacher Education* 26 (2): 75–80.
Books-A-Million. 2017. "Books-A-Million Interviews: Rick Riordan on Writing, Fiction, and Mythology." *Chapters: A Books-A-Million Blog.* April 17, 2017. http://blog.booksamillion.com/author-spotlight/author-interviews/2017/04/books-million-interviews-rick-riordan-writing-fiction-mythology/.
boyd, danah. 2007. "Why Youth ♥ Social Network Sites: The Role of Networked Publics in Teenage Social Life." In *Youth, Identity, and Digital Media*, edited by David Buckingham, 119–42. Cambridge, MA: MIT Press.
Busse, Kristina, and Karen Hellekson. 2006. "Introduction: Work in Progress." In *Fan Fiction and Fan Communities in the Age of the Internet: New Essays*, edited by Karen Hellekson and Kristina Busse, 5–32. Jefferson, NC: McFarland & Co.
Cabello-Hutt, Tania, Patricio Cabello, and Magdalena Claro. 2018. "Online Opportunities and Risks for Children and Adolescents: The Role of Digital Skills, Age, Gender and Parental Mediation in Brazil." *New Media & Society* 20 (7): 2411–31.
Castro, Ingrid E. 2005. "Children's Agency and Cinema's New Fairy Tale." In *Sociological Studies of Children and Youth, Volume 11*, edited by David A. Kinney and Katherine Brown Rosier, 215–38. Amsterdam: Elsevier.
———. 2016. "Children, Innocence, and Agency in the Films of Steven Spielberg." In *Children in the Films of Steven Spielberg*, edited by Adrian Schober and Debbie Olson, 121–40. Lanham, MD: Lexington Books.
———. 2017. "Contextualizing Agency in High-Structure Environments: Children's Participation in Parent Interviews." In *Researching Children and Youth: Methodological Issues, Strategies, and Innovations—Sociological Studies of Children and Youth, Volume 22*, edited by Ingrid E. Castro, Melissa Swauger, and Brent Harger, 149–73. Bingley: Emerald.
———. 2019. "The Spirit and the Witch: Hayao Miyazaki's Agentic Girls and Their (Intra)Independent Generational Childhoods." In *Representing Agency in Popular Culture: Children and Youth on Page, Screen, and In Between*, edited by Ingrid E. Castro and Jessica Clark, 255–82. Lanham, MD: Lexington Books.
Clark, Jessica, and Ingrid E. Castro. 2019. "ZuZu's Petals and Scout's Mockingbirds: The Legacy of Children's Agency in Popular Culture." In *Representing Agency in Popular Culture: Children and Youth on Page, Screen, and In Between*, edited by Ingrid E. Castro and Jessica Clark, xi–xxxi. Lanham, MD: Lexington Books.
Coker, Catherine. 2012. "The Angry! Textual! Poacher! Is Angry! Fan Works As Political Statements." In *Fan Culture: Theory/Practice*, edited by Katherine Larsen and Lynn Zubernis, 81–96. Newcastle Upon Tyne: Cambridge Scholars Publishing.
Corsaro, William A. 2009. "Peer Culture." In *The Palgrave Handbook of Childhood Studies*, edited by Jens Qvortrup, William A. Corsaro, and Michael-Sebastian Honig, 301–15. Hampshire: Palgrave Macmillan.
———. 2015. *The Sociology of Childhood* (4th ed.). Thousand Oaks, CA: SAGE.

Derecho, Abigail. 2006. "Archontic Literature: A Definition, A History, and Several Theories of Fan Fiction." In *Fan Fiction and Fan Communities in the Age of the Internet: New Essays*, edited by Karen Hellekson and Kristina Busse, 61–78. Jefferson, NC: McFarland & Co.

Dresang, Eliza T. 1999. *Radical Change: Books for Youth in a Digital Age*. New York, NY: H.W. Wilson Company.

Duffet, Mark. 2013. *Understanding Fandom: An Introduction to the Study of Media Fan Culture*. New York, NY: Bloomsbury.

FOPJ (Fans of Percy Jackson). 2017a. *Facebook*. June 3, 2017. https://www.facebook.com/fansofpercyjackson1/photos/a.315183935234266/1362711347148181/?type=3&theater.

———. 2017b. *Facebook*. June 11, 2017. https://www.facebook.com/fansofpercyjackson1/photos/a.315183935234266.74351.306530739432919/1372738829478766/?type=3&theater.

———. 2017c. *Facebook*. June 4, 2017. https://www.facebook.com/fansofpercyjackson1/photos/a.315183935234266/1363903703695612/?type=3&theater.

Frankel, Sam. 2012. *Children, Morality and Society*. New York, NY: Palgrave Macmillan.

Hunt, Peter, and Millicent Lenz. 2001. *Alternative Worlds in Fantasy Fiction*. New York, NY: Continuum.

Ito, Mizuko, Heather Horst, Matteo Bittanti, danah boyd, Becky Herr Stephenson, Patricia G. Lange, C.J. Pascoe, Laura Robinson, Sonja Baumer, Rachel Cody, Dilan Mahendran, Katynka Martínez, Dan Perkel, Christo Sims, and Lisa Tripp. 2008. *Living and Learning with New Media: Summary of Findings from the Digital Youth Project*. Chicago, IL: John D. and Catherine T. MacArthur Foundation.

Jackson, Rosemary. 1981. *Fantasy: The Literature of Subversion*. London: Routledge.

James, Allison, and Adrian James. 2012. *Key Concepts in Childhood Studies* (2nd ed.). Thousand Oaks, CA: SAGE.

James, Allison, Chris Jenks, and Alan Prout. 1998. *Theorizing Childhood*. Cambridge: Polity Press.

The Janissary Collective. 2014. "Fandom as Survival in Media Life." In *The Ashgate Research Companion to Fan Cultures*, edited by Linda Duits, Koos Zwaan, and Stijn Reijnders, 77–90. Oxon: Routledge.

Jeffrey, Craig. 2012. "Geographies of Children and Youth II: Global Youth Agency." *Progress in Human Geography* 36 (2): 245–53.

Jenkins, Henry. 1998. "Introduction: Childhood Innocence and Other Modern Myths." In *The Children's Culture Reader*, edited by Henry Jenkins, 1–40. New York, NY: New York University Press.

———. 2006a. *Fans, Bloggers, and Gamers: Exploring Participatory Culture*. New York, NY: New York University Press.

———. 2006b. *Convergence Culture: Where Old and New Media Collide*. New York, NY: New York University Press.

———. 2013. *Textual Poachers: Television Fans and Participatory Culture* (classic ed.). New York, NY: Routledge.

———. 2015. "'Cultural Acupuncture': Fan Activism and the Harry Potter Alliance." In *Popular Media Cultures: Fans, Audiences and Paratexts*, edited by Lincoln Geraghty, 206–29. Hampshire: Palgrave Macmillan.

Jenkins, Henry, Mizuko Ito, and danah boyd. 2016. *Participatory Culture in a Networked Era: A Conversation on Youth, Learning, Commerce, and Politics*. Cambridge: Polity Press.

Jenkins, Henry, Ravi Purushotma, Margaret Weigel, Katie Clinton, and Alice J. Robison. 2009. *Confronting the Challenges of Participatory Culture: Media Education for the 21st Century*. Cambridge, MA: MIT Press.

Jenkins, Henry, Sangita Shresthova, Liana Gamber-Thompson, Neta Kligler-Vilenchik, and Arely Zimmerman. 2016. *By Any Media Necessary: The New Youth Activism*. New York, NY: New York University Press.

Johansen, K.V. 2005. *Quests and Kingdoms: A Grown-Up's Guide to Children's Fantasy Literature*. New Brunswick: Sybertooth.

Kahne, Joseph, Nam-Jin Lee, and Jessica T. Feezell. 2013. "The Civic and Political Significance of Online Participatory Cultures Among Youth Transitioning to Adulthood." *Journal of Information Technology & Politics* 10 (1): 1–20.

Katz, Jon. 1996. "The Rights of Kids in the Digital Age." *Wired*. July 1, 1996. https://www.wired.com/1996/07/kids-2/.

Kenny, Erin. 2019. "'Ship Wars' and the OTP: Narrating Desire, Literate Agency, and Emerging Sexualities in Fanfiction of *The 100*." In *Child and Youth Agency in Science Fiction: Travel, Technology, Time*, edited by Ingrid E. Castro and Jessica Clark, 181–205. Lanham, MD: Lexington Books.

Lister, Ruth. 2007. "Why Citizenship: Where, When and How Children?" *Theoretical Inquiries in Law* 8 (2): 693–718.

Livingstone, Sonia, and Ellen Helsper. 2010. "Balancing Opportunities and Risks in Teenagers' Use of the Internet: The Role of Online Skills and Internet Self-Efficacy." *New Media & Society* 12 (2): 309–29.

Lurie, Alison. 1990. *Don't Tell the Grown-Ups: The Subversive Power of Children's Literature*. Boston, MA: Little, Brown and Company.

Lynn, Ruth N. 2005. *Fantasy Literature for Children and Young Adults: A Comprehensive Guide* (5th ed.). Santa Barbara, CA: Libraries Unlimited.

Mayall, Berry. 2002. *Towards a Sociology for Childhood: Thinking from Children's Lives*. Buckingham: Open University Press.

McNair, Maria D. 2018. "How Children's Literature Became Everybody's Literature." *The Boston Globe*. May 5, 2018. https://www.bostonglobe.com/ideas/2018/05/05/how-children-literature-became-everybody-literature/uRYv5qPURpoEMC4tIq7rAJ/story.html.

Moreau, Elise. 2019. "What Does 'Bae' Mean?" *Lifewire*. June 26, 2019. https://www.lifewire.com/what-does-bae-mean-3485960.

O'Neill, Michael. 2015. "'We Put the Media in (Anti)Social Media': Channel 4's Youth Audiences, Unofficial Archives and the Promotion of Second-Screen Viewing." In *Popular Media Cultures: Fans, Audiences and Paratexts*, edited by Lincoln Geraghty, 17–38. Hampshire: Palgrave Macmillan.

PMTAI (Pottermore—More Than An Insider). 2017a. *Facebook.* June 11, 2017. https://www.facebook.com/PMTAI/photos/a.200314160068922/1102507613182901/?type=3&theater.
———. 2017b. *Facebook.* June 12, 2017. https://www.facebook.com/PMTAI/photos/a.200314160068922/1104145009685828/?type=3&theater.
———. 2017c. *Facebook.* June 5, 2017. https://www.facebook.com/PMTAI/photos/a.200314160068922/1097711213662541/?type=3&theater.
———. 2017d. *Facebook.* June 5, 2017. https://www.facebook.com/PMTAI/posts/1097720893661573.
———. 2017e. *Facebook.* June 1, 2017. https://www.facebook.com/PMTAI/photos/a.200314160068922/1093909427376053/?type=3&theater.
———. 2017f. *Facebook.* June 1, 2017. https://www.facebook.com/PMTAI/photos/a.200314160068922/1093909427376053/?type=3&theater.
———. 2017g. *Facebook.* June 1, 2017. https://www.facebook.com/PMTAI/photos/a.200314160068922/1093909427376053/?type=3&theater.
———. 2017h. *Facebook.* June 1, 2017. https://www.facebook.com/PMTAI/photos/a.200314160068922/1093909427376053/?type=3&theater.
———. 2017i. *Facebook.* June 4, 2017. https://www.facebook.com/PMTAI/photos/a.200314160068922.30486.200302240070114/1095127750587554/?type=3&theater.
———. 2017j. *Facebook.* June 4, 2017. https://www.facebook.com/PMTAI/photos/a.200314160068922.30486.200302240070114/1095127750587554/?type=3&theater.
———. 2017k. *Facebook.* June 1, 2017. https://www.facebook.com/PMTAI/photos/a.200314160068922.30486.200302240070114/1092594800840849/?type=3&theater.
———. 2017l. *Facebook.* June 6, 2017. https://www.facebook.com/PMTAI/photos/a.200314160068922/1097712283662434/?type=3&theater.
———. 2017m. *Facebook.* June 1, 2017. https://www.facebook.com/PMTAI/photos/a.200314160068922/1092595940840735/?type=3&theater.
———. 2017n. *Facebook.* June 9, 2017. https://www.facebook.com/PMTAI/photos/a.200314160068922.30486.200302240070114/1100799603353702/?type=3&theater.
———. 2017o. *Facebook.* June 8, 2017. https://www.facebook.com/PMTAI/posts/1099956290104700.
———. 2017p. *Facebook.* June 13, 2017. https://www.facebook.com/PMTAI/photos/a.200314160068922/1104146233019039/?type=3&theater.
———. 2017q. *Facebook.* June 14, 2017. https://www.facebook.com/PMTAI/photos/a.200314160068922/1105153909584938/?type=3&theater.
Reynolds, Kimberley. 2007. *Radical Children's Literature: Future Visions and Aesthetic Transformations in Juvenile Fiction.* Hampshire: Palgrave Macmillan.
———. 2011. *Children's Literature: A Very Short Introduction.* Oxford: Oxford University Press.
Rosenblatt, Louise M. 1978. *The Reader, the Text, the Poem: The Transactional Theory of the Literary Work.* Carbondale, IL: Southern Illinois University Press.

Slack, Andrew. 2010. "Cultural Acupuncture and a Future for Social Change." *The Huffington Post*. July 2, 2010. http://www.huffingtonpost.com/andrew-slack/cultural-acupuncture-and_b_633824.html.

Standlee, Alecea. 2017. "Digital Ethnography and Youth Culture: Methodological Techniques and Ethical Dilemmas." In *Researching Children and Youth: Methodological Issues, Strategies, and Innovations—Sociological Studies of Children and Youth, Volume 22*, edited by Ingrid E. Castro, Melissa Swauger, and Brent Harger, 325–48. Bingley: Emerald.

Stetka, Bret. 2014. "Why Everyone Should Read Harry Potter." *Scientific American*. September 9, 2014. https://www.scientificamerican.com/article/why-everyone-should-read-harry-potter/.

Thomas, Bronwen. 2011. "What Is Fanfiction and Why Are People Saying Such Nice Things About It?" *Storyworlds: A Journal of Narrative Studies* 3 (1): 1–24.

Treneman, Ann. 2000. "J.K. Rowling, the Interview." *The Times*. June 30, 2000. http://www.accio-quote.org/articles/2000/0600-times-treneman.html.

valentine, kylie. 2011. "Accounting for Agency." *Children & Society* 25 (5): 347–58.

Vezzali, Loris, Sofia Stathi, Dino Giovannini, Dora Capozza, and Elena Trifiletti. 2015. "The Greatest Magic of Harry Potter: Reducing Prejudice." *Journal of Applied Social Psychology* 45 (2): 105–21.

Portals/Time

Chapter 8

Girls' Agency through Supermobility

The Power of Imagined Futures in Young Adult Fantasy Literature

Ida Fadzillah Leggett

Girls are often perceived as "women in training" who are relatively powerless to control the forces affecting their lives. However, in young adult (YA) fantasy literature girls engage in—and are shaped by—alternate identity narratives in which young female protagonists occupy dominant positions that are active, interesting, and important. Using Laini Taylor's Daughter of Smoke and Bone YA fantasy trilogy (2011–2014), I examine how Taylor's creation of a powerful heroine creates a space of imagination that allows her girl readers to imagine new, more agentic identities for themselves. Specifically, I explore how Taylor's manipulation of place, time, and mobility presents a form of "supermobility" for seventeen-year-old female protagonist Karou, and through Karou's access to new geographies, new mobilities, and corresponding new identities, girls can conceive themselves as similarly empowered beings. I argue the ability to imagine new, powerful selves is itself a form of agency that allows girls to engage in alternately scripted gendered expectations and lay claim to the spaces and times of their lives that extend beyond the cosmopolitan and global.

This chapter demonstrates that girls' concepts of identity are powerfully reimagined through their exposure to Karou's ability to occupy and engage space and time while she is propelled at magical speeds across landscapes, kingdoms, species, lifetimes, and life and death. With supermobility, Karou gains control of her future and redefines her agency. I argue that her story fosters readers' "mobility imaginaries," the "socially shared schemas of cultural interpretations about migratory movements that mediate reality and help form identifications of self and other" (Salazar 2010, 56). While most commonly found in reference to cross-border migrations, the concept of mobility imaginaries is also useful in the examination of how fictional landscapes shape girls' ideas about their future movements and possibilities.

For real-life youth, agency can be measured (in part) by achieving mobility and thus controlling their own time and occupied spaces. As children move from one identity to another, "always and necessarily 'being and becoming,'" they are partly enacting their agency through the action of deliberate, controlled movement across webs of significance that branch out to different forms of their present and future selves (Uprichard 2008, 303). The ability to move effortlessly from one place to the next and to claim time in the process is an important aspect of children's agency because while such mobility is not necessarily available to children, it is deeply desired by them. As Frederiksen and Dalsgård (2014) posit in their exploration of youth and temporality, when youth picture their possible futures, what matters is not necessarily the outcome but their imagined possibilities. Thus, understanding the complexities of mobility as an element of real girls' desires and imagined possibilities, intertwined with fictional girls' supermobility in YA fantasy novels, demonstrates the significance of the imaginary on girls' possible future identities.

THE STORY AND THE GIRL

Literature about—and actively consumed by—girls is one avenue through which girls explore "girlhood." Literature provides a safe site for the negotiation of female identities that might not be available in the real world, allowing girls to imagine possible worlds through their immersion with the text (Blackford 2004; Curry 1998; Ryan 2001). Constructions of YA fantasy protagonists, who are usually strong, motivated, young, and female, increasingly overlap with real-life media images of powerful girls like Malala Yousafzai (who at fifteen became a leading proponent for girls' universal education after being shot by the Taliban) and Greta Thunberg (a sixteen-year-old leader of global climate change reform). In this cultural moment of political "girl power," girls are reshaping concepts of gender in line with their cultural, historical, material, and social circumstances, in part by conceptualizing real-life heroines as similar to fictional protagonists (Adams 2009; Willis 2009). For example, in Willis's (2009) research, girls interviewed said their female heroes were various characters found in fictional narratives. Willis (2009) concludes that when these girls referred to such narratives, "they often described a re-imaging of 'girlhood' characterized by spaces in which girls are not bound by normative rules or roles of a society" (106–7).

Girls' imagined realities thus contain links to the world of YA fantasy literature with its powerful young heroines and their promise of empowerment in an increasingly dangerous world. Because of this link and through interacting with the text, girls' imaginations can craft relational models of identity and crisis management since reading offers "a chance to meet characters worth observing and to witness how they manage conflict, peril, and adventure" (Tatar 1987, 18). While Tatar (1987) is referring specifically to fairy tales, Bruhm and Hurley (2004) point out that "Both the best fairy tales and children's/young adult (YA) fiction teach readers to think for themselves through stories that 'make interest' beyond the colonizing narratives of normativity" (xx).

In addition to the possibility of girls' empowerment, the consumption of YA narratives reflects new forms of engagement with the world. For example, teens and young adults do more than passively read YA novels: the YA book community engages in fantasy narratives through video games, YouTube videos, and cosplay; attends comic cons to meet their favorite "producers" of fantasy universes (authors, actors, and show runners, for example), with readers modifying their appearance to match their favorite characters; and spends considerable sums of money on product merchandise. They also participate in fan-oriented chat groups, read and write online reviews of YA books, create fan fiction, and directly contact authors, publishers, and film producers in the hopes of influencing future storylines or the casting of their favorite characters for book to film adaptations. As Weinberger (2016) states, "When it comes to the book world, no segment is as powerful as the Young Adult book community. They get blockbuster movies, channels full of TV adaptations, more merchandise than you can imagine, and one of the strongest online fandoms around." These examples indicate that young people are engaging with their favorite stories through interactive processes, their participation embedded within the content of favorite YA fiction, which results in a very large, influential, and interconnected community.

Young people consume literature voraciously and are personally enriched by the stories; girl readers, in particular, are shaped by fictional narratives in unique ways (see Bettis and Adams 2005; Day 2013; Kearney 2011; Warner 2014; Wu, Mallan, and McGillis 2013). Children absorb stories by engaging in different virtual spaces and social media sites, as well as infusing their own identities into the characters and seeing those identities reflected back in the characters' journeys (Thomas 2007). This multiplicity and "interactive" engagement with literature is key to the influence of YA fantasy novels on readers, and also perhaps an indication of why certain aspects of fantasy seem to work so well with new generations of digital natives. As Thomas (2007) states, "For children, there is no such dichotomy of online and offline, or virtual and real—the digital is so much intertwined into their lives and psyche that the one is entirely enmeshed with the other" (163). Perhaps partly because of such interactivity with fictional narratives, in fantasy literature children's imaginations become less attached to the "real" and focus more on what is "possible" since in fantasy almost anything is possible. Children's engagement with literacy in the digital age reflects new "practices in which young people are actively constructing multimodal texts, manipulating the affordances of technology for a range of pleasurable purposes, and experimenting with new ways of constructing, expressing and communicating their identities," an important aspect of understanding contemporary childhood (Thomas 2007, 182).

While children certainly engage with literature interactively, some scholars wonder how YA narratives influence their audiences, for as Sarah Hentges (2018) writes, "the mountain of evidence that illustrates the power and influence of texts makes this more a question of how, and to what ends, than it is a question of whether texts can change us or changes the world" (199). She adds that YA heroines "grow consciousness in the realm of their stories; readers grow consciousness through reading, reflecting, discussing, and imagining" (Hentges 2018, 228). Similarly, Jessica L. Willis (2009) states of her interviews with tween girls, "When I asked girls who they would identify as a female hero and why, a thematic pattern emerged in which they cited characters from science fiction, adventure, animated and fantasy narratives," demonstrating girls' "deployments of agency in the imaginary" (105 & 112). YA narratives are thus imagined and actively consumed in ways that blur the need to differentiate between fact and fiction, and fictional stories of power and agency go on to influence real girls' concepts of identity.

My theories of how YA fantasy narratives help readers "grow consciousness" are crafted around Laini Taylor's trilogy: *Daughter of Smoke and Bone* (2011), *Days of Blood and Starlight* (2012), and *Dreams of Gods and Monsters* (2014). Taylor's series was met with critical and popular success, beautifully written with unique characters and an unpredictable storyline. I was especially drawn to the richly textured worlds that Taylor builds, and ruminated on them days and even years after the last page was turned. On her blog, the author describes *Daughter of Smoke and Bone* thusly: "There are weird tattoos and giant marionettes; art school, mustaches, and vintage ballet costumes; scary knives, naked ex-boyfriends, and vengeance; heartbreak, a masquerade, a light dusting of sugar, a wishbone on a cord, a cafe full of statues wearing gas masks, plentiful creatures, necklaces made of teeth" (Taylor 2011b).

The series details the adventures of azure-haired Karou, who is an art student in Prague. Though Karou is human, she can also magically make small wishes come true. She was raised by her adoptive monster family (beings known as Chimaera) headed by her guardian, Brimstone. Brimstone has human arms and torso, but beastly aspects for every other part: "below the waist he became *elsething*" (Taylor 2011a, 39). Karou is routinely sent on global errands to purchase teeth from unsavory characters, traveling through mysterious portals in Brimstone's home that open to other places on Earth. Karou does not know anything about her own background, what the teeth are for, or the origins of her Chimaera family, but she plays her part happily and dutifully.

Karou's life changes when she meets Akiva, an angel (or Seraphim) with fiery eyes. She discovers that her real identity has lain hidden within her the whole time: Brimstone uses teeth to resurrect Chimaera souls into new bodies, and Karou's (human) body holds the resurrected soul of Madrigal, who was Akiva's forbidden love and executed for that love seventeen years earlier. Karou thus learns of her origins as Chimaera—who are at war with the Seraphim in a parallel universe—and regains her memories as Madrigal. *Days of Blood and Starlight* continues Karou's story as she struggles to come to terms with her resurfaced hybrid identity as Chimaera/human, with the plot primarily taking place in a castle in Ourzazate, Morocco, "a region of palm oases, camels, and kasbahs at the fringes of the Sahara desert" (Taylor 2012, 138). Karou learns to navigate the dangerous landscapes of Earth and of Eretz, the world of the Chimaera and Seraphim only accessible through rips in the sky. She finds out more about the long war between the Seraphim and the Chimaera, and the reader learns about Akiva's hard life, his half-siblings, the closeness they share as soldiers through blood and battle, and Akiva's slow realization that war is not singular. The book ends with Akiva and his siblings escaping after their failed coup attempt against the Seraphim Empire to end the war. *Dreams of Gods and Monsters* brings the reader full-circle back to Earth, with a ragtag group of renegade angels and monsters coming together to save Eretz and Earth from total annihilation by the Seraphim. This final book in the series brings machine-gun-toting angels into full view of the world and introduces Eliza Jones, a "twenty-four-year-old doctoral student on a tiny budget," who slowly comes to the realization that she is an earthly descendant of a powerful alien society (Taylor 2014, 3). Karou and Akiva organize their respective troops, inspire harmony between the Chimaera and the Seraphim, quell revolts, and, with Eliza's help, save the world.

AGENCY AND CULTURE

Karou has a journey of self-discovery and "becoming." Through her thoughts, actions, and travels she gains and demonstrates agency—feminist agency in particular. Feminist agency is often linked to a variety of psychosocial developments in fictional characters:

> The most powerful way that feminist children's novels reverse traditional gender roles ... is by their reliance on the protagonist's agency .... The protagonist

is more aware of her own agency, more aware of her ability to assert her own personality and to enact her own decisions, at the end of the novel than she has been at the beginning . . . . The feminist protagonist need not squelch her individuality in order to fit into society. Instead, her agency, her individuality, her choice, and her nonconformity are affirmed and even celebrated. (Trites 1997, 6–7)

However, agency is complex and needs to be examined in detail to add to current anthropological research (my academic specialty) that considers the culture of children and youth globally (see Fadzillah 2003, 2005; Khosravi 2008; Levinson 2001; Liu 2011; Soto 2018).

The concept of agency has multiple layers of significance and is "possibly *the* key concept of Childhood Studies" (James and James 2012, 3). Prout and James (1997) establish some of the basic tenets, positing that "Children are and must be seen as active in the construction and determination of their own social lives, the lives of those around them and of the societies in which they live" (8). James (2011) defines children's agency as "what it means to act" (43), and Theis (2001) states that children practice agency when they "take an active part in creating and organizing their environment, making decisions, having their own views, interests, skills, and abilities" (100). In agreement, Oswell (2016) sees children's agency in their abilities to be active, participative, and politically demonstrative. Additionally, Prout and James (1997) theorize children's agency as important "not just in its construction, but also in its active reconstruction" (9). Regarding this "active reconstruction," Buckingham (2019) finds agency "is not a fixed quality, but one that is actively *produced* in different social contexts and defined in quite different ways," and "involves factors such as individual choice, autonomy, self-determination, and creativity, but it also implies *power*—the power to produce an effect, to have influence, to make a difference in the world" (284).

The practice theory of agency, as applied to children, posits that "In every practice in which they participate, they produce self-positioning actively and with considerable situation variability" (Bollig and Kelle 2016, 41). Bollig and Kelle (2016) suggest that the researcher considers "the differential forms of children's agency as an effect of encounters between different practice ensembles, their choreography and their interconnection" (42). The construction and reconstruction of life by children is an important point in my research, because it implies that agency is about acting, but can also be found in currently changing social structure accompanied by children's desire to effect change. As Oswell (2016) writes, "The determination of social structure, but also the power of agency to change that structure, are instantiated in the present time" (21).

Raithelhuber (2016) sums up recent discussions of agency as "the idea that someone or something is endowed with a capacity or potential to do things and to make a difference," with agency connected "to intentionality, thus representing intention or some sort of consciousness, or at least a form of practical reflexivity" (93). The concept of children's agency, in particular, places strong emphasis not just on the act, but on the social, with agency found to be "not a quality that children possess by nature; instead, it is produced in conjunction with a whole network of different human and non-human actors, and is distributed among these" (Esser et al. 2016, 9). Therefore, children's agency is evidenced in their actions, their ability to act, their connections to their social networks, their potential, and thoughts of their actions and abilities. Here, I argue that desires and imaginations associated with possible positive change—perhaps especially in children—are also agentic. Thus, while agency exists in "being" a certain way, I believe that for girls their agency is found in the potential to control their "becoming": "what" one becomes, "when" one becomes, and "where" one comes into being. We cannot witness or guide this transformation in real life since time is always in the present for the viewer, but in reading fantasy literature and constructing our imaginations, such potential control over "becoming" is an empowering, agentic ability with untapped potential.

Specifically, my analysis finds that the agency of girls in fantasy stories presents itself through an "ontological narrative," defined as "the stories that social actors use to make sense of—indeed, in order to act in—their lives . . . . Ontological narratives make identity and the self something that one *becomes*" (Somers 1992, 603). Regarding the Smoke and Bone series, I use Castoriadis's (1987) concept of agency, wherein the idea of the symbolic as the realm of instituted meaning is replaced with the idea of the "social imaginary," its radical flux creating a condition of possibility from which many outcomes, ideas, and identities could arise. The social imaginary connects well to "agentive realism," which Barad (2007) posits is the process of "mattering," with agency engaged by our own perceptions of the transaction between matter and meaning. Further, as Trites (2018) explains, "Gendered bodies are not simply material objects; they are constantly redefined as agents through the discursive processes of mattering" (12). This concept of agency in the abstract (rather than what is found in concrete action) is significant because it prioritizes the aspect of "becoming." Thus, I believe one effect of the Smoke and Bone series on its girl readers is that it provides a new model of "becoming," specifically through experiencing space and time via supermobility, which can influence how readers imagine their own possibilities in the real world.

SUPERMOBILITY AND IMAGINARIES

The concept of space is complex, a "bundle of trajectories" within which different people, things, memories, buildings, and histories come together to create "place," a "simultaneity of stories-so-far" (Massey 2005, 9 & 47). For children's geographies scholars, childhood is recognized as "spatially as well as temporally specific" (Holloway and Valentine 2000, 10). This understanding of space and place is significant to the argument at hand, especially when discussing space and place in children's story-influenced imaginaries. In the Smoke and Bone series, Laini Taylor sets the scene for readers by harnessing the potentiality of "soft cities," reflecting a landscape that is both real and imagined. "The soft city of illusion, myth, aspiration, nightmare . . . is as real, maybe more real, than the hard city one can locate on maps" (Raban 1974, 2). Within soft cities, just as within fantasy stories, anything is possible.

Karou is a youth who engages with the soft city in imaginative ways: she plays a ghost on Prague's vampire tour, sports a Fu Manchu mustache at the Moustache Bar, and constantly draws figures from the landscape in her sketchbook. She is also action-oriented, with the scars to prove it: she is trained to fight, carries a knife, and has been shot several times. Most significantly, Karou moves across great spaces frequently and effortlessly; hence, her self-proclaimed label of being a "hither-and-thither girl." She lived restlessly in Manhattan and then in Hong Kong before settling in Prague. She uses portals to quickly travel to Paris, San Francisco, Morocco, and Saigon on her errands for Brimstone. Karou also "had claim to no nationality. Her papers were all forgeries, and her accents . . . were all fakes" (Taylor 2011a, 27). She is fluent in fifteen languages—she magically collects them as her favorite birthday presents. Thus, she is a character whose identity and agency are tied to her global mobility, restlessness, and acumen.

The concept of a more agentic imaginary—of one's place in the world transforming into highly active engagement with the world—is further reflected in research on societies that demonstrate changing ideas of and desires for mobility. Frederiksen and Dalsgård's (2014) definition for the imaginary works well here: "an open field of possibilities [where the] mere fact that it has not happened yet makes it fertile ground for the imagination. It is in what they imagine that agency is located" (9). Rudolf Mrázek (2002) examines how "unseemly technologies" like railroads introduced during colonial Dutch rule in Batavia changed how native Indonesians saw themselves in relation to the rest of the world. Specifically, he looks at how "the late-colonial sense of touching the ground with one's feet or wheels on trains or cars, as well as roads, velocity, and the conceptualization of moving" transformed "natives" into modern subjects (Mrázek 2002, xvi).

Wardlow (2006) explores how Huli women in Papua New Guinea alter their status within the Huli community by becoming "passenger women": those who leave their traditional compounds controlled by fathers or husbands, traveling across the land on modern buses in direct contradiction of cultural gender norms. Not only are these women traversing long distances by themselves, they are also peppering their conversations with modern pidgin words, wearing Western apparel like sunglasses and flip-flops, and breaking other traditions (for example, using modern contraceptives). Becoming a passenger woman—with its easy mobility across a range of spaces and associated statuses—makes these women "modern." Another example is Handman's (2017) research on the Guhu-Samane, also of Papua New Guinea. In the last few decades, the Guhu-Samane converted to Christianity, but many are experiencing a crisis of faith: they prayed unsuccessfully for years for an asphalt road (and cars) that could connect them to the neighboring villages, and now see their continued difficult trek on foot for hours through the unpaved jungle as proof that there is no Christian God. If a road was built and they were able to get to places faster and in a more modern fashion, they argue, that would be proof that the space of their valley is now part of a Christian kingdom.

Moving forward to examples of the imaginary specifically found in global girls' lives, Soto's (2018) work on Mexican and Mexican American teenage girls' "migrant imaginaries" demonstrates how much of their agency is located within their imagined futures. These girls "enact new imaginaries, temporalities, and spatialities from which new ways of being women emerge" (Soto 2018, 11). And finally, my own research (Fadzillah 2003) posits an interesting connection between rural Thai girls' sense of agency through their ability to travel via public buses, jeepneys, motorbikes, and bicycles to the big city of Chiang Mai or Bangkok to sell or to buy things. Further, they dream of flying to Michigan to get rewarded for their superior Amway sales, or to Taipei or Tel Aviv to visit their migrant parents, or to Paris or London to achieve sophisticated work positions (Fadzillah 2005). Desires for international, successful futures push these girls to long for a "cosmopolitan" life far from their natal villages, part of the logic that pulls Thai girls into the international prostitution industry.

These anthropological examples demonstrate that real life contains "triggers" around mobility that can cause a shift from traditional, to modern, to international citizenship. Technologies of mobility and travel also shape ideas pertaining to the shift from "child to adult"; for children, especially youth, the possibility of mobility is transformational. These technologies of mobility and travel are of particular significance to girlhood since real-life girls chafe at their relative immobility in relation to enforced limitations on the spaces they are traditionally allowed to occupy. From this perspective, cultural field examples are useful in understanding girls' own perspectives on their practice of agency: they dream of freedom, defined as the ability to become a more significant part of the "real world" (more adult, more responsible, more civilized, more global). Thus, the images and narratives of supermobility provided to youth through YA fantasy literature can shape imaginaries of the future, as perceived by readers: ideas of supermobility can add to girls' sense of their own capacities to be agentic. As Hentges (2018) writes, YA fantasy heroines are "a part of a culture of possibilities" (16). She further posits that "YA dystopia specifically, can play an important role in the futures we imagine" (Hentges 2018, 17).

THE FAIRY TALE

The style and imagery of fairy tales consistently appear in YA fantasy, weaving novels from ancient storytelling traditions. Fairy tales are usually characterized as stories that occur a long time ago in a place far away (or an unknown place); feature magic or marvels and symbolic objects that possess great power; contain stereotypical characters representing extremes of good and evil; and end happily, or, at least, justly (Lindahl 2018). Fairy tales are some of the oldest forms of narrative storytelling, and one of their most powerful qualities is the inclusion of aspects that address universal meanings and specific cultural details (Lindahl 2018). These tales often feature "magical, transformative characters, forces, and events," and "its giants, witches, and dragons appear magical to the tale tellers and listeners, but in the eyes of the *Marchen* [German for 'tale'] hero they appear normal . . . the hero rarely shows awe in encountering magic" (Lindahl 2018, 12). The fairy tale form continues to be active and popular in today's YA fantasy literature, perhaps because YA fantasy narratives share the general formula of fairy tales that "tend to feature children who grow into adulthood by leaving home, conquering magical adversaries, and/or passing special tests" (Lindahl 2018, 13).

In her fantasy series, Laini Taylor creates a magical fairy tale experience for the reader, first through wedging the reader into the narrative by crafting the character of Karou as a story within the story. Karou is already established as a creature of modern fairy tales since she travels effortlessly to faraway places through magic portals, makes wishes come true, and is a descendant of magical beings. However, there are additional literary signifiers: Karou sports multiple tattoos (including one on each wrist spelling out "true" and "story") and she is described as moving "like a poem" (Taylor 2011a, 8 & 18). When Akiva (her love interest) first glimpses Karou wandering the Marrakesh souk, he cannot believe what he sees: "It was like stepping into the pages of a book—a book alive with color and fragrance, filth and chaos—and the blue-haired girl moved through it all like a fairy through a story, the light treating her differently than it did others, the air seeming to gather around her like held breath. As if this whole place were a story about her" (Taylor 2011a, 78). Razgut, a broken creature as old as time, narrates the moral of Karou's life: "She tastes like fairy tales. Swan maiden at midnight . . . . She tastes like hope" (Taylor 2011a, 117). Thus, Taylor presents Karou as a hybrid of various fairy tale protagonists come to life, and this hybridity manifests within Karou a fantasy-based agency. Through this framing of the main character, the reader is incorporated into the fantastic spaces of imagination and is submerged into the story.

Before we can fully understand Karou's story, however, we must combine it—much like Brimstone does—with the story of Madrigal, a beautiful and noble Chimaera: "Her horns were a gazelle's, black and ridged, flowing up off her brow and back in a scimitar sweep. Her legs shifted at the knees from flesh to fur, the gazelle portion giving them an elegant, exaggerated length, so that when she stood to her full height she was nearly six feet, not including horns, and an undue portion of that was leg" (Taylor 2011a, 319). Akiva first encounters Madrigal as he lies dying in the aftermath of battle. He sees her walking toward him, "unaccountably beautiful," and he is "dream-lost . . . beyond wondering whether this was real. It could be a dying dream, or she could be a reaper sent from the next life to cull his soul" (Taylor 2011a, 269–70). So, if Karou is like a fairy tale, then Madrigal is like a dream, a beautiful monster of horns and hooves.

Madrigal reflects a common fairy tale trope in which animals are portrayed as humans, "including nonhuman animals dressing as humans and vice versa, as well as magical somatic transformations between human and nonhuman forms" (Greenhill and Allen 2018, 225). Through this hybridity, "Fairy tales extend transbiology to include transgenic magic, in which nonhuman and human biological characteristics combine" (Greenhill and Allen 2018, 225). The hybrid creature and her narrative of monstrosity can be seen to function "as metaphors for the teen girl's negotiation of her changing body along with her search for identity and autonomy" (Talafuse 2014, 1; see also Clark and Castro 2019). Characters' girl-animal bodies can also give them agency when they are silenced at the level of the human, allowing them more abilities to accomplish tasks and create endings impossible to achieve by singular, simple humans (Viswanath 2019). An imaginative construction not just of possible worlds, but possible bodies, can therefore demonstrate a more sympathetic consideration of other/ed bodies—animals, sexualities, disabilities— in readers' lives, a move toward confronting and accepting otherness that is a powerful act of agency (Lassén-Seger 2006). While the hybrid "monstrous feminine" has been examined in detail (see Clark and Castro 2019; Talafuse 2014), in this case, Karou/Madrigal is less a monster and more a creature of words and stories, a body of signifiers of the real and fantastic in tales, memories, and dreams.

Laini Taylor also focuses the reader's attention on the fantastic as unknowable and liminal, rather than the expected and static. For example, as explained previously, Brimstone's beastly aspects are described as "*elsething*," and when Karou asks how the magical portals work, Brimstone brusquely responds that they lead to "*elsewhere*." While these are brief examples, they are an efficient tool to shift the reader's eyes away from the real and explainable and onto something different just out of readers' everyday reach. The Smoke and Bone novels' framing of landscape is partly based on the perspective of place as ungrounded and consistently shifting. Karou, for example, is a constant world traveler and has no geographic base: "Home. The word always had air quotes around it" (Taylor 2011a, 422). Meanwhile, Karou's Prague apartment is merely a place for momentary rest in between ventures into the in-between plane; thus, home itself becomes an in-between space.

Without a definitive geographic starting point, Taylor anchors the stable and solid not to places, but to people. Zuzana, Karou's best friend, is a quintessentially human teenage girl, as demonstrated through her mannerisms and speech. She is the protective friend who stays until the end, the useful friend who makes things happen, the funny friend who keeps things real, and the hip friend who uses teen-speak and actions completely appropriate to her age and generation. For example, when Zuzana is first introduced to handsome Akiva she blurts out: "Oh, hell. Must. Mate. Immediately" (Taylor 2011a, 236). After this encounter, she has T-shirts screen-printed that proclaim: "I MET AN ANGEL IN MOROCCO AND ALL I GOT WERE THESE LOUSY SCARS" and "I SAW AN ANGEL AND YOU DIDN'T. SUCK IT, RAPTURE-MONKEYS!" (Taylor 2012, 153). When Karou considers fleeing from her troubles, Zuzana says, "You are not just going to vanish like this, Karou. This isn't some goddamn Narnia book" (Taylor 2012, 291), a playful reference to C.S. Lewis's (1950) fantasy land. And when Karou does run away, Zuzana emails her: "Gone to ANOTHER WORLD. I always knew you were a freaky chick, but I never saw this one coming . . . most important, do they have chocolate there?" (Taylor 2014, 10). Zuzana provides the counterweight of reality in this fairy tale narrative, and acts as the stand-in for real girls reading the books; her presence also fashions fantasy into something that is immediately recognizable and thus comfortable to teenage girls peering into Karou's uncanny life.

TIME

Another way Laini Taylor refocuses the reader from the real to the fairy tale is by playing with time. First, though, she establishes the normal: the story opens with a day that seems "just like another Monday, innocent but for its essential Mondayness, not to mention its Januaryness" (Taylor 2011a, 1). The scene is set in the realm of the teenage "ordinary": "Karou's own footsteps and the feather of steam from her coffee mug, and she was alone and adrift in mundane thoughts: school, errands" (Taylor 2011a, 1). But, by the second novel Taylor includes time that is disorienting on multiple levels; for example, during dreams "that invade the space between seconds, proving sleep has its own physics—where time shrinks and swells, lifetimes unspool in a blink, and cities burn to ash in a mere flutter of lashes" (Taylor 2012, 43). In the final book of the series, Taylor (2014) describes the day the Seraphim show themselves on Earth, using time as the reference point: "On this day in history—the ninth of August—time cleaved abruptly into 'before' and 'after,' and no one would ever forget where they were when 'it' began" (11). Akiva muses on possible futures: "There is the past, and there is the future. The present is never more than the single second dividing one from the other. We live poised on that second as it's hurtling forward—toward what?" (Taylor 2014, 79). But, time reorients itself slowly and begins again with encounters between Madrigal/Karou and Akiva. Long before her death, Madrigal and Akiva contemplate a life without war, and Madrigal states, "This is the beginning, here . . . . We are the beginning" (Taylor 2011a, 169). Akiva also recounts a conversation with Madrigal, when she tells him the human tale of the golem: "It was a thing shaped of clay in the form of a man, brought to life by carving the symbol aleph into its brow. Aleph was the first letter of an ancestral human alphabet, and the first letter of the Hebrew word truth; it was the beginning" (Taylor 2011a, 296). The first time he sees Karou, Akiva realizes "she was his aleph, his truth and beginning" (Taylor 2011a, 296). As aleph is the first letter of the ancestral alphabet, Madrigal/Karou is to him about beginnings, and also about hope for a better future.

However, it is Eliza Jones who is the very manifestation of time, for she is the direct descendant of an alien species and carries all knowledge of past, present, and future in her body. Once she fully accepts her abilities, she "beheld Time itself laid open before her, unzipped like a strand of DNA. Knowable. Possibly even navigable" (Taylor 2014, 474). Eliza is thus a conduit into future possibilities and the most powerful being of all. Interestingly, she brings with her the capacity to not just effortlessly travel across space but also across time—the ultimate supermobility. Laini Taylor thus ties time to hope, and going back to "the beginning" in the future presents the possibility of second chances for all involved. Through her literary imagery combined with her characters' abilities, Taylor creates an imaginary for her readers in which time, space, and travel can be controlled, an empowering act. For as Zeiher and colleagues (2007) state, "Time and space related agency, as well as representations of time and space, are driving forces in social change, and social change occurs in temporal and spatial phenomena" (11).

Within childhood studies, time is recognized as an important aspect of agency, wherein agency can be seen as "a temporally embedded process of social engagement, informed by the past . . . but also oriented toward the future" (Emirbayer and Mische 1998, 962; Närvänen and Näsman 2007). Increasingly, children in real life are spatially and temporally confined to child-specialized spaces (like playgrounds and schools) and stricter time structures, a process of "domestication" with a shift of activities away from unregulated external spaces to protected internal spaces (Hengst 2007; Zeiher et al. 2007). In addition to domestication, children are also experiencing "insularization," in which the unitary spaces available to earlier generations of children are now fragmented and scattered, requiring greater mobility so as to be crossed (Hengst 2007). Within this perspective of childhood, parental control of children's activities in time and space provides an example of children's lack of agency (Närvänen and Näsman 2007). Thus, Laini Taylor's imaginative expansion of travel and identity across time and space can serve to provide a temporally embedded model of agency to engage children's, and specifically girls', desires and imaginations.

One powerful force that disrupts time and space in the Smoke and Bone series is the ability of people to be revived after death, creating an experience of time that can be unending and an understanding of age that can be irrelevant. Reincarnation, especially of Chimaera souls into human bodies (as in the case of Madrigal/Karou), is an example of "literary metamorphosis," as detailed by Maria Lassén-Seger (2006). She states that "the fascination of literary metamorphosis is that it enacts an adventure that takes the protagonists, not necessarily out of this world, but out of their human bodies" (Lassén-Seger 2006, 1). So, bodies become signifiers rather than biological truths since one body can hold several lifetimes (and ages) of relationships, moralities, dreams, and futures: a state of being that requires constant renegotiation of what it is to be "human" (Lassén-Seger 2006). This act of renegotiation, in addition to the ability to control one's age and lifetimes, is quite agentic, for control over one's body implies a control over one's identity. For example, in terms of childhood, general society interprets aging and time as the process of growth and development, informed by constructivist guidelines of what adults believe to be appropriate for the respective age of the child (Corsaro 2015). Therefore, being able to command one's body through control over one's age results in the capacity to redirect society's perspective toward children's heightened abilities and reconsider children's regularly undervalued status. And since agency presupposes time as necessary for acquiring knowledge, and experiences as the basis for reflexivity, interpretation, and action, a person's supposed "age" makes a difference in terms of interpreting and enacting agency (Närvänen and Näsman 2007).

Another related element of supermobility is apparent in the reincarnated body's ability to contain multiple individuals, multiples experiences, and multiple ages: because seventeen-year-old Karou is also seventeen-year-old Madrigal (dead seventeen years now), time and age become interwoven and complicated. The beginning is not the beginning, and we learn that the end is not the end but the creation of a new chronology altogether. Therefore, the ability to resurrect souls troubles time, for bodies (and their ages) are irrelevant: Brimstone says dismissively, "Bodies were just bodies, just things" (Taylor 2011a, 328). Thus, in the Smoke and Bone series a character can have an old soul in a teenage body, which is important given that "bodily transformations are extremely interesting phenomena in regard to aged and gendered identities, both in real life and in fiction. Growing up does not necessarily take years. It may take only one significant moment. One significant transformation" (Lehtonen 2013, 1).

Bodily transformations like the processes of aging and changing, the limits of identity and selfhood, and the boundaries of living and dying can address fundamental human concerns, as well as lay bare different kinds of power relations (Lehtonen 2013). For example, when Karou is forced into conflict, she experiences an identity shift that transforms her from a teenager at school into a seasoned warrior within multiple universes. In this case, young people are also adults, accompanied by adult responsibilities and abilities. Taken to its logical conclusion, the possibility of reincarnation means that anyone can have power over their own lives, even children, since they likely carry with them adult experiences. Establishing agency as a temporally embedded process that is both situational and relational within this reincarnated model of life ("always agency toward something," Emirbayer and Mische 1998, 973), agency is "enfolded" into youth since Taylor's children are individuals who carry many lifetimes worth of experiences and relationships in one body.

Lehtonen (2013) argues that there is something specifically gendered within bodily transformations since these movements "offer various perspectives on a girls' changing body and agency and provide links between real-life and fantastic discourses of gender, power . . . growing up and aging" (5). In the fantasy genre, bodily transformations are not merely considered natural; instead, these movements are often expected and desired outcomes that work to establish a new line of traditions, customs, and youth-centered cultures to which the young protagonist (and her readers) can relate. As in fairy tales, such transformations are illustrated as the awakening of something (or someone)—as truths or identities or destinies—that have always been present but must be "triggered." I perceive transformation in Taylor's series as reflective of how young people in real life think about their own connections to their future, adult selves: they wait for an awakening to reveal their destinies, their callings, and their paths in the world.

SPACE

In his analysis of globalization, James Clifford (1988) reflects on the resultant "clash" of spaces that bring the "exotic . . . uncannily close" (13). He calls this clash "dis-orientation," and part of what causes this dis-orientation is that culture—or cultural difference—is recognized as "no longer a stable, exotic otherness" but is as familiar as our own backyard (Clifford 1988, 14). Central to contemporary childhood, especially among Western youth, is their identification with global spaces and cross-cultural interminglings; currently, youth desire and experience such global citizenship at much higher and faster rates than older generations (Coe 2005; Cole 2008; Durham 2008). Thus, the presentation of fantastic mobility in popular YA fantasy narratives—of sprouting wings, magical doors that connect to faraway places, traversing parallel universes, or exploring the galaxy—should garner special attention to the genre. Modern fantasy series like Smoke and Bone reflect youth's global senses of space, place, and travel across "youthscapes," as well as express their dreams and desires through "mobility imaginaries" (Maira and Soep 2005; Salazar 2010). Laini Taylor presents Karou occupying a fictional landscape while traveling the whole world, maneuvering through spaces that actually exist, but are depicted as fantastical and dreamlike as though from a child's vivid and limitless imagination. Taylor's fictive imaginary emphasizes magic found in the dream of what is possible in the fantastic realm.

As explained, Taylor begins Karou's story in Prague, using a soft city description that is an amalgam of realities and fictions, heroes and villains: "The streets of Prague were a Fantasia scarcely touched by the 21st century, or 20th or 19th, for that matter. It was a city of optimists and dreamers, it's medieval cobbles once trod by golems, mystics, invading armies . . . . The wind carried a memory of magic, revolution, violins, and the cobbled lanes meandered like creeks" (Taylor 2011a, 24). Spaces filled with European historical lore abound in Karou's daily life: she goes to school at the Art Lyceum of Bohemia, situated "in a pink Baroque palace where famously, during the Nazi occupation, two young Czech nationalists had slit the throat of a Gestapo commander and scrawled *liberty* with his blood" (Taylor 2011a, 5). Karou and Zuzana's favorite hangout spot is Poison Kitchen, a dark and hidden café. To reach Poison Kitchen is a fairy tale journey in itself, moving down winding roads and through misty arches, and the interior that awaits manages to incorporate elements of the interesting and fantastic, filled with Roman statues of life-size gods, nymphs with missing arms and wings, and giant horse statues sporting World War I gas masks. In her spatial descriptions, Taylor accomplishes a kind of "dis-orientation," a fictional "clash of spaces" by portraying the real world as so exotic that even a fantasy locale like the city of Astrae seems real, with its "Palaces, arcades, fountains, all pearl marble quarried in Evorrain, broad boulevards paved in quartz, overreached by the honey-scented boughs of Gilead. It perched above its harbor on striated cliffs, with the emerald Mirea coast as far as the eye could see" (Taylor 2011a, 280). Connecting these worlds and cities are portals; therefore, Karou lives in a city that is a heady combination of past, present, and fantasy, traveling anywhere in this world or beyond in mere seconds across the great divide.

Once the truth of her origin as Madrigal/Karou is revealed, Karou uses her rudimentary magic and wishes for the ability to fly, and from that moment on her agency is expressed in soaring action as she searches for her family and the truth about her life. The landscape is now expanded to illustrate the characters' "super-global" worlds—youth's origins, in this fantasy context, include other planets and parallel worlds. This super-global network is one that is easily accessible for Karou (though not to others); she figures out how to breach guarded entrances into Eretz through rips in the sky. The sky as border and the rips as doors reflect a common device in YA fantasy fiction; as Hentges (2018) writes, "Almost every book/series has some version of a wall. The intent is safety, the effect is illusion and often oppression. The wall works in conjunction with the corrupt power structure, but it is also a symbol on its own. One thing about walls that YA dystopia makes clear: they get broken down" (118). And the Smoke and Bone series, with the demonstration of supermobility through the protagonists' movements, presents the actions necessary for youth to break down walls as an agentic means to cross into and over many worlds. This youth-oriented agency prizes mobility and superhuman speed. So, mobility, travel, and the ability to adjust to spaces lost and found provide an endless field within which characters can redefine what is possible.

Breached and reconfigured borders in the Smoke and Bone series are also demonstrated through the main characters' dismantling of traditional expectations and rules of nations and cultures. The presence of (at least) three different worlds allows the young characters to break from traditional institutions, expectations, and cultures. In the real world, understanding kinship is how children learn their place in their society (Montgomery 2009). Thus, to start (become) something new, one must first break with traditional kinship ties and rules. And, if girls are able to separate from such traditional expectations, they can reconstruct their teen girlhood identities in ways they see fit within their new global—and universal—world. YA novels describe the characteristics of global girls as the most beautiful (across the heavens, animals, and humans) and desirable (across time and space). YA global girls like Karou perceive beauty in all their worlds; they want peace and freedom (unlike elders, who only want war), and they connect disparate groups together because global girls represent new ideas, new solutions, and new freedoms. Agency is thus accentuated as empowerment across time and space, beyond traditional expectations and into untold futures. Agency becomes the ability to control expectations and create new traditions, something only possible if one can claim the entire world or universe as one's point of origin, rather than a singular tradition, family, culture, or timeline.

CONCLUSION: CHILDHOOD, HOPE, AND IMAGINED FUTURES

Children's connection to space is different than that of adults, who control occupied places through their legal mobility: adults own cars and motorbikes, they can take the subway by themselves, and they can fly unimpeded to far-away places. Children and youth frequently do not have access to that sort of easy mobility—they have to stay in school, they do not have access to a driver's licenses, they do not own motorized vehicles, they cannot travel solo, and, for the most part, they must go where they are told until they reach a certain age (and, as we know, those ages vary widely between and within nations). Thus, children's agency is legally and culturally limited, but their desire for mobility is strong and shapes imaginaries of their futures. Desire might influence their concrete decisions, but, more importantly, this desire shapes their perspectives of the world and their places within society. Therefore, in imaginary worlds, an expansion and reconceptualization of the very concept of childhood and the abilities and futures of children are created and reimagined.

By dissolving real-life narratives into the fairy tale and dis-orientating the reader with the presence of fantastic creatures, spaces, and possibilities, Laini Taylor's Smoke and Bone series fuses Karou's supermobility across space, time, and bodies onto the reader's own experience of identity. This interconnection introduces the reader to a new agentic narrative through which the ability of the fictional protagonist to transcend geographic and age boundaries can be connected to the reader's real-life mobile possibilities. Through a presentation of Karou's abilities, the reader's imaginary of possible futures is bridged between the fantastic and the real. Karou's supermobility is of particular significance since today's children and youth are faced with limits to their real-life mobility that many desire to transcend. This mobile imaginary can give children the taste of freedom, within which they might envision "self" as becoming anybody, anywhere (Strandell 2007). For girls, specifically, encounters with such fantasy narratives allow for "the possibility of adolescent women readers 'experiencing' the realities of young adulthood vicariously through the narrators' stories" (Day 2013, 18). Girls' agency in the imaginary provides a space for conceptualizing girlhood in ways that transform and morph dichotomized notions of gender (Willis 2009). With mobility imaginaries, girls can experience potential future lives and make decisions in the present toward or away from various potential futures.

This chapter's emphasis is on space as it interacts with time, especially in terms of moving into the future. Others have focused more specifically on how the future is a significant motivator for girls (see McCall 2015; Zannettino 2008). Karou's name means "hope," which is noteworthy because, as Cole and Durham (2008) point out, youth "see hope as an active and even agentive orientation toward the future" (15). The hope created through Taylor's writing and focus on dis-orientations is one that guides the reader toward a future that is filled with anxiety-free adventure coupled with the normalization of new versions of childhood practices and identities. Importantly,

> Looking at hope and its enactments in everyday life allows us to examine not just the spatial dimensions of these flows but also the ways they enter into the temporalities of people's lives and relationships . . . . Conceived in this way, hope is political, a sentiment that diversely situated actors deploy to link, challenge, or reconfigure domestic, national, and transnational relationships. (Cole and Durham 2008, 16)

Cole and Durham (2008) further write that "Children and youth create the future . . . children and youth's practices, sometimes inadvertently, generate new ways of thinking, feeling, and being that carry into the future" (18). I demonstrate that Laini Taylor's novels, though they dwell within the imaginary, give girls agency in the form of new narratives that steer them to different, possible futures.

I believe one reason her novels are popular is because girls fully connect with the imaginary worlds and the imagined futures the books create. Girls globally are highly influenced by imagined lives and imaginary worlds. My previous research chronicles how Thai village girls are inspired by their own future possibilities through the images of their absent parents' lives as portrayed in letters, postcards, phone calls, and photographs from faraway lands (Fadzillah 2003). They want to be part of cosmopolitan city life, strongly influenced by secondhand accounts to imagine urban, international lives for themselves with Western clothes, makeup, mopeds, speaking English, and having foreign boyfriends. These places have differently magical and fantastical aspects to them; for example, in their dreams people are very tall and very handsome, and far-off locales are very cold and very snowy. But, for girls in the West, these people and places are not "exotic" or unknown, instead they are mundane. In many ways, since such places exist in the spaces Western girls physically occupy, their imaginations must propel them even further afield to find spaces that inspire their dreams and desires. For Western girls today, YA books set in other realms are just the beginning of this search;

for example, girls are also intricately connected to new technologies and products such as social media networks and communities and fan fiction sites where they can write their own versions of fantastical stories. These girls' real lives are mobile, perpetually connected, lived outside of schooltime, artistic, and filled with the imaginary because in the spaces girls occupy, they consider their desires, dreams, and fantasies to be as important as the real, the mundane, and the everyday. Through fantasy stories and enchanting future possibilities, girls outside of Western privilege can also imagine alternative—and better—futures for themselves. Fantasy series like Smoke and Bone present new narratives of possible lives, providing potential futures that might be slightly too far to grasp, but near enough to imagine.

REFERENCES

Adams, Annmarie. 2009. "The Power of Pink: Children's Bedrooms Since World War II." Paper Presented at the Society for the History of Children and Youth Conference. University of California, Berkeley, July 10–12, 2009.

Barad, Karen. 2007. *Meeting the Universe Halfway: Quantum Physics and the Entanglement of Matter and Meaning*. Durham, NC: Duke University Press.

Bettis, Pamela J., and Natalie G. Adams. 2005. "Landscapes of Girlhood." In *Geographies of Girlhood: Identities In-Between*, edited by Pamela J. Bettis and Natalie G. Adams, 1–16. New York, NY: Routledge.

Blackford, Holly V. 2004. *Out of This World: Why Literature Matters to Girls*. New York, NY: Teachers College Press.

Bollig, Sabine, and Helga Kelle. 2016. "Children as Participants in Practices: The Challenges of Practice Theories to an Actor-Centred Sociology of Childhood." In *Reconceptualising Agency and Childhood: New Perspectives in Childhood Studies*, edited by Florian Esser, Meike S. Baader, Tanja Betz, and Beatrice Hungerland, 34–47. New York, NY: Routledge.

Bruhm, Steven, and Natasha Hurley. 2004. "Curiouser: On the Queerness of Children." In *Curiouser: On the Queerness of Children*, edited by Steven Bruhm and Natasha Hurley, ix–xxxviii. Minneapolis, MN: University of Minnesota Press.

Buckingham, David. 2019. "Afterword: Agency and Representation in Children's Media Culture." In *Representing Agency in Popular Culture: Children and Youth on Page, Screen, and In Between*, edited by Ingrid E. Castro and Jessica Clark, 283–8. Lanham, MD: Lexington Books.

Castoriadis, Cornelius. 1987. *The Imaginary Institution of Society*. Cambridge: Polity.

Clark, Jessica, and Ingrid E. Castro. 2019. "Girl Zombies and Boy Wonders: The Future of Agency is Now!" In *Child and Youth Agency in Science Fiction: Travel, Technology, Time*, edited by Ingrid E. Castro and Jessica Clark, 1–21. Lanham, MD: Lexington Books.

Clifford, James. 1988. *The Predicament of Culture: Twentieth-Century Ethnography, Literature, and Art*. Cambridge, MA: Harvard University Press.

Coe, Cati. 2005. *Dilemmas of Culture in African Schools: Youth, Nationalism, and the Transformation of Knowledge*. Chicago, IL: University of Chicago Press.

Cole, Jennifer. 2008. "Fashioning Distinction: Youth and Consumerism in Urban Madagascar." In *Figuring the Future: Globalization and the Temporalities of Children and Youth*, edited by Jennifer Cole and Deborah Durham, 99–124. Santa Fe, NM: School of Advanced Research Press.

Cole, Jennifer, and Deborah Durham. 2008. "Introduction: Globalization and the Temporality of Children and Youth." In *Figuring the Future: Globalization and the Temporalities of Children and Youth*, edited by Jennifer Cole and Deborah Durham, 3–24. Santa Fe, NM: School of Advanced Research Press.

Corsaro, William A. 2015. *The Sociology of Childhood* (4th ed.). Thousand Oaks, CA: SAGE.

Curry, Renee R. 1998. "'I Ain't No FRIGGIN' LITTLE WIMP': The Girl 'I' Narrator in Contemporary Fiction." In *The Girl: Constructions of the Girl in Contemporary Fiction by Women*, edited by Ruth O. Saxton, 95–106. New York, NY: St. Martin's Press.

Day, Sara K. 2013. *Reading Like a Girl: Narrative Intimacy in Contemporary American Young Adult Literature*. Jackson, MS: University Press of Mississippi.

Durham, Deborah. 2008. "Apathy and Agency: The Romance of Agency and Youth in Botswana." In *Figuring the Future: Globalization and the Temporalities of Children and Youth*, edited by Jennifer Cole and Deborah Durham, 151–78. Santa Fe, NM: School of Advanced Research.

Emirbayer, Mustafa, and Ann Mische. 1998. "What Is Agency?" *American Journal of Sociology* 103 (4): 962–1023.

Esser, Florian, Meike S. Baader, Tanja Betz, and Beatrice Hungerland. 2016. "Reconceptualising Agency and Childhood: An Introduction." In *Reconceptualising Agency and Childhood: New Perspectives in Childhood Studies*, edited by Florian Esser, Meike S. Baader, Tanja Betz, and Beatrice Hungerland, 1–16. New York, NY: Routledge.

Fadzillah, Ida. 2003. *You Take the Good and Leave the Rest Behind: Northern Thai Adolescent Girls and Their Narratives of Future Possibilities*. Doctoral Dissertation: University of Illinois, Urbana-Champaign. http://hdl.handle.net/2142/85252.

———. 2005. "The Amway Connection: How Transnational Ideas of Beauty and Money Affect Northern Thai Girls' Perceptions of Their Future Options." In *Youthscapes: The Popular, the National, the Global*, edited by Sunaina Maira and Elisabeth Soep, 86–102. Philadelphia, PA: University of Pennsylvania Press.

Frederiksen, Martin D., and Anne L. Dalsgård. 2014. "Introduction: Time Objectified." In *Ethnographies of Youth and Temporality: Time Objectified*, edited by Anne L. Dalsgård, Martin D. Frederiksen, Susan Højlund, and Lotte Meinert, 1–21. Philadelphia, PA: Temple University Press.

Greenhill, Pauline, and Leah C. Allen. 2018. "Animal Studies." In *The Routledge Companion to Media and Fairy-Tale Cultures*, edited by Pauline Greenhill, Jill T. Rudy, Naomi Hamer, and Lauren Bosc, 225–34. New York, NY: Routledge.

Handman, Courtney. 2017. "Walking Like a Christian: Roads, Translation, and Gendered Bodies as Religious Infrastructure in Papua New Guinea." *American Ethnologist* 44 (2): 315–27.

Hengst, Heinz. 2007. "Metamorphoses of the World within Reach." In *Flexible Childhood? Exploring Children's Welfare in Time and Space*, edited by Helga Zeiher, Dympna Devine, Anne T. Kjørholt, and Harriet Strandell, 95–119. Odense: University Press of Southern Denmark.

Hentges, Sarah. 2018. *Girls on Fire: Transformative Heroines in Young Adult Dystopian Literature*. Jefferson, NC: McFarland & Company.

Holloway, Sarah L., and Gill Valentine. 2000. "Children's Geographies and the New Social Studies of Childhood." In *Children's Geographies: Playing, Living, Learning*, edited by Sarah L. Holloway and Gill Valentine, 1–26. London: Routledge.

James, Allison. 2011. "Agency." In *The Palgrave Handbook of Childhood Studies* (paperback ed.), edited by Jens Qvortrup, William A. Corsaro, and Michael-Sebastian Honig, 34–45. Hampshire: Palgrave Macmillan.

James, Allison, and Adrian James. 2012. *Key Concepts in Childhood Studies*. Thousand Oaks, CA: SAGE.

Kearney, Mary C. 2011. "Introduction: Girls' Media Studies 2.0." In *Mediated Girlhoods: New Explorations of Girls' Media Culture*, edited by Mary C. Kearney, 1–14. New York, NY: Peter Lang.

Khosravi, Shahram. 2008. *Young and Defiant in Tehran*. Philadelphia, PA: University of Pennsylvania Press.

Lassén-Seger, Maria. 2006. *Adventures into Otherness: Child Metamorphs in Late Twentieth-Century Literature*. Turku: Åbo Akademi Press.

Lehtonen, Sanna. 2013. *Girls Transforming: Invisibility and Age-Shifting in Children's Fantasy Fiction Since the 1970s*. Jefferson, NC: McFarland & Company.

Levinson, Bradley A.U. 2001. *We Are All Equal: Student Culture and Identity at a Mexican Secondary School, 1988–1998*. Durham, NC: Duke University Press.

Lindahl, Carl. 2018. "Definition and History of Fairy Tales." In *The Routledge Companion to Media and Fairy-Tale Cultures*, edited by Pauline Greenhill, Jill T. Rudy, Naomi Hamer, and Lauren Bosc, 11–19. New York, NY: Routledge.

Liu, Shao-hua. 2011. *Passage to Manhood: Youth Migration, Heroin, and AIDS in Southwest China*. Stanford, CA: Stanford University Press.

Maira, Sunaina, and Elisabeth Soep. 2005. "Introduction." In *Youthscapes: The Popular, the National, the Global*, edited by Sunaina Maira and Elisabeth Soep, xv–xxxv. Philadelphia, PA: University of Pennsylvania Press.

Massey, Doreen. 2005. *For Space*. London: SAGE.

McCall, Stephanie D. 2015. "Recognition and Knowledge: Mapping the Promises and Seductions of Successful Female Futures." *Girlhood Studies* 8 (3): 88–102.

Montgomery, Heather. 2009. *An Introduction to Childhood: Anthropological Perspectives on Children's Lives*. Malden, MA: Wiley-Blackwell.

Mrázek, Rudolf. 2002. *Engineers of Happy Land: Technology and Nationalism in a Colony*. Princeton, NJ: Princeton University Press.

Närvänen, Anna-Liisa, and Elisabet Näsman. 2007. "Time, Identity, and Agency." In *Flexible Childhood? Exploring Children's Welfare in Time and Space*, edited by Helga Zeiher, Dympna Devine, Anne T. Kjørholt, and Harriet Strandell, 69–92. Odense: University Press of Southern Denmark.

Oswell, David. 2016. "Re-Aligning Children's Agency and Re-Socialising Children in Childhood Studies." In *Reconceptualising Agency and Childhood: New Perspectives in Childhood Studies*, edited by Florian Esser, Meike S. Baader, Tanja Betz, and Beatrice Hungerland, 19–33. New York, NY: Routledge.

Prout, Alan, and Allison James. 1997. "A New Paradigm for the Sociology of Childhood? Provenance, Promise and Problems." In *Constructing and Reconstructing Childhood: Contemporary Issues in the Sociological Study of Childhood* (2nd ed.), edited by Allison James and Alan Prout, 7–33. Oxon: Routledge.

Raban, Jonathan. 1974. *Soft City*. New York, NY: The Harvill Press.

Raithelhuber, Eberhard. 2016. "Extending Agency: The Merit of Relational Approaches for Childhood Studies." In *Reconceptualising Agency and Childhood: New Perspectives in Childhood Studies*, edited by Florian Esser, Meike S. Baader, Tanja Betz, and Beatrice Hungerland, 89–101. New York, NY: Routledge.

Ryan, Marie-Laure. 2001. *Narrative As Virtual Reality: Immersion and Interactivity in Literature and Electronic Media*. Baltimore, MD: Johns Hopkins University Press.

Salazar, Noel B. 2010. "Towards an Anthropology of Cultural Mobilities." *Crossings: Journal of Migration and Culture* 1 (1): 53–68.

Somers, Margaret R. 1992. "Narrativity, Narrative Identity, and Social Action: Rethinking English Working-Class Formation." *Social Science History* 16 (4): 591–630.

Soto, Lilia. 2018. *Girlhood in the Borderlands: Mexican Teens Caught in the Crossroads of Migration*. New York, NY: New York University Press.

Strandell, Harriet. 2007. "New Childhood Space and the Question of Difference." In *Flexible Childhood? Exploring Children's Welfare in Time and Space*, edited by Helga Zeiher, Dympna Devine, Anne T. Kjørholt, and Harriet Strandell, 49–68. Odense: University Press of Southern Denmark.

Talafuse, Elizabeth J. 2014. *I Am the Monster: Self and the Monstrous Feminine in Contemporary Young Adult Literature*. Doctoral Dissertation: Texas A & M University. https://oaktrust.library.tamu.edu/handle/1969.1/153218.

Tatar, Maria. 1987. *The Hard Facts of the Grimms' Fairy Tales*. Princeton, NJ: Princeton University Press.

Taylor, Laini. 2011a. *Daughter of Smoke and Bone*. New York, NY: Little, Brown and Company.

———. 2011b. "Daughter of Smoke and Bone, Revealed. Twice. (!!!!!)." *lainitaylor.com*. March 9, 2011. http://www.lainitaylor.com/2011/03/daughter-of-smoke-and-bone-revealed.html.

———. 2012. *Days of Blood and Starlight*. New York, NY: Little, Brown and Company.

———. 2014. *Dreams of Gods and Monsters*. New York, NY: Little, Brown and Company.

Theis, Joachim. 2001. "Participatory Research with Children in Vietnam." In *Children and Anthropology: Perspectives for the 21st Century*, edited by Helen B. Schwartzman, 99–109. Westport, CT: Bergin & Garvey.

Thomas, Angela. 2007. *Youth Online: Identity and Literacy in the Digital Age*. New York, NY: Peter Lang.

Trites, Roberta S. 1997. *Waking Sleeping Beauty: Feminist Voices in Children's Novels*. Iowa City, IA: University of Iowa Press.

———. 2018. *Twenty-First-Century Feminisms in Children's and Adolescent Literature*. Jackson, MS: University Press of Mississippi.

Uprichard, Emma. 2008. "Children As 'Being and Becomings': Children, Childhood and Temporality." *Children & Society* 22 (4): 303–13.

Viswanath, Tharini. 2019. "Girl-Animal Metamorphoses: Voice, Choice, and (Material) Agency of the Transforming Female Body in Young Adult Literature." *Jeunesse: Young People, Texts, Culture* 11 (1): 112–38.

Wardlow, Holly. 2006. *Wayward Women: Sexuality and Agency in a New Guinea Society*. Berkeley, CA: University of California Press.

Warner, Marina. 2014. *Once Upon a Time: A Short History of Fairy Tale*. Oxford: Oxford University Press.

Weinberger, Aliza. 2016. "What's the Best YA Series? Our #OneTrueYA Bracket Will Find Out." *Mashable.com*. May 25, 2016. https://mashable.com/2016/05/25/young-adult-series-bracket/#ja1j2UWAn8q3.

Willis, Jessica L. 2009. "Girls Reconstructing Gender: Agency, Hybridity and Transformations of 'Femininity.'" *Girlhood Studies* 2 (2): 96–118.

Wu, Yan, Kerry Mallan, and Roderick McGillis. 2013. "Introduction: The World Is Never Too Much with Us." In *(Re)Imagining the World: Children's Literature's Response to Changing Times*, edited by Yan Wu, Kerry Mallan, and Roderick McGillis, xi–xvii. New York, NY: Springer.

Zannettino, Lana. 2008. "Imagining Womanhood: Psychodynamic Processes in the 'Textual' and Discursive Formation of Girls' Subjectivities and Desires for the Future." *Gender and Education* 20 (5): 465–79.

Zeiher, Helga, Dympna Devine, Anne T. Kjørholt, and Harriet Strandell. 2007. "Introduction." In *Flexible Childhood? Exploring Children's Welfare in Time and Space*, edited by Helga Zeiher, Dympna Devine, Anne T. Kjørholt, and Harriet Strandell, 9–24. Odense: University Press of Southern Denmark.

Movement/Power

Chapter 9

Being Scared in the Dark

Paradoxes, Perils, and the Promise of Fantasy for Urban Girls of Color

Ingrid E. Castro and Ana Lilia Campos-Manzo

A classic children's nursery rhyme claims girls are made of sugar and spice and everything nice. In reality, girls navigate through and negotiate with the places, spaces, and people of their lives, often facing environments and trials that are anything but nice. With purpose, girls evaluate their surroundings while traversing societally dictated freedoms and limitations. They weigh gains and costs, pleasures and doubts in the effort to address their own needs and desires, accompanied by deep considerations of their personal and extended communities' strengths and shortcomings. Girls of color particularly face such laborious work. In this complicated exchange, elements of their age, gender, race/ethnicity, and socioeconomic status combine with qualities/qualifiers of their families, neighborhoods, and cities. Each reflecting on one another, these identifiers and descriptors dictate where girls of color are permitted to be present, be visible, be active, be vocal. Their streets and their homes are inextricably linked to how the rest of the world sees them and, indeed, how they see themselves. In consort, the views of those residing inside and outside their cityscapes temporally and ideologically construct girls' movements, resulting in the production of a thorny, multileveled paradox of fear. This chapter explores how girls of color experience fear in their everyday lives and, more specifically, how they employ fantasy as a coping mechanism within their emplaced girlhoods.

FEAR DURING CHILDHOOD AND ADOLESCENCE

Fear is present in all members of any society but varies in level and type according to age. There are fears that purportedly span across all world cultures, in various doses. Dozier (1998) states the most common fears among us all are animals (particularly spiders and snakes), heights, and small spaces. Other common fears/phobias include thunder, deep water, strangers, public/open spaces, public speaking, and darkness (Dozier 1998). That said, younger children tend to have the most fears, many of which align with the above lists. In accordance with the generalizability of fears among varied populations, "Children from very different nationalities, cultures, and socio-economic backgrounds experience similar fears at the same ages" (Kruuse and Kalmus 2017, 252). In studies of children under the age of ten, major fears include darkness, danger/death, injuries/medical issues, the unknown, animals, imaginary creatures, television, failure/criticism, strangers, being alone, natural phenomena/disasters, nightmares, and separation from parents (Gullone 1999; Lahikainen et al. 2003, 2006; Salcuni et al. 2009; Sayfan and Lagattuta 2008; Slaughter and Griffiths 2007).

Connected to children's integral processes of development, and cited as one of the four basic emotions they immediately experience and express, in the early years many children's fears are influenced by their environments, imaginations, and instincts (Gullone 1999; Kruuse and Kalmus 2017; Lahikainen et al. 2003; Michalčáková et al. 2013; Sayfan and Lagattuta 2008). The number of fears children have peaks by age four; over the next years children experience heighted fears of darkness, death, being alone, and threats to their personal safety/violence (Chaiyawat and Jezewski 2006; Dozier 1998; Kruuse and Kalmus 2017). As children age, their fears change, whereby their fears become less connected to immediate environmental stimuli (for example, a small child crying when left alone in a room), as well as fearing less of the imaginary and more of the realistic (Chaiyawat and Jezewski 2006; Dozier 1998; Kruuse and Kalmus 2017; Michalčáková et al. 2013). As children's fears decrease with frequency and intensity, becoming less prominent with lower incidences, they begin to understand that fears are temporary, utilizing knowledge that their fears depend on their minds, perceptions, and mediation of their emotions (Gullone 1999; Salcuni et al. 2009; Sayfan and Lagattuta 2009). While children learn and enact coping strategies for their fears, eleven- through thirteen-year-old children experience heightened fears related to their school environment, school peers, and school performance (Kruuse and Kalmus 2017; Michalčáková et al. 2013). By adolescence, youth report more fears pertaining to new situations and come to hold more abstract fears connected to their futures, including general but intensified fears of injury or losing people close to them (Michalčáková et al. 2013).

While all children experience fear, the bulk of studies agree that girls are more fearful than boys. Specifically, after the age of seven, girls are significantly more likely than boys to fear animals, danger, injury, and death (Lahikainen et al. 2003; Salcuni et al. 2009). Attributed to gender role stereotyping, girls are more likely than boys to outwardly display fear and report their fears with greater intensity and frequency; in addition, girls are more likely to use avoidance (fleeing, hiding) instead of approach (attacking) coping strategies (Gordon and Riger 1989; Gullone 1999; Sayfan and Lagattuta 2009).[1] These behaviors and reactions are due to children being taught that "girls are allowed to fear . . . boys are not" (De Groof 2008, 286). This socialization process codes girls "to be vulnerable and helpless" (avoid risk, display cautiousness, and be in need of protection), and boys "to be fearless or even aggressive" (take risks, display physical strength, and be protectors) (De Groof 2008, 286). These gender differences continue into adolescence, when some researchers find higher levels of fear for girls at school, particularly when transitioning to new schools and in regard to participation, risk taking, and achievement in specific course subjects (see Addington and Yablon 2011; Streitmatter 1997). As youth enter adulthood, differences in fear levels between females and males continue, whereby women are more fearful than men.

GENDERED FEARS PLAGUING GIRLHOOD AND WOMANHOOD

Inextricably intertwined, women are fearful of crime, danger, strangers, public spaces, and sexual assault (Day 1999; Franklin and Franklin 2009; Lane and Fisher 2009; Pain 2001; Yodanis 2004). These fears are part of female socialization processes, when at a young age girls, not boys, are taught to fear strangers—an "exaggerated" fear of unknown men approaching them in unknown places with the threat of sexual assault or child molestation (Christensen, Mygind, and Bentsen 2015; Franklin and Franklin 2009; Gordon and Riger 1989; Valentine 1989). Called "the female fear" or "women's geography of fear," most studies find that differences in women's socioeconomic status, age, and/or race/ethnicity do not impact higher levels of girls and women's fears compared to boys and men, with molestation, rape, sexual violence, and harassment underlying all females' heightened levels of fear (Gordon and Riger 1989; Lane and Fisher 2009; Pain 2001; Popkin, Leventhal, and Weismann 2010; Valentine 1989; Warr 1990). With "stranger danger," gender-oppressive, moral panic messages imparted by families, educational institutions, and media outlets, girls and women are subjected to severe social control with the goal of putting them in their "place" (Day 1999; Leonard 2007; Pain 2001). Paradoxically, *feeling threatened and alone affects girls and women's relationships with others, causing behavior restrictions and self-isolation; but, their feelings of fear and perceived risk are reduced through social support and connection with others* (Barecca 2011; Dozier 1998; Gordon and Riger 1989; Franklin and Franklin 2009).[2] Given that the strongest underlying component of these interrelated fears is the fear of death, girls and women's movements in society are limited and so there is a need to explore their feelings toward and usage of public space (Gordon and Riger 1989; Madriz 1997a; Valentine 1989).

Girls and women's fears of crime, violence, and physical and sexual assault are exponentially increased in urban locales. To the extreme, tales of the "urban jungle" and the "dark city" present cityscapes as an otherized crime-riddled place, propelling females' feelings of anxiety and unease (Bonnett 2002, 351; Bromley and Stacey 2012). Women believe that streets, alleys, and parks are the most dangerous places in cities, with downtown areas putting them at highest risk for victimization via sexual assault (Gordon and Riger 1989). Experiences with sexual harassment in cities "bolster the idea of public places and strangers as unpredictable and threatening, and reinforce women's spatial perceptions of their own vulnerability" (Pain 1997, 237). As a result, women frequently avoid these spaces, in effect living "under a self-imposed curfew," refusing to walk on city streets or travel to unfamiliar areas of cities while fearing the crimes of robbery, rape, and murder (Gordon and Riger 1989; Madriz 1997a, 13). Here, we find an eternal cycle, an element anchoring the paradox of fear, since unfamiliar environments provoke fear of crime (Tomanović and Petrović 2010; Warr 1990). So then, *how can girls and women emotionally navigate their fears of cityscapes if its streets are never to become familiar?*

Additionally, a racialized and socioeconomic fissure occurs when women (and by proxy girls) can afford to avoid various city spaces. Women who own cars or have expendable money for taxi, Uber, and Lyft fares can choose to sidestep feared urban locales (Pain 1997). Related, borders are drawn between white, "crimeless," cities that are viewed as safe and visited with supposed ease, while brown, "crime-ridden," dangerous cities are avoided (see Day 1999; Madriz 1997a; Pain 1997). Obviously, only certain individuals can employ such evasion tactics or fall outside of the (purported) phenotypically racialized equation of cities to crime. As a paradoxical result of these class, race, and space differences, *middle- and upper-class women are less afraid of crime (while at the same time portrayed as the innocent victims of these very crimes) and poorer women of color are henceforth more afraid of crime* (Madriz 1997a, 1997b).

PARENTS, CHILDREN, AND FEAR
OF THE URBAN LANDSCAPE

The fear of cities and urban violence transfers to fears for children, whereby rules regarding children's safety are strongly encouraged and enforced (Dozier 1998). In particular, middle-class children find their movements in cities restricted, while embodying more spatial resources for general mobility (Dillabough and Kennelly 2010; Furedi 2002; Madriz 1997b). Dillabough and Kennelly (2010) state that middle- and upper-class children "are often driven home in cars, live in property owned by their families or walk home through leafy neighbourhoods and have little cause to worry about the 'dangers' of inner-city life" (149).[3] Mirroring women, in yet another paradox of fear (labeled the "control-fear" paradox), *children who come from families with less material capital and opportunities for socioeconomic mobility experience increased social vulnerability and fear of crime, while children who hail from families with assets, wealth, and power have more control over their mobility and safety and exhibit less fear of crime* (Gullone 1999; Franklin and Franklin 2009, 98). With the pointed effort of restricting Westernized children (particularly middle-class children) from experiencing urban terrain, "the city has developed from a public space to a private, adult place, one which they, as children, have little access to" (James, Jenks, and Prout 1998, 48).

Today's parents express generalized concerns pertaining to incidences of crime in public spaces; as a result, parents' control over children's social, physical, and spatial experiences—while constructing children as vulnerable, in danger, and threatened—dictate greater fear socialization for children (Matthews, Limb, and Taylor 2000; Pain 2001). Corsaro (2015), Katz (2005), and Wyness (2006) all state that parents' heightened fears of child victimization are a result of adult guilt and anxieties pertaining to feeling out of control in adult changing worlds, thus not related to how children agentically perceive their own social worlds. Following parent supervision and modeling, many children come to hold similarly fearful views of urban public spaces and believe interaction with strangers is dangerous and risky (Christensen and O'Brien 2003; Furedi 2002; Mayall 2002; Vornanen, Törrönen, and Niemelä 2009). Children, therefore, are sensitive to their surroundings and frequently ambivalent about their cities, or, worse, are likely to avoid or dislike certain urban areas, becoming adept at labeling them as "good" or "bad" places (Bromley and Stacey 2012; Christensen, Mygind, and Bentsen 2015, 596; Christensen and O'Brien 2003).

Through establishing public spaces of the city as "off limits" via parental and media moral panics, children are relegated to diminishing, smaller spaces of interaction and movement. Connected to the prevailing hyperprotectionist discourses of our time, the public spaces of cities are surveilled and regulated with ever-increasing control, all in the effort to be sure children are not "found in the wrong place at the wrong time" (Hopkins 2010; James, Jenks, and Prout 1998, 52; Swauger, Castro, and Harger 2017). Removing children from urban public places transforms cityscapes into adult spaces, a "progressive reconceptualization of children and space" (Hopkins 2010; James, Jenks, and Prout 1998, 51). By configuring urban public space into urban adult space, parents are allotted the freedom to restrict children's activities and access, resulting in segregated city spaces that reflect children's removal from the streets (James, Jenks, and Prout 1998; Pain 2003; Skelton 2000; Zeiher 2003). This exercise in power leads children to be separated and excluded from the larger (adult) world; regrettably, in the process insularized and islanded children also become separated and excluded from each other (Buckingham 2000; Zeiher 2001, 2003).

THE "UNDESIRED" CITYSCAPE AS HOME

Labeling urban areas as dangerous and marking out youth as "undesirable occupants" of urban spaces greatly impacts children who reside in these cities; in particular, youth of color are cut off from access to the neighborhoods and streets they call home (Breitbart 1998, 307). Police reinforce such boundaries, threatening the safety of children of color through hypersurveillance, harassment, and enforcement (Campos-Manzo, Flores et al. 2020; Rios 2011). Following, we ask, what specifically happens to girls of color living in cities? Since public space is traditionally defined as adult male space under patriarchal rule, women and children are delivered tacit and overt messages that they are not welcome there. As a result, girls find their movements restricted and constrained, made all the more invisible in public urban spaces due to patriarchal and fear-based associations between vulnerability and femininity (Breitbart 1998; Malone and Hasluck 2002; Mayall 2002; Miller 2008; Percy-Smith 2002; Spilsbury 2005).

Relegated to exist outside the margins of cityscapes, excluded girls of color are placed under extreme personal and social limitations, a problematic process given public space and its streets are inherently connected to urban youth's identity constructions and contestations (Hopkins 2010; Pain 2001). Additionally, *when they do venture into the urban landscape, they are placed in high-stress, highly surveilled scenarios with higher likelihood of victimization*, given the sexualized/innocent paradox that surrounds girls of color (see Miller 2008). To borrow from Barrie Thorne's (1987) seminal work, we must ask, then, "Where are the girls of color?" And, following, how do girls of color experience and navigate fear and dangerous situations?

METHODOLOGY: SOCIO-SPATIAL TOURS

To center the experience of girls of color in a society that is adult, white, and male-dominated, we combined critical race and "doing research with children" methodologies, and added a gendered children's geographies lens for analyses (see Campos-Holland 2017; Denov and Gervais 2007; Skelton 2000; Thorne 1993). Fifty-seven girls of color, ten to seventeen years old, participated in semi-structured interviews. IRB approval, parental consent, and girls' assent was acquired prior to the interviews, which took place during the summer of 2013 and the summer of 2015. The girls are of African American, Puerto Rican, Jamaican American, and multiethnic descent, all from a racially and socioeconomically segregated metropolitan area in the northeast of the United States. As part of the interview, the girls used Google Maps to give interviewers a participant-driven virtual tour of the socio-spatial environments where they experience their everyday lives.[4]

Specifically, participants navigated from home(s)[5] to park(s), school(s), religious space(s), shops, the community youth center(s) where they were interviewed, other community organization(s), and all the in-between spaces within and across cities and suburbs. The interviewer asked: What do you think about this place? What have been your experiences with peers here? And, what about adults? While not directly asked about fears, the topic emerged through image elicitation, primarily as participants virtually moved from place to place through the streets. At which point, the interviewer asked follow-up questions: What did you think about the situation? How did you feel? Have there been other similar situations? After completion of the interviews, the data was transcribed and checked for accuracy. A thematic analysis of the 153 reported instances of fear was conducted using Atlas.ti.[6] Coding was developed separately and collaboratively via a discussion approach (see Auerbach and Silverstein 2003).

MOM KNOWS BEST

Families show concern for girls' safety and limit their movements in neighborhoods and cities. As is the case with most children, regardless of housing location, their parents, and mothers particularly, have great influence on these girls' everyday lives. The fear girls hold is imparted from their parents' desire to keep them from harm, exhibited through parental control over their bodies and the establishment of boundaries around their (un)lived urban spaces (Christensen and Prout 2003; Leverett 2011; Madriz 1997a; McIntyre 2000; Pain 2001). While discussing her mother's rules, Astrici,[7] 15, African American, states: "Well, I have to tell her where I'm going, what time I'm gonna be back . . . the majority of the time she doesn't let me out of the house. I really don't get out the house a lot. But if I do, oh my God, I cherish it to the moment. I have the most fun I could possibly have." Research finds that urban parents, in particular, are the most restrictive of children's mobility (Barnes et al. 2006). According to Astrici, her mother's control limits all of her mobility, to the point where she is predominantly forced to remain indoors. We also see the great desire of girls to experience their urban cityscapes—Astrici "cherishes every moment" she is allowed out, free to be a child beyond her mother's fear-based parenting range. The stranger danger warnings mothers relay start at early ages, anchored in their fear of children's victimization (Christensen and Prout 2003; Valentine 1997). Reflecting on the Aurora, Colorado mass public shooting at *The Dark Knight* (2012) movie premiere, Noodles, 11, African American, explains how her feelings of fear translate from her mother: "I feel really scared. Like I need to hide in a hiding spot. My mom said there's a lot of crazy people out there. So, don't be out-there, out-there." Parental responsibilities to keep children safe and sound are spurred by media moral panics and expectations of the home world's responsibility for children's well-being while in the public world (Mayall 2002; Wyness 2006). Children internalize their parents' fear-based messages about the dangers in their neighborhoods and cities, and through this process may come to share their parents' heightened anxieties when exploring unknown areas beyond their homes; knowing their place—"where and where not to go, what to do and when"—becomes "inscribed into the environment" (Blundell 2016; Matthews 2003, 108; Salvadori 2002; Tomanović and Petrović 2010). Due to lack of knowledge about their immediate, "lived," surroundings, urban children are at a severe disadvantage (Salvadori 2002).

Many girls in our study reside in neighborhoods considered more dangerous due to higher rates of poverty, crime, and violence. In such neighborhoods, parents can be particularly challenged to find effective strategies for keeping children safe from victimization (Franklin and Franklin 2009; Spilsbury 2005). The girls explain the presence of gunshots and drugs in their neighborhoods:

> I was younger and it was in the summer. My aunt was backing out and [we heard] firecrackers, but it was early in the morning. This guy was backing up really fast and we saw this boy running. So, we was like, "Oh, it's gunshots." We drove down, down in our driveway and ducked in the car. We just waited a while, 'til it seemed safe. (Ashley, 14, Jamaican and African American)

Nobody could go over [to the park in my neighborhood], 'cuz it's not a really good place ... there's shooting. So, my dad usually takes me to other parks that he feels is safer. (Kween, 14, Trinidadian and Puerto Rican)

I don't feel too safe [in my neighborhood]. A lot of things happen on my street: people getting into fights, a lot of shootings, a lot of violence. My mom doesn't like the idea of me going outside. She's like, "Oh my god. You should be home [from school] earlier. I don't like what's going on outside." (Elaine, 14, African American)

One day, somebody was shooting outside [my home]. So, my mom put us inside the house and pushed us under the couch. It was crazy. (Pricella, 15, Mexican and Caucasian)

The girls' experiences with violence in their neighborhoods reflect parents' fear for their children's exposure to such elements. Often, children in cities are highly constrained by parents controlling their outdoor activities, particularly if there is greater incidence of drug activity in their streets or when children witness crime or violence near their homes (Cahill 2000; Chawla and Malone 2003; Shehan 1999; Skelton 2000). The girls' exposure to neighborhood crime involves the internalization of fear. Vanessa, 14, Puerto Rican, says she is "scared of my neighborhood, because they be shootin'." Dawn, 10, African American, states that people in her neighborhood "smoke, have a gang, do drugs, stuff like that," which makes her feel "scared that someone will come to attack me, 'cuz it's such a bad neighborhood." In contrast, other girls come to experience a normalization of crime in their daily lives. Bubbles, 11, Puerto Rican and Caucasian, explains she is "scared" because she hears "a lot of gunshots like all the time. I always hear that ... I hear it with my brother and my mom, my cousins, [but] we just don't acknowledge it. We just leave it alone."

Girls face the double construction and double burden of being both children and female in poorer urban neighborhoods. Girls are frequently kept in the home, only allowed out with other children or adults, and sometimes not ever allowed outdoors (Mackett et al. 2007; Madriz 1997a; Mayall 2002; Spilsbury 2005). In addition to Astrici, other interviewees comment that they never leave their homes. Barbie, 17, African American and Filipino, details:

That makes me mad and it scares me, because I like to be outside. I don't like to be stuck in the house. I have freedom. So, I'm going to use it. And I like to be outside freely to do what I please. But I can't be outside like that because people will kill at any time of the day. They won't care what time it is, like, daytime, nighttime, evening time, morning time; they don't care! If they're gonna do something, they're gonna do it. And that's just—it's sad but it's true.

Barbie highlights another paradox of fear in the lives of urban girls: *they are relegated to their homes for fear of violence, but being imprisoned there is just as scary.* Similar to urban youth in other studies (see Malone and Halsuck 2002, 92; McIntyre 2000, 68; Way 1998, 51), the girls in our work reinforce the saying, "you never know, anything can happen on the street." Esther Madriz (1997a) heard her young female participants echo Barbie's "frustration of living in a high-crime area and facing the possibility of being a victim of a crime every time 'you get to step out of your house'" (45). This ultimate constraint weighs heavily on girls. If they are allowed out of doors, they are merely allotted (or allot themselves) the "freedom" to stay within small areas near their homes (blacktops, yards, or a few blocks) and/or go to friends' homes if accompanied by someone else. Two girls reveal the limited play, socialization, and movement placed on them in their violent neighborhoods:

> I could just play in the driveway with my brother. We didn't have friends come, [because] they lived far away. (Tamrah, 13, African American)

> It's bad though. It's a bad neighborhood. Not bad, bad; but it's like, it's just ghetto. It's a ghetto street, though. I don't usually come out there that much . . . . Well, I do, but I always go in the parking lot, 'cuz there's always people yelling and cussing. They be talkin' really loud. And I'm like, "Can you go somewhere, like in the house? Why you yelling outside?" [But], some of my friends live on my street. So, I just hang out with them. And sometimes they come in my house and then we just talk. (Elaine, 12)[8]

Therefore, girls' social lives are immobilized by parental fears (and their own fears) to stay safe. As Tamrah and Elaine explain, siblings and peers are similarly constrained through parental rules and dislike of the violent activities in their neighborhoods. Because of stranger danger, fear of assault, drug culture, and localized violence, girls are likely to spend time in their friends' homes or in their own homes with friends in comparison to being outside on urban streets (Cahill 2000; Malone and Hasluck 2002; Matthews, Limb, and Taylor 2000). As is evident from girls like Dawn, Astrici, and Elaine, in addition to gun presence, children are sensitive to other elements they consider to be indicators of violence, particularly drugs, loud voices, fighting, aggressive dogs, gangs, and booming music in their neighborhoods—all of which combine to signal, for these girls, urban environments are unwelcoming and "bad."

Parents keep children indoors because of perceptions that they are too naïve, immature, and incompetent, believing children do not have the social skills to "recognize potentially dangerous situations and deal with them appropriately" (James 2013; Mayall 2002; Valentine 1997, 70). Following, in repetition of a paradox of fear outlined earlier, *it is difficult "to imagine how a child can become streetwise without being allowed on the streets"* (Furedi 2002, 117). In response to this critique, some parents understand children's freedoms and independence are necessary and accept that urban dangers are beyond their control; in such families, parents attempt to gradually introduce their growing children to these outdoor, urban, sometimes violent, environments (Elsley 2011; James 2013; Leverett 2011; Mayall 2002). Erica, 12, Puerto Rican, explains that in her neighborhood, "People be doing drugs and I don't like that. My mom don't want us to do it, but she wants us to look at people who ruin their life because of that. I think it's good, because we're actually getting a hint." The parenting Erica experiences reveals a mother's stance that her children should view and understand some of the ramifications of drug addiction in their neighborhood in the effort to curb prospective drug use. Erica agentically vocalizes appreciation of her mother's belief that children should see and understand social problems in real time.

Children's views of parents' limitations on their behaviors are at once clear and paradoxical. They believe parents are correct in limiting their movements, stating parents are doing what they can to protect them from the seen and unseen dangers in their immediate environments. Nicole, 13, Puerto Rican, appreciates parents' protective efforts, stating they are keeping children safe "from being out on the streets, from growing up . . . not letting them mess up, keeping them grounded." Youth may feel safer with such parental efforts, supervision, and monitoring, raising their confidence through a belief their likelihood of victimization is reduced, but they paradoxically *recognize protections by parents can "only do so much to keep children 'on the right path'"* (Hopkins 2010; Mayall 2002; McIntyre 2000, 111; Yuan, Dong, and Melde 2017). Elaine explains how the violence in her neighborhood is inescapable:

> There's always crime going on, but not too much crime, not like much of serious crime . . . it's always fights or this person doin' this or doin' that . . . . [People] say, "There's always bad things going on your street. I'm always hearing that the police is over there." It doesn't happen all the time, but often it happens. I always wanted to move off that street, 'cuz it's really not good. But it's not just my street, it's [nearby] too.[9]

In Elaine's observations, the violence and crime of her neighborhood is ever-present, though not too "serious." Other girls who live on "not good" streets similarly downplay the crime in their neighborhoods. When asked what other people think of her neighborhood, Bubbles had trouble providing an answer: "I think that they think it's—I think—I dunno what I think. I think they think that it's good. Yeah, 'cuz it's a nice neighborhood." Residents of these girls' city, compared to those living in neighboring suburbs and cities, experience higher rates of violence, drugs, and other crimes (Federal Bureau of Investigation 2014). These illicit elements, along with the fear of victimization, impact the girls' perceptions of safety, erasing them from their local streets (similar to Cope 2008; McIntyre 2000).

While simultaneously complying with the rules, children may feel their parents are both overly fearful and strict. Astrici details the frequent exchange she has with her mother over gender-based rules:

> Mommy doesn't let me over boys' houses. Ever [*in a whisper*]. I mean, I understand why. I get it, but at the same time, I think it's a little dramatic. She's like:
> "What if their parents leave and they might try to force you to do something."
> "I understand that, but we're not going to though."
> "You don't know that!"
> "Okay! Alright! Oh, okay."
> It's annoying. It really is annoying. It's just like, I understand. It's like, I know that. They're not going to do anything.

Research shows that children will not inform their parents of bad experiences for fear of heightened restrictions in the wake of truth-telling (Seymour 2015; Valentine 1997). Mirroring the statements of their parents, children likewise view their parents as naïve, incompetent, and overemotional; as a result, limiting information flow serves an intergenerational and agentic protective function from children toward their parents (Castro 2019; Hopkins 2010; Valentine 1997). Children may also believe safety is part of their own personal responsibility and that parents' attempts to protect them are futile, eventually leading children to turn to peers, not parents, for help and advice (Sharkey 2006; Valentine 1997). For example, Star, 13, Jamaican American, continues to visit her friend's house even though her mother does not want her to go:

> There's this one friend, I think her street is terrible. Her neighborhood is terrible. I witnessed a car chase on the street, a fight, everything. Her neighborhood is terrible. My mom does not like me over there at all, but I love being at her house. Her house is fun in general, but her neighborhood sucks. It's scary being out on the streets, on her front porch. I feel so unsafe, anything could happen over there. It is scary.

In Astrici's exchange with her mother and Star's desire to visit with her friend over her mother's wishes, we see children generationally negotiate and manage adult feelings and demands while agentically honoring their own emotions and embodying self-proclaimed competencies (Barnes et al. 2006; Castro 2017; Hopkins 2010; Seymour 2015; Valentine 1997). To note, very few of the girls confess to keeping brushes with violence from their parents, nor do any state their parents are naïve or incompetent. Though, María, 14, Puerto Rican, admits to recently hiding her movements from her mother: "That's the worst part. I can't even walk. Like yesterday, I ended up running back to the [youth center] from the corner. It's like, 'Whew' [*relieved*]. [On my way back home], once I got near the apartment building, I started walking casually so I didn't look like I was out of breath when [my mom] sees me." María does not want to be caught walking the city streets because her mother insists on driving her everywhere.[10] In this instance, María's movements do not follow her mother's wishes. She feels fear, but at the same time nothing puts her in immediate peril. In fact, we find that in cases when the girls faced real danger, victimization, or potential violence, they immediately told parents of their experiences and fears.

Restricting children's movements on a daily basis takes quite a bit of time and effort. Mothers, in particular, are in charge of such work, and many women try to ensure children do not spend time outside alone. The presence of unaccompanied children in the neighborhood is viewed as dangerous (James 2013; Pain 1997). To alleviate such fears, mothers or caretakers (aunts, grandmothers, etc.) must walk with or drive children to bus stops, schools, afterschool centers, sporting events, parks, friends' houses, and the like. Parents and caretakers' hypervigilant efforts are physically and emotionally draining, not to mention demanding of their personal time (Gillis 2008; Katz 2005; Madriz 1997b; Pain 1997). If they cannot accompany them, mothers and caretakers impart words of warning to children. As Tiara, 13, African American, explains: "When we leave the house and everything, [my grandmother says], 'Be careful. Don't talk to strangers. Don't get into any trouble.'" Taking these broad messages into account, children must similarly put in tremendous effort to avoid violence and adhere to their parents and caretakers' rules (Sharkey 2006).

Thus, the girls in this study often depend on their mothers for transportation and company when leaving their homes. They are very aware of the spatial restrictions and limitations mothers place on their movements, even if they are allowed to go certain places on their own:

- I would go [to the park] with my mom, but I wouldn't go alone. (Dawn)
- My mom doesn't like me going that far. (Pricella)
- My mom comes, picks me up. (María)
- Not [ride my bike] around the block or anything, because my mom won't let me do that. She lets me walk over [to the youth center] though! (Erica)
- I can't walk by myself [to the library], but I'll go sometimes with my cousins, or my mom will walk with me or drive me or something.... No matter where it is, she just doesn't really like me to be by myself.... She doesn't want anything bad to happen to me. (Bubbles)

With such constraints, mothers also recognize the paradox of keeping their girls indoors under strict mobility rules for the bulk of their childhoods since *women hold personal knowledge that the home is frequently a space where children are most in danger of accidents and violence* (Pain 1997, 2001). Barbie reembodies the fearful, concerned, and protective messages of her mother, stating that she, too, would not let her own children (or by proxy her younger siblings) roam the neighborhood for fear of victimization (see Madriz 1997a; Morrow 2011). Speaking of a neighborhood park, Barbie admits: "I wouldn't wanna bring my child there when I have kids. A lot of families hang out there. But that don't make a difference for me. My family, well, uh-uh [no]. I would not bring my family there." Similar to women in urban areas who avoid being alone and desire protection from others, particularly men (Madriz 1997a, 1997b; Warr 1990), Tiara feels very uneasy when alone in her own home and neighborhood: "I like being with a lot of people, 'cuz I don't like being by myself. It makes me feel alone sometimes. [I'm like], 'Let's go in there 'cuz she's in there.' So, I like being with a lot of people I know."

Tucker and Matthews (2001) explain, "Where girls occupy public spaces they may be seen by adults as being the 'wrong' gender in the 'wrong' place, being exposed to risks in such 'unsafe' spaces" (163). Mothers are especially vigilant in keeping their children safely indoors once the sun sets over the city, transferring their own fearful messages of darkness by not going out at night themselves (McIntyre 2000; Pain 1997; Tuan 1980). The definitions of "wrong" place and "wrong" gender are particularly salient at night: darkness dictates the most unsafe situations and spaces for urban girls. Girls in our study fear darkness in their neighborhoods more than daylight, and at times their fears of events that take place in the dark transfer into a generalized fear of their cityscapes.

> I don't know [about my neighborhood]. It's okay, I guess. I don't really be outside at night. I don't be outside that late, 'cuz I don't want to. (Dee, 11, Puerto Rican)

> I liked the fact that.... I never really went outside. So, I never hung out in the neighborhood. It was weird. It just, I didn't feel comfortable. I felt comfortable, but I felt uncomfortable once the dark hit out. When it started to fade, I didn't want to go outside. It just felt like so many people were loud and rambunctious. You never know what was gonna happen. (María)

> It's creepy quiet, though, especially at night. You know, creepy quiet? Like, there's neighborhoods that are quiet, and they have a street, and our neighborhood is dead silent, like creepy quiet. I don't think we should move, though. I like it during the daytime when everyone's outside. (Tamrah)

Younger females show heightened reactions to being alone at night and, in general, poorer urban children equate dark or abandoned places with violence; in fact, they may fear these areas more than their parents (Bromley and Stacey 2012; Madriz 1997a; McIntyre 2000; Tomanovič and Petrovič 2010; Warr 1990). Research repeatedly shows that children, and girls in particular, try not to leave their homes alone for any reason, especially at night. We find Dee, María, and Tamrah experience night as unpredictable and uncomfortable, staying inside and avoiding dark and deserted streets in order to feel safe (see also Cahill 2000; van der Bergt 2015; Way 1998). Here, we point to another paradox of urban girls' fears since *the girls find urban "creepy quiet" darkness just as scary, if not scarier, than urban "loud and rambunctious" darkness*.

VOICING THE UNTHINKABLE

The girls tell many stories during their interviews. Some of these stories are funny, some silly, some mundane, but many are tragic, harrowing, and sad, culminating in one word: limiting. Intersectionally, the following additive equation greatly influences their tales of the cityscape: urban people feel quite vulnerable, females feel more at risk than males, girls have more stranger danger messages instilled in them at earlier ages, and girls of color are at the highest risk for victimization (Gordon and Riger 1989; Hopkins 2010; Pain 2003). Girls are not only more fearful in general, they are specifically more fearful and frightened when they are in the city alone (Matthews 2003; Warr 1990). In fact, urban females of color believe that "if they called for help no one would respond," requiring them to constantly be on guard for potential threats while occupying their cityscape (Day 1999; Gordon and Riger 1989, 51). This secondary effect is due to another paradox of fear: *females are portrayed through socialization and the media as physically, emotionally, and societally vulnerable, which makes perpetrators, especially males, view them as easy targets* (Madriz 1997a). The formative experiences of poorer girls of color being victimized in the streets powerfully increases their levels of social fear and anxiety and greatly influences their (non)public lives and (im)mobility (Addington and Yablon 2011; Hopkins 2010; Skelton 2000). Is it no wonder, then, that the girls in our study experience a range of fearful emotions while retelling stories of victimization when walking to school, walking home from a party, walking home from work, or walking around the neighborhood?

Researchers and scholars frequently take the stance that various urban dangers for children are overblown through media panics. Time and again, neighborhood warnings recited by adults to children of kidnapping, murder, and pedophilia (to mention a few) are referred to as "imaginary" dangers (Barnes et al. 2006, 68; Christensen, Mygind, and Bentsen 2015, 597; Malone and Hasluck 2002, 101; Salvadori 2002, 194; Webster 2003, 112), "wild" stories (Matthews 2003, 108), "hyperboles" (James, Jenks, and Prout 1998, 51), and "urban myths" (Matthews 2003, 108) that focus "attention on horrific yet relatively rare incidents" (Leverett 2011, 14). While we are sure that these types of stories are blown out of proportion for suburban, white, affluent children, we also know that urban, black and brown, poorer children are forgotten in such media discourse, pushed outside of the margins of popular, albeit inflated, reporting, their tragedies made invisible (see Campos-Manzo et al. 2019; Sternheimer 2006). To be fair, some of these same and other academics (see Barnes et al. 2006; Madriz 1997b; Malone and Hasluck 2002; Miller 2008; Morrow 2011; Webster 2003) recognize that stories of danger are partly or wholly found in neighborhood history and experienced truth, based on actual, lived, and, at times, frequent victimization. Others go further, stating that while these stories may describe "minor incidences," the risks girls face in public spaces should not be dismissed or labeled as "irrational" (Pain 2003, 166; Yodanis 2004, 657). Another paradox of fear, we believe that *some researchers downplay such happenings in the lives of girls in the attempt to promote the agency of children.* However, while such efforts to frame out freer spaces and lives for children are important, these girls' stories are not hearsay. In fact, eight of the fifty-seven girls in our study gave first-person accounts of sexual harassment, stalking, or kidnapping attempts. Certainly, their experiences are real, not imaginary myths, and we must recognize their agency, voice, and physical and emotional negotiations of the environment within such traumas, not outside of them.

Occasionally, girls are forced to make choices on where to walk based on their physical locations and time allotments. Like any other person, they use shortcuts to get to one place from another, reflecting insider knowledge of their neighborhoods, making urban spaces their own to fit their immediate needs (Christensen, Mygind, and Bentsen 2015). However personally fulfilling this process might be, children also experience these routes as "frightening and unpleasant" (Morrow 2011, 67). Often, children who use shortcuts traverse through parks and alleyways to get to where they need to be. Children frequently cite parks as spaces of urban fear and trepidation, mirroring their views of the streets through the claim "anything really could happen" (Malone and Hasluck 2002; Morrow 2011; O'Brien 2003; Valentine 1997, 78). Moreover, female fears of urban parks escalate when darkness falls (Bromley and Stacey 2012; Gordon and Riger 1989; van der Burgt 2015; Webster 2003). Barbie details the park she sometimes must walk through: "I'm scared of that park. Two people died in there. People got killed and raped and thrown in the pond. [One man was] high off 'danger dust' and he thought he could walk on water. So, he just decided to walk on the pond [and] he got pulled in. The water pulled him in, sucked him in, and he was just in water. So sad." Given the stories of danger and death attached to this locale, Barbie cuts through the park "very quick, very, very quick. I don't want nobody to see me." Barbie's attempt to move quickly and unnoticed is similar to women in Gordon and Riger's (1989) study, wherein females perceived their urban parks as very dangerous and unsafe due to rapes and assaults, with one woman explaining that if she must go through the park she first "'surveys the area' and then walks quickly through" (13). In other scenarios, girls use a tactic to be simultaneously aware and detached—"mind your own business." Youth in Cahill's (2000) study detailed the mind your own business stance: "keep walking, do not start trouble, keep to yourself, keep your own opinion, keep your comments to yourself, and do not act stupid with people you do not know" (264). Roxanne, 17, African American and Native American, details employing this method when traversing her friend's "bad" neighborhood:

> There's more stuff to do in her neighborhood, a lot more people. We walk around, probably run into a couple friends. It's a kind of bad neighborhood in a way; but, if you mind your business it's a fine neighborhood. There's a lot of bums on the street. It's really, really dirty, a lot of drug activity. We just do our own thing, don't get in other people's faces.

For Roxanne and Barbie, if they choose to be outside in dangerous locations, there is a protocol to follow for self-protection and preservation. In their efforts to be simultaneously unnoticed and present in these places, the girls reflect attempts to not be victims of their environments, agentically resisting and challenging their personal fears and societal definitions of urban spaces as "bad" (see Hopkins 2010).

Girls of color are at a heightened risk of sexual harassment and sexual crimes in urban locales (Miller 2008). Girls fear sexual harassment on the streets, which usually includes verbal abuse (e.g., propositioning), but can also extend to physical sexual abuse (e.g., flashing) (Percy-Smith 2002; Valentine 1989, 1997). Following, these fears for safety put females on high-alert and constantly on their guard from the threat of verbal, sexual, and physical attackers (Bromley and Stacey 2012; Gordon and Riger 1989; Morrow 2003; Pain 1997). Verbal and physical sexual harassment has great impact on urban girls' independence and mobility, given "the demoralizing effects of omnipresent and constant harassment and the pressure to become sexually active at younger ages" (Malone and Hasluck 2002; Popkin, Leventhal, and Weismann 2010, 716; Valentine 1989). These types of female victimization weigh very heavily on girls; for example, in her one-hour forty-minute interview, Erica thrice details verbal sexual harassment she incurs in her neighborhood. Certainly at the forefront of why she dislikes her neighborhood and why she limits her own movements within, Erica tells us:

[On why Erica does not like anyone in her neighborhood]:
They're not even no kids. They's grown up. Every single time I walk through the street, they like, "Heyyy whassup, girl? Where you goin' today? You busy?"
Interviewer: Who says that to you?
Some G—some random guy.
Interviewer: Is it the same guy?
Different guys and the same guys, when they want to.
Interviewer: And how old are they?
Older than me, twice as older.

[On frequency of harassment and Erica's father's reaction]:
I can't even go outside without some guy insulting me. Well, tryna flirt.
Interviewer: What do you say back?
I just walk. I just keep walking.
Interviewer: And your mom and dad, have you told them this?
Yup. My dad said, "Let me find out something."
Interviewer: What does that mean, though?
He's gonna do something bad.
Interviewer: But you don't even know who the guys are, do you?
He does. He knows.

[On quality of her neighborhood and Erica's mother's reaction]:
Where I live, pure bad. I don't like it. I don't like even going—I don't like even getting out the house. I only like doing it in the morning, because everybody's sleeping.
Interviewer: What do you mean by flirt, like they yell at you? Or—
They try to ask me, "Ooh, whatcha gonna do tonight, you gonna do something?" And I just did what my Mom told me, I just keep walking, don't pay attention.
Interviewer: How does it make you feel, though?
I just don't pay attention to it. It makes me feel like nothing, makes me feel nothin'.

As a reminder, Erica is twelve years old. The continuous neighborhood victimization she faces because of her racialized and gendered positionality on the street is profound. Popkin, Leventhal, and Weismann (2010) explain: "The difference in pressure to engage in sex is especially significant for very young girls, who in high-poverty neighborhoods begin experiencing harassment and pressure during early adolescence, for example, at age 12 or 13 . . . the pressures for sexual activity are much greater, the threats more blatant, and the risk of victimization very real" (720 & 728). Too often, girls lose appreciation of their bodies to male victimizers' commodification and cooptation of female forms that are not theirs to have. Made to be something feared, girls are forced to remove their bodies from everyday public spaces; as Erica says, she only goes outside early in the morning when these men are sleeping, absent from the neighborhood she fears and yet calls home.

Following the tyranny of sexual harassment, female fears attach to the dangers male harassers and attackers represent; most frequently, child molestation and rape (Glassner 1999; Gordon and Riger 1989; Madriz 1997a, 1997b). These feelings lead to girls' anxiety when strangers walk too closely, particularly at night (Gordon and Riger 1989; Matthews 2003; Morrow 2011). Star, Tamrah, and Tiara all tell long and detailed stories of being followed home by adults; Star and Tamrah at night, Tiara during the day.[11] In a rarer twist, Star's account details a "crazy lady" with a dog who followed her home, taking purchase on the back porch until her mother came home and confronted the woman. Star says that once she made it inside, "I was hiding under my covers for a long time. I was so scared . . . . I was just in shock. I was like, 'Oh my god. I'm so scared.' 'Cuz anything could've happened. She could've been looking in our windows. She could've been stalking us for a long time. So, I'm just upstairs thinking—scared." Tiara and Tamrah's experiences connect to the finding that commute-specific movement, such as walking from school or taking public transportation, contributes to youth fears (Addington and Yablon 2011). Tamrah was chased home from school one winter night by an older man, and she says now when walking home she "feels bad. Especially at nighttime, I keep looking back." Tiara explains how she felt walking home from school one day, and how the event influences her fear of others now that time has passed:

> Sometimes I get nervous by seeing—I don't like when people walk so close to me. One day this guy kind of followed me home. And when I got to my house to go into the driveway, he stood in front of the driveway to see where I was going and it made me nervous. But that was a one-time thing . . . [I felt] nervous, scared . . . . Now I feel kind of comfortable, because I haven't seen that man and since I don't walk to school during summer. I don't walk anywhere anymore; well, I take the bus and everything with my sister, but we don't really walk anywhere.

In Tiara's story, we once again see how girls' movements are limited by male perpetrators. In every way, her sense of comfort does not come to resolution. Just because she has not "seen that man" does not mean he is not out there, lurking. And just because she can use the bus to travel with her sister does not mean she is fully mobile, or wholly free. Star additionally tells of a pedophile who lives on her block:

> I don't know if he was a rapist, I don't know if he was a molester, but he's something in-between that. He took little kidnapped girls and stuff like that. And there's a lot of little kids on our street. They're mostly girls. And he always sits right in front of his house, and stop and talk. I'm like, "I'm okay." I'll stand there, just me and my sister. I think he's on house arrest, 'cuz I always see him outside with a bracelet on. And he only goes, like he can barely go anywhere. You'll see him coming with a few grocery bags, but it will only be like 10 minutes that he's gone. He can't be out long. He's always in his house or sitting on the front porch, looking out the window. My neighborhood's creepy, but then again, it's better than some other neighborhoods.

Pain (2003) states that urban girls in her study related "minor incidents outside involving weirdoes and perverts" (165). Star's story, in our estimation, is not minor. The feelings of trepidation she and her sister experience every time they walk down their street frightens them, obviously influencing Star's portrayal of her neighborhood as "creepy." Additionally, we again witness the strategy of walking with other people to buffer fear, wherein urban vulnerability of girls is offset by company, usually relatives or friends (van der Bergt 2015).

As previously discussed, the "brute effect of darkness" compounds girls' fears in their "racialised geography" of the street and city (Warr 1990, 905; Webster 2003, 112).[12] "Urban darkness has long been described in negative terms—for instance, as the 'dark side'—and the 'forces of darkness' have been conceived as the opposite of that which enlightens and illuminates" (van Liempt, van Aalst, and Schwanen 2015, 410). As a result, girls feel less safe at night, fearing events that might happen in unlit alleys, on dark streets, and with strange, "dangerous others" lurking in the shadows. Girls learn and are taught to take precautionary measures when in urban public locations at night, ensuring they limit their movements, stay close to home, and are not by themselves once the sun sets (see Madriz 1997b; Malone and Hasluck 2002; Watt and Stenson 1998; Yadonis 2004). One clear rule of the street is that if girls have to walk at night, they must not do so alone:

> Because if you outside and you get kidnapped, or anything like that, then you gonna be hurt. 'Cuz you never should walk outside by yourself. You should always have something beside you, or somebody beside you, that know how to fight or anything like that . . . . If I get to be with my cousins [at night], we be going to the park, places. (Carmela, 12, African American)

I walk with my friends, but sometimes it's just scary when it gets this dark, and you don't want to walk by yourself. So, you just have to get with other people, especially at a certain age. (Angie, 13, African American)

I be here [at the youth center] until nine o'clock. My friend—he walks me home, so it's better. He's fifteen. So, I feel better when I'm walking with someone. I don't like walking alone. I'm never walking alone. Only if I need to go to the store. In some cases, I don't like walking home alone at nighttime, because I be scared. (Vanessa)

So, walking alone is viewed as dangerous, and being accompanied by someone allows the girls a small sense of relief, believing they are protected from unknown but predicted threats. Matthews, Limb, and Taylor (2000) found that 61 percent of all girls in their study were afraid of the streets when alone, but only 32 percent were fearful if accompanied by friends. The latter enabled girls in their study more movement in cities, particularly at night. Some girls, like Vanessa, Carmela, and Angie, state they never go outside without friends or family. Vanessa specifically feels more at ease since her escort is both male and older than she, providing a perceived extra buffer against would-be attackers.

The final way girls are victimized in their city streets and neighborhoods is by men trying to kidnap them. Again, even though many experts state this event is very unlikely, much more media hype than reality, one of the girls in our study, María, shared a harrowing story of when it happened to her walking home alone at night. Child abduction is the most feared type of male victimization by children, as well as by parents. In fact, Glassner (1999) states that surveys indicate three out of four parents fear a stranger will kidnap their child. Girls are particularly fearful of being abducted from city streets by strangers in cars and vans (Bromley and Stacey 2012; Valentine 1997). María says she was nearly abducted when "It was dark, dark." Here is her experience:

I was walking home from [afterschool care] and a guy slipped out his car. He asked me to get in. At first, I dismissed him. Then he said it again. [I was] like, "Sir, I have to get home." And I continued walking. I started walking faster. The guy slows down his car, stops his car, gets out of the car and yells at me, "Get in my goddamn car!" And, like I said, I just kept walking. He was like, "I know you hear me!" And kept, he then, I'm walking faster and faster. I'm further away from the car. But the guy starts to chase me. So, I ended up running away. Like, I had to keep running. And I ended up running—I literally passed my house trying to get rid of this guy. And I finally got rid of him. And I basically stood at the train stop. Down, all the way down the street—yeah, all the way down there.[13] Tryna get away from this, getting, I got to the train stop. And I basically just sat there for a while. And waited to make sure he was gone, with all these people getting off the train. And then I walked home again. . . . I don't like talking about it. It reminds me that I could have been kidnapped, raped, or killed.

This ordeal is not an urban myth, not an imagined story, not hyperbole. Here is the story of one out of the fifty-seven girls telling us of kidnapping. We suggest one in fifty-seven is not rare and it is hard to digest. The trauma María still carries with her on a daily basis hinges, partly, on the disappointment she feels because police can do nothing. Since it was night and she was running for her life, "There was nothing we could do. I never looked, got a license plate. It was all black. So, it was dark out and everything. I never really got to see details." Without these important facts, the police cannot act on the incident report she made with her mother. In further trauma, María says the failure to catch this man "made me feel a lot more uncomfortable walking down the street, even in daylight. 'Cuz my fear was, what if—I didn't see the guy's face—what if he remembers my face and I don't remember his?" Importantly, María escaped the kidnapper by using emplaced agency and neighborhood familiarity. Even in the midst of the worst kind of fear, she remembered the train station located past her house, a safe place that would be populated, not isolated, at night (see Nansen et al. 2015). María's sophistication, expertise, and ability to utilize of-the-moment strategies and her local, urban knowledge of the social and temporal landscape to minimize the possibility of kidnapping is what saved her (Christensen and Prout 2003; Leonard 2007; van der Bergt 2015). In her efforts to avoid kidnapping, we find reflected in María girls' connection with spaces that "invoke powerful feelings, including those associated with . . . safety and/or danger" (Leverett 2011, 9).

In the life stories of María, Erica, Vanessa, Tiara, Barbie, Star, Tamrah, and countless other girls, we witness a long trail of true fear. Fear of the dark is not a remnant of early childhood bedtime stories; it is the result of being watched, followed, creeped upon by real men. Significantly, prior to María telling us the story of her near-capture, she expressed nihilistic thoughts, wondering what life would be like for her mother if she was dead. Kirkpatrick Johnson and Mollborn (2009) state, "When young people witness or experience violence and fear for their safety in their daily lives, it can raise the possibility (and sometimes the reality) of the end of one's life being nearer" (44). We are reminded of a small but striking quote found in Niobe Way's (1998) work with urban youth of color—Marie, a ninth grader from the Dominican Republic, asserts, "life is a child of death. You know?" (168). Girls of color are kept from the streets of their neighborhoods, imprisoned in their homes because of the fear of seen and unseen victimizers and violence, leading us to agree with Marie. Their lives are forever burdened by controlling images of their positionality as victims of crime, strangers, and violence (Madriz 1997a). Urban girls of color experience childhoods that are at once confined by and confined to "the predatory public space" of cityscapes, their racialized geographies with limited mobility "importantly and problematically" weighing on "young people's quality of life" (Horton, Kraftl, and Tucker 2011, 45; James, Jenks, and Prout 1998, 52).

TAKING BACK THE NIGHT: THE POWER OF FANTASY, PLAY, AND POPULAR CULTURE

The girls in our study carry the fear of night on their bodies. Their memories of neighborhoods past and present hang heavily on their backs, the weight of which restrains them from moving freely or serenely across their cityscape homes. Kelly Barnhill's fantasy book for children, *The Girl Who Drank the Moon* (2016), provides an apt description of these girls' experiences: "She was an old woman. She was a girl. She was somewhere in between. She was all of those things at once" (381). Yes, they are girls, but they are also in some ways older, facing dangers that some adults chalk up to rumor, but youths know are not the imagined monsters of their childhood. Instead, these are the real monsters of girls' lived journeys yesterday, today, and tomorrow. Some of the girls speak of their neighborhoods and homes as prisons, with violence and crime preventing them from fully experiencing life. At the same time, girls still have hope: Tamrah assures, "But we still living!" and Barbie exclaims, "But we still alive!" Of all the girls, Barbie, in particular, has such a positive outlook on her future. She says:

> I know I'm going to be successful. I'm not going to live somewhere near here, I ain't. I wanna live in a big city in a big house [*whispering*], big house, big house in the south. If not in the south, I wanna be, I dunno, I'm scared to go somewhere where I've never been just because I've never been. But I have to experience it to know. Yeah, I'm excited for life. I am. I just can't wait to see myself in five years.

Similar to the poor youth of color in Way's (1998) work, the girls tell stories of "frightening, even chilling, events happening in their neighborhoods . . . and about being successful in the future" (170). Barbie hopes so much for her future self, while still embracing living in a city. This emplacement is yet another paradox of fear for urban girls—*while they experience such hardships in the city during their childhoods, they still look forward to living there as an adult*. Maybe not their city, but a city nonetheless. In the meantime,

Barbie welcomes her fear; she says she is scared, but she knows that feeling is a part of growth to get to a better place, a brighter future than the one she might have in the city of her youth. In this hope, we understand that girls can potentially look forward to fear if it is of their own making—fear of the unknown is not necessarily something they need to run from.

Girls fear the dark because it is constructed as a time fraught with questions and danger. What loud noise wakes her up in the middle of the night, and is it gunfire? What lascivious man is lurking around that next corner? What car contains someone intending to snatch her from the street, preventing her from taking the next trepidatious step across the cityscape? While researchers broadly agree that fear of the dark decreases as children age (see Chaiyawat and Jezewski 2006; Salcuni et al. 2009), the girls in our study do not have such a luxury. In fact, we argue their fear of the dark increases as they age. Together, the girls experience a geography of fear that combines dark, dimly lit alleys, streets, and neighborhoods with their changing adolescent and racially otherized bodies. In our final paradox of fear, *the girls still recognize that darkness is both necessary and cathartic in small amounts* (Howarth 2014). During the socio-spatial tours that took place at the youth center, one third of the girls mentioned the locker room there. This place takes on special importance for the girls, a space where they can reconstruct their identities and embrace the dark with their peers, finding the comfort *in* fear, not the danger *of* fear.

LaLa, 12, Jamaican and African American, tells us what girls do in the locker room is "a secret"; but, unable to contain her excitement, she says the locker room is "where we go crazy! Go crazy and play a scary game. That's the hangout room for girls. We do anything that's outside 'cuz there's no counselors, and [no] cameras." In LaLa's depiction of the girls' locker room and what the girls do with it, we find that such spaces enable youth to recreate their girlhoods as "a secret and protected world" (James 1993, 89). The locker room and what happens in there was the only piece of information most girls seemed reluctant to discuss during their socio-spatial tours. In fact, Elaine got so nervous when the topic of the girls' locker room came up, she immediately asked for some water. That being said, Noodles and Bubbles both reveal that girls play Bloody Mary in the locker room. Noodles explains: "Last year, they used to do the Bloody Mary thing in the girls' bathroom. Turn off the lights. It's like this ghost that comes up in the mirror. So, they turn off the lights and go, 'Bloody Mary and close your eyes,' and then look at the mirror, something comes up. Some scary face comes up on the mirror." Bubbles says the whole point of the Bloody Mary game is that "it's fun" when "all the girls, they always get scared." Similarly, Coffee, 12, African American, details playing Slender Man in the girls' locker room:

We're always in there when we don't want to do something; it's really fun, because we just always hang around . . . .We would all hide in this little corner and . . . .we would play this game, Slender Man . . . . [Our friend] makes it scary and she doesn't mind always being the person that tries to get us. So, one minute she's in one place and you can see her shadow, and the next she's gone, she vanishes. It's crazy. And sometimes it's completely dark in there, you can't, there are times, sometimes, we see something or we can see still in the dark and then there's those times where it's completely pitch-black and you can't see anything. It's even scarier and we just hide in this little corner.

Children's pop culture fantasy games like Slender Man and Bloody Mary seem scary to younger participants like Bubbles, Noodles, and Coffee. Turning off all the lights and running around the girls' locker room "involves both the excitement and the joy of mastering a risky and potentially dangerous situation, and the thrill of being on the dangerous edge, fully aware of the possible outcome of fear" (Sandseter 2009, 94). The girls take the dark, their "space of fearfulness" (Pain 2001, 904), and transform it into a place of play—boldly, defiantly, and agentically facing their fears in a safe location with friends. In this process, girls' fear and danger is self-made and their games can, therefore, be terminated at any point. Crucially, there is a beginning and an end to their fear of darkness in the girls' locker room. They can always turn the lights back on.

The girls' locker room is an enclosed space, but not too small (according to Star). The location and what the girls do with it signifies a "girl place" where they can resist adult and parental efforts to control their movements since it is a space outside of their households, somewhere private yet still part of a somewhat public realm (Hopkins 2010; Tucker and Matthews 2001, 167; Skelton 2000). Elaine claims, "there's always stuff going on in the girls' locker room." However, NaeNae, 12, African American, informs us that the girls' locker room is only open in the summer months; during the school year, it is closed off to them. She explains, "This is the hangout spot during the summertime," where girls "listen to music, dance, and chill." Actions, NaeNae assures the interviewer, that "wouldn't be appropriate" for girls outside, in public. So, during the summer girls appropriate the space for their own uses, utilizing their agency to be freer than they are allowed to be otherwise (see Smith and Barker 2000). In addition, descriptions of the room's usage from Bubbles, Elaine, Noodles, Coffee, and NaeNae show us that children have a "remarkable capacity for responding to shifting, unexpected, often fleeting opportunities for expression [that is] . . . remarkably responsive, with a fantastical mixing of the material and the imaginary" (Jones 2000, 41–2). Similar to Tracey Skelton's (2000) research, the girls' locker room "is a place for them, somewhere they feel central and important. It provides an alternative to some of the stifling domestic settings and the contested spaces of the streets" (96).

Exactly like our participants, Smith and Barker (2000) find that girls try to claim spaces in afterschool clubs where they can sing and talk in private, usually without interruption from boys. In performing their true identities to one another, not the ones they must construct for protection in their neighborhoods and streets, the girls are finally free to be themselves (Hopkins 2010). Having fun, playing, and being rowdy are important aspects of life for girls; they value the short times when and small spaces where they, and their friends, are beyond the reach of adults and the lives they are forced to lead outside of the margins but still inside the city (Mayall 2002; Merten 2005; Skelton 2000). Of all the girls, Star was the most forthcoming about the girls' locker room. In the following description, we get a very clear idea of just how much the place means to them and just how much they need the space to feel like girls, even though she admits they "are not supposed to go in there." In between detailing their scary games in the dark, Star emotes:

> Everything goes on in the girls' locker room. That's when all the girls come together. We talk, we turn off the light, and we play this little scary thing, the game . . . . We twerk in there. We dance in there. We sing in there. We talk in there. We take pictures in there. It's our spot, where girls can be girls. And that's when the whole group, where we hang. That's where we get in trouble . . . . And we be loud. We be recordin' foolishness. Yeah, I like being in the girls' locker room.

The girls creatively enact their bodies and voices to agentically claim a meaningful social space in the locker room, employing a combination of pop culture, fantasy, and play. Popular culture reflects struggles of identity, desire, pleasure, power, and community for urban girls, and so the locker room becomes a "symbolic gateway"—a transformative space that, through the hopeful imagination and "limitless possibilities" found in fantasy, enables the girls to gain "meaningfulness . . . in the present moment" (Dillabough and Kennelly 2010, 197; Kearney 2011, 2; Willis 2009, 106 & 107). The girls mine elements of popular culture to express their "girl power," embracing fantasy and play to challenge their generalized portrayal as passive victims (Bae 2011; Kearney 2011). Agency, here, is a strategic resource used by the girls, for in the context of the imaginary and fantasy they reclaim their girlhood identities and peer culture, no longer bound by the hegemonic norms or racialized messages that target them on the streets (Kearney 2011; Willis 2009). Dillabough and Kennelly (2010) state that "complex emotion and cultural antagonisms" found in the landscapes of urban youth "[drive] young people's fantasy constructions and play some part in the very making of young cultures" (151). For urban youth, fantasy is blurred with reality "as young people's desires are enacted and performed in the everyday of confined spaces" (Dillabough and Kennelly 2010, 78).

Related, Skelton (2000) stresses that it is important to honor the "spaces and places where teenage girls can perform aspects of their identities and play around with meanings of femininity" (82). The girls we spoke with use this space to its maximum capacity; given there are no adult staff or cameras in the girls' locker room, they seize the opportunity to be free from adult surveillance and their highly regulated home worlds (see Wyness 2015). In this way, the locker room, and the variety of activities girls use it for, indicates its importance as "a mode of survival" that depends on the girls finding times and places to play, hope, and build new communities with peers outside the streets of their neighborhoods (Breitbart 1998, 325). Star's statement, "It's our spot where girls can be girls. And that's when the whole group, where we hang" echoes Carol, one of the girls in Skelton's (2000) study—"we have a really good laugh some of the time, we can just giggle and be together here, there's no trouble, you can just be yourself" (97). Following, Skelton (2000) states these spaces, friendships, and activities allow urban girls "significant freedom and mobility in an otherwise deprived and impoverished environment" (97). The girls in our study agentically create new ways of interacting with space in the locker room, subversively raging against the controlling adultist and environmental influences found elsewhere in their lives (see Hacket, Procter, and Seymour 2015). While this time and space is so important to the girls, we must recognize it is temporary. As explained, the locker room is merely available for entre three months out of the year, and within those fleeting days, only when they can sneak away from surveilling adult staff. Additionally, it is only tween girls (in the 10–12 age range) who mention the girls' locker room during interviews. Whether older girls outgrow the space or whether they protect the secret of the locker room with more conviction, we do not know.

In speaking of the streets, Matthews, Limb, and Taylor (2000) assert, "These are places where young people can piece together their own identities, celebrate an emotional sense of togetherness and stand apart, if only temporarily, from the adult world which surrounds them" (77). We do not find this statement to be true for the girls in our study—renegotiating their identities or finding spaces of solace on the public streets is not always realistic for them. Their presence on the street is sometimes seen as "out of place," excluded from adult society, leading urban girls to recreate and repurpose private spaces for what might otherwise be public identity performances if they lived elsewhere (Buckingham 2000; Cope 2008; Hopkins 2010; Yarwood and Tyrrell 2012). As Hopkins (2010) so eloquently explains: "Where young people grow up, the places they encounter and the localities that they negotiate during their everyday lives have significant consequences for who they are, where they can and cannot go, and who they may become. Place matters and geography makes a difference" (272). As proof, Elaine offers the very insightful observation that the locker room, with the safety and camaraderie it provides girls and their peer culture, is the place where "we track our social lives." With high crime rates, the cityscape of the girls dictates that their movements are restricted to such an extent that they are relegated to smaller and smaller spaces and times of living. Yet, whether it be the blacktops outside their homes, early morning hours of diminished male populations on the streets, or three months' respite in a girls' locker room, the girls still persevere. They utilize agentic strategies to seek out possibilities of joining other girls in fantasy play and in fear, facing the encroaching darkness with hope that tomorrow will bring more light. For, if they are afforded the opportunity to give testimony of their lives, and if we listen closely, no one can further deny their stories are imagination or myth. There is truth in their struggle and there is pain in their fear, but therein lies many youth's journeys across the urban plain.

NOTES

1. Similar effects are found between women and men—Barecca (2011) states that while men respond to fear with anger, women respond with anxiety that presents through symptoms of illness (e.g., allergies, cramps, stomachaches, headaches, and dizziness).

2. Perhaps underlying this paradox, Tuan (1980) asserts fear is integral to close human connection. He explains that if fear and threat is removed, the "bonds of community tend to weaken" (Tuan 1980, 211). Similarly, Kruuse and Kalmus (2017) state that moderate fears are useful for children's development, as fear leads them to "learn by experimenting, testing limits, and experiencing the consequences of their behavior" (260).

3. Adding to the unequal risks found between poorer and wealthier children, Barnes and colleagues (2006) state that pedestrian casualties are greatest for poorer children and children of color. Affluent families' use of cars for safe transport in the effort to protect their own children from harm places mounting risks on poorer children since the latter are more likely to walk to school and cross many streets during the week as pedestrians (Barnes et al. 2006).

4. See Campos-Holland, Dinsmore, and Kelekay (2016) for more on this research process.

5. Participants in this sample experience high levels of residential mobility and some have parents living in separate homes, either within their hometown or across cities and suburbs.

6. Atlas.ti is software by Scientific Software Development GmbH that we used to assist in our qualitative analysis.

7. All girls' legal names are replaced with self-selected pseudonyms.

8. Elaine was interviewed in both 2013 and 2015. While her earlier quote is from the second interview at 14, this quote from Elaine and all that follow are from the first interview at 12.

9. In addition to restricting girls' use of public spaces, caring adults in the girls' lives (parents, other relatives, and teachers) find access routes to better environments for the girls, such as the surrounding suburbs that have lower crime rates (Campos-Manzo et al. 2018), higher-performing schools (Campos-Manzo, Ramos et al. 2020), and safer public spaces (e.g., parks, malls, and sidewalks). At the time of the interviews, 7/57 girls lived in the suburbs and 12/57 girls attended schools in the suburbs. As for all the girls, 21/57 have lived in the suburbs and 44/57 have attended suburban schools at some point in their lives. However, attending suburban schools is unstable since access to inter-district programs for city students is constantly changing, the predominantly white peer culture in suburban schools is aggressive against students from the city, and students struggling academically or socially are pushed back to city schools. As for access to housing, rents and property values are higher in the suburbs, with most families that gain access to suburban housing eventually returning to the city.

10. See later account of María's near abduction as explanation for her mother's vigilant watchfulness.

11. For lack of space, Star and Tamrah's full accounts of being followed are not related here.

12. To note, children's suburban neighborhoods also present as darker, dilapidated, and abandoned when buildings and public spaces are not maintained and are neglected (Tomanović and Petrović 2010).

13. María is referring to the Google Map she and the interviewer are looking at during the interview.

REFERENCES

Addington, Lynn A., and Yaacov B. Yablon. 2011. "How Safe Do Students Feel at School and While Traveling to School? A Comparative Look at Israel and the United States." *American Journal of Education* 117 (4): 465–93.

Auerbach, Carl F., and Louise B. Silverstein. 2003. *Qualitative Data: An Introduction to Coding and Analysis*. New York, NY: New York University Press.

Bae, Michelle S. 2011. "Interrogating Girl Power: Girlhood, Popular Media, and Postfeminism." *Visual Arts Research* 37 (2): 28–40.

Barecca, Gina. 2011. "Women's Fears vs. Men's Fears Part 2: Do Women Use Fear As a Penance for Power?" *Psychology Today*. September 23, 2011. https://www.psychologytoday.com/us/blog/snow-white-doesnt-live-here-anymore/201109/womens-fears-vs-mens-fears-part-2.

Barnes, Jacqueline, Ilan Katz, Jill E. Korbin, and Margaret O'Brien. 2006. *Children and Families in Communities: Theory, Research, Policy and Practice*. West Sussex: John Wiley & Sons.

Barnhill, Kelly. 2016. *The Girl Who Drank the Moon*. Chapel Hill, NC: Algonquin Young Readers.

Blundell, David. 2016. *Rethinking Children's Spaces and Places*. London: Bloomsbury.

Bonnett, Alastair. 2002. "The Metropolis and White Modernity." *Ethnicities* 2 (3): 349–66.

Breitbart, Myrna M. 1998. "'Dana's Mystical Tunnel': Young People's Designs for Survival and Change in the City." In *Cool Places: Geographies of Youth Cultures*, edited by Tracey Skelton and Gill Valentine, 305–27. London: Routledge.

Bromley, Rosemary D.F., and Robert J. Stacey. 2012. "Feeling Unsafe in Urban Areas: Exploring Older Children's Geographies of Fear." *Environment and Planning A: Economy and Space* 44 (2): 428–44.

Buckingham, David. 2000. *After the Death of Childhood: Growing Up in the Age of Electronic Media*. Cambridge: Polity Press.

Cahill, Caitlin. 2000. "Street Literacy: Urban Teenagers' Strategies for Negotiating Their Neighbourhood." *Journal of Youth Studies* 3 (3): 251–77.

Campos-Holland, Ana. 2017. "Sharpening Theory and Methodology to Explore Racialized Youth Peer Cultures." In *Researching Children and Youth: Methodological Issues, Strategies, and Innovations—Sociological Studies of Children and Youth, Volume 22*, edited by Ingrid E. Castro, Melissa Swauger, and Brent Harger, 223–47. Bingley: Emerald.

Campos-Holland, Ana, Brooke Dinsmore, and Jasmine Kelekay. 2016. "Virtual Tours: Enhancing Qualitative Methodology to Holistically Capture Youth Peer Cultures." In *[New] Media Cultures, Communication and Information Technologies Annual, Studies in Media and Communications, Volume 11*, edited by Laura Robinson, Jeremy Schulz, Shelia R. Cotten, Timothy M. Hale, Apryl A. Williams, and Joy L. Hightower, 225–60. Bingley: Emerald.

Campos-Manzo, Ana L., Marisol Flores, Denise Pérez, Zoe Halpert, and Kevin Zevallos. 2020. "Unjustified: Youth of Color Navigating Police Presence Across Sociospatial Environments." *Race and Justice* 10 (3): 297–319.

Campos-Manzo, Ana L., Allison M. Mitobe, Christiana Ignatiadis, Emily W. Rubin, and Joanna Fischer. 2019. "Collective Pain: Youth of Color Facing the Aftermath of Mass School Shootings." In *Handbook of Research on School Violence in American K-12 Education*, edited by Gordon A. Crews, 179–207. Hershey, PA: IGI Global.

Campos-Manzo, Ana L., Luis E. Ramos, Grace Hall, and Christina Ignatiadis. 2020. "(Dis)connected: Youth Peer Culture During a Racial/Ethnic Integration Reform." In *The Complex Web of Inequality in North American Schools: Investigating Educational Policies for Social Justice*, edited by Gilberto Q. Conchas, Briana M. Hinga, Miguel N. Abad, and Kris D. Gutiérrez, 99–120. New York, NY: Routledge.

Castro, Ingrid E. 2017. "Contextualizing Agency in High-Structure Environments: Children's Participation in Parent Interviews." In *Researching Children and Youth: Methodological Issues, Strategies, and Innovations—Sociological Studies of Children and Youth, Volume 22*, edited by Ingrid E. Castro, Melissa Swauger, and Brent Harger, 149–73. Bingley: Emerald.

———. 2019. "The *Emergence* of Agency After Bionuclear War: Posthuman Child–Animal Possibilities." In *Child and Youth Agency in Science Fiction: Travel, Technology, Time*, edited by Ingrid E. Castro and Jessica Clark, 251–72. Lanham, MD: Lexington Books.
Chaiyawat, Waraporn, and Mary A. Jezewski. 2006. "Thai School-Age Children's Perception of Fear." *Journal of Transcultural Nursing* 17 (1): 74–81.
Chawla, Louise, and Karen Malone. 2003. "Neighbourhood Quality in Children's Eyes." In *Children in the City: Home, Neighbourhood and Community*, edited by Pia Christensen and Margaret O'Brien, 118–41. Oxon: Routledge.
Christensen, Julie H., Lærke Mygind, and Peter Bentsen. 2015. "Conceptions of Place: Approaching Space, Children and Physical Activity." *Children's Geographies* 13 (5): 589–603.
Christensen, Pia, and Margaret O'Brien. 2003. "Children in the City: Introducing New Perspectives." In *Children in the City: Home, Neighbourhood and Community*, edited by Pia Christensen and Margaret O'Brien, 1–12. Oxon: Routledge.
Christensen, Pia, and Alan Prout. 2003. "Children, Place, Space and Generation." In *Childhood in Generational Perspective*, edited by Berry Mayall and Helga Zeiher, 133–54. London: Institute of Education, University of London.
Cope, Meghan. 2008. "Patchwork Neighborhood: Children's Urban Geographies in Buffalo, New York." *Environment and Planning A: Economy and Space* 40 (12): 2845–63.
Corsaro, William A. 2015. *The Sociology of Childhood* (4th ed.). Thousand Oaks, CA: SAGE.
Day, Kristen. 1999. "Embassies and Sanctuaries: Women's Experiences of Race and Fear in Public Space." *Environment and Planning D: Society and Space* 17 (3): 307–28.
De Groof, Saskia. 2008. "And My Mama Said…The (Relative) Parental Influence on Fear of Crime among Adolescent Girls and Boys." *Youth & Society* 39 (3): 267–93.
Denov, Myriam, and Christine Gervais. 2007. "Negotiating (In)Security: Agency, Resistance, and Resourcefulness Among Girls Formerly Associated with Sierra Leone's Revolutionary United Front." *Signs: Journal of Women in Culture and Society* 32 (4): 885–910.
Dillabough, Jo-Anne, and Jacqueline Kennelly. 2010. *Lost Youth in the Global City: Class, Culture and the Urban Imaginary*. New York, NY: Routledge.
Dozier Jr., Rush W. 1998. *Fear Itself: The Origin and Nature of the Powerful Emotion That Shapes Our Lives and Our World*. New York, NY: St. Martin's Press.
Elsley, Susan. 2011. "Out of the Way: Children, Young People and Outdoor Spaces." In *Children and Young People's Spaces: Developing Practice*, edited by Pam Foley and Stephan Leverett, 102–15. Hampshire: Palgrave MacMillan.
Federal Bureau of Investigation. 2014. "Uniform Crime Report (UCR)." https://www.fbi.gov/about-us/cjis/ucr/ucr.
Franklin, Cortney A., and Travis W. Franklin. 2009. "Predicting Fear of Crime: Considering Differences Across Gender." *Feminist Criminology* 4 (1): 83–106.

Furedi, Frank. 2002. *Culture of Fear: Risk-Taking and the Morality of Low Expectation* (revised ed.). London: Continuum.

Gillis, John R. 2008. "Epilogue: The Islanding of Children—Reshaping the Mythical Landscapes of Childhood." In *Designing Modern Childhoods: History, Space, and the Material Culture of Children*, edited by Marta Gutman and Ning de Coninck-Smith, 316–30. New Brunswick, NJ: Rutgers University Press.

Glassner, Barry. 1999. *The Culture of Fear: Why Americans Are Afraid of the Wrong Things*. New York, NY: Basic Books.

Gordon, Margaret T., and Stephanie Riger. 1989. *The Female Fear*. New York, NY: The Free Press.

Gullone, Eleonora. 1999. "The Assessment of Normal Fear in Children and Adolescents." *Clinical Child and Family Psychology Review* 2 (2): 91–106.

Hackett, Abigail, Lisa Procter, and Julie Seymour. 2015. "Introduction: Spatial Perspectives and Childhood Studies." In *Children's Spatialities: Embodiment, Emotion and Agency*, edited by Abigail Hackett, Lisa Procter, and Julie Seymour, 1–17. Hampshire: Palgrave Macmillan.

Hopkins, Peter E. 2010. *Young People, Place and Identity*. Oxon: Routledge.

Horton, John, Peter Kraftl, and Faith Tucker. 2011. "Spaces-in-the-Making, Childhoods-on-the-Move." In *Children and Young People's Spaces: Developing Practice*, edited by Pam Foley and Stephan Leverett, 40–57. Hampshire: Palgrave MacMillan.

Howarth, Michael. 2014. *Under the Bed, Creeping: Psychoanalyzing the Gothic in Children's Literature*. Jefferson, NC: McFarland & Company.

James, Allison. 1993. *Childhood Identities: Self and Social Relationships in the Experience of the Child*. Edinburgh: Edinburgh University Press.

———. 2013. *Socialising Children*. Hampshire: Palgrave Macmillan.

James, Allison, Chris Jenks, and Alan Prout. 1998. *Theorizing Childhood*. Cambridge: Polity Press.

Jones, Owain. 2000. "Melting Geography: Purity, Disorder, Childhood and Space." In *Children's Geographies: Playing, Living, Learning*, edited by Sarah L. Holloway and Gill Valentine, 29–47. London: Routledge.

Katz, Cindi. 2005. "The Terrors of Hypervigilance: Security and the Compromised Spaces of Contemporary Childhood." In *Studies in Modern Childhood: Society, Agency, Culture*, edited by Jens Qvortrup, 99–114. Hampshire: Palgrave MacMillan.

Kearney, Mary C. 2011. "Introduction: Girls' Media Studies 2.0." In *Mediated Girlhoods: New Explorations of Girls' Media Culture*, edited by Mary C. Kearney, 1–14. New York, NY: Peter Lang.

Kirkpatrick Johnson, Monica, and Stefanie Mollborn. 2009. "Growing Up Faster, Feeling Older: Hardship in Childhood and Adolescence." *Social Psychology Quarterly* 72 (1): 39–60.

Kruuse, Kristiina, and Veronika Kalmus. 2017. "Supernatural Creatures, Accidents, and War: Young Children's Television-Related Fears and Coping Strategies." *Television & New Media* 18 (3): 252–68.

Lahikainen, Anja R., Tiina Kirmanen, Inger Kraav, and Merle Taimalu. 2003. "Studying Fears in Young Children: Two Interview Methods." *Childhood* 10 (1): 83–104.

Lahikainen, Anja R., Inger Kraav, Tiina Kirmanen, and Merle Taimalu. 2006. "Child-Parent Agreement in the Assessment of Young Children's Fears." *Journal of Cross-Cultural Psychology* 37 (1): 100–19.

Lane, Jodi, and Bonnie S. Fisher. 2009. "Unpacking the Relationship Between Gender and Fear of Crime: Explaining Why There Are Similarities and Differences." *Journal of Contemporary Criminal Justice* 25 (3): 260–3.

Leonard, Madeleine. 2007. "Trapped in Space? Children's Accounts of Risky Environments." *Children & Society* 21 (6): 432–45.

Leverett, Stephan. 2011. "Children's Spaces." In *Children and Young People's Spaces: Developing Practice*, edited by Pam Foley and Stephan Leverett, 9–24. Hampshire: Palgrave MacMillan.

Mackett, Roger, Belinda Brown, Yi Gong, Kay Kitazawa, and James Paskins. 2007. "Children's Independent Movement in the Local Environment." *Built Environment* 33 (4): 454–68.

Madriz, Esther. 1997a. *Nothing Bad Happens to Good Girls: Fear of Crime in Women's Lives*. Berkeley, CA: University of California Press.

———.1997b. "Latina Teenagers: Victimization, Identity, and Fear of Crime." *Social Justice* 24 (4): 39–55.

Malone, Karen, and Lindsay Hasluck. 2002. "Australian Youth: Aliens in a Suburban Environment." In *Growing Up in an Urbanising World*, edited by Louise Chawla, 81–109. Paris: United Nations Educational, Scientific and Cultural Organization.

Matthews, Hugh. 2003. "The Street As a Liminal Space: The Barbed Spaces of Childhood." In *Children in the City: Home, Neighbourhood and Community*, edited by Pia Christensen and Margaret O'Brien, 101–17. Oxon: Routledge.

Matthews, Hugh, Melanie Limb, and Mark Taylor. 2000. "The 'Street As Thirdspace.'" In *Children's Geographies: Playing, Living, Learning*, edited by Sarah L. Holloway and Gill Valentine, 63–79. London: Routledge.

Mayall, Berry. 2002. *Towards a Sociology for Childhood: Thinking from Children's Lives*. Berkshire: Open University Press.

McIntyre, Alice. 2000. *Inner-City Kids: Adolescents Confront Life and Violence in an Urban Community*. New York, NY: New York University Press.

Merten, Don E. 2005. "Transitions and 'Trouble': Rites of Passage for Suburban Girls." *Anthropology & Education Quarterly* 36 (2): 132–48.

Michalčáková, Radka, Lenka Lacinová, Hana Kyjonková, Ondřej Bouša, and Martin Jelínek. 2013. "Fears in Czech Adolescents: A Longitudinal Study." *Journal of Early Adolescence* 33 (8): 1072–90.

Miller, Jody. 2008. *Getting Played: African American Girls, Urban Inequality, and Gendered Violence*. New York, NY: New York University Press.

Morrow, Virginia. 2003. "Improving the Neighbourhood for Children: Possibilities and Limitations of 'Social Capital' Discourse." In *Children in the City: Home, Neighbourhood and Community*, edited by Pia Christensen and Margaret O'Brien, 162–83. Oxon: Routledge.

———. 2011. "Researching Children and Young People's Perspectives on Place and Belonging." In *Children and Young People's Spaces: Developing Practice*, edited by Pam Foley and Stephan Leverett, 58–72. Hampshire: Palgrave MacMillan.

Nansen, Bjorn, Lisa Gibbs, Colin MacDougall, Frank Vetere, Nicola J. Ross, and John McKendrick. 2015. "Children's Interdependent Mobility: Compositions, Collaborations and Compromises." *Children's Geographies* 13 (4): 467–81.

O'Brien, Margaret. 2003. "Regenerating Children's Neighbourhoods: What Do Children Want?" In *Children in the City: Home, Neighbourhood and Community*, edited by Pia Christensen and Margaret O'Brien, 142–61. Oxon: Routledge.

Pain, Rachel. 1997. "Social Geographies of Women's Fear of Crime." *Transactions of the Institute of British Geographers* 22 (2): 231–44.

———. 2001. "Gender, Race, Age and Fear in the City." *Urban Studies* 38 (5–6): 899–913.

———. 2003. "Youth, Age and the Representation of Fear." *Capital & Class* 27 (2): 151–71.

Percy-Smith, Barry. 2002. "Contested Worlds: Constraints and Opportunities in City and Suburban Environments in an English Midlands City." In *Growing Up in an Urbanising World*, edited by Louise Chawla, 57–80. Paris: United Nations Educational, Scientific and Cultural Organization.

Popkin, Susan J., Tama Leventhal, and Gretchen Weismann. 2010. "Girls in the 'Hood: How Safety Affects the Life Chances of Low-Income Girls." *Urban Affairs Review* 45 (6): 715–44.

Rios, Victor M. 2011. *Punished: Policing the Lives of Black and Latino Boys*. New York, NY: New York University Press.

Salcuni, Silvia, Daniela Di Riso, Claudia Mazzeschi, and Adrianna Lis. 2009. "Children's Fears: A Survey of Italian Children Ages 6 to 10 Years." *Psychological Reports* 104 (3): 971–88.

Salvadori, Ilaria. 2002. "Between Fences: Living and Playing in a California City." In *Growing Up in an Urbanising World*, edited by Louise Chawla, 183–200. Paris: United Nations Educational, Scientific and Cultural Organization.

Sandseter, Ellen B.H. 2009. "Children's Expressions of Exhilaration and Fear in Risky Play." *Contemporary Issues in Early Childhood* 10 (2): 92–106.

Sayfan, Liat, and Kristin H. Lagattuta. 2008. "Grownups Are Not Afraid of Scary Stuff, but Kids Are: Young Children's and Adults' Reasoning About Children's, Infants', and Adults' Fears." *Child Development* 79 (4): 821–35.

———. 2009. "Scaring the Monster Away: What Children Know About Managing Fears of Real and Imaginary Creatures." *Child Development* 80 (6): 1756–74.

Seymour, Julie. 2015. "Approaches to Children's Spatial Agency: Reviewing Actors, Agents and Families." In *Children's Spatialities: Embodiment, Emotion and Agency*, edited by Abigail Hackett, Lisa Procter, and Julie Seymour, 147–62. Hampshire: Palgrave MacMillan.

Sharkey, Patrick T. 2006. "Navigating Dangerous Streets: The Sources and Consequences of Street Efficacy." *American Sociological Review* 71 (5): 826–46.

Shehan, Constance L. 1999. "No Longer a Place for Innocence: The Re-Submergence of Childhood in Post-Industrial Societies." In *Through the Eyes of the Child:*

Revisioning Children as Active Agents of Family Life, edited by Constance L. Shehan, 1–17. Stamford, CT: JAI Press.

Skelton, Tracey. 2000. "'Nothing to Do, Nowhere to Go?': Teenage Girls and 'Public' Space in the Rhondda Valleys, South Wales." In *Children's Geographies: Playing, Living, Learning*, edited by Sarah L. Holloway and Gill Valentine, 80–99. London: Routledge.

Slaughter, Virginia, and Maya Griffiths. 2007. "Death Understanding and Fear of Death in Young Children." *Clinical Child Psychology and Psychiatry* 12 (4): 525–35.

Smith, Fiona, and John Barker. 2000. "'Out of School', in School: A Social Geography of Out of School Childcare." In *Children's Geographies: Playing, Living, Learning*, edited by S. L. Holloway and G. Valentine, 245–56. London: Routledge.

Spilsbury, James C. 2005. "'We Don't Really Get to Go Out in the Front Yard' – Children's Home Range and Neighborhood Violence." *Children's Geographies* 3 (1): 79–99.

Sternheimer, Karen. 2006. *Kids These Days: Facts and Fictions About Today's Youth*. Lanham, MD: Rowman & Littlefield.

Streitmatter, Janice. 1997. "An Exploratory Study of Risk-Taking and Attitudes in a Girls-Only Middle School Math Class." *The Elementary School Journal* 98 (1): 15–26.

Swauger, Melissa, Ingrid E. Castro, and Brent Harger. 2017. "The Continued Importance of Research with Children and Youth: The 'New' Sociology of Childhood 40 Years Later." In *Researching Children and Youth: Methodological Issues, Strategies, and Innovations—Sociological Studies of Children and Youth, Volume 22*, edited by Ingrid E. Castro, Melissa Swauger, and Brent Harger, 1–7. Bingley: Emerald.

Thorne, Barrie. 1987. "Re-Visioning Women and Social Change: Where Are the Children?" *Gender and Society* 1 (1): 85–109.

———. 1993. *Gender Play: Girls and Boys in School*. New Brunswick, NJ: Rutgers University Press.

Tomanović, Smiljka, and Mina Petrović. 2010. "Children's and Parents' Perspectives on Risks and Safety in Three Belgrade Neighbourhoods." *Children's Geographies* 8 (2): 141–56.

Tuan, Yi-Fu. 1980. *Landscapes of Fear*. Oxford: Basil Blackwell.

Tucker, Faith, and Hugh Matthews. 2001. "'They Don't Like Girls Hanging Around There': Conflicts Over Recreational Space in Rural Northamptonshire." *Area* 33 (2): 161–8.

Valentine, Gill. 1989. "The Geography of Women's Fear." *Area* 21 (4): 385–90.

———. 1997. "'Oh Yes I Can.' 'Oh No You Can't': Children and Parents' Understandings of Kids' Competence to Negotiate Public Space Safely." *Antipode* 29 (1): 65–89.

van der Burgt, Danielle. 2015. "Spatial Avoidance or Spatial Confidence? Young People's Agency in the Active Negotiation of Risk and Safety in Public Space." *Children's Geographies* 13 (2): 181–95.

van Liempt, Ilse, Irina van Aalst, and Tim Schwanen. 2015. "Introduction: Geographies of the Urban Night." *Urban Studies* 52 (3): 407–21.

Vornanen, Riita, Maritta Törrönen, and Pauli Niemelä. 2009. "Insecurity of Young People: The Meaning of Insecurity as Defined by 13–17-Year-Old Finns." *Young: Nordic Journal of Youth Research* 17 (4): 399–419.

Warr, Mark. 1990. "Dangerous Situations: Social Context and Fear of Victimization." *Social Forces* 68 (3): 891–907.

Watt, Paul, and Kevin Stenson. 1998. "The Street: 'It's a Bit Dodgy Around There': Safety, Danger, Ethnicity and Young People's Use of Public Space." In *Cool Places: Geographies of Youth Cultures*, edited by Tracey Skelton and Gill Valentine, 249–65. London: Routledge.

Way, Niobe. 1998. *Everyday Courage: The Lives and Stories of Urban Teenagers*. New York, NY: New York University Press.

Webster, Colin. 2003. "Race, Space and Fear: Imagined Geographies of Racism, Crime, Violence and Disorder in Northern England." *Capital & Class* 27 (2): 95–122.

Willis, Jessica L. 2009. "Girls Reconstructing Gender: Agency, Hybridity and Transformations of 'Femininity.'" *Girlhood Studies* 2 (2): 96–118.

Wyness, Michael. 2006. *Childhood and Society: An Introduction to the Sociology of Childhood*. Hampshire: Palgrave MacMillan.

———. 2015. *Childhood*. Cambridge: Polity Press.

Yarwood, Richard, and Naomi Tyrrell. 2012. "Why Children's Geographies?" *Geography* 97 (3): 123–8.

Yodanis, Carrie L. 2004. "Gender Inequality, Violence Against Women, and Fear: A Cross-National Test of the Feminist Theory of Violence Against Women." *Journal of Interpersonal Violence* 19 (6): 655–75.

Yuan, Yue, Beidi Dong, and Chris Melde. 2017. "Neighborhood Context, Street Efficacy, and Fear of Violent Victimization." *Youth Violence and Juvenile Justice* 15 (2): 119–37.

Zeiher, Helga. 2001. "Children's Islands in Space and Time: The Impact of Spatial Differentiation on Children's Ways of Shaping Social Life." In *Childhood in Europe: Approaches— Trends—Findings*, edited by Manuela Du Bois-Reymond, Heinz Sünker, and Heinz-Hermann Krüger, 138–59. New York, NY: Peter Lang.

———. 2003. "Shaping Daily Life in Urban Environments." In *Children in the City: Home, Neighbourhood and Community*, edited by Pia Christensen and Margaret O'Brien, 66–81. Oxon: Routledge.

Index

500 Hats of Bartholomew Cubbins, The, 44

abuse, 26, 29–30n7, 42, 84, 120–24, 133, 160, 161, 167, 180, 181, 188, 243. *See also* sexual violence; violence
acceptance, 15–18, 23, 24, 53, 56, 58, 73, 77, 87, 88, 96, 97, 103–6, 108, 119, 127, 136–38, 154, 157, 158, 161, 165, 180, 182, 187, 193n20, 211, 213, 232, 236, 237, 250
access, 102, 104, 105, 106, 112n11, 119, 129, 174–78, 180, 182, 184, 189, 201, 205, 217, 218, 231, 232, 255n9
activism, 27, 174, 186, 190, 191, 193n26. *See also* rights; social justice
Adler, Patricia A., 106
Adler, Peter, 106
adultism, 24, 112n14, 253; adult culture, 5, 119, 120, 132–33, 141n2, 143–44n18, 174, 176, 177, 183, 186, 188, 189, 190, 191; adult expectations, 16, 17, 43, 46, 50, 61, 65, 99, 103, 104, 106, 151, 234, 238, 239
adventure, 9–12, 14, 15, 17, 18, 24, 28, 29n3, 126, 151, 178, 179, 203, 204, 214, 219
Adventures in Babysitting, 111n6

agentive realism, 207, 219
aging, 6, 14, 16, 25, 46, 98, 100, 129, 142n8, 212, 218, 227, 228, 229, 244, 247, 250, 253; age-shifting, 8, 9, 16, 18, 214–15
Aykroyd, Dan, 12
Alanen, Leena, 154
Albus Dumbledore, 112n9, 123, 126, 130, 140, 143n14, 181, 186, 191–92n4
Alice in Wonderland, 5
aliens, 27, 205, 213
alone, 28, 106, 110, 111n2, 120, 156, 165, 213, 228, 230, 239–41, 246–48; loneliness, 43, 65, 76, 120–21
altruistic agency, 104, 109. *See also* moral agency
angel/devil construction, 23, 122, 183. *See also* good/bad construction
angels, 27, 205, 212
animals, 74, 76, 134, 193n21, 211, 217, 228, 229; pets/dogs, 45, 47, 62, 88, 122, 123, 126, 236, 245
Annabeth Chase, 152–53, 183, 192n10, 192n13
Apollo, 151, 152, 161–63; 164, 168n9, 168n10, 192n11; *Trials of Apollo: The Dark Prophecy*, 152, 155, 162; *Trials of Apollo: The Hidden Oracle*, 162, 164
Astin, Sean, 13–15

263

Astoria, Oregon, 9, 12
Atomic City, 58
atomic power, 58–61
Attention Deficit Hyperactivity Disorder (ADHD), 152–53, 167, 179
audience, 6, 11, 41, 42, 44, 50, 52, 53, 56, 61, 63, 64, 97, 98, 100, 102, 104, 107, 109, 111n1, 111n3, 154, 156, 175, 204
Aurora, Colorado, 234
Aurors, 138, 145n24, 193n23
auteur, 15
autonomy, 29n4, 151, 153, 156, 163, 164, 167, 177, 188, 206, 211

Bangles, The, 13, 30n8
Bartimaeus Sequence, The, 191n1
Beatniks, 44, 45
being/becoming, 7, 8, 16, 20, 23, 45, 106, 126, 202, 205, 207, 209, 218, 231
belonging, 7, 8, 11, 15, 22, 24–26, 117, 125, 133, 135, 140, 141, 143n17
Benefits of Looking Ahead, 43
bikes, 11, 29n3, 85, 209, 239
biographical object, 80
Bloody Mary, 250–51
Blundell, David, 118, 139
bodies, 6, 16, 19–23, 29n4, 59, 101, 127–28, 131, 138, 143n16, 151–53, 158–61, 163, 167n6, 205, 207, 211, 213, 214, 215, 218, 234, 245, 249, 250, 252; embodiment, 19, 20, 27, 137, 162, 165, 240
borders, 16, 201, 217, 230
boyd, danah, 174, 190
boyhood, 25, 29n3, 41, 42, 45, 47, 49–51, 53, 57–60; and adults, 42, 43, 46, 55, 65, 66n8; consumerism, 42, 49, 51, 56–59, 63; delinquency, 43, 44, 46, 52, 55, 58, 65, 66n4, 122; maturity, 42, 43, 46, 47, 49, 51, 52, 56, 61, 67n11; music, 42, 45–48, 52, 60–62, 65, 66n1, 67n11, 67n12;

science, 56–59, 67n10; sports, 45, 47, 51, 58, 62. *See also* gender; girlhood
Boy Scouts of America, 57
Breakfast Club, The, 111n6
Buckingham, David, 5, 8, 22, 97, 206
Buffy the Vampire Slayer, 26, 100–2, 109, 110, 112n11, 112n13; chosen one narrative, 101, 110
building, 78, 108, 120, 124, 126, 133, 136, 204–5, 208, 212, 216–17, 253
bullying, 31n11, 55, 99, 106, 122, 137, 180
Burton, Tim, 12

Caldecott Medal, 6
Campbell, Joseph, 98
Campbell, Lori M., 20, 99, 101
capabilities, 6, 7, 19, 73, 78, 97, 101, 103, 109, 137, 183, 189
capitalism, 9, 12, 25, 29–30n7, 53, 54, 57, 62, 63
Captain Video and His Video Rangers, 58
caring children, 8, 25, 84–86, 88
cars, 13, 30n8, 208, 209, 218, 230, 231, 247, 254n3
Castoriadis, Cornelius, 207
Castro, Ingrid E., 8, 13, 19, 29n1, 29n3, 29n4, 31n13, 31n15, 31n18, 67n10, 88, 99, 104, 111n2, 112n2, 121, 143n14, 158, 177–78, 183, 192n7
censorship, 3, 66n7, 174
CGI (Computer-Generated Imagery), 12, 29n4
Charlie/Willy Wonka and the Chocolate Factory, 11, 29n2
childhood studies, 6–8, 11, 19, 21, 22, 89, 95, 206, 214
Child Messiah, 165
children's geographies, 7, 19, 23, 24, 26, 117–19, 130, 208, 233
children's islanding, 26, 120–24, 128, 130, 139–41, 232. *See also* protectionism; Zeiher, Helga

children's/YA literature, ix, 5–6, 16, 26, 27, 95, 97, 98, 101, 109–10, 139, 153, 154, 173–75, 177, 179, 189, 201, 203, 218, 219; as a "low" art form, 5–7. *See also* reading down
Chilling Adventures of Sabrina, The, 100
chimaera, 27, 204, 205, 211, 214
choice, ix, 8, 20, 23, 26, 28, 73, 75, 76, 77, 79, 81, 82, 85, 87, 88, 96, 99, 100, 103, 106, 119, 137, 143n15, 151–54, 163–66, 167n6, 168n9, 168n13, 173, 179, 180, 183, 185, 189, 206, 230, 242, 243
Chomsky, Noam, 98, 112n7
Chowdhury, Radhiah, 165. *See also* Child Messiah
Christensen, Pia H., 130, 153
Chronicles of Narnia, The, 191n1
citizenry, 3–4, 8, 9, 10, 15, 18, 22, 24, 28, 42, 51, 56, 58, 103, 140, 175, 189–91, 209, 216; "citizenship from below," 10
city, 17, 71, 89, 112n11, 134, 216, 217, 219, 227, 230–32, 234, 239–41, 246, 247, 249, 250, 252, 254, 255n9; urban, 27–28, 219, 230–32, 234–37, 240–43, 246, 248, 249, 252–54
City of Ember, The, 97
Clear and Present Danger, 111n5
Clifford, James, 216
clothing, 17–18, 30n8, 44, 46, 51, 56, 57, 80, 82, 85, 86, 121, 124, 135, 211, 219
Columbia Pictures, 41, 62–64, 66n7
Columbus, Chris, 9
comics, 51, 58, 101, 179, 185, 203
communication, 75–79, 81, 88, 132–33, 143n17, 160, 174, 186, 190, 204
community, 26, 100, 107, 109, 120, 123, 128, 136, 137, 139, 203, 209, 220, 227, 233, 252, 253, 254n2; fan communities, 173–93

company, 25, 28, 31n19, 96, 106, 124, 138, 141, 236, 239, 246, 247; imaginary companions, 73–89
compromise, 140, 160
conflict, 15, 26–27, 58, 83, 88, 96, 98, 99, 103, 106, 109, 112n11, 126–27, 140, 151, 157, 159, 160, 184, 203, 215, 236
consumerism, 29–30n7, 41, 42, 49, 55, 56–59, 63–64, 75; consumers, 110, 111, 154; product tie-ins, 11, 12, 63, 65
context, 7, 9, 19, 21–22, 24, 26, 27, 31n16, 46, 55, 58, 65, 78–81, 84, 86, 97, 119, 134, 175, 176, 177–80, 182, 184, 186, 188, 189, 191, 206, 217, 252
control, 7, 17, 25, 31n18, 44, 46, 47, 50, 59, 60, 61, 76, 100–103, 110, 122, 129, 132–34, 143n16, 159–61, 163, 166, 167, 174, 175, 179, 189, 201, 202, 207, 209, 213, 214, 218, 229, 231–35, 237, 249, 251, 253
coronavirus/COVID–19, ix, 3, 11
Corsaro, William A., 5, 8, 50, 60, 73, 74, 78, 103–5, 119, 176–77, 186, 231. *See also* interpretive reproduction
cosplay, 203
creativity, 5, 7, 9, 15, 24–28, 43, 62, 78, 86, 87, 102–4, 118, 119, 139, 143n17, 163, 165, 175, 176, 179, 185, 190, 191, 206, 252
crime, 10, 43, 104, 193n21, 229, 230, 231, 234, 235–38, 243, 249, 254, 255n9
Csapo, Eric, 154, 167n2
cultural object, 78–79
culture, 5, 8, 9, 15, 23–26, 28, 29–30n7, 74, 75, 87, 95, 98, 99, 104–6, 109, 119, 120, 128, 130, 132, 133, 140, 156, 167, 173–77, 179, 180, 184, 185, 188–91, 205, 206, 210, 215–18, 228, 236, 237, 252–53. *See also*

material culture; peer culture; play culture; popular culture

danger, 9, 22, 27, 100, 101, 104–6, 109, 112n9, 121, 122, 127, 128, 134, 141n4, 160, 202, 205, 228–34, 236, 237, 239–43, 245–51. *See also* safety

Dark Knight, The, 234

darkness, 6, 22, 27, 28, 109, 123, 134, 135, 142n8, 143–44n18, 144n22, 228, 230, 240–54, 255n12. *See also* light; night

Davi, Robert, 11

death, 30n8, 61, 100, 107, 109, 112n9, 135–37, 141–42n4, 143n15, 193n25, 201, 213–15, 228–30, 243, 248

Deathly Hallows (items), 130, 143n15; Elder Wand/Wand of Destiny/Deathstick, 143n15; Invisibility Cloak, 130–31, 138, 143n14, 143n15, 143n16, 145n25; Resurrection Stone, 143n15

Decision of Christopher Blake, The, 58

del Toro, Guillermo, 25, 96, 98, 101, 105, 108, 111n3

Dementors, 134, 141n4, 185, 188, 193n21

democracy, 140, 157

Design for Death, 43

desire, 15, 17, 20, 22, 24, 25, 31n17, 47, 54, 65, 75, 82, 84, 86, 87, 88, 122, 129, 133, 151, 161, 163, 164, 202, 206–9, 214–16, 218, 219, 220, 227, 233–34, 237, 238, 240, 252–53

destiny, 46, 59, 96, 101, 112n9, 122, 126, 143n15, 165, 166, 215; fate, 8, 62, 164–66, 168n12, 180

deviance, 21, 122, 144n20

Día de los Muertos, 30–31n11

disability, 19, 26, 211

discrimination, 6, 27, 30–31n11, 156, 184; stereotypes, 18, 29n4. *See also* diversity; race/ethnicity

Divergent, 109

diversity, 26, 101, 151, 155, 158, 174, 177, 179, 182, 183, 184, 186, 187, 189, 192n11, 219; minority groups, 175, 176, 177, 184, 187. *See also* discrimination; LGBTQ; race/ethnicity

Dobby the house elf, 123, 131, 137, 138; house elves, 184

Donner, Richard, 11–15, 29n5, 29n6, 30n9

Don't Knock the Rock, 65

Draco Malfoy, 125, 134, 137, 144n21, 145n25, 180, 188, 191n4

dragons, 127, 210

Dr. Benjamin Spock, 44–47, 52

dream, x, 5, 24–25, 42, 43, 45, 46, 51, 54–55, 77, 120, 164, 209–10, 211, 213, 214, 216, 219, 220, 249; nightmare, 45, 126, 208, 228

Dr. Seuss. *See* Geisel, Theodor

drugs, 234–38, 243

Dumbledore's Army (the D.A.), 132–33, 134, 144n20

Dursleys, the, 120, 122–24, 142n5, 143n13; Dudley Dursley, 120–22, 124, 137, 141n4

dyslexia, 152–53, 167, 179

Eastwood, Clint, 12

Ebert, Roger, 12, 14

Eder, Donna, 102, 109

education, 43, 44, 58, 133, 178, 184, 185, 189, 202, 229. *See also* Hogwarts; school

Eisenhower, Dwight David, 58

Emirbayer, Mustafa, 22, 215

emotionality, 6, 11, 20–23, 25, 74, 78, 89, 99, 109, 123, 125–28, 130, 131, 133, 136–39, 143n13, 160–61, 180, 181, 183, 184, 187, 191, 228, 230, 238, 239, 241, 242, 249–54

empowerment, 26, 27, 42, 95, 97, 100–102, 109–11, 151, 153, 157–59, 161, 167, 173, 174, 189, 201–3, 207, 213, 218, 249–54. *See also* power

Enclave, 109

encouragement, 10, 28, 43, 44, 46, 153, 177, 179, 181, 182, 184, 191
English, O. Spurgeon, 44
essentialism, 6, 22
E.T. the Extra-Terrestrial, 12, 15, 29n3, 29n4
Every Heart a Doorway, 15–24

fable, 3, 136
Facebook, 26, 179
Fairey, Shepard, 30n8
fairness and equality, 17, 26, 27, 60, 99, 106, 129, 141, 158, 178, 186, 190, 193n26
fairy tale, 3, 4, 6–9, 15, 23, 27, 28, 30n8, 95, 203, 210–12, 215, 216, 218; fairies, 16, 18, 31n20, 30–31n11
family, ix, 7, 9, 16, 25, 29n4, 42, 46, 54, 57–58, 61, 66n6, 84, 86, 88, 106, 122–25, 127, 128, 142n5, 143n13, 143n15, 151–68, 217, 218, 227, 229, 231, 240, 247, 255n9; family relationships and structures, 6, 11, 24, 26, 29–30n7, 31n19, 76, 79, 81, 87, 88, 101, 102, 120, 122, 123, 125, 126, 142n6, 151–68, 184, 204–5, 233, 237, 254n3; nuclear family, 25, 42, 44, 52, 53, 54, 56, 62. *See also* generation; parents; siblings
fan communities, 26, 173–91, 203–4; fan studies, 175; fan texts, 175–81, 185–90, 203–4
Fantastic Beasts and Where to Find Them, 183
fantasy genre, 3–9, 11, 19, 20, 23, 24, 26–28, 97, 117, 154, 164, 174, 175, 178, 207, 208, 215, 216, 220, 249
fathers, 25, 44, 46, 48, 52–59, 65, 128, 129, 130, 131, 136, 138, 141–42n4, 142n5, 143n12, 143n14, 143–44n18, 145n26, 152, 155, 157, 159, 160–62, 164, 166, 167, 168n9, 181, 187, 192n6, 209, 244. *See also* family; mothers; parents

fear, 6, 7, 27–28, 30–31n11, 46, 47, 53, 58, 122, 123, 140, 142n8, 156, 163, 177, 184, 185, 193n20, 193n23, 227–55
Feldman, Corey, 11, 13
Feldt, Laura, 154
femininity, 18, 46, 183, 211, 232, 253. *See also* girlhood; masculinity
feminism, 109–10, 158, 205–6
The 5,000 Fingers of Dr. T, 41, 44–66; *Crazy Music* (rerelease), 65; critical reception, 41, 55, 62–64, 66n3; marketing, 63–65; popular reception, 41–42, 45, 64–66. *See also* Geisel, Theodor; Kramer, Stanley
Fingerson, Laura, 158, 163, 167n6
fluidity, 6, 8, 16, 19, 23, 25, 109, 158–60, 168n8, 179
Flynn, Richard, 95
Ford, Harrison, 12
Foucault, Michel, 75, 161
Frankel, Sam, 177
freedom, 4, 5, 16, 19, 27, 29n4, 43, 45, 47, 50, 51, 54, 58–60, 73, 99, 105, 121, 124, 125, 142–43n10, 145n27, 160, 165–67, 177, 186, 210, 217, 218, 227, 232–37, 242, 246, 249–54
friends, ix, 3, 9, 12, 16, 18, 25, 26, 28, 29–30n7, 47, 95, 96, 98, 102, 106, 107, 109, 110, 112n11, 117–45, 161, 162, 167, 175, 178, 185, 191–92n4, 192n6, 192n8, 192n13, 212, 236, 238, 239, 243, 246, 247, 251, 252, 253; imaginary friends, 73–89. *See also* peer culture; peer group
Frozen, 3
future, 8, 15, 16, 27, 41, 43, 47, 51, 53, 58, 62, 101, 117, 140–41, 157, 164, 165, 167, 201, 202, 209, 210, 213–15, 218–20, 228, 249, 250

Gad, Josh, 3, 11, 30n9
Geisel, Theodor, 41–43, 45, 49, 50, 52–54, 65–66; politics, 42–43, 65; views

on childhood, 43, 45, 49, 61–62, 65–66, 66n5
gender, 8, 9, 16–19, 26, 27, 31n18, 31n20, 56, 66–67n8, 75, 82, 87, 102, 104, 109, 110, 142n5, 142–43n10, 151, 158–61, 167–68n7, 168n8, 179, 181–83, 186, 192n11, 201, 202, 205–7, 209, 215, 218, 227, 229–30, 232, 233, 238, 240, 244. See also boyhood; girlhood
generation, 7, 8, 9, 10, 11, 12, 15–16, 24, 46, 130, 131, 132, 134, 143n15, 143–44n18, 189, 192n11, 203, 212, 214, 216; generational agency, 8, 22, 42, 48, 51, 54–55, 59, 60, 64, 140, 143n14, 143n14, 165, 238; generational relationships, 6, 11, 14, 26, 44, 45, 48, 51, 162, 177, 189, 192n7
"Gerald McBoing Boing," 43
giants, 184, 210; André the Giant, 30n8; Rubeus Hagrid, 124
girlhood, 9, 27, 31n18, 202–3, 209, 217, 218, 227, 229–30, 250–54. See also boyhood; gender
Girl Who Drank the Moon, The, 249
Giver, The, 97
Glassner, Barry, 247
global, 8, 26, 27, 51, 189, 201, 202, 204, 206, 208–10, 216–19
good/bad construction, 23, 24, 25, 30–31n11, 83, 87, 122, 210, 231, 235–37, 243, 244. See also angel/devil construction
Goonies, The, 9–15, 28, 29n5, 29n6, 29–30n7, 30n9
Graveyard Book, The, 191n1
Greece, 25, 80, 87; Greek, 25, 81, 87, 151–53, 155, 156, 162, 179, 185, 192n10
Guardians of the Galaxy, The, 192n17
guns, 29n4, 111, 174, 205, 234–36, 250

Hannah, Daryl, 29n4
Harris, Paul L., 78
Harry Potter, 9, 26, 97, 98, 99, 107, 110, 112n9, 117–45, 165, 166, 168n12, 174, 178, 180–84, 188, 191–92n4, 193n19; *and the Chamber of Secrets*, 122, 123, 125, 128, 192n16; *and the Deathly Hallows*, 127, 130, 132, 133, 134, 137, 138, 145n26; *and the Goblet of Fire*, 127, 142n8, 192n15; *and the Half-Blood Prince*, 131, 138; *and the Order of the Phoenix*, 123, 125, 129, 131, 132, 135, 136, 139, 141n4, 181; *and the Prisoner of Azkaban*, 126, 181, 193n20; *and the Sorcerer's Stone*, 122. See also Hogwarts
Haviland, Virginia, 5
Haynes, Peter Lynd, 66n6
health, 74, 84, 85, 86, 119, 153, 159, 254n1; depression, 159, 185, 193n21; mental health, 135, 180, 181, 187, 188, 193n22
Healy, Mary, 48, 66n6
Hellboy, 111n3
Hengst, Heinz, 156
Hentges, Sarah, 9, 204, 210, 217
Hermione Granger, 98, 117, 123, 125–36, 138, 139, 141, 142n5, 142n6, 142n9, 142–43n10, 143–44n18, 144n20, 144n21, 145n25, 180, 181, 191–92n4, 192n8
heroes, 8, 25–26, 41, 58, 97, 100, 101, 108–10, 164, 165, 166, 168n12, 183, 201, 202, 204, 210
Heroes of Olympus: The Lost Hero, 153, 168n11, 192n11; *Heroes of Olympus: The Blood of Olympus*, 192n10
heteronormativity, 16, 25, 159
High Noon, 41
His Dark Materials, 191n1
Hogwarts, 26, 117, 120, 122–25, 127–31, 133–36, 138–41, 142n8, 143n11, 143n16, 143–44n18, 145n25, 145n27, 178, 183–85, 188, 191–92n4, 192n6, 192n15; final battle,

134, 148; Four Houses, 120, 125, 126, 130, 132, 134, 137, 138, 142n7, 145n25; Hogwarts Express, 124–25, 135, 145n25; Room of Requirement, 131–34, 143n16, 144n20; sorting, 125; Triwizard Tournament, 127, 142n8, 192n15. *See also* education; Harry Potter; Ministry of Magic; school
holistic, 8, 11, 15, 24, 28
Hollander, Frederick, 55
Holloway, Sarah L., 119
Hollywood, California, 12, 24, 41–43, 62, 65, 66n7
home, 9, 12, 15–19, 22–25, 31n12, 42, 44, 46, 49, 56, 59, 62, 63, 83, 84, 102, 104, 111n2, 112n7, 112n13, 119–23, 125, 126, 129, 130, 132–34, 138, 141, 142n5, 142n6, 142n7, 143n12, 155–57, 158, 174, 210, 212, 227, 231–36, 238–41, 244–49, 251, 253, 254, 254n5; homelessness, 119, 155, 167n5, 179
hope, x, 6, 10, 15, 16, 24, 27, 28, 42, 43, 50, 51, 63–65, 89, 123, 134, 151, 153, 164, 165, 173, 177, 185, 203, 211, 213, 219, 249–54
Horton Hears a Who, 43
Hugo Award, 15
humanism, 6
Hunger Games, The, 109
hybridity, 18, 31n15, 205; animal-human hybrids, 211

identity, 7, 8, 12, 15–24, 26–28, 31n15, 42, 51, 58, 78, 80, 97, 99, 102, 103, 105, 112n9, 117, 119, 120, 125, 127, 131, 133, 140, 141, 143n11, 151, 156, 158–60, 165, 168n8, 178, 179, 182, 183, 192n11, 201–5, 208, 211, 214, 215, 217–19, 232, 249–54; inner attributes, 15, 18, 20, 30n10, 59, 78, 79, 126. *See also* personality
ideologies, 7, 104, 119, 120, 154, 155, 165, 177, 183, 186, 187, 189, 227

imagination, 5, 12, 25, 42, 50, 55, 57, 62, 64, 66, 97, 105, 180, 191, 203, 207, 208, 211, 214, 216, 219, 228, 249–54
Inferno, the, 9, 12, 29n6
innocence, 4, 8, 13, 15, 17, 21, 31n18, 58, 101, 121–22, 183, 189, 230, 232
institutional triangle, 7, 104, 119, 141n1. *See also* Helga Zeiher
interpretive reproduction, 5, 23, 26, 78, 103, 119–20, 128, 129, 131–33, 139, 140, 141, 176, 177, 181, 185, 190; interpretation, 75, 78, 118, 119, 176, 177. *See also* William A. Corsaro
intersectionality, ix, 4, 26, 151, 156, 167, 241
intraindependence, 192n7
Ito, Mizuko, 175, 190

James, Adrian L., 43, 176
James, Allison, 18, 31n16, 43, 73, 127, 128, 176, 185, 187, 206
jealousy, 126–27, 143–44n10, 153, 192n8
Jenkins, Henry, 22, 186, 190
Jenks, Chris, 73, 185, 187
Jensen, An-Magritt, 155, 157
Jones, Owain, 28
journey, 9, 10, 18, 26, 28, 127, 156, 203, 205, 216, 249, 254. *See also* travel

Kane Chronicles: The Red Pyramid, 156, 163
Khrushchev, Nikita, 57
kidnapping, 241, 242, 246–48
kinship, 217. *See also* family
Kirkpatrick Johnson, Monica, 248
knights, 86, 87, 101
knowledge, 9, 24, 27, 31n13, 60, 98, 100, 101, 103, 112n9, 119, 130, 132, 133, 136, 139, 155, 161, 165, 175–77, 185, 187, 213, 214, 228, 234, 240, 242, 248

270 Index

Kraftl, Peter, 19, 31n15
Kramer, Stanley, 41–42, 45, 62–63

language, 75, 83, 88, 112n7, 128, 143n17, 151, 154, 208
Lassén-Seger, Maria, 214
latchkey kids, 95, 111n2
laughter, 137–38, 253
Lauper, Cyndi, 11, 12, 13, 15, 28, 30n8; *The Goonies 'r' Goon Enough* music video, 12, 13, 30n8
leaders, 8, 10, 13, 96, 100, 104, 105–8, 133, 166, 186, 193n23, 202
Lee, Nick, 7
Lehtonen, Sanna, 9, 215
Leonard, Madeleine, 77, 84, 87, 88, 156, 157
Lewis, C.S., 212
LGBTQ, 159, 162, 167, 178, 181, 182, 192n11; asexuality, 18–19; genderfluidity, 158–59; transgender, 18, 158–59; sexual orientation, 18–19, 181. *See also* sexuality
library, 239; Library of Congress U.S. National Film Registry, 12
light, 28, 30–31n11, 101, 108, 134, 137–38, 144n22, 210, 240, 246, 248, 250–54; lightning, 127–28, 141–42n4, 156. *See also* dark
liminality, 16, 18, 27, 101, 105, 110, 133–34, 142n5, 212
Lincoln, Bruce, 154
Lindahl, Carl, 210
locality, 18, 28, 31n16, 79, 127, 132, 133, 142n5, 144n20, 216, 219, 230, 238, 243, 248, 253. *See also* place, space
locker room, 250–54
Lost, 97, 111n6
love, 7, 17, 29n4, 29–30n7, 79, 80, 84, 120, 123, 134–39, 142–43n10, 144n22, 157, 161, 162, 163, 167n5, 182, 187, 191–92n4, 205, 210, 238
loyalty, 16, 56, 64, 95, 102, 125–27, 142n7, 191–92n4, 192n12

Lucas, 30n7
Luna Lovegood, 26, 126, 134–39, 141, 144n20, 144n22, 145n26

Madriz, Esther, 236, 241
magic, 4, 8, 16, 25–27, 95, 96, 99–105, 107, 108, 111n4, 112n11, 120, 122–24, 128, 130, 131, 133, 136–39, 143–44n18, 145n23, 145n27, 152, 187, 192n15, 193n19, 201, 210–12, 216, 217, 219; magician, 152, 163. *See also* portals
Magnus Chase, 151, 155, 158–61, 166, 167n5; *and the Gods of Asgard: The Hammer of Thor*, 158, 167–68n7; *and the Gods of Asgard: The Ship of the Dead*, 161, 166, 167n5; *and the Gods of Asgard: The Sword of Summer*, 152, 155, 158–59
maps, 129, 174, 208; Google Maps, 233, 255n13; Marauder's Map, 130–31; 143n16, 144n19; treasure map, 9, 10, 13, 86
masculinity, 18, 46–47, 53, 59, 102, 106, 110, 127, 183, 192n17. *See also* boyhood; femininity
material culture, 6, 8, 11, 12, 24–26, 29n3, 29–30n7, 57, 58, 61, 64, 67n10, 79–80, 123, 129–31, 134, 143n17, 174, 231, 251
Matilda, 191n1
mattering, 11, 14, 19, 99, 176, 177, 182, 189, 202, 207, 254
Matthews, Hugh, 240, 247, 253
Mayall, Berry, 103, 141, 162, 176, 177, 185, 187
McGuire, Seanan, 15, 16, 31n20
meaning, 6, 19, 20, 23, 25, 27, 57, 75, 78–80, 88, 102, 106, 108, 119, 123–25, 128, 132, 133, 138–39, 140, 144n22, 176, 177, 178, 187, 190, 207, 210, 252, 253
media, 56–58, 109, 111, 111n1, 156, 158, 159, 175, 178, 179, 183, 191, 193n23, 202, 229, 231, 234, 241,

242, 247; social media, 24, 26, 176, 179, 189, 190–91, 192n14, 203, 220
Men, The, 41
Menniger, William C., 44
micro-childhoods, 77
Milner Jr., Murray, 127, 143n11, 144n20
"mind your own business," 243
Ministry of Magic, 120, 130, 132, 136, 138, 141n2, 145n23, 145n24, 185, 188, 193n23; Educational Decree, 132, 139. *See also* Harry Potter; Hogwarts
mirrors, 250–51; "looking-glass self," 137; mirroring, 18, 45, 83, 128, 136, 173, 182, 191, 231, 238, 242
Mische, Ann, 22, 215
mobility, 9, 19–21, 27, 29n3, 97, 130, 160, 231, 234, 236, 240, 241, 243, 246, 249, 253, 254n5; mobility imaginary, 201, 208–9, 214, 216, 218–19; social mobility, 41, 42, 49, 54, 56; supermobility, 201, 214–18; *See also* movement; stillness
modernity, 4, 16, 23, 24, 26, 28, 57, 95, 98, 119, 158, 191–92n4, 208–10, 216
Mollborn, Stefanie, 248
monster, 59, 100, 111n3, 128, 156, 157, 192n12, 204, 205, 249; beautiful monster/monstrous feminine, 22, 211; Frankenstein's monster, 22
Moore, Victor, 46
moral agency, 21–24, 59, 60, 85, 99, 103, 105, 106, 110, 120, 127–28, 133, 176, 177, 182, 184, 186–90. *See also* altruistic agency
moral panic, 229, 231, 234
Morrow, Virginia, 88
mortal world, 15, 16, 22, 151, 152, 154, 162, 163, 166, 167
mothers, 25, 46–49, 51, 52, 53, 61, 66n12, 80, 83, 84, 87, 89, 100–103, 123, 129, 137, 141–42n4, 145n26, 155–57, 159, 160, 164, 187, 191–92n4, 233–41, 244, 245, 248, 255n10. *See also* family; fathers; parents
movement, 10, 17, 19–22, 25, 27, 85, 117, 201, 202, 215, 217, 227, 230–33, 236, 237, 239, 244–46, 247, 251, 254. *See also* mobility; stillness
Mrázek, Rudolf, 208
muggle, 120, 121, 123, 124, 141n2, 187, 188, 193n19
myth, 4, 8, 24, 26, 27, 99, 109, 151–56, 159, 166, 167, 167n2, 168n12, 179, 185, 208, 242, 248, 254

narratives, 7, 12, 15, 16, 24, 27, 55, 95, 99, 100, 101, 105, 106, 110, 111n2, 139, 142–43n10, 144n21, 154, 158, 164, 165, 182, 183, 201–4, 207, 210, 211, 212, 218, 219, 220; ontological narrative, 207; YA narratives, 203–4, 216
national agency, 42, 58–60, 64
Nebula Award, 15
negotiation, 26, 42, 58, 83, 102, 104, 115, 118, 129, 140, 141, 158, 160, 162, 164, 167, 176, 177, 178, 182–87, 190, 202, 211, 214, 227, 238, 242, 253
neighborhood, 7, 27, 121, 227, 231–50, 252, 253, 255n12
Netflix, 25, 29n3, 95, 96, 100, 105, 111n1
networks, 8, 106, 109, 110, 131, 132, 174, 177, 182, 207, 217, 220; television network, 3
Neville Longbottom, 133, 138, 141, 144n20, 144n21, 145n25
"new" sociology of childhood, 7, 8, 19, 26, 55, 73, 117–20, 152
New Yorker, The, 5
Nietzsche, Friedrich, 165
Nieuwenhuys, Olga, 75
night, 30n9, 96, 112n11, 130, 131, 211, 235, 240–41, 244–48, 249, 250;

taking back the night, 28, 249–52. *See also* darkness
Nikolajeva, Maria, 4
Nixon, Richard, 57
normalization, 66n4, 77, 100, 103, 122, 155, 159, 160, 163, 181, 182, 210, 212, 219, 235

Order of the Phoenix (group), 129, 133, 143n12
orphan, 155, 187, 188
Oswell, David, 30n7, 206

Paderewski, Ignacy Jan, 51, 61
pain, 111n3, 136, 254
Pain, Rachel, 246
Pan's Labyrinth, 111n3
paracosms, 75, 81, 86
paradox, 15, 21, 27–28, 227, 230–32, 236, 237, 240–42, 249, 250, 254n2
parents, 6, 9, 10, 15–19, 26, 27, 31n17, 42–44, 46, 47, 51, 56, 62, 65, 76–77, 80, 83, 87–89, 96–99, 102–6, 122, 137, 142n5, 142n8, 144–45n18, 144n20, 152, 153, 155–58, 160–62, 167, 187, 193n19, 209, 214, 219, 228, 231–39, 241, 247, 251, 254n5, 255n9; parenting (1950s), 43, 44, 59–62. *See also* family; fathers; mothers
parks, 3, 230, 233, 235, 239, 240, 242–43, 246, 255n9
participation, 23, 26, 27, 59, 73, 77, 85, 89, 98, 103, 104, 109, 117–19, 124, 140, 141, 143–44n18, 158, 174–78, 180, 184, 187–91, 203, 206, 229; participatory research, 7, 80–81, 118, 179, 233
passivity, 16, 17, 21, 46, 56, 73, 99, 118, 119, 121, 176, 203, 252
Patronus, 134, 185, 193n21
peer culture, 5, 7, 9, 24, 26, 42, 60, 64, 74, 78, 103–9, 117–20, 123–41, 143n11, 143n17, 144n20, 176–77, 252, 254, 255n9; peer network, 104–9. *See also* friends; peer group
peer group, 7, 9–10, 14, 15, 26, 101, 102, 103, 106, 107, 108, 109, 110, 120, 126–31, 133, 136, 137, 143–44n18, 144n20, 145n25, 176. *See also* friends; peer culture
Percy Jackson, 151–53, 155, 157, 158, 165–67, 179, 181–82, 183, 185–86, 192n10, 192n11, 192n12, 192n13; *and the Olympians: The Last Olympian*, 157–58; *and the Olympians: The Lightning Thief*, 152–53, 155; *and the Olympians: The Titan's Curse*, 166
performance, 8, 16, 18, 28, 30n8, 60, 61, 66n3, 104, 180, 228, 249–54
personality, 15, 30n10, 75–80, 82–83, 87, 106, 137–39, 142n7, 206
personification, 74–75
perspective, 4, 45, 47, 48, 62, 73, 96, 118, 119, 143n11, 152, 161, 162, 174–77, 184, 185, 187–90, 209, 212, 214, 215, 218
Peter Pan, 9
Peter Pettigrew/Wormtail, 143–44n18
Piaget, Jean, 117
Pippi Longstocking, 83, 87
pirates, 9, 30n7, 30n8, 86, 87
place, 7, 16–18, 20, 23, 24, 28, 30–31n11, 73, 81, 87, 99, 111, 117–22, 128–34, 139, 143n11, 158, 186, 201, 208–12, 216–55; children's place, 27, 104–5, 112n14, 167n5. *See also* locality; space
play, 3, 5, 7, 11, 24, 25, 27–28, 29–30n7, 42, 46, 47, 55, 58, 73–77, 80–89, 119, 180, 182, 191, 203, 212, 214, 236, 249–54; games, 3, 11, 27, 77, 80, 83, 85–89, 111n6, 203, 250–52; play culture, 11, 29–30n7. *See also* toys
political approaches, 3, 4, 27, 105, 118, 158, 162, 173, 176, 177, 182, 183,

185, 186, 189, 190, 191, 202, 206, 219
Pond, Julia, 165, 166, 168n12
popular culture, 11, 12, 28, 30n8, 49, 58, 80, 98, 190, 249–53
portals, 8, 15–20, 27, 31n12, 31n20, 99, 100, 107, 110, 205, 208, 210, 212, 217; doors as, 15–18, 20, 22–24, 30n10, 31n17, 31n19, 216, 217
possibility, 4, 7, 18, 22–24, 27, 28, 173, 202, 203, 207–10, 213, 215, 218, 219, 220, 236, 248, 252, 254
posthuman, 31n18, 112n12
power, 7, 8, 10, 11, 14, 15, 17, 19, 21, 25, 26, 27, 28, 31n18, 43, 44, 95, 97–101, 103–11, 123, 130, 133, 140, 141, 143n15, 143–44n18, 151–65, 167, 174, 176, 177, 182, 184, 187, 189, 201–6, 210, 211, 213, 215, 217, 231, 232, 241, 248, 249–54. *See also* empowerment
practice theory, 206
Prague, Czech Republic, 204, 208, 212, 216
Presley, Elvis, 65
princess, 18, 95
Princess Bride, The, 30n8
"Private Snafu," 43
prophecy, 151, 165–66, 168n13; Hall of Prophecy, 136
protection, 9, 20, 21, 31n19, 96, 99–104, 106, 111n4, 118, 125, 127, 129, 130, 132–34, 141n4, 142n6, 143n13, 151, 157–58, 162, 166, 174, 188, 212, 229, 231–37, 238, 240, 243, 247, 250, 252, 253, 254n3
protectionism, 5, 6–7, 24, 29n4, 109, 121–24, 130, 140–41, 142n8, 183, 214, 232. *See also* children's islanding
Prout, Alan, 31n15, 73, 130, 185, 187, 206
psychology, 6, 8, 45, 46, 56, 58, 75, 89, 111, 117, 136

public, 11, 41–42, 49, 53, 58, 109, 118–19, 121, 174, 179, 186, 190, 209, 228–32, 234, 240–42, 245, 246, 249, 251, 253, 255n9, 255n12. *See also* place; space
Punch, Samantha, 21–22, 23

quests, 26, 86, 96–98, 136, 151, 152, 156, 162, 165
Qvortrup, Jens, 121

race/ethnicity, 26, 29n4, 51, 80, 101, 155–56, 167, 179, 192n11, 227–54. *See also* discrimination, diversity
Rasmussen, Kim, 104–5, 112n14, 134, 141n1
reaction shots, 29n6
reading down, 5, 6, 98
reality, 4, 5, 16, 20, 23, 45, 55, 60, 62, 73, 75, 104, 118, 128, 129, 155, 162, 173, 201, 202, 212, 216, 247, 248, 253; real world, 3, 15, 17, 19, 23, 27, 31n12, 31n17, 42, 49, 76, 78, 83, 99, 128, 140, 160, 173, 174, 184, 185, 186, 188–91, 202, 205, 207, 210, 216, 217, 218, 227
reception, 11, 25, 41, 64, 65, 98
Red Queen, 110
reincarnation, 214–15
religion, 26, 27, 154, 179, 186
Remus Lupin, 143n18, 181, 182, 184, 192n6, 193n20
resistance, 23, 27, 49, 87, 88, 98, 102, 103, 106, 128–34, 139, 143n16, 160–61, 163, 173, 180, 188, 189, 193n23, 243, 251
responsibility, 43, 54, 56, 60, 65, 88, 99, 102, 103, 106, 109, 156, 166, 178, 181, 210, 215, 234, 238, 240, 251
Reunited Apart, 11, 12, 30n9
Revolutionary United Front (RUF), 109
rights, 3–4, 8, 9, 57, 73, 102, 120, 158, 167n6, 180, 183, 185–91, 193n26. *See also* activism; fairness and equality; social justice; United

Nations Convention on the Rights of the Child
Riordan, Rick, 26, 151–59, 165, 166, 179, 181
Rock, Rock, Rock, 65
Rocket Man, The, 58
role models, 46, 48, 55, 97, 159, 181, 187
Ronald Weasley, 123–31, 134–36, 138, 139, 141, 142n5, 142n6, 142n9, 142–43n10, 143n18, 144n20, 144n21, 145n25, 181, 192n8, 192n15, 192n16, 193n25
Rowling, J.K., 26, 97–99, 103–4, 107, 110, 112n9, 117, 123, 129, 142n5, 142–43n10, 144n20, 144n21, 144n22, 145n26, 193n22
Rubens, Paul, 12
Rubin, Lillian B., 136

safety, 9, 20, 103, 104, 121–23, 128, 130, 141, 156, 158, 159, 166–67, 167n5, 202, 217, 228, 230–38, 240, 241, 243, 246–49, 251, 254, 254n3. *See also* danger
Schlesinger Jr., Arthur, 59
school, 3, 6, 7, 15–18, 20, 22, 24–26, 30n10, 30–31n11, 31n20, 50, 57, 64, 74, 82, 88, 96, 97, 99–100, 102–6, 111n2, 112n9, 117, 119, 120–24, 127, 128, 130, 134, 137, 139–41, 142n5, 142n8, 143n11, 143n17, 143–44n18, 145n27, 159, 174, 188, 191–92n4, 204, 213–16, 218, 220, 228, 229, 233, 235, 239, 241, 245, 251, 252, 254n3, 255n9; boarding school, 15–17, 22, 131; classrooms, 58, 131, 153; teachers, 16, 25, 41, 45, 46, 48–50, 52, 53, 59, 103–5, 109, 112n9, 130, 139–41, 144n20, 145n27, 255n9. *See also* education; Hogwarts
secrecy, 26, 95, 101, 103–5, 109, 111n1, 111n4, 112n9, 128–33, 140, 143n17, 143–44n18, 144n20, 145n23, 192n10, 250, 253

segregation, 5, 232, 233
Sendak, Maurice, ix, 5–7
Serling, Rod, x, 3–4
Severus Snape, 131, 143n18, 145n26, 180, 191–92n4
sexual harassment, 229, 230, 232, 242–45
sexuality, 16, 18–19, 26, 30–31n11, 46, 53, 158, 163, 167n6, 179, 181, 182, 183, 192n11, 211. *See also* LGBTQ
sexual violence, 229–30, 242–46, 248. *See also* abuse; violence
shapeshifting, 159–61, 167n7, 168n8; Polyjuice Potion, 138
sharing, 7, 9, 11, 15, 24–26, 60, 74, 77, 79, 103, 105–7, 124–27, 129, 131, 132, 135–38, 140, 141, 143–44n18, 144n20, 154, 175–76, 180, 182, 184, 185, 187, 191, 201, 234
Sharkey, Patrick K., 19
"shipping," 182, 191–92n4
siblings, 56, 81, 82, 88, 130, 151, 152, 155–57, 160, 161, 163, 166, 192n15, 192n16, 205, 235, 236, 240, 245, 246; twins, 18, 22, 31n19, 134; Weasley twins, 129, 130, 134, 143n18. *See also* family; parents
silence, 19–21, 45, 109, 118, 134, 211, 240; silencer, 57–60. *See also* voice
Singer, Dorothy G., 76
Singer, Jerome E., 76
Sirius Black, 129, 136–37, 142n5, 143n12, 143–44n18, 145n26, 182, 192n6
Skelton, Tracey, 251, 253
Slender Man, 250–51
smallness, 5, 6, 8, 28, 29n1, 66n4, 103, 120–22, 166, 231, 236, 247, 250–52, 254
social agency, 17, 97, 107, 108, 177, 181, 182, 184–86, 190
social change, 8, 27, 156, 189, 213.
social justice, 26–27, 100, 104, 173, 174, 177, 183–85, 187–90. *See also* activism; rights

socialization, 7, 31n20, 42, 45, 46, 49, 73, 97, 104, 117–18, 162, 229, 231, 236, 241
social norms, 4, 7, 43, 45, 56, 62, 101, 173, 176, 177, 181, 182, 184, 186–91, 209, 252
soft city, 208, 216
solidarity, 26, 27, 125–27, 182
Soto, Lilia, 209
space, 5–8, 11, 15, 16, 18, 20, 23–25, 28, 43, 75, 104, 105, 109, 117–24, 128–34, 140, 158, 173–91, 201, 202, 207–9, 213, 214, 216, 227–54. *See also* locality; place
Space Children, 58
Space Patrol, 58
spatial agency, 26, 42, 43, 45, 50, 54–55, 57, 60, 64, 97, 118, 130, 136, 219, 235, 243, 249–54
Spielberg, Steven, 9, 12–15, 29n3, 29n4, 29n5, 30n9, 99
Splash, 29n4
Spyrou, Spyros, 21
Star Trek Beyond, 192n17
Star Wars, 97
stillness, 20–21. *See also* mobility; movement
Stonewall Award, 158–59
strangers, 228–31, 234, 236, 239, 241, 245, 247, 249
Stranger Things, 29n3, 97, 111n6
streets, 27, 119, 135, 155, 216, 227, 230, 232–44, 246–48, 250, 252–54, 254n3
structure, ix, 7, 8, 17, 19, 22, 28, 46, 65, 73, 98, 99, 102, 105, 107–11, 112n12, 118, 119, 121, 132, 139–40, 142–43n10, 145n27, 152, 155–58, 163, 167, 173–77, 184, 187, 206, 214, 217
struggle, ix, 8, 15, 18, 26, 45, 49, 65, 96, 100–103, 107, 140, 174, 178, 185, 205, 252, 254, 255n9
suburbs, 29n3, 29–30n7, 44, 59, 66n1, 233, 242, 254n5, 255n9, 255n12

surveillance, 121, 232, 253
survival, 109, 124, 141n4, 157, 187, 253
sympathy, 30n10, 53, 83, 85, 86, 100, 107, 183, 211

Tatar, Maria, 203
Taylor, Laini, 27, 201, 204, 208, 210–19
teamwork, 9–10, 25, 44, 95, 105–10, 132–33, 161, 163
technology, 4, 29n4, 57, 67n10, 118, 174, 175, 177, 178, 189–91, 203–4, 208, 209, 220
Thor: The Dark World, 192n17
Thorne, Barrie, 232
Thunberg, Greta, 202
time, 3–7, 10, 11, 12, 15–17, 19, 21, 23–25, 27, 28, 30n8, 44, 47, 58, 73, 75, 76, 80, 83, 84, 88, 96, 99, 102, 106, 111, 112n10, 118–20, 122–25, 127, 131, 132, 134, 136, 138, 141, 141n3, 142n5, 144n20, 154–57, 159, 160, 178, 187, 189, 191–92n4, 201, 202, 206, 207, 211, 212–15, 217–19, 232, 234, 235, 236–40, 242, 244–48, 250–54, 255n9
To Catch a Thief, 111n5
toys, 29–30n7, 51, 57, 59, 63, 74, 75, 78, 80, 81, 83, 86, 87, 89; figures, 25, 29–30n7, 81, 82, 86; dolls, 25, 75, 78–83, 86, 88; stuffed animals, 25, 74, 75, 78–81, 83, 86, 88, 89
train, 124, 125, 145n25, 208, 247–48
transformation, 5, 16, 18, 25, 27, 28, 46, 66n4, 78, 99, 101, 126, 133, 138, 140, 141, 176, 185, 189, 190, 207–11, 215, 218, 232, 250–54
travel, 15–18, 20, 23, 24, 27, 142n5, 156, 204–5, 208–14, 216–18, 230, 245. *See also* journey; mobility; portals; walking
treasure, 9, 12, 25, 86, 87, 88
Trites, Roberta S., 205–6, 207
Trollhunters, 95–112
tropes, 12, 111, 211

trust, 15, 26, 56, 99, 102, 104, 105, 112n9, 126–28, 129, 133, 136, 143n17, 143–44n18, 144n19, 144n20, 163, 167
Tuan, Yi-Fu, 254n2
Twilight Zone, The, 3–4
Twitter, 179

uncanny, 28, 100, 212
underworld, 16, 17, 20, 30–31n11, 31n17, 100
United Nations Convention on the Rights of the Child, 8, 73
Uprichard, Emma, 7

Valentine, Gill, 23, 119, 122
valentine, kylie, 176
Vallone, Lynne, 95
vampires, 22, 100, 208
victim, 84, 165, 189, 230–32, 234, 236–45, 247–49, 252
viewer age ratings, 12, 112n8
violence, 27, 43, 100, 109, 110, 180, 183, 186, 228, 231, 234–41, 248, 249. *See also* abuse; sexual violence
Vogler, Christopher, 98
voice, 7, 8, 19, 21, 22, 42, 43, 47, 50, 57, 103, 106, 136–37, 154, 157–59, 163, 167, 176, 178, 187, 189, 190, 236, 242, 252. *See also* silence
Voldemort, 107, 123, 127, 128, 133, 134, 137, 139, 141–42n4, 142n8, 142n9, 144n18, 144n21, 144n22, 145n25, 178, 187, 191–92n4, 192n5, 192n16, 193n23; Death Eaters, 123, 133, 137, 141-42n4; horcruxes, 127, 130, 124n9, 143n10, 145n25
vulnerability, 21, 28, 31n18, 45, 84, 109, 110, 127, 128, 137, 140, 153, 183, 229, 230, 231, 232, 241, 246

walking, 85, 86, 230, 231, 239, 241–48, 254n3

war, 41, 42, 43, 44, 54, 109, 205, 213, 215, 217; and consumerism, 44, 53–55, 57, 58, 64, 66n2; Cold War, 41–42, 48, 50, 51, 58, 62; The Great Depression, 42, 44, 54, 56; Hitler, Adolf, 49, 50, 52, 65, 182; World War I, 216; World War II, 43, 46, 50, 52, 56, 59, 188
Wardlow, Holly, 209
Warming, Hanne, 51
Way, Niobe, 125, 248, 249
Wee Free Men, The, 191n1
Whedon, Joss, 100, 112n11
Where the Wild Things Are, 5–6
Whyte Jr., William H., 49
Wihstutz, Anne, 84
Willis, Jessica L., 202, 204
Wilson, Sloan, 49
Wizard of Oz, The, 11, 41
work, 8, 9, 14–16, 22, 24, 27, 30n8, 30n9, 43, 44, 47, 53, 54, 56, 65, 97, 99, 100, 103, 104, 105–11, 111n3, 122, 140, 142n7, 145n23, 145n24, 151, 156, 161, 163–65, 175, 188, 193n26, 209, 227, 236, 239, 241
writing, ix, 3, 5–6, 11, 65, 97, 132, 143n17, 174–78, 180, 185, 186. *See also* fan communities
WWF, 13, 30n8
Wylie, Philip, 46
Wyness, Michael, 29n1, 106, 109, 231

Xena the Warrior Princess, 109

Yousafzai, Malala, 202
youthscapes, 216
YouTube, 11, 179, 203

Zamani-Gallahar, Eboni, 158–59
Zeiher, Helga, 26, 121–22, 141n1, 213. *See also* children's islanding
Zipes, Jack, 4

About the Contributors

Ana Lilia Campos-Manzo is Associate Professor of Sociology at Connecticut College in New London, CT. She received her PhD in Sociology from the University of Iowa. She specializes in childhood and adolescence with a focus on youth peer cultures and the lived experiences of youth of color; criminology, with interests in the emergence of laws and parents under correctional supervision; and qualitative methods, specifically developing research tools that prioritize underrepresented voices of children of color and recognize the significance of research contexts.

Michele D. Castleman is Associate Professor of Education at Heidelberg University in Ohio, where she teaches courses on English methods, the teaching of writing, and young adult and children's literature. She has a PhD in Literature for Children and Young Adults from The Ohio State University. She also writes young adult novels and is represented by Kristy Hunter at The Knight Agency.

Ingrid E. Castro is Professor of Sociology and Chair of the Sociology, Anthropology, and Social Work Department at Massachusetts College of Liberal Arts. She earned a PhD in Sociology with Graduate Certificates in Cinema Studies and Women & Gender Studies from Northeastern University. She is an interdisciplinary childhood studies and sociology scholar with research interests in children and youth, cinema studies, popular culture, gender/race/class, and qualitative methods. She is lead editor of *Researching Children and Youth: Methodological Issues, Strategies and Innovations—Sociological Studies of Children and Youth, Volume 22* (2017), and coeditor of *Representing Agency in Popular Culture—Children and Youth on Page, Screen, and In Between* (2019) and *Child and Youth Agency in Science*

Fiction: Travel, Technology, Time (2019). Her most successful moments are when she completes *The New York Times* Sunday Crossword Puzzle with no hints or mistakes.

Sophia Kremmydiotou is a kindergarten teacher. She holds a degree in preschool education from the Department of Early Childhood Education of the National and Kapodistrian University of Athens and a Master of Arts in "Educational Sciences: Creative Educational Environments and Playing in Education" from the Department of Early Childhood Education of the University of Thessaly in Greece.

Peter W. Y. Lee is an independent scholar and historian in modern American culture. He earned his doctorate in History and Culture from Drew University in 2017, with an emphasis on American culture during the Cold War. Peter writes extensively on American popular culture, as reflected in his edited volumes *Exploring Picard's Galaxy: Essays on Star Trek: The Next Generation* (2018) and *A Galaxy Here and Now: Historical and Cultural Readings of Star Wars* (2016). His most recent edited work is *Peanuts and American Culture: Essays on Charles M. Schulz's Iconic Comic Strip* (2019), and his forthcoming book is *From Dead Ends to Cold Warriors: Constructing American Boyhood in Postwar Hollywood Films*.

Ida Fadzillah Leggett is Associate Professor of Anthropology in the Department of Sociology and Anthropology at Middle Tennessee State University. She received her doctorate in Cultural Anthropology from the University of Illinois, Urbana-Champaign in 2003, for which she conducted field research in Northern Thailand on teenage girls and the effects of education and globalization on their "life strategy narratives." Her research and publications center on childhoods, immigration, refugees, girlhood, food, education, prostitution, and health outcomes.

Kostas Magos is Associate Professor in the Department of Early Childhood Education of the University of Thessaly in Greece. He earned his PhD from the Department of Early Childhood Education at the National and Kapodistrian University of Athens (Greece). His scientific interests focus on the theory and praxis of intercultural dimensions in early childhood education and in the role of play in children's development.

Tara Moore spent many hours paging through brittle Victorian periodicals while she earned her PhD in English from the University of Delaware. She now teaches writing and young adult literature courses as Visiting Assistant Professor of English at Elizabethtown College in beautiful central

Pennsylvania. She published two books about Christmas culture, *Victorian Christmas in Print* (2009) and *Christmas: The Sacred to Santa* (2014). She also edited *The Valancourt Book of Victorian Christmas Ghost Stories* (2016). Her recent scholarship examines representations of adoption and girl warriors in young adult literature, and her essays appear in *The ALAN Review*, *SIGNAL*, and various edited collections.

Parinita Shetty is a second-year doctoral researcher in Education at the University of Leeds, England. She has worked with young people and children's books in India in various ways—as an author, a bookseller in a children's bookshop, a reading program developer, and a coordinator of a children's literature festival. She completed her MEd in children's literature and literacies at the University of Glasgow, Scotland, in 2017. Her research interests include children's literature, intersectionality, fan podcasts, public pedagogy, digital media, online fan communities, and critical literacy. She studies fan communities as both a researcher and a fan. She should currently be writing, but is probably watching *Doctor Who*.

Breck Young earned his BA in Art from the University of Delaware. A surrealist, his medium of choice is oil on canvas. In addition to making art, he is a fan of the Philadelphia Eagles and Philadelphia Flyers and is an avid freshwater aquarist.

www.ingramcontent.com/pod-product-compliance
Lightning Source LLC
Chambersburg PA
CBHW050859300426
44111CB00010B/1308